General Issues
in Literacy/Illiteracy

General Issues in Literacy/Illiteracy

A Bibliography

**Compiled by
John Hladczuk,
William Eller,
and Sharon Hladczuk**

Bibliographies and Indexes in Education, Number 8

GREENWOOD PRESS
New York • Westport, Connecticut • London

In print Nov. 2001

016.374
H644g

Library of Congress Cataloging-in-Publication Data

Hladczuk, John.
   General issues in literacy/illiteracy : a bibliography / compiled
by John Hladczuk, William Eller, and Sharon Hladczuk.
      p. cm.—(Bibliographies and indexes in education, ISSN
0742-6917 ; no. 8)
   Includes bibliographical references.
   ISBN 0-313-27327-8 (lib. bdg. : alk. paper)
      1. Literacy—United States—Bibliography. I. Eller, William.
II. Hladczuk, Sharon. III. Title. IV. Series.
Z5814.I3H56   1990
[LC151] ·
016.374'012—dc20   89-28646

British Library Cataloguing in Publication Data is available.

Library of Congress Catalog Card Number: 89-28646
ISBN: 0-313-27327-8
ISSN: 0742-6917

First published in 1990

Greenwood Press, Inc.
88 Post Road West, Westport, Connecticut 06881

Printed in the United States of America

The paper used in this book complies with the
Permanent Paper Standard issued by the National
Information Standards Organization (Z39.48-1984).

10 9 8 7 6 5 4 3 2 1

*This book is dedicated to all those who are working
in literacy efforts throughout the world.*

Contents

Acknowledgements

We would like to thank Loomis Mayer, Christina Smith, Stan Sobolewski, Adam Epstein, Jason Epstein, Amy Epstein and A.J. Hladczuk in helping us bring the bibliography to its final form.

General Issues in Literacy:
An Introduction

The question - and issue - of literacy and illiteracy not only means different things to different people and groups, it also has both a varied focus and applicability within the structure and organization of these people and groups.

This was not always the case; there was a time when literacy simply, generally - and perhaps even exclusively - meant the ability to read, to be what is called functionally literate. Yet, the ramifications of increasing modernization coupled with the technological explosion have resulted in major and significant changes in the way we have come to conceptualize and understand literacy.

In other words, literacy went the way of the family doctor, from general applicability to specialization. It has gone from "plain-old" literacy to scientific literacy, adult literacy, functional literacy, computer literacy, technological literacy, braille literacy, biliteracy, aliteracy, job literacy, visual literacy, graphic literacy, video literacy, and media literacy.

The terms computer literacy, and technological literacy were first listed as desciptors by ERIC in April and September of 1982, respectively.

E.D. Hirsch, Jr., in his recent book, Cultural Literacy: What Every American Needs To Know is urging that the schools begin teaching cultural content - cultural literacy - to its students.

We've come a long way from the Horn Books and the McGuffey Readers - not to mention the seemingly idyllic lives of Dick, Jane and Spot.

In a good many ways, literacy has ceased to be simply a pursuit and has all too quickly become a responsibility. This responsibility effects us as individuals and citizens, and particularly as professionals. Thus, in a world which is becoming increasingly more - and not less - complex, educators cannot step back from the rush of complexity.

In method courses and seminars, educators have to be abreast of the various aspects of literacy so that would-be teachers can better reach and teach their would-be students to "read".

The 12 April 1988 Education Life supplement to the New York Times featured an article entitled, "Redesigning the American Teacher". That's fine, but you can have immediate input into the redesign by educating your own would-be teachers to the complexity of literacy and the responsibility that its multiple facets requires from all of us.

Using This Bibliography

When attempting to use this bibliography one must remember, first, that the topic of literacy has great breadth and depth to it, and, second, that there are some things which this bibliography attempts to achieve, and there are some things which this bibliography does not attempt to achieve.

To begin, this bibliography has attempted to be comprehensive; it is not, however, exhaustive. Second, this bibliography should not be assumed to deal with the subject of adult education. True, the user may find materials on adult literacy, adult reading programs and the like. We have, however, tried to "walk the line," so to speak, between literacy and adult education **without** falling into the domain of the latter.

The table of contents, and thus the organization of the book, is relatively straightforward and should basically be user-friendly. The issues in literacy and illiteracy are arranged alphabetically so as to facilitate logical use.

In addition, it is important that the user understand that although we have tried to organize this bibliography in an efficient manner, there still remains the need to cross-check parts of the bibliography so that users can maximize their search. In a case where, for example, one might be interested in the relationship between computer literacy and adults, one would not only have to check under computer literacy but under adult literacy, adult reading programs, evaluation of literacy, and perhaps even functional illiteracy.

Finally, although this bibliography is discrete and therefore stands alone for the purpose that it serves, it is important to point out that this literacy bibliography has a companion bibliography volume entitled, Literacy/Illiteracy in the World (Hladczuk, Eller, and Hladczuk, Greenwood, 1989). This companion volume deals with the subject of literacy organized along the lines of International and National Research in literacy.   The International Research section is subdivided into sections pertaining to cross-cultural, cross-national, world literacy, and world regional research in literacy. The National Research section lists countries alphabetically with the United States being further subdivided into a "general" section, followed by a state-by-state alphabetical listing.   Finally, Chapter Two deals with illiteracy and UNESCO, while Chapter Three presents entries pertaining to literacy in the Third World.   Thus, the serious researcher would not only want to cross-check within the areas of this bibliography, but would also be advised to cross-check with the companion volume.   Take, for example, the subject of computer literacy in Australia.   One could first check the chapter on Computer Literacy in this volume.   Then, one could move over to the companion volume and check Australia under the National Research section.   This approach would result in the most efficient use of this bibliography.

General Issues
in Literacy/Illiteracy

1

Adult Literacy

1.1   Adult Literacy: Developments. London: H.M.S.O., nd.

1.2   "Adult Literacy in Industrialized Countries." Convergence 15, (1982): 74-76.

1.3   "Adult Literacy Programs and Development." School and Society 97, (February 1969): 119.

1.4   "Adult Literacy Success Story." Education 152, 13(September 29, 1978): 285.

1.5   "Adult Literacy: The First Decade." Education 165, 19 (May 10, 1985): iv.

1.6   Ahmed, Mushtaq. "Retention of Literacy Skills In Adults." Literacy Work 2, 4(May 1973): 43-54.

1.7   Ahmed, Mushtaq. Teaching Adults To Read and Write; A Guide Book For Literacy Teacher. New Delhi: Ministry of Education, 1967.

1.8   Alessi, Stephen M., et al. "Effectiveness of a Computer-Based Reading Comprehension Program For Adults." Journal of Educational Technology Systems II, 1(1982-1983): 43-57.

1.9   Arnold, Arthur, and Webb, Bob. "Literacy Symposium: The Development of Remedial English Classes - an Exercise in Professional Cooperation." Adult Education (London) 47, (January 1975): 285-296.

1.10   Aspects of Adult Illiteracy. N.P.: n.p., 1974.

1.11   August, Bonne T. "Teaching Writing in the Adult Literacy
        Program." Adult Literacy and Basic Education 3, 2(Summer
        1979): 139-144.

1.12   Bacon, Margaret. "What Adult Literacy Teachers Need To Know
        About Strategies For Focusing a Comprehension." Lifelong
        Learnings: The Adult Years 6, 6(February 1983): 4-5.

1.13   Bailey, N.J. "Reading Instruction For Basic Adult Literacy."
        International Reading Conference Papers 14, (1970): 306-320.

1.14   Balmuth, Miriam. "Recruitment and Retention in Adult Basic
        Education: What Does The Research Say?" Journal of Reading
        31, 7(April 1988): 620-623.

1.15   Bartley, D.E., and James, C. "Teacher Training in Adult Basic
        Education - TESOL: A Step to Eradicate Illiteracy in Standard
        English." Modern Language Journal 56, (October 1972): 374-377.

1.16   Bataille, Leon, ed. A Turning Point For Literacy: The Spirit and
        Declaration of Persepolis. Oxford: Pergamon Press, 1976.

1.17   Ben-Tovim, Margaret, and Kedney, R.J. Aspects of Adult
        Illiteracy: A Collection of Papers. N.P.: Cheshire County
        Council, 1974.

1.18   Bhola, H.S. "The Politics of Adult Literacy Promotion: An
        International Perspective." Journal of Reading 31, (April 1988):
        667-671.

        Examines the changing ideologies of adult literacy campaigns,
        projects and programs. Reviews world illiteracy from a global
        perspective. Presents statistics pertaining to the number of
        illiterates and illiteracy rates in 1985 for the adult population
        aged 15 and over. Also offers a political model of literacy for
        development. Concludes with the question of what can the
        teachers of reading do in the schools.

1.19   Bhola, H.S. "Needed Research in Adult Literacy for Policy
        Makers and Planners." Adult Education 31, 3(Spring 1981): 169-
        176.

1.20   Bhola, H.,S. "Policy Analysis of Adult Literacy Versus Universal
        Primary Education: Child Is Father of Man and Man of the
        Child." Viewpoints in Teaching and Learning 55, (Fall 1979): 22-
        35.

1.21   Bhola, Harbans S. "A Policy Analysis of Adult Literacy
         Promotion In The Third World: An Accounting of Promises
         Made and Promises Fulfilled." International Review of
         Education 30, 3(1984): 249-264.

1.22   Bhola, Harbans S. "Why Literacy Can't Wait: Issues for the
         1980's." Convergence 14, 1(1981): 6-23.

1.23   Bonanni, C. "Adult Literacy: An Hypothesis For A New
         Approach." Indian Journal of Adult Education 32, 7(July 1971):
         2-4, 19-20.

1.24   Bonanni, C. "Writing Versus Reading In Traditional and
         Functional Adult Literacy Processes." Literacy Discussion 2,
         2(Spring 1971): 191-197.

1.25   Bonniwell, Hilton T. "Selection Principles and Categories For
         Adult Basic Education Materials." Continuing Education 5,
         3(July1972): 6-7.

1.26   "Books for Adult Literacy Work." Books in School 2, 1-
         2(December 1978): 71.

1.27   Boraks, Nancy. "Research and Adult Literacy Programs." Adult
         Literacy and Basic Education 5, 1(Spring 1981): 5-11.

1.28   Bower, John. "Functional Adult Education for Rural People:
         Communication, Action Research and Feedback." Convergence
         10, 3(1977): 34-43.

1.29   Bowren, Fay F. "Adult Reading Needs Adult Research Models."
         Journal of Reading 31, 3(December 1987): 208-212.

1.30   Boyd, Robert D., and Martin, Larry G. "A Methodology For The
         Analysis of The Psychosocial Profiles of Low Literate Adults."
         Adult Education Quarterly 34, 2(Winter 1984): 85-96.

1.31   Boyd, Robert Dean. A Methodology For The Analysis Of The
         Psychological Profiles of Low-Literate Adults. N.P.: n.p., 1981.

1.32   Braund, Diane. "Teacher-pupil Relationships in Adult Literacy
         Tuition." British Journal of Sociology of Education 6, 2(June
         1985): 185-207.

1.33   Brock, Christine. "Breaking the Failure Barrier." Australian
         Journal of Reading 6, 3(August 1983): 105-107.

1.34   Bryant, Antusa S., and Bryant, Benjamin F. "Helping The Adult
            Student Achieve Better Comprehension." Minnesota Reading
            Quarterly 16, 3(February 1972): 137-143.

1.35   Bryant, Antusa S., and Bryant, Benjamin. "Some Considerations
            In Teaching Adults To Read." Minnesota Reading Quarterly 16,
            1(October 1971): 11-14.

1.36   Butter, Sheila. "Fighting Illiteracy - The Role of Library
            Technicians." Canadian Library Journal 43, 6(December 1986):
            419-422.

1.37   Campos, S.N. Adult Literacy In National Development: A Case
            Study of A Developing Country. Norwich, England: Geo
            Abstracts, Ltd., 1980.

1.38   Cass, Angelica W. "Materials and Methods For Adult Literacy
            Programmes." Literacy Discussion 2, 3(Summer 1971): 9-25.

1.39   Cervero, Ronald M. "Is a Common Definition of Adult Literacy
            Possible?" Adult Education Quarterly 36, 1(Fall 1985): 50-54.

1.40   Cervero, Ronald M. "Assessment in Adult Basic Education: A
            Comparison of the APL and GED Tests." Adult Education 31,
            2(Winter 1981): 67-84.

1.41   Chall, J.S., et al. "Adult Literacy: New and Enduring Problems."
            Phi Delta Kappan 69, (November 1987): 190-196.

1.42   Chall, Jeanne S. "Reading Development in Adults." Annals of
            Dyslexia 37, (1987): 240-251.

1.43   Chang, K.L. "Linking Content Area Reading To Adult Literacy
            and Basic Education." Adult Literacy and Basic Education 9,
            2(1985): 68-79.

1.44   Charnley, A.H., and Jones, H.A. Concepts of Success In Adult
            Literacy. Cambridge: Huntington Publishers, 1981.

1.45   Check, J.F., and Toellner, S. "Reading Patterns of Adults."
            Reading Improvement 21, (Summer 1984): 82-88.

1.46   Ciancio, J. "Literacy: The Basic Skill." Vocational Education
            Journal 63, (March 1988): 41-42.

1.47   Coleman, Jean Ellen. "ALA's Role in Adult and Literacy
            Education." Library Trends 35, 2(Fall 1986): 207-217.

1.48   Coles, G.S. "Adult Illiteracy and Learning Theory: A Study of
            Cognition and Activity." Science & Society 47, (Winter
            1983/1984): 451-482.

1.49   Coles, Gerald S. "Can ABE Students be Identified as Learning
            Disabled?" Adult Literacy and Basic Education 4, 3(Fall 1980):
            170-180.

1.50   Cooper, Max. "An Investigation of Two Types of Material for
            Teaching Reading To Mentally Retarded Delinquent and
            Illiterate Male Adults." Ph.D. dissertation, New York
            University, 1945. W 1945, p. 42.

1.51   Cornell, T. "Characteristics of Effective Occupational Literacy
            Programs." Journal of Reading 31, (April 1988): 654-656.

1.52   Cortright, Richard Watkins. "A Study of Different Styles of
            Educational Materials for Adult New Literates." Ed.D.
            dissertation, The American University, 1967. 28/04-A, p.1259.

1.53   Crane, John M. "Adult Literacy - A Continuing Need." Adult
            Education 56, 2(September 1983): 147-152.

1.54   Cranney, A. Garr. "The Literature of Adult Reading: Selected
            References." Journal of Reading 26, 4(January 1983): 323-331.

1.55   Curriculum Guide To Adult Basic Education. N.P.: n.p., 1966.

1.56   Curry, Robert L. "Adult Literacy - - Progress and Problems." 1966.
            ED 012 215.

1.57   Darch, C. and Kameenui, E.J. "Teaching LD Students Critical
            Reading Skills: A Systematic Replication." Learning Disability
            Quarterly 10, (Spring 1987): 82-91.

1.58   Diekhoff, George M., and Diekhoff, Karen Bembry. "The Adult
            Literacy Program Attrition Problem: Identification at Intake."
            Adult Literacy and Basic Education 8, 1(1984): 34-47.

1.59   Directory of Adult Education Periodicals - Seventh Revised
            Edition. Paris: UNESCO, 1985. ED 263 308.

1.60   Donohue, Dan, et al. Guidelines For Teaching The 'Under-educated' Adult. Olympia, Washington: State Superintendent For Public Instruction, 1966. ED 012 411.

1.61   Drane, Richard Stephen. "The Effects of Participation Training on Adult Literacy Education in a Mental Hospital." Ph.D. dissertation, Indiana University, 1967. 28/06-A, p. 2057.

1.62   Dutton, Donnie, and Seaman, Don F. "Audio-Visual Aids In Adult Literacy Education." Literacy Discussion 2, 3(Summer 1971): 27-42.

1.63   Elam, E. H. "Who Can Read?" Adult Education Bulletin 3, (January 1939): 15-16.

1.64   Elsey, Barry. "Volunteer Tutors in Adult Education." Studies in Adult Education 12, 2(October 1980): 134-142.

1.65   Fagan, William T. "Adult Illiterates Processing Narrative and Expository Text." English Quarterly 20, 2(Summer 1987): 95-105.

1.66   Fields, E.L. "Industry-Based Programs: A Growing Source For Adult Literacy Development." Lifelong Learning 10, (September 1986): 7-9.

1.67   Fingeret, Arlene. Adult Literacy Education: Current and Future Directions. Columbus, Ohio: Ohio State University, National Center For Research In Vocational Education, 1984.

1.68   Fingeret, A., ed. "Adult Literacy." (symposium). Lifelong Learning 6, (April 1983): 13-27.

1.69   Finlay, Judy, et al. "Instruction for Illiterates: The Initial Teaching Alphabet." Australian Journal of Adult Education 21, 1(April 1981): 15-18.

1.70   Fisher, James C. "The Literacy Level Among Older Adults: Is It a Problem?" Adult Literacy and Basic Education 11, 1(1987): 41-50.

1.71   France, Marycarolyn G., and Weeks, Jane Warren. "Parents Who Can't Read: What The Schools Can Do." Journal of Reading 31, 3(December 1987): 222-227.

1.72   Freire, Paulo. "The Adult Literacy Process As Cultural Action For Freedom." Harvard Educational Review 40, 2(May 1970): 205-225.

1.73   Forester, Anne D. "Learning To Read and Write at 26." Journal of Reading 31, 7(April 1988): 604-613.

1.74   Furter, Pierre. "Adult Education: Its Clients." Prospect 2, 3(Autumn 1972): 314-320.

1.75   Gamliel, Amram. Educational Imperatives In Adult Literacy. Newton Center, Massachusetts: Gamliels, 1985.

1.76   Geeslin, Robert H., and York, Patricia W. "Literacy Skills As A Barrier To Inservice Training" Journal of Reading Behavior 3, 3(Summer 1971): 9-12.

1.77   Goffinet, Sylvie-Anne. "Analyse du Processus de Production de L'Analphabetisme a Travers Le Discours des Analphabetes Adultes." International Review of Education 33, 2(1987): 213-227.

1.78   Gold, P.C. and Horn, P.L. "Achievement In Reading, Verbal Language, Listening Comprehension and Locus of Control of Adult Illiterates In a Volunteer Tutorial Project." Perceptual and Motor Skills 54, (June/Part 2 1982): 1243-1250.

1.79   Gold, P. C. and Johnson, J. A. "Prediction of Achievement In Reading, Self-esteem, and Verbal Language By Adult Illiterates In A Psychoeducational Tutorial Program." Journal of Clinical Psychology 38, (July 1982): 513-522.

1.80   Gorman, T. P. "A Survey of Attainment and Progress of Learners in Adult Literacy Schemes." Educational Research 23, 3(June 1981): 190-198.

1.81   Gorman, W. E. "Illiteracy in the '60's; Look at Adult Education." Illinois Education 55, (January 1967): 204-205.

1.82   Goudreau, Nancy. "Improve Your Adult Literacy Instruction by Vitalizing The Research: Part II." Lifelong Learning 10, 4(January 1987): 11-14.

1.83   Goudreau, Nancy. "Improve Your Adult Literacy Instruction by Vitalizing The Research." Lifelong Learning 10, 3(November 1986): 17-20.

1.84   Grimsley, William. "Promising Practices In In-Service
            Education - Teachers of Adults." International Reading
            Association Conference Proceedings, Part 1, 13(April 1968): 418-
            422.

1.85   Grubaugh, S. "Teaching Functional Words To Adult Students
            Through Meaningful Vocabulary Methods." Adult Literacy and
            Basic Education 7, 1(1983): 1-12.

1.86   Guthrie, John T. "Research: Script To Print." Journal of Reading
            25, 7(April 1982): 716-719.

1.87   Hall, Bud, and Stock, Arthur. "Trends in Adult Education Since
            1972." Prospects 15, 1(1985): 13-26.

1.88   Hall, MaryAnne, and Coley, Joan D. "Needs in Reading
            Instruction in Adult Basic Education." Adult Leadership 24,
            3(November 1975): 103-104.

1.89   Hand, S. E., and Puder, William H. A Preliminary Overview Of
            Methods And Techniques In Adult Literacy And Adult Basic
            Education. Tallahassee, Florida: Florida State University, 1967.
            ED 021 158.

1.90   Harman, David. Community Fundamental Education. N.P.:
            n.p., 1974.

1.91   Hayes, Ann, et al. An Investigation of Materials and Methods
            For The Introductory Stage of Adult Literacy Education. Chicago:
            Adult Education Council of Greater Chicago, 1967. ED 014 629.

1.92   Heathington, Betty S. "Expanding The Definition of Literacy for
            Adult Remedial Readers." Journal of Reading 31, 3(December
            1987): 213-217.

1.93   Henneberg, Susan, "What Do You Mean, You Can't Read?"
            English Journal 75, 1(January 1986): 53-55

1.94   Hoffman, Lee McGraw. "ABE Reading Instructions: Give Them
            Something To Read. " Community College Review 8,
            1(Summer 1980): 32-37.

1.95   Hughes, Betty. "Adult Literacy: A Project Explained." Spoken
            English 9, (September 1976): 87-91.

1.96   Hvitfeldt, Christina. "Traditional Culture, Perceptual Style, and
        Learning: The Classroom Behavior of Hmong Adults." Adult
        Education Quarterly 36, 2(Winter 1986): 65-77.

1.97   Identifying Problems Affecting Adult Literacy Training Programs
        In The CENTO Region. N.P.: CENTO Seminar on Illiteracy,
        Teheran, 1963.

1.98   Ilsley, P.J. "Policy Formulation in Adult Literacy Voluntarism."
        Adult Literacy and Basic Education 9, 3(1985): 154-162.

1.99   Ilsley, Paul J. "Including Educationally Deprived Adults in the
        Planning of Literacy Programs." New Directions for Continuing
        Education, 26(June 1985): 33-42.

1.100   Ilyin, Donna. "What Can Be Done to Help the Low Ability
        Student?" System 11, 2(1983): 163-179.

1.101   Imel, S. "Adult Literacy Education." (Eric Report) Adult Literacy
        and Basic Education 9, 2(1985): 106-116.

1.102   Impact! Adult Literacy + Language Skills. Reading,
        Massachusetts: Addison-Wesley Publishing Co., Inc., 1982.

1.103   Inter-American Seminar on Illiteracy and Adult Education;
        Summary report. Paris: UNESCO, 1950.

1.104   International Conference on Adult Education (4th, Paris, France,
        March 19-29, 1985). Final Report. Paris: UNESCO, 1985. ED 262
        166.

1.105   Irish, Gladys H. "Maximizing Functional Competencies and
        Basic Skills: Lessons of a Special Project." Adult Literacy and
        Basic Education 4, 1(Spring 1980): 17-22.

1.106   Jackson, S. "The Adult Illiterate." Special Education 47,
        (September 1958): 30-31.

1.107   Johnson, M. "Reading and Writing: Adults." TESL Talk 6,
        (June 1975): 1-11.

1.108   Jones, Edward V. Reading Instruction For The Adult Illiterate.
        Chicago: American Library Association, 1981.

1.109   Kahn, Akhter Hameed. "My Fifty Years of Literacy and Adult
        Education." Convergence 19, 1(1986): 39-47.

1.110   Kambuwa, G.P.A. A Guide To Teaching Adult Literacy. N.P.:
             n.p., 1971.

1.111   Kapel, M.B. "Improving Reading Competence of City Housing
             Authority Personnel: a Diversified Approach." Lifelong
             Learning 8, (November 1984): 16-20.

1.112   Kaufman, Laura. "Adults Learn to Grow Better Cotton in Pilot
             Literacy Project; Adult Literacy Programme Will Follow Pilot
             Scheme." Times Higher Education Supplement 15, (January 21,
             1972): 10; 16, (January 28, 1972): 10.

1.113   Kazemek, F.E. "The Self As Social Process: The Work of George
             Herbert Mead and Its Implications For Adult Literacy
             Education." Adult Literacy and Basic Education 12, 1(1988): 1-13.

1.114   Kazemek, F.E. "Adult Literacy Education: an Ethical Endeavor."
             Adult Literacy and Basic Education 8, 2(1984): 61-72.

1.115   Kazemek, Francis E. "'I Wanted to be a Tencra to Help Penp to I
             ...': Writing For Adult Beginning Learners." Journal of Reading
             27, 7(April 1984): 614-619.

1.116   Kazemek, Francis E., and Rigg, Pat. "Four Poets: Modern Poetry
             in The Adult Literacy Classroom." Journal of Reading 30,
             3(December 1986): 218-225.

1.117   Kazemek, Francis E., and Rigg, Pat, comps. Adult Literacy.
             Newark, Delaware: International Reading Association, 1984.

1.118   Kedney, R. J. "Educational Objectives in Adult Literacy
             Provision." Studies in Adult Education 8, (April 1976): 1-14.

1.119   Kedney, Robert John, ed. Illiterate In The Community Adult.
             Bolton, England: Bolton College of Education, 1975.

1.120   King, Kenneth J. "Research on Literacy and Work among the
             Rural Poor." Convergence 12, 3(1979): 42-54.

1.121   King, R. "Adult Literacy: Problem and Challenge." Lutheran
             Education 123, (January/February 1988): 168-172.

1.122   Kingston, Albert J. "Does Literacy Really Enhance the Lives of
             the Elderly?" Reading World 21, 3(March 1981): 169-171.

1.123   Kirsch, Irwin S., and Guthrie, John T. "Adult Reading Practices for Work and Leisure." Adult Education Quarterly 34, 4(Summer 1984): 213-232.

1.124   Kitz, William R. "Adult Literacy: A Review of The Past and A Proposal For The Future." Remedial and Special Education 9, 4(July-August 1988): 44-50.

1.125   Kolenbrander, R.W. "The Reagan Administration: Adult Literacy, Present Policy and Future Possibilities." Lifelong Learning 11, (September 1987): 13-15.

1.126   Kolenbrander, Ronald W. 'Adult Illiteracy, The Reagan Administration, and The Corporate Response: A Policy Study." Ph.D. dissertation, Kansas State University, 1986. 47/11A, p. 3944.

1.127   Kolinsky, Regine; Cary, Luz; and Morais, Jose, "Awareness of Words As Phonological Entities: The Role of Literacy." Applied Psycholinguistics 8, 3(September 1987): 223-232.

1.128   Kossack, Sharon. "Use The News: People's Choice." Journal of Reading 30, 2(November 1986): 168-170.

1.129   Kozol, Jonathan. "Fight Illiteracy with Volunteer Youth." Journal of Experiential Education 5, 2(Summer 1982): 17-22.

1.130   Lakey, Chris. "The Non-Reading Adult: Some Personality Characteristics." CORE: Collected Original Resources in Education 3, 3(October 1979): On nos. 1 & 2 of 17 microfiches (83 Frames).

1.131   Lamorella, Rose Marie, et al. "Teaching The Functionally Illiterate Adult: A Primer." Reading Horizons 23, 2(Winter 1983): 89-94.

1.132   Lawrence, Margaret, et al. "School and Community - -. Partners In Education: Helping Parents Help Their Children." Instructor 82, 1(August-September 1972): 63-66.

1.133   Laubach, Robert S. Teacher Attitude Assessment Model For Adult Literacy Trainers. Washington, D.C.: Laubach Literacy Inc., 1966. EP 010 860.

1.134   Learning Never Ends. N.P.: International Seminar on Workers and Adult Education, 1965.

1.135   Lee, Chris. "Basic Training in the Corporate Schoolhouse." Training 25, 4(April 1988): 27-30, 32, 33-36.

1.136   Lehr, F. "Reading Programs for the Older Adult: ERIC/RCS." Journal of Reading 28, (December 1984): 276-278.

1.137   Lehr, Fran. "ERIC/RCE: Adult Literacy." Journal of Reading 27, 2(November 1983): 176-179.

1.138   Lerche, Renee S. Effective Adult Literacy Programs. New York: Cambridge Book Company, 1985.

1.139   Lewis, J.W. "Adult Literacy Attacked." Adult Leadership 15, (May 1966): 15-16.

1.140   Limage, Leslie J. "Prospects For Adult Literacy In A Period of Economic Austerity." Comparative Education 24, 1(1988): 61-73.

1.141   Limage, Leslie J. "Adult Literacy Policy and Provision In An Age of Austerity." International Review of Education 32, 4(1986): 399-412.

1.142   Lindsey, Jimmy D., and Jarman, Leasa T. "Adult Basic Education: Six Years after Kavale and Lindsey's Literature Review." Journal of Reading 27, 7(April 1984): 609-613.

1.143   "Literacy Program is a Revelation for Non-Reading Adults (IBM's Interactive Adult Literacy Program called Principles of the Alphabet Literacy System)." T.H.E. Journal 15, (September 1987): 81-82.

1.144   Lizarzaburu, Alfonso E. "ALFIN, an Experiment in Adult Literacy Training in a Society in Transition." Prospects 6, (1976): 103-110.

1.145   Long, Huey B. "Adult Basic Education in Colonial America." Adult Literacy and Basic Education 7, 2(1983): 55-68.

1.146   Lorenzetto, Anna. "The Cultural Dimension of Adult Education: Permanent Education." Convergence 6, 3-4(1973): 67-75.

1.147   Luebke, Paul T., ed. Identifying Problems Affecting Adult Literacy Training Programs In The CENTO Region; Report. Teheran: General Department of Adult Education, 1964.

1.148   Lyman, Helen Huguenor. "Reading Materials For Adults With Limited Reading Experience." Library Trends 20, 2(October 1971): 326-349.

1.149   MacDonald, Bernice. Literacy Activities In Public Libraries; A Report of A Study of Services To Adult Illiterates. Chicago: American Library Association, 1966.

1.150   MacFarlane, Tom. "Curriculum Innovation in Adult Literacy: The Cost of Insularity." Studies in Adult Education 10, 2(October 1978): 153-160.

1.151   Mack, Faite Royjier-PonceFonte. "The Illiteracy Concept: Defining the Critical Level." Reading Horizons 19, 1(Fall 1978): 53-60.

1.152   Macker, Donald W. "Serving the Undereducated." Threshold in Secondary Education 2, 1(Spring 1976): 18-19.

1.153   Mageean, P., and Wilson, R. Assessment In Adult Literacy: The Profiling Alternative. Adelaide: Adelaide College of TAFE, 1987.

1.154   "Major Trends In Adult Education During The Last Ten Years: Analysis and Major Problems." Indian Journal of Adult Education 34, 4(April 19730; 13-14.

1.155   Malus, S. "The Logical Place To Attain Literacy." Library Journal 112, (July 1987): 38-40.

1.156   Manning, Diane Thompson. "Everyday Materials Improve Adults' Reading." Journal of Reading 21, 8(May 1978): 721-724.

1.157   Mark, Jorie Lester. "In Pursuit of Adult Literacy." Lifelong Learning 8, 7(May 1985): 4-5.

1.158   Mattran, Kenneth J. "From Illiteracy to Literacy: A Case Study." Reading Psychology 2, 3(July 1981): 165-172.

1.159   McQuaid, Grace. "How One English County Fosters Language Learning of Adults." English Quarterly 12, 4(Winter 1979-1980): 95-100.

1.160   McWilliams, Lana J. "Riding and Reading." Journal of Reading 22, 4(January 1979): 337-339.

1.161   Meyer, Sister Jean. "Reading Improvement For Urban-Area
            Adults." Journal of Reading 14, 3(December 1970): 183-186.

1.162   Meyer, Valerie. "Lingering Feelings of Failure: An Adult
            Student Who Didn't Learn to Read." Journal of Reading 31,
            3(December 1987): 218-221.

1.163   Mikulecky, L. and Newman, A. "Adult Literacy (Symposium)."
            Journal of Reading 31, (April 1988): 602-630.

1.164   "MOBRAL: Un Modelo Para La educacion de Aldutos?
            Convergence 7, 1(1974): 61-70.

1.165   Mocker, Donald. "Take School Out of ABE." Lifelong Learning;
            The Adult Years 1, 5(January): 12-13.32.

1.166   Morriss, E.C. "Articulation and Adult Elementary Education."
            Journal of Adult Education 7, (April 1935): 238-41.

1.167   Mudd, Norma. "I Know What You Mean . . . (I Think!)."
            Support for Learning 2, 1(February 1987): 17-21.

1.168   Mulira, Enoch E. Adult Literacy and Development: A
            Handbook For Teachers of Adults. Kampala: East African
            Literature Bureau, 1975.

1.169   Munns, K. L. "Why Can't Johnny's Parents Read?" Reading
            Improvement 19, (Summer 1982): 144-148.

1.170   Nadler, Leonard. "Literacy - Beyond The Classroom." Literacy
            Discussion 3, 1(March 1972): 25-33.

1.171   National Center For Research In Vocational Education Staff.
            Adult Literacy. Columbus, Ohio: Ohio State University,
            National Center For Research In Vocational Education, 1985.

1.172   Newman, A.P. "Volunteers Keep an Adult Basic Education
            Tutoring Program VITAL (Volunteers in Tutoring Adult
            Learners)." Educational Horizons 60, (Spring 1982): 109-110.

1.173   Newman, Anabel P. Adult Basic Education. N.P.: n.p., 1980.

1.174   Nickerson, Raymond S. "Adult Literacy and Technology."
            Visible Language 19, 3 (Summer 1985): 311-355.

1.175   Noor, Abdun. "Managing Adult Literacy Training." Prospects
         12, 2(1982): 163-184.

1.176   Norman, Charles A. and Malicky, Grace. "State in the Reading
         Development of Adults." Journal of Reading 30, 4(January
         1987): 302-307.

1.177   Norman, C.A. and Malicky, G. "Literacy as a Social
         Phenomenon: Implications for Instruction." Lifelong Learning
         9, (May 1986):   12-15.

1.178   O'Brein-Twohig, Bridget. "Cambridge House Literacy Scheme."
         Adult Education (London) 45 (September 1972): 146-149.

1.179   Olsen, T. "International Adult Education; ERIC/RCS Report."
         Journal of Reading 16, (April 1973): 584-589.

1.180   Olson, David R. "Interpreting Texts and Interpreting Nature:
         The Effects of Literacy on Hermeneutics and Epistemology."
         Visible Language 20, 3(Summer 1986): 302-317.

1.181   O'Neill, Julie. "Literacy Groups in a Probation Department."
         Adult Education 55, 1(June 1982): 49-54.

1.182   Orefice, Paolo. "Permanent Education and Functional Literacy."
         Literacy Work 2, 4(May 1973): 29-30.

1.183   Park, Rosemarie J. "Three Approaches to Improving Literacy
         Levels." Educational Horizons 66, 1(Fall 1987): 38-41.

1.184   Park, Rosemarie J. "Language and Reading Comprehension: A
         Case Study of Low-Reading Adults." Adult Literacy and Basic
         Education 7, 3(1983): 153-163.

1.185   Payne, Ryder, and McTeague, Frank. "Developing Literacy Skills
         in Adolescents and Adults." TESL Talk 7, 4(September 1976):
         60-82.

1.186   Peach, Richard Veale. "A Reading and Writing Initiation
         Program Administered In The Homes of Moderately and
         Severely Retarded Illiterates." Ph.D. dissertation, Kansas State
         University, 1978. 39/05A, p. 2873.

1.187   Peck, Cynthia Van Norden, and Kling, Martin. "Adult Literacy
         in the Seventies: Its Definitions and Measurement." Journal of
         Reading 20, 8(May 1977): 677-682.

1.188   Peters, Verne. "An Ambulance Emergency: Learning to Read."
             Phi Delta Kappan 62, 9(May 1981): 668-669.

1.189   Pipho, C. "Sorting Out The Data On Adult Literacy." Phi Delta
             Kappan 69, (May 1988): 630-631.

1.190   Pitman, James. "Adult Literacy." Literacy Discussion 3, 3-
             4(September-December 1972): 337-356.

1.191   "Population Education Materials Developed for The Most Needy
             in Society." Population Education Newsletter and Forum,
             26(1987): 3-6.

1.192   "The Problem of Drop-outs." Indian Journal of Adult Education
             41, 9(September 1980): 4-9, 32.

1.193   Pugh, Roy. "Modeling Behavior in the Tutor-Trainer
             Relationship." Australian Journal of Reading 6, 3(August 1983):
             128-136.

1.194   Rainsberry, Linda, ed. Out of the Shadows: Adult Literacy
             Guide. Toronto: TVOntario, 1983.

1.195   Ramirez, Sylvia. "Project Literacy: KGO-TV Fights Local
             Illiteracy." Television Broadcast 9, 11(November 1986): 50-55.

1.196   Read, C., and Ruyter, L. "Reading and Spelling Skills in Adults
             of Low Literacy." Remedial And Special Education 6,
             (November/December 1985): 43-52.

1.197   Richardson, J.S. "Networking For Adult Literacy: A Position
             Statement." Adult Literacy and Basic Education 12, 1(1988): 27-
             32.

1.198   Richardson, Judy S. "Language Experience for Adult Beginning
             Readers: Sometimes it Work!" Lifelong Learning 4, 8(April
             1981): 12-13, 20.

1.199   Richardson, Judy S., and Harbour, Kathy. "These Are a Few of
             Our Favorite Things." Lifelong Learning 6, 1(September 1982):
             18-19, 31.

1.200   Rigg, Pat. "Petra: Learning to Read at 45." Journal of Education
             167, 1(1985): 129-139.

1.201   Rigg, Pat, and Kazemek, Francis. "Literacy and Elders; What We Know and What We Need To Know." Educational Gerontology 9, 5-6(September-December 1983): 417-424.

1.202   Riley, T. "Adult Literacy Provision: An Overview." Journal of Applied Educational Studies 4, (Summer 1975): 20-27.

1.203   Ringley, Tay, et al. "Three Adult Education Projects: Local History Sparks ABE Class; Teleteacher; Project TARA: An Approach to AE." Lifelong Learning 2, 9(May 1979): 18-21, 25.

1.204   Roberts, J.T. "Adult Literacy." Adult Education (London) 46, 6(March 1974): 10-12.

1.205   Robertson, Elizabeth. "Adult Literacy in Fife - Some Student Profiles." Scottish Journal of Adult Education 2, 1(Autumn 1975): 15-19.

1.206   Robinson, Richard David. "An Investigation Into The Use of The Cloze Procedure With A Group of Functionally Illiterate Adults." Ed. D. Dissertation, University of Georgia, 1971. 32/07-A, p. 3572.

1.207   Rogers, Joy J. "Readability as a Source of Perceived Failure in Adult Literacy Instruction." Lifelong Learning 10, 4(January 1987): 26-29.

1.208   Ross, Bev. "Help For The Adult Literacy Tutor." Access Magazine, (September-November 1983): 15.

1.209   Roth, Edith. "APL: A Ferment in Education." American Education 12, 4(May 1976): 6-9.

1.210   Roueche, John E. "Between a Rock and A Hard Place: Meeting Adult Literacy Needs. " Community and Junior College Journal 54, 7(April 1984): 21-24.

1.211   Ryan, John. "Some Key Problems in Adult Literacy." Prospects 15, 3(1985): 375-381.

1.212   Sanford, Julie P., and Crawley, Frank E. "The Forum." Science Teacher 44, 4(April 1977): 25-26.

1.213   Schmidt, David L. "Does Rapid Reading Training Really Work?" Training and Development Journal 26, 2(February 1972): 26-29.

1.214   Schneiderman, Paula. "Active Reading Techniques System
             (ARTS): A Method for Instruction of Functionally Illiterate
             Adults." Urban Education 13, 2(July 1978): 195-202.

1.215   "School For Parents." Reading Newsreport 5, 6(April 1971): 26-
             29.

1.216   Shrivastava, Om. "Language Issues in Adult Education." Indian
             Journal of Adult Education 41, 6-7(June-July 1980): 33-36.

1.217   Sisco, Burt. "The Undereducated: Myth or Reality." Lifelong
             Learning 6, 8(April 1983): 14-15, 24, 26.

1.218   Smith, James V. "Reading, Writing and Recurrency: Some
             Reflections On The Adult Literacy Question." Education in The
             North 16, (1979): 51-56.

1.219   Steuart, Richard Calvert. "An Evaluation of The Educational
             Effectiveness of Selected Adult Basic Education Literacy
             Materials." Ph. D. dissertation, The University of Wisconsin,
             1968. 29/12-A, p. 4269.

1.220   Suggestions For Research In Adult Literacy; Meeting of Experts
             On Research In Literacy. (UNESCO House, 8-12 July 1968). Paris:
             UNESCO, 1968. ED 029 191.

1.221   Taylor, N. et al. "Study of Low-Literate Adults: Personal,
             Environmental and Program Considerations." Urban Review
             12, (Summer 1980): 69-77.

1.222   Thistlethwaite, Linda. "The Adult Disabled Reader - An
             Independent Learner?" Lifelong Learning 7, 3(November 1983):
             28.

1.223   Trismen, Donald A. "Adult Readers: Activities and Goals."
             Paper presented at the Meeting of the American Educational
             Research Association, Chicago, Illinois, 1972. ED 061 024.

1.224   Turner, Terilyn C. "An Overview of Computers In Adult
             Literacy Programs." Lifelong Learning 11, 8(June 1988): 9-12.

1.225   Valentine, Thomas. "Adult Functional Literacy as a Goal of
             Instruction." Adult Educational Quarterly 36, 2(Winter 1986):
             108-113.

1.226   Verner, Coolie. "Basic Factors in Learning to Read and Write."
             Literacy Disussion 5, 4(Winter 1974): 583-596.

1.227   Versluys, J.D.N. "Why Do You Want To Read?" Prospects 2,
             2(Summer 1972): 202-205.

1.228   Vijagendra, T. "Adult Education Integrates Literacy, Health and
             Conscientization: The Mandar Story." Convergence 15, 2(1982):
             35-42.

1.229   Wainwright, Gordon. "Rapid and Efficient Reading: A BASIC
             Approach to Training for Managers and Others in Reading
             Efficiency. Part Two." Industrial Training International 10,
             3(March 1975): 81-83.

1.230   Walker, Becky, et al. "Use The News." Journal of Reading 30,
             7(April 1987): 652-653.

1.231   WCOTP Training Workshop. "The Role of Teachers
             Organizations In Adult Literacy Education." Including Report
             on WCOTP Adult Education Meeting. "Relationship of Lifelong
             Education To The Work of The Public Schools." (Seoul, Korea,
             1966). N.P.: World Confed-eration of Organizations of The
             Teaching Profession, 1966. ED 017 750.

1.232   Weibel, Marguerite Crowley. "Use The Public Library With
             Adult Literacy Students." Journal of Reading 27, 1(October
             1983): 62-65.

1.233   Weingand, Darlene E. "The Library-Learner Dynamic in a
             Changing World." Library Trends 35, 2(Fall 1986): 187-196.

1.234   Weintraub, Herbert. "Dedicated Computers: A Promising
             Solution For Adult Academic Literacy." Technological Horizons
             In Education 10, 2(November 1982): 93-94.

1.235   Wells, Alan. "Adult Literacy: Closer Working With FE."
             NATFHE Journal, 9(December 1979): 12-14.

1.236   White, Kath. "Conflict, Principles and Practice in Adult
             Literacy." Australian Journal of Reading 6, 3(August 1983): 117-
             127.

1.237   Wiese, M.J.J. "Why Adult Education? For Literacy." Adult
             Education Bulletin 6, (August 1942): 176-177.

1.238   Youngman, Frank. "Adult Literacy and the Mode of
             Production." International Journal of Lifelong Education 4,
             2(April-June 1985): 149-161.

1.239   Zarembinski, Clem. The Relationship of The Adult Basic
             Education Student's Authoritarian Attitude and His Learning
             Potential. Tempe, Arizona: Arizona State University, College of
             Education, 1970. ED 041 213.

2

Adult Reading Programs

2.240   "Adult Literacy Programs and Development." School and
           Society 97, 2315(February 1969): 119.

2.241   Alessi, Stephen M., et al. "Effectiveness of a Computer-Based
           Reading Comprehension Programs for Adults." Journal of
           Educational Technology Systems 11, 1(1982-1983): 43-57.

2.242   Ambardar, A.K. "Reading Efficiency: Analysis of Techniques for
           Adult Readers." Reading Improvement 21, (Spring 1984): 21-27.

2.243   Anderson, C.A. "In Adult Basic Reading Programs, Are We
           Teaching Students or Systems?" Adult Leadership 16,
           (November 1967): 179-181.

2.244   Andrews, J.D., et al. "Readability in The Adult Reader."
           Teaching English in The Two-Year College 10, (Winter 1984):
           185-189.

2.245   Askov, E.N., and Cole, P.G. "Computer Assisted Instruction for
           Teaching Adults Beginning Reading." Adult Literacy and Basic
           Education 9, 2(1985): 57-67.

2.246   Bacon, Margaret. "What Adult Literacy Teachers Need to Know
           About Strategies for Focusing on Comprehension." Lifelong
           Learning 6, 6(February 1983): 4-5.

2.247   Barnes, Robert F. "A Review and Appraisal of Adult Literacy
           Materials and Programs." ED 003 519.

2.248   Baucum, Kenneth L. The ABC's of Literacy: Lessons From
           Linguistics. Teheran: International Institute For Adult Literacy
           Methods, 1978. ED 154 335.

2.249   Brown, Don A. "A Literacy Program For Adult Illiterates." 1968.
             EP 010 437.

2.250   Carey, Susan. "15 NonFiction Books For Developing Adult
             Readers." Journal of Reading 27, 6(March 1984): 520-522.

2.251   Coates, R.H. "Preparing Adults for Rapid Change." NEA
             Journal 55, (December 1966): 23-25.

2.252   Cornell, Thomas. "Characteristics of Effective Occupational
             Literacy Programs." Journal of Reading 31, 7(April 1988): 654-
             656.

             Discusses the need and characteristics of effective occupational
             literacy programs. Also offers suggestions for reading specialists
             who what to help develop these kinds of programs. The
             characteristics of effective occupational literacy programs are: 1.)
             maintain organization's mission; 2.) teach skills and enhance
             knowledge within a meaningful context; 3.) increase time on
             task through active involvement; and 4.) use a competency-
             based mastery learning system.

2.253   Cranney, A. Garr. "Two Decades of Adult Reading Programs:
             Growth, Problems, and Prospects." Journal of Reading 26,
             5(February 1983): 416-422.

2.254   Devereux, W.A. "Adult Literacy Campaign in the United
             Kingdom." Convergence 10, 1(1977): 10-19.

2.255   Diekhoff, George M. "An Appraisal of Adult Literacy Programs:
             Reading Between The Lines." Journal of Reading 31, 7(April
             1988): 624-630.

2.256   Diekhoff, G.M., and Diekhoff, K.B. "The Adult Literacy Program
             Attrition Problem: Identification At Intake." Adult Literacy and
             Basic Education 8, 1(1984): 34-47.

2.257   Fields, Ernest L. "Industry-based Programs: A Growing Source
             For Adult Literacy Development." Lifelong Learning 10,
             1(September 1986): 7-9.

2.258   Fineman, M.P. "Project: LEARN-Adults Become Readers."
             Library Journal 112, (March 1, 1987): 45-46.

2.259   "From Illiterate To Adult Reader In 11 Hours (Using Words In Colour)." Teachers Journal (Victoria) 51, (May 1968): 125-126.

2.260   Gillis, M.K., and Longnion, Bonnie. "Materials Preferences and Reading Goals of Adult Beginning Readers." Adult Literacy and Basic Education 6, 2(Summer 1982): 85-90.

2.261   Given, N. "The British Concept of Success in Adult Literacy." Adult Literacy and Basic Education 8, 2(1984): 102-107.

2.262   Heathington, B.S., et al. "Characteristics of Adult Beginning Readers Who Persisted in a Volunteer Tutoring Program." Lifelong Learning 7, (February 1984): 20-22.

2.263   Heathington, Betty S., et al. "An Inventory To Assess Adult Beginning Readers' Beliefs, Feelings, and Behavious Regarding Reading." Adult Literacy and Basic Education 10, 1(1986): 37-46.

2.264   Johnson, Laura, ed. Reading and The Adult Learner. Newark, Delaware: International Reading Association, 1979.

2.265   Khater, M.R. "Adult Literacy Programme." International Journal of Adult and Youth Education 14, 1(1962): 5-11.

2.266   Kilgannon, John R. "I.T.A. - Is It The Adult Way To Literacy?" Teacher 6, 21(19 November 1965): 12-13.

2.267   Koenke, Karl. "ERIC/RCS: Teaching Adults To Read: Exhortations, Explanations, and Examples." Journal of Reading 22, 6(March 1979): 552-555.

2.268   Lamorella, Rose Marie, et al. "Teaching The Functionally Illiterate Adult: A Primer." Reading Horizons 23, 2(Winter 1983): 89-94.

2.269   Lewis, E.P., and Ness, M.J. "Basic Education Class Aids Adults." Wisconsin Journal of Education 99, (December 1966): 10-12.

2.270   Lizarzaburu, Alfonso E. "ALFIN, An Experiment in Adult Literacy Training in a Society in Transition." Prospects 6, 1(1976): 103-110.

2.271   Lupton, D. E. "Meeting Current Reading Needs; In Adult Literacy Programs." Conference on Reading - University of Chicago 27, (1965): 20-23.

2.272   Lyman, Helen H. Reading and The Adult New Reader. Chicago: American Library Association, 1976.

2.273   Meltzer, Bernice. "Using Experience To Teach Reading Skills To Adults." Journal of Reading 23, 3(December 1979): 251-253.

2.274   Meyer, Valerie. "Prime-O-Tec: A Successful Strategy For Adult Disabled Readers." Journal of Reading 25, 6(March 1982): 512-515.

2.275   Meyer, Valerie, and Keefe, Donald. "The Laubach Way To Reading: A Review." Lifelong Learning 12, (September 1988): 8-10.

2.276   Miller, Phyllis A. "Using Annual Reports For Adult Literacy Improvement." Journal of Reading 32, 1(October 1988): 25-29.

2.277   Mocker, Donald W. "Cooperative Learning Process: Shared Learning Experience in Teaching Adults To Read." Journal of Reading 18, 6(March 1975): 440-444.

2.278   Newman, Anabel P. Adult Basic Education: Reading. Boston: Allyn and Bacon, 1980.

2.279   Nickse, Ruth S., et al. "An Intergenerational Adult Literacy Project: A Family Intervention/Prevention Model." Journal of Reading 31, 7(April 1988): 634-642.

2.280   O'Malley, Paulette F., and Haase, Ann Marie Bernazza. "Retaining The Returning Adult In a Reading Program." Reading Horizons 21, 3(Spring 1981): 200-205.

2.281   "Open To Suggestion." Journal of Reading 23, 5(February 1980): 390-391.

2.282   Perin, Dolores. "Schema Activation, Cooperation, and Adult Literacy Instruction." Journal of Reading 32, 1(October 1988): 54-62.

2.283   Pidgeon, Douglas. "A Self-Instructional Programme For Teaching Adults To Read English." Literacy Work 5, 3(Fall 1976): 47-55, 57, 59.

2.284 Prins, Jan Vanryswik. "A Study To Determine Reasons of Adult Drop Out of an Adult Basic Education Literacy Program." Ed. D. dissertation, Wayne State University, 1972. 33/05-A, p. 2063.

2.285 Rauch, Ester N. "Pornography: A Special Pedagogical Tool For A Special Adult Group: Staff Room Interchange." College Composition and Communication 29, 4(December 1978): 390-392.

2.286 Richards, M. "End of Term Adult Reading Report, Result: Inadequate." Times Higher Education Supplement 322, (January 6, 1978): 8.

2.287 Richards, M. "Questionaires Sent To Tutors For Adult Literacy Project." Times Higher Education Supplement 319, (December 16, 1977): 4.

2.288 Richardson, J. S. "Language Experience For Adult Beginning Readers: Sometimes It Works!" Lifelong Learning 4, (April 1981): 12-13.

2.289 Rigg, P. "Petra: Learning To Read at 45." Journal of Education 167, 1(1985): 29-39.

2.290 Rigg, Pat, and Kazemek, Francis E. "For Adults Only: Reading Materials For Adult Literacy Students." Journal of Reading 28, 8(May 1985): 726-731.

2.291 Schmidt, Susan. "A History of ABE Services in Public Libraries." Drexel Library Quarterly 14, 4(October 1978): 5-13.

2.292 Schneiderman, Paula. "Without Reading You Ain't Nothing." Lifelong Learning: The Adult Years 1, 1(September 1977): 16-18.

2.293 Siegel, Martin A. "Computer Based Education in Prison Schools." Journal of Educational Technology Systems 7, 3(1978-1979): 239-256.

2.294 Stevens, J. "BBC Adult Literacy Project." Convergence 10, 1(1977): 20-28.

2.295 Thistlethwaite, Linda. "Teaching Reading To The ABE Student Who Cannot Read." Lifelong Learning: The Adult Years 7, 1(September 1983): 5-7, 28.

2.296   Turner, Terilyn C. "Using The Computer For Adult Literacy
             Instruction." Journal of Reading 31, 7(April 1988): 643-647.

2.297   Wells, A. "Adult Literacy and Basic Education: The British
             Experience." Adult Literacy and Basic Education 9, 1(1985): 1-10.

2.298   Young, Deborah, and Irwin, Martha. "Integrating Computers
             into Adult Literacy Programs." Journal of Reading 31, 7 (April
             1988): 648-652.

3

Aliteracy

3.299   Aliteracy, People Who Can Read But Won't. N.P.: n.p., 1984.

3.300   Decker, Barbara Cooper. "Aliteracy: What Teachers Can Do To
         Keep Johnny Reading." Journal of Teacher Education 37,
         6(November-December 1986): 55-58.

         Discusses the phenomenon of aliteracy, those people who can
         read but choose not to. Explores the causes of aliteracy.
         Examines reading instruction in other countries. Presents a
         number of suggestions for preventing aliteracy. Suggestions
         include making reading relevant, emphasize the
         reading/writing connection, and foster creative and intelligent
         thinkers.

3.301   Giordno, D.J. "Aliterates: Students Who Can Read, But Won't."
         New Jersey Education Association Review 59, (March 1986): 28-
         30.

3.302   Hale, Robert D. "Musings." Horn Book Magazine 62, 3(May-
         June 1986): 352-353.

3.303   Thimmesch, Nick, ed. Aliteracy: People Who Can Read But
         Won't. A Conference Sponsored by The American Enterprise
         Institute For Public Policy Research (Washington, D.C. ,
         September 20, 1982). AEI Symposia 83C. Washington, D.C.:
         American Enterprise Institute For Public Policy Research, 1984.
         ED 240 543.

4

Bibliographies on Illiteracy and Literacy

4.304   Adult Education and Creation of Rural Press For The Newly Literate. Tehran: International Institute For Adult Literacy Methods, 1972.

4.305   Adult Literacy II: A Select Bibliography 1978 to 1981. Canberra: National Library of Australia, 1981.

4.306   Adult Literacy In Africa - Nigeria, Rhodesia, South Africa, Sudan, Tanzania. Literacy Bibliographies 23. Teheran: International Institute For Adult Literacy Methods, 1980. ED 198 475.

4.307   Alfabetizacion y Educacion de Adultos. N.P.: n.p., 1983.

4.308   Annotated Bibliography Of Materials For Teachers Of Americanization And Literacy Classes. Columbus, Ohio: Ohio State University, Bureau of Education Research and Service, 1958.

4.309   Arsulich, Michael. Microcomputers In Education. Selected Bibliography. N.P. : n.p., 1982. ED 226 719.

4.310   Askov, Eunice N., and Lee, Joyce W., comps. An Annotated Bibliography of Adult Basic Education Instructional Materials. State College, Pennsylvania: Pennsylvania State University, 1974. ED 123 610.

4.311   August, Bonne. Getting Started: Adult Education, Reading, and Writing. An Annotated List of Bibliographies For Youth and Adult Literacy Programs. New York: Literacy Assistance Center, 1984. ED 260 179.

4.312   Azzouz, Azzedine, et al. Selected Bibliography of Educational
             Materials: Algeria, Libya, Moracco, Tunisia. Volume 7, Number
             3, 1973. Tunis, Tunisia: Agence Tunisienne de Public Relations,
             1973. ED 110 403.

4.313   Barnes, Robert F., and Hendrickson, Andrew. Graded Materials
             For Teaching Adult Illiterates. Columbus, Ohio: Ohio State
             University Center For Adult Education, 1965.

4.314   Bates, M., and Zimmerman, J. Adult Basic Education: An
             Annotated List of Resources. Brisbane: Division of Technical
             and Further Education, 1987.

4.315   Berg, Joann La Perla, and Wallace, Virginia A. A Selected
             Bibliography of Functional Literacy Materials For Adult
             Learners. Upper Montclair, New Jersey: Montclair State College,
             1980. ED 199 551.

4.316   Bibliographic Guide To Functional Literacy, A. Washington, DC:
             National Institute of Education, 1979. ED 189 197.

4.317   Bibliography of Reading Materials For Basic Reading and English
             As A Second Language Syracuse, New York: Literacy
             Volunteers, Inc., 1977. ED 188 466.

4.318   Bibliography For Use In The Preparation of Materials For Adult
             Literacy Education In Brazil, A. Tallahassee, Florida: Florida
             State University, 1967. ED 019 550.

4.319   Butler, Mike. "Selected Annotated Bibliography." Action in
             Teacher Education 5, 4(Winter 1983-1984): 63-79.

4.320   Chmaj, Deborah R., and Wolde, Menbere, comps. The Laubach
             Collection: Consisting of The Personal Papers of Frank C.
             Laubach and The Organizational Documents of Laubach Literacy,
             Inc., in The Archives of Continuing Education in Syracuse
             University Libraries. Syracuse, New York: Syracuse University
             Libraries, 1974. ED 166 363.

4.321   Clarke, Ann, comp. Adult Literacy: A Catalogue of Material In
             The Library of The College of Librarianship Wales. Aberystwyth:
             College of Librarianship Wales, 1977.

4.322   Collection of Selected Summaries From Books and Periodicals In
             The Field of Literacy and Adult Education Received by the

IIALM During The First Half of The Year 1984. Teheran: International Institute For Adult Literacy Methods, 1986. ED 276 968.

4.323   Copple, Christine. Computers In The Secondary Mathematics Curriculum. N.P.: n.p., 1981. ED 204 144.

4.324   Documents From The Experimental World Literacy Programme. Paris: UNESCO, 1979.

4.325   Documents On Adult Education and Literacy: A Bibliography of Selected Documents. Bangkok, Thailand: UNESCO, 1971. ED 052 451.

4.326   Emeru, Sarah Snell. Mexico's Marginal Peoples - Informal Eduction Projects. N.P.: n.p., 1984.

4.327   Family Planning And Literacy. London: International Planned Parenthood Federation, 1977. ED 146 022.

4.328   Favre, Dominique, comp. Bibliographie Sur L'alphabetisation. Lyon, France: CRDP, 1977.

4.329   French, Joyce N., comp. Adult Literacy. N.P.: n.p., 1987.

4.330   Functional Literacy and Illiterate Immigrants. Tehran: International Institute For Adult Literacy Methods, 1972.

4.331   Graff, Harvey J. Literacy In History: An Interdisciplinary Research Bibliography. New York: Garland Publishing. 1981.

4.332   Griswold, Karen. Bibliography of Professional Materials: Literacy, Reading, Writing. New York: Literacy Assistance Center, 1985. ED 260 181.

4.333   Hay, Wendy, comp. Adult Literacy In Britain: An Annotated Bibliography. London: Library Association, 1978.

4.334   Healey, Phyllis M. Biobliography of The Summer Institute of Linguistics, Papua New Guinea Branch, 1956-1972. N.P.: n.p., 1973.

4.335   Heiser, Jane-Carol. Literacy Resources: An Annotated Checklist For Tutors & Librarians. Baltimore, Maryland: Pratt, Enoch, Free Library, 1983.

4.336   Honig, Bill, et al. "A Year-End Look at The Books of 1987."
               American School Board Journal 174, 12(December 1987): 23-25,
               32-45.

4.337   Joseph, Grace, comp., et al. A Selected ERIC Bibliography On
               Teaching English As A Second Language To The Illiterate. CAL-
               ERIC/Cll Series on Languages and Linguistics, No. 25.
               Arlington, Virginia: ERIC Clearinghouse on Languages and
               Lingusitics, 1975. ED 105 779.

4.338   Kazemek, Francis E., and Rigg, Pat, eds. Adult Literacy. Newark
               Delaware: International Reading Association, 1984.

4.339   Korkmas, Ann, and Waite, Marian, comps. Adult Literacy; A
               Bibliography of Materials Suitable For Public Library Collections.
               Dallas, Texas: Dallas Public Library, 1976. ED 129 288.

4.340   Korpi, Barbara, comp. Materials For Teaching Adult Functional
               Literacy In North Dakota; Annotated Bibliography.
               Occupational Knowledge, Community Resources, Government
               and Law, Consumer Economics, Health. Dickinson, North
               Dakota: Dickinson Public School District 1, 1979. ED 199 479.

4.341   L'Alphabetisation Fonctionnelle. N.P.: Centre Universitaire de
               Cooperation Economique et Sociale, 1972.

4.342   Literacy, Adult Education & Social Sciences: A Bibliography List,
               Vol. 1, No. 2, October-December 1983. Teheran: International
               Institute For Adult Literacy Methods, 1984. ED 244 256.

4.343   Literacy, Adult Education & Social Sciences: A Bibliography List,
               Vol. 1, No.1, January 1982 - September 1983. Teheran:
               International Institute For Adult Literacy Methods, 1984. ED 244
               255.

4.344   Literacy and Basic Education: A Selected, Annotated
               Bibliography. Annotated Bibliography #3. East Lansing,
               Michigan: Michigan State University, Education Information
               Center, 1981. ED 232 824

4.345   Literacy Documentation. Volume VII, Number 1, 1978.
               Teheran: International Institute For Adult Literacy Methods,
               1978. ED 169 207.

4.346   Literacy Documentation. Volume 5, Number 1. Teheran:
          International Institute For Adult Literacy Methods, 1976. ED
          122 139.

4.347   Literacy Documentation: An International Bulletin For Libraries
          and Information Centres. Volume 3, Number 4. Teheran:
          International Institute For Adult Literacy Methods, 1974. ED
          105 278.

4.348   Literacy Documentation: An International Bulletin For Libraries
          and Information Centres. Volume II, Nos. 3-4, August-
          November 1973. Teheran: International Institute For Adult
          Literacy Methods, 1973. ED 089 093.

4.349   Literacy Education. Paris: UNESCO, 1950.

4.350   Literacy Evaluation. Literacy Bibliographies 8. Teheran:
          International Institute For Adult Literacy Methods, 1977. ED 169
          209.

4.351   Literacy Teaching; A Selected Bibliography. Paris: UNESCO,
          1956.

4.352   Literacy Teaching. Specialised Bibliography B5. London: British
          Council, 1975. ED 113 948.

4.353   Marrapodi, Maryann. Booting Up: A Computer-Assisted
          Bibliography. An Annotated List of Educational Computer
          Software For Youth and Adult Literacy Programs. New York:
          Literacy Assistance Center, 1984. ED 260 180.

4.354   McGee, Leo, and Neufeldt, Harvey G., comps. Education of The
          Black Adult In The United States: An Annotated Bibliography.
          Westport, Connecticut: Greenwood Press, 1985. ED 266 233.

4.355   Miller, Inabeth. Micro-computers And The Media Specialist:
          An Annotated Bibliography. Syracuse, New York: ERIC
          Clearinghouse on Information Resources, 1981. ED 222 182.

4.356   Motivation. Literacy Bibliographies 15. Teheran: International
          Institute For Adult Literacy Methods, 1978. ED 169 208.

4.357   Murane, Elizabeth. Bibliography of The Summer Institute of
          Linguistics. Ukarumpa, Papua New Guinea: The Institute, 1975.

4.358   Nazzaro, Lois B., ed. <u>Annotated Bibliography, January 1, 1971</u>. Philadelphia, Pennsylvania: Free Library of Philadelphia, 1971. ED 054 783.

4.359   Nelson, Nancy Wong, ed. <u>Back To Basics; 1977 Fall Reading Institutes</u>. New Brunswick, New Jersey: Rutgers, The State University, 1977. ED 145 397.

4.360   Nussbaum, Mary J. <u>Adult Literacy In The Developing Countries: A Bibliography</u>. N.P.: n.p., 1971. ED 044 638.

4.361   O'Brien, Roberta Luther, comp. <u>Books For Adult New Readers. Second Revised Edition</u>. Cleveland, Ohio: Project LEARN, 1984. ED 257 957.

4.362   O'Brien, Roberta Luther, comp. <u>Books For Adult New Readers. Second Revised Edition</u>. Cleveland, Ohio: Cleveland Area Metropolitan Library System, 1980. ED 201 738.

4.363   Patrick, Heather, comp. <u>Bibliography of The Summer Institute of Linguistics, Papua New Guinea Branch, 1956-1980</u>. N.P.: n.p., 1981

4.364   <u>Past Literacy. Literacy Bibliographies 6</u>. Teheran: International Institute For Adult Literacy Methods, 1977. ED 169 210.

4.365   <u>Problem of Drop-outs, The</u>. N.P.: n.p., 1980.

4.366   Purvis, Jeffrey. "Places to Begin: A Bibliographic Sketch of Linguistics, Conposition and Literacy." <u>Writing Instructor</u> 4, 3(Spring 1985): 144-150.

4.367   Reder, Stephen M. <u>A Bibliographic Guide To Functional Literacy</u>. N.P.: n.p., 1979.

4.368   Rivera, William, and Laubach, Robert S., comps. <u>Literacy In The 70's: An Annotated Bibliography</u>. Syracuse, New York: Syracuse University Publications, 1980. ED 195 660.

4.369   <u>Rural Libraries</u>. N.P.: n.p., 1979.

4.370   Smith, Edwin H., and Bradtmueller, Weldon G. <u>A Selected Annotated Bibliography of Instructional Literacy Materials For Adult Basic Education</u>. Tallahassee, Florida: Division of Vocational, Technical and Adult Education, 1968.

4.371   Sokolova, Emilija S., and Metlina, Sotija I. "Participation of
          Youth in Educational Development." Educational
          Documentation and Information, 229 (1983): 1-71.

4.372   Spencer, Marion D., and Chemerys, Mary K., eds. Bibliography
          of Literacy Materials, 3rd Edition. Kalamazoo, Michigan:
          Kalamazoo Library System, 1967.

4.373   Versluys, J.D.N., ed. Research In Adult Literacy: A Bibliography.
          Teheran: International Institute For Adult Literacy Methods,
          1977.

4.374   Von Rhu Me, Ma. Mran' Ma Nuin Nam Ca Tat Mrok Re Chuin
          Ra Ca Cu Ca Ran, 1964-80. N.P.: n.p., 1981.

4.375   Wagner, S. "Several Publications on Literacy Education."
          Prospects (Paris, France) 14, 3(1984): 429-431.

4.376   Ward, Betty A., and Brice, Edward W. Literacy and Basic
          Elementary Education For Adults; A Selected Annotated
          Bibliography. Washington, D.C.: Department of Health,
          Education, and Welfare, 1961. ED 048 559.

4.377   Work, William. "Toward Comprehensive Communication
          Literacy: ERIC Report." Communication Education 27,
          4(November 1978): 338-342

5

Biliteracy

5.378   Canbourne, Brian. "Process Writing and Non-English Speaking
           Background Children." Australian Journal of Reading 9,
           3(August 1986): 126-138.

5.379   Cummings, Jim. Language and Literacy Learning In Bilingual
           Instruction: Policy Report. Washington, D.C.: National
           Institute of Education, 1983. ED 245 575.

5.380   Fishman, Joshua A. "Ethnocultural Dimensions in The
           Acquisition and Retention of Biliteracy." Journal of Basic
           Writing 3, 1(Fall-Winter 1980): 48-61.

           Examination of five schools wherein the stress is on biliteracy,
           the acquisition of literacy in two languages. Reviews the various
           kinds of biliteracy. Presents ethnofunctional, ethnopedagogic,
           ethnolinguistic, and ethnographic comparisons. Concludes with
           a discussion of the early childhood acquisition of biliteracy, and
           the author's contention that societal biliteracy is unproblematic.

5.381   Goodman, Kenneth, et al. Reading In The Bilingual Classroom:
           Literacy and Biliteracy. Washington, D.C.: National Institute of
           Education, 1979. ED 181 725.

5.382   Guebert, Linda. "Learning To Read In A Second Language."
           TESL Talk 15, 1-2(Winter-Spring 1984): 52-59.

5.383   Horowitz, Rosalind. "Orality and Literacy in Bilingual-
           Bicultural Contexts." NABE: The Journal For The National
           Association For Bilingual Education 8, 3(Spring 1984): 11-26.

5.384   McEvedy, Rosanna. "Some Social, Cultural and Linguistic Issues
           in Teaching Reading To Children Who Speak English as a

Second Language." Australian Journal of Reading 9, 3(August 1986): 139-152.

5.385   Niyekawa, Agnes M. Biliteracy Acquisition and Its Socio-Cultural Effects. Professional Papers N-1. Washington, D.C.: National Institute of Education, 1980. ED 222 082.

5.386   Penfield, Joyce. "ESL Literacy and The New Refugees: Priorities and Considerations" Adult Literacy and Basic Education 10, 1(1986): 47-57.

5.387   Ronan, Eileen. "Commentary: English as a Second Language." Journal of Reading 29, 5(February 1986): 388-390.

5.388   Swearingen, C. Jan. "The Literacy Conundrum: The Bilingual/Bicultural Boom and The Language Teacher." CEA Critic 42, 3(March 1980): 12-16.

6

Computer Literacy

A.   GENERAL

6.A.389   Abernathy, Sandra M., and Pettibone, Timothy J. "Computer
          Literacy and Certification: What States Are Doing."
          Technological Horizons in Education 12, 4(November 1984):
          117-119.

6.A.390   Adams, K. "Computers and Home Economics." Journal of The
          Home Economics Association of Australia 18, 1(April 1986): 5-8.

6.A.391   Ahl, David H. "School Uses of Microcomputers." Creative
          Computing 9, 10(October 1983): 185-186.

6.A.392   Akst, Geoffrey. "Computer Literacy: An Interview with Dr.
          Michael Hoban." Journal of Development & Remedial
          Education 8, 2(1984): 31.

6.A.393   Albro, Paul. "Evolution of a Successful Faculty Computer
          Literacy Project." CAUSE/EFFECT 10, 2(March 1987): 24-27.

6.A.394   Albury, D. "Technological Gatekeepers." Times Higher
          Education Supplement 783, (November 6, 1987): Supplement
          XIV.

6.A.395   Alexander, Wilma Jean. "Microcomputers: Impact on Society
          and Education." Business Education Forum 35, 8(May 1981): 19-
          21.

6.A.396   Allen, C.A., and Rude, R.T. "Computer Literacy and Writing:
          Complementary Processes for all Subjects." New England
          Reading Association Journal 21, (Winter 1986): 33-36.

6.A.397   Allison, L. A Practical Introduction To Denotational Semantics.
           New York: Cambridge University Press, 1987.

6.A.398   Amador, Sherrill L. "Adult Computer Literacy: A Marketing
           Opportunity with Financial Rewards." New Directions for
           Continuing Education, 29(March 1986): 79-87.

6.A.399   Anderson, Cheryl A. "Computer Literacy: Changes for Teacher
           Education." Journal of Teacher Education 34, 5(September-
           October 1983): 6-9.

6.A.400   Anderson, Jonathan. Computing In Schools: An Australian
           Perspective. Australian Education Review Number 21.
           Hawthorn, Australia: Australian Council For Educational
           Research, 1984. ED 246 860.

6.A.401   Anderson, Ronald E., et al. "In Defense of a Comprehensive
           View of Computer Literacy - A Reply to Luehrmann."
           Mathematics Teacher 74, 9(December): 687-690.

6.A.402   Anderson, Ronald M. "A New Approach To Computer Literacy
           For Elementary Teachers and Others." Collegiate
           Microcomputer 1, 4(November 1983): 341-437.

6.A.403   Andrews, Wayne, and Nourie, Alan. "Enhancement of
           Computer Literacy Through a Library Computer Study Area."
           Library Software Review 7, 2(March - April 1988): 108-115.

6.A.404   Arden, Eugene. "Beyond Computer Literacy." College Board
           Review, 139(Spring 1986): 27-28.

6.A.405   Aron, Helen. "The Impact of Computers on Literacy." Lifelong
           Learning 6, 4(December 1982): 8-9, 22-23.

6.A.406   Ashbrook, Richard M. "What Will We Do For The Poor,
           Disadvantaged, and Computer Illiterate." Instructional
           Innovator 29, 3(March 1984): 48.

6.A.407   Austin, Gilbert R., and Lutterodt, Sarah A. "The Computer at
           School." Prospects 12, 4(1982): 421-438.

6.A.408   Austin, Richard H. "A Study of Computer Impact on Society
           and Computer Literacy Courses and Materials." Journal of
           Educational Technology Systems 7, 3(1978-1979): 267-274.

6.A.409   Auten, Anne. "ERIC/RCS: Computer Literacy, Part III: CRT Graphics." Reading Teacher 35, 8(May 1982): 966-969.

6.A.410   Baker, Elaine. "From Victrola To Microcomputer: Rural Libraries and New Technology." Library Journal 109, 12(July 1984): 1288-1293.

6.A.411   Balajthy, Ernest. "A Preservice Training Module in Microcomputer Applications For Teaching Reading." Journal of Reading 30, 3(December 1986): 196-200.

6.A.412   Bangasser, Vi. "Computer Literacy For Seventh Grade." Computer Teacher 10, 7(March 1983): 66-68.

6.A.413   Banwart, R. "Planning a Change? Focus First on Goals." Electronic Education 5, (March 1986): 12-13.

6.A.414   Barbour, Andrew. "Computing in America's Classrooms 1984: The New Computer Literacy Emerges." Electronic Learning 4, 2(October 1984): 100.

6.A.415   Barger, Robert Newton. "Computer Literacy: Toward a Clearer Definition." Technological Horizons in Education 11, 2(October 1983): 108-112.

6.A.416   Barnes, Cynthia C. "Teaching Computer Literacy : A Nontraditional Approach." Journal of Education For Business 61, 7(April 1986): 311-314.

6.A.417   Barnes, Martha. "Computer Literacy: An Introduction." Top of The News 39, 3(Spring 1983): 237-240.

6.A.418   Barton, J.M. "Literacy is Not Enough: The Computer As a Bridge Between Psychological Research and Educational Practice." The Journal of Computers in Mathematics and Science Teaching 5, (Fall 1985): 2-3

6.A.419   Batte, M.T. et al. "Assessing The Concept of Computer Literacy: A Case Evaluation in The College of Agriculture." AEDS Journal 19, (Summer 1986): 255-269.

6.A.420   Beal, Barry B., and Cole, Dennis W. "Staff Development and Computer Literacy." Journal of Staff Development 4, 2(November 1983): 14-19.

6.A.421   Beall, B.S. "Computer Literacy For Health Educators." Health Education 14, (October 1983): 19-22.

6.A.422   Bear, George G. "Teaching Computer Ethics: Why, What, Who, When, and How." Computers in The Schools 3, 2(Summer 1986): 113-118.

6.A.423   Beauchamp, K.G. "Schools Computer Education in Australia." British Journal of Educational Technology 13, 1(January 1982): 56-64.

6.A.424   Bell, A.H. "Twenty Questions You've Always Wanted To Ask About Computers." Curriculum Review 21, (May 1982): 142-143.

6.A.425   Bell Frederick H. "Implementing Instructional Computing and Computer Literacy in a School or College." AEDS Journal 15, 4(Summer 1982): 169-176.

6.A.426   Bell, Frederick H. "Computer Literacy, School Mathematics and Problem Solving: Three For The Price of One." AEDS Journal 12, 4(Summer 1979): 163-170.

6.A.427   Bennett, Ruth L. "Final Steps To Computer Literacy." CALICO Journal 1, 2(September 1983): 10-13.

6.A.428   Besag, F.P., and Levine, L.P. Computer Literacy For Teachers. London: Sage Publications, 1984.

6.A.429   "Best Way To Teach Computer Literacy,The" Electronic Learning 3, (April 1984): 37-44.

6.A.430   Better, Jennifer, and Miller, Marilyn. "Computer Literacy and Staff Development." Teacher Education Quarterly 10, 4(Fall 1983): 31-41.

6.A.431   Bingham, M.H. "Preparing For Any Job - 1994." Electronic Education 4, (November/December 1984): 14-15.

6.A.432   Bitter, Gary. "The Road To Computer Literacy. Part V: Objectives and Activities for Grades 10-12." Electronic Learning 2, 5(February 1983): 54, 56, 60.

6.A.433   Bitter, Gary G. "The Road To Computer Literacy. Part IV:
           Objectives and Activities for Grades 7-9." Electronic Learning 2,
           4(January 1983): 40, 42, 46, 48.

6.A.434   Bitter, Gary G "The Road To Computer Literacy. Part III:
           Objectives and Activities for Grades 4-6." Electronic Learning 2,
           3(November-December 1982): 44-48, 90-91.

6.A.435   Bitter, Gary G. "The Road To Computer Literacy. Part II:
           Objectives and Activities for Grades K-3." Electronic Learning 2,
           2(October 1982): 34-37, 85-86.

6.A.436   Bitter, Gary G., and Davis, Shelley J. "Measuring The
           Development of Computer Literacy Among Teachers." AEDS
           Journal 18, 4(Summer 1985): 243-253.

6.A.437   Blurton, Craig. "Integrating The New 'Basic" - Computer
           Literacy - Into The Science Curriculum." Journal of Computers
           in Mathematics and Science Teaching 3, 3(Spring 1984): 7-14.

6.A.438   Bock, Almon C., II. "Computer Literacy and The Business
           Manager." School Business Affairs 50, 5(May 1984): 70-71.

6.A.439   Bostock, S.J., and Seifert, R. V. "Curriculum Development in
           Computer Literacy." Studies in The Education of Adults 16,
           (October 1984): 20-31.

6.A.440   Bostock, S.J., et al. "The Effects of Learning Environment and
           Gender on The Attainment of Computer Literacy." Studies in
           The Education of Adults 19, (April 1987): 37-45.

6.A.441   Bowen, Blannie E., et al. "Theme: Using Microcomputers in
           Agricultural Education." Agricultural Education Magazine 57,
           10(April 1985): 4-23.

6.A.442   Bowman, R.F., Jr. "Computer Literacy: A Strategy For
           Cultivating Consensus." T.H.E. Journal 13, (June 1986): 60-62.

6.A.443   Bowman, R.F., Jr. "Computer Literacy: An Interactive Model
           For Courseware, Hardware, and Faculty Development."
           Educational Technology 23, (April 1983): 42-43.

6.A.444   Bowman, Richard F. "Computer Literacy: A Strategy For
           Cultivating Consensus." Technological Horizons in Education
           13, 10(June 1986): 60-62.

6.A.445   Braun, P. "How To Make Computer Literacy Cost-Effective (The Answer is BASIC)." TechTrends 30, (November/December 1985)

6.A.446   Bright, George W., and Clark, W. Bruce. "A Model Computer Literagy Course For Pre-Service Teachers at The University of Calgary." Journal of Computers in Mathematics and Science Teaching 6, 1(Fall 1986): 47-49.

6.A.447   Bruder, I. "Ed Schools: Literacy Requirements Stagnant, But More Offer Degrees." Electronic Learning 7, (April 1988): 18-10.

6.A.448   Bruder, I. "California Teachers Need Extra Courses in Computer Literacy For Credential." Electronic Learning 7, (April 1988): 16-17.

6.A.449   Calfee, Robert. "Computer Literacy and Book Literacy: Parallels and Contrasts." Educational Researcher 14, 5(May 1985): 8-13.

6.A.450   Campbell, Donald, and Campbell, John H. "Microcomputer Mania . . . Avoid The Pitfalls." Journal of Business Education 58, 3(December 1982): 89-92.

6.A.451   Camuse, Ruth, ed. Fourth Annual Microcomputer In Education Conference: Literacy Plus. Rockville, Maryland: Computer Science Press, Inc., 1984.

6.A.452   Carleer, G. J. "Computer Literacy in The Netherlands." Computer and Education 8, 4(1984): 401-405.

6.A.453   Carpenter, T.P., et al. "Current Status of Computer Literacy: NAEP Results For Secondary Students." Mathematics Teacher 73, (December 1980): 669-673.

6.A.454   Cartwright, G.P. "Technology Compentencies For Special Education Doctoral Students." Teacher Education and Special Education 7, (Spring 1984): 82-87.

6.A.455   Cerych, Ladislav. "Computers in Education: Major Problems and Key Policy Options." European Journal of Education 17, 4(1982): 421-423.

6.A.456   "Challenges of The Emerging Technologies." Momentum 13, (December 1982): 3.

6.A.457   Chamberlin, Leslie J. "Technophobia vs. Technomania." USA
            Today 112, 2462(November 1983): 50-51.

6.A.458   Chapline, Elaine B., and Turkel, Susan. "The Impact of a
            Computer Literacy Program on Affective Variables." Journal of
            Computers in Mathematics Science Teaching 5, 3(Spring 1986):
            30-33.

6.A.459   Charp, Sylvia. "Effectiveness of Computers in Instruction."
            Viewpoints in Teaching and Learning 57, 2(Spring 1981): 13-22.

6.A.460   Chaudhry, Farouk I., and Fakhro, Samir Q. "Computer
            Education in Bahrain's Secondary Schools (A Pilot Project)."
            Computers and Education 10, 4(1986): 439-443.

6.A.461   Cheng, Tina T., et al. "A Validation Study of The Computer
            Literacy Examination: Cognitive Aspect." AEDS Journal 18,
            3(Spring 1985): 139-152.

6.A.462   Christ, Frank. "Computers in Learning Assistance Conters and
            Developmental Education: Beginning to Explore." Journal of
            Developmental & Remedial Education 6, 1(Fall 1982): 10-13.

6.A.463   Christie, Betti J., and Dolan, Dan. "Montana's Task Force on
            Computer Education." Technological Horizons in Education 10,
            2(November 1982): 91-92.

6.A.464   "Citizens Committee Attacks Use of Computers To Teach Basic
            Skills." Educational Technology 22, (June 1982): 7-9.

6.A.465   Clark, C.H. "Computer Literacy and the '57 Chevy." TechTrends
            31, (January 1986): 40.

6.A.466   Clark & Lambrecht. Information Processing: Concepts,
            Principles & Procedures. Cincinnati, Ohio: South-Western
            Publishing Co., 1985.

6.A.467   "Clarkson First College to Require Computer Literacy."
            Technological Horizons in Education 10, 3(January 1983): 14.

6.A.468   Clement, Frank J. "Affective Considerations in Computer-Based
            Education." Educational Technology 21, 4(April 1981): 28-32.

6.A.469   Clemmensen, D.R. "In-Service Workshops Help Develop
            Computer Literacy Among Business Educators." Business
            Education Forum 39, (March 1985): 27-29.

6.A.470   Clouse, R. Wilburn. "Computer Literacy and Children."
Canadian Library Journal 41, 1(February 1984): 26-29.

6.A.471   Clouse, R. Wilburn and Savage, Edward M. "Educational Policy
Issues Related To Computer Literacy in Rural School Systems,"
Journal of Educational Technology Systems 10, 4(1981-1982): 343-
356.

6.A.472   Cole, Anthony Z., and Riser, Robert. "East Tennessee State's
Initiative in Computer Literacy For Faculty Members."
Technological Horizons in Education 14, 10(June 1987): 60-63.

6.A.473   Collins, Carmen. "Interactive Literacy: The Connection between
Reading and Writing The Computer." Collegiate
Microcomputer 3, 4(November 1985): 333-338.

6.A.474   Collis, Betty. "Reflections on Inequities in Computer Education:
Do The Rich Get Richer?" Education and Computing 1,
3(September 1985): 179-186.

6.A.475   "Computer Connection (Learning Link Project of New Haven,
Connecticut Public School System and Southern New England
Telephone), The." Early Years 14, (April 1984): 34.

6.A.476   "Computer Countdown . . . Teacher Literacy." Instructor 92,
8(April 1983): 38-40, 44, 48, 55.

6.A.477   Computer Literacy. New York: Gordon Press, 1986.

6.A.478   Computer Literacy. Nottingham, England: East Midland
Education Council, 1986.

6.A.479   "Computer Literacy." Balance Sheet 64, 4(March-April 1983):
231-233.

6.A.480   "Computer Literacy In '84: Pepperdine Prepares." California
Higher Education 1, 1(September 1982): 21-22.

6.A.481   Computer Literacy Themes and Skills. Sheffield, England:
Career and Occupational Information Centre, 1985.

6.A.482   "Computer Literacy vs. 'Real' Literacy." English Journal 72,
(October 1983): 24-27.

6.A.483   "Computer Skills Required For Graduation." <u>New York State School Boards Association Journal,</u> (March 1983): 3.

6.A.484   "Computers and The Gifted." <u>G/C/T</u> 30, (November/December 1983): 7-14.

6.A.485   "Computers For The Gifted." <u>G/D/T,</u> No.36 (January/February 1985): 29, 31-46.

6.A.486   Conklin, Joyce. "New Technology and The Curriculum." <u>Thrust For Educational Leadership</u> 16, 5(February-March 1987): 18-20.

6.A.487   Connolly, P. "Our Fascination With Electronic Technology is Myopic - and Quintessentially American." <u>Chronicle of Higher Education</u> 25, (September 22, 1982): 48.

6.A.488   Corwin, Rebecca Brown. "Looking For A Model Computer Literacy Training." <u>Journal of Staff Development</u> 4, 2(November 1983): 6-13.

6.A.489   Craighead, Donna, and Switzer, Mary Ellen. "Is Typing The Key to Computer Literacy?" <u>Instructor</u> 93, 2(September 1983): 178-180, 202.

6.A.490   Crook, Charles, and Steele, John. "Self-Selection of Simple Computer Activities by Infant School Pupils." <u>Educational Psychology</u> 7, 1(1987): 23-32.

6.A.491   Culbertson, J.A. "Whither Computer Literacy?" <u>Yearbook</u> (National Society For The Study of Education)85th, pt. 1(1986): 109-131.

6.A.492   Culp, G.H. "'Computer-using' Teachers and Programming Knowledge: Must Reality Deter Creativity?" <u>Educational Technology</u> 26, (February 1986): 39-41.

6.A.493   Cushing, David. "Computer Literacy for Managers: The New Challenge in HRD." <u>Training</u> 20, 2(February 1983): 22-26, 31-32.

6.A.494   Cutts, Dannie E., et al. "Administrator Microliteracy: A Challenge for The '80's." <u>NASSP Bulletin</u> 66, 455(September 1982): 53-59.

6.A.495   Cybertronics International, Inc. Cyber Logo Turtle: A First Step
           In Computer Literacy. Englewood Cliffs, New Jersey: Reston,
           1984.

6.A.496   "Databank: Experts on Educational Uses of Computers." Music
           Educators Journal 69, 5(January 1983): 71-73.

6.A.497   David, Chen, and Rafi, Nachmias. "The Design and
           Implementation of an Introductory Computer Literacy Course
           For Teachers and Educational Decision-Makers." Technological
           Horizons in Education 11, 4(January 1984): 113-116.

6.A.498   Davis, N.C. "Computer Literacy For The Special Student: A
           Personal Experience." Teaching Exceptional Children 16,
           (Summer 1984): 263-265.

6.A.499   Davis, Nancy C. "Yes, They Can! Computer Literacy For Special
           Education Students." Computing Teacher 10, 6(February 1983):
           64-67.

6.A.500   Dayton, A.H. "Let's Stop Playing The Computer Con Game."
           English Journal 75, (February 1986): 107-109.

6.A.501   Dearborn, Donald E. "Computer Literacy." Educational
           Leadership 41, 1(September 1983): 32-34.

6.A.502   DeGraff, J.T. "Notes on Computer Literacy: Another Catch-all
           Phrase?" International Journal of Instructional Media 12,
           3(1985): 185-195.

6.A.503   Deken, Joseph. The Electronic Cottage: Everyday Living With
           Your Personal Computer In The 1980's. New York: Morrow,
           Williams, & Company, 1981.

6.A.504   Dellow, D.A. "Computer Literacy - a 21st Century Debate."
           Electronic Education 4, (January 1985): 24-25.

6.A.505   Denenberg, Stewart A. "Using a Semantic Information Network
           to Develop Computer Literacy." Journal of Computer-Based
           Instruction 7, 2(November 1980): 33-40.

6.A.506   Denenberg, Stewart A. "An Alternative Curriculum for
           Computer Literacy Development." AEDS Journal 13, 2(Winter
           1980): 156-173.

6.A.507   DeVault, M.V. "Riding The Tide: Guiding Computer Education
           in The Elementary School." Curriculum Review 24,
           (November/ December 1984): 40-43.

6.A.508   Devon, R.F. "Microcomputer Literacy As Remedial Education."
           English Education 75, (December 1984): 138-141.

6.A.509   Dewar, Jacqueline M. "Incorporating Computer Literacy into a
           Mathematics Course For Preservice Elementary Teachers."
           Mathematics and Computer Education 20, 3(Fall 1986): 155-157.

6.A.510   Dewey, P.R. "Computers, Fun, & Literacy." School Library
           Journal 29, (October 1982): 118.

6.A.511   Dickerson, L., and Pritchard, W.H., Jr. "Microcomputers and
           Education: Planning For The Coming Revolution In The
           Classroom." Educational Technology 21, (January 1981): 7-12.

6.A.512   Diem, Richard A. "Preparing For The Technological Classroom:
           Will We Meet The Challenge?" Educational Technology 24,
           3(March 1984): 13-15.

6.A.513   Diessner, Rhet, et al. "English Fluency via Computers at Yakima
           Tribal School." Journal of American Indian Education 25,
           1(October 1985): 17-24.

6.A.514   D'Ignazio, Fred. Small Computers. New York: Watts, Franklin,
           Inc., 1981.

6.A.515   Dinkmeyer, D., Jr., and Carlson, J., eds. "Kids + Computers."
           Elementary School Guidance & Counseling 18, (October 1983):
           3-63.

6.A.516   Ditlea, Steve, ed Digital Deli: The Lunch Group. New York:
           Workman Publishing Company, Inc., 1984.

6.A.517   Dittmer, Allan. "Computer Language - Literacy or Litter."
           English Journal 73, 1(January 1984): 42-45.

6.A.518   D'Onofrio, Marianne J., and Slama, Mark E. "An Investigation
           of the Relationship Between Computer Literacy and The Home
           and School Environments of Students in Business Education."
           Delta Pi Epsilon Journal 26, 2(Fall-Winter 1984): 132-143.

6.A.519   Dorrah, H. "Closing The Gap: A Teacher-Centered Approach to
           In-Service Computer Literacy Training." American Secondary
           Education 16, 1(1987): 15-19.

6.A.520   Douziech, Richard, and English, Jim. <u>Computer Literacy Activities For Elementary & Middle School Students</u>. Eugene, Oregon: International Council For Computers In Education, 1983.

6.A.521   Drumm, David. <u>The Computer In Training & Development</u>. Boston: International Human Resources Development Corporation, 1985.

6.A.522   D'Souza, P.V. "Computer Literacy inToday's Society." <u>Educational Technology</u> 25, (August 1985): 34-35.

6.A.523   DuCharme, R. G., and Vulgamore, M.L. "Richmond's Goal: 100% Computer Literacy." <u>American School & University</u> 54, (May 1982): 11-13.

6.A.524   Duckenfield, C. "Computer Literacy - Crisis or False Alarm?" <u>Electronic Education</u> 3, (February 1984): 35.

6.A.525   Duncan, C.S. "Compulit: Computer Literacy For Tacoma." <u>Library Journal</u> 109, (January 1984): 52-54.

6.A.526   Durbak, Ivan R., and Sadnytzky, Nicholas O. "The Hidden Crisis in Education: Faculty Computer Illiteracy." <u>Community College Review</u> 12, 1(Summer 1984): 7-13.

6.A.527   Duttweiler, P.C. "Barriers To Optimum Use of Educational Technology." <u>Educational Technology</u> 23, 11(November 1983): 37-39.

6.A.528   Eisele, James E. "A Case For Universal Computer Literacy." <u>Journal of Research and Development in Education</u> 14, 1(Fall 1980): 84-89.

6.A.529   Ekins, Roger Robin. "Computer Illiterate, and Proud of It." <u>Community and Junior College Journal</u> 56, 2(October-November 1985): 28-31.

6.A.530   Ekman, B. "How To Start A Computer Literacy Program In An Elementary School." <u>Phi Delta Kappan</u> 70, (September 1988): 78-79.

6.A.531   Elliott, C. "Latent Computer Literates." <u>Media & Methods</u> 19, (September 1982): 24-25.

6.A.532   Ellis, James D. "A Rationale For Using Computers in Science
           Education." American Biology Teacher 46, 4(April 1984): 200-
           206.

6.A.533   Emihovich, Catherine, and Miller, Gloria E. "Learning Logo:
           The Social Context of Cognition." Journal of Curriculum
           Studies 20, 1(January - February 1988): 57-70.

6.A.534   Ewing, Jeanne B., et al. "Adult Education and Computer
           Literacy: A New Challenge." Lifelong Learning 10, 3(November
           1986): 21-23.

6.A.535   "Exemplary Programs in Computer Literacy." Instructional
           Innovator 29, 1(January 1984): 56.

6.A.536   Farrell, C.S. "Guilford Studies Computer Proficiency as
           Requirement For Graduation." Chronicle of Higher Education
           25, (February 2, 1983): 2.

6.A.537   Farrell, Pat. "Computer Literacy: What Does It Mean?" Journal
           of Physical Education, Recreation & Dance 55, 4(April 1984): 54-
           55.

6.A.538   Farris, Pamela J., and Vedral, Nancy M. "Computers and Six
           Pacs: An Infused Approach to Computer Literacy At The
           Preservice Level." Innovative Higher Education 9, 1(Fall-
           Winter 1984): 30-35.

6.A.539   Fary, Barbara A. "Computer Literacy For Staff Development."
           AEDS Journal 17, 4(Summer 1984): 1-8.

6.A.540   Fisher, Glenn. "Developing a District-Wide Computer-Use
           Plan." Computing Teacher 10, 5(January 1983): 52-59.

6.A.541   Fisher, Glenn. "Bringing Computers Into The Classroom." PTA
           Today 8, 3(December-January 1982-1983): 10-12.

6.A.542   Fleit, Linda. "Overselling Technology: Suppose You Gave a
           Revolution And Nobody Came?" CAUSE/EFFECT 10, 3(May
           1987): 4-8.

6.A.543   Flemister, M.G. "Computer Edification Programs: A Class For
           The Teacher." Journal of Research on Computers In Education
           20, (Spring 1988): 213-225.

6.A.544   "Focus On Computer Literacy," Business Education Forum 39, (October 1984): 5-6.

6.A.545   Foell, Nelson A. "A New Concern For Teacher Educators: Computer Literacy." Journal of Teacher Education 34, 5(September-October 1983): 19-22.

6.A.546   Ford, Brian J. COMPUTE! Why? When? How? Do I Need To? North Pomfret, Vermont: David & Charles, Inc., 1985.

6.A.547   Franklin, James L. "What's a Computer Doing in My Music Room?" Music Educators Journal 69, 5(January 1983): 29-32.

6.A.548   Fruin, M.F., and Bakshi, A.S. "How We Can Teach Computer Literacy At The University." Educational Technology 24, (August 1984): 12-14.

6.A.549   Furlong, Mary S. "Strengthening The Classroom Teacher Through Microcomputer Technology." Momentum 14, 3(September 1983): 12-14.

6.A.550   Gahala, Estella. "Computer Literacy: A Comprehensive Program At Lyons Township High School." Journal of Staff Development 4, 2(November 1983): 20-28.

6.A.551   Ganske, Ludwig, and Hamamoto, Pauline. "Response To Crisis: A Developer's Look At The Importance Of Needs Assessment To Teacher Educators In The Design Of Computer Literacy Training Programs." Educational Communication and Technology: A Journal of Theory, Research, and Development 32, 2(Summer 1984): 101-113.

6.A.552   Gantt, Vernon W. "Computing Literacy in The University of The Future." Association For Communication Administration Bulletin, 51(January 1985): 51-53.

6.A.553   Gawronski, Jane D. "Computer Literacy and School Mathematics." Mathematics Teacher 74, 8(November 1981): 613-614.

6.A.554   Geisert, G. "Workshop: Keys To Computer Literacy, A." Early Years 14, (October 1983): 41-43.

6.A.555   Gelder, Amanda, and Maggs, Alex. "Direct Instruction Microcomputing In Primary Schools: Manipulation of Critical

Instructional Variables." <u>Research in Science and Technological Education</u> 1, 2(1983): 221-238.

6.A.556   Gennaro, E.D., et al. "Computer Literacy is a Family Affair." <u>Instructional Innovator</u> 28, (January 1983): 17-18.

6.A.557   Germain, J.M. "Teaching Computer Literacy Without Computerese (at Lacey Township High School, N.J.)." <u>Curriculum Review</u> 27, (September/October 1987): 7-8.

6.A.558   Giacoma, Pete. "Computers, Computer Literacy, and Access in The Children's Room." <u>Top of The News</u> 41, 1(Fall 1984): 53-59.

6.A.559   Glenn, Allen D. "Computer Literacy Among College of Education Faculty." <u>Educational Perspectives</u> 22, 4(Winter 1984): 24-26.

6.A.560   "Glossary of Computer Terms." <u>Music Educators Journal</u> 69, 5(January 1983): 79-81.

6.A.561   Goens, George A. "Getting To The Core of The Apple-Gap." <u>Phi Delta Kappan</u> 65, 2(October 1983): 130-131.

6.A.562   Goldberg, A.L. "The Eclectic Technologist: Computer Literacy or Technological Literacy?" <u>Educational Technology</u> 24, (July 1984): 33-34.

6.A.563   Golden, R.E. "Caution and Skepticism Are Needed On The Road To Computer Literacy." <u>Chronicle of Higher Education</u> 27, (December 7, 1983): 80.

6.A.564   Goldman, T. <u>Groundworks For Data Processing & Computer Literacy Courses</u>. New York: McGraw-Hill, Inc., 1986.

6.A.565   Goodson, Bobby, et al. "Building a Software Library: How Do You Create A Library of Software That Meets Your Needs - and Doesn't Break Your Budget?" <u>Electronic Learning</u> 3, 2(October 1983): 77-87.

6.A.566   Goody, Roy W. <u>Microcomputer Fundamentals</u>. Chicago: SRA, 1980.

6.A.567   Gordon, H. G., et al. "Ten Myths About Microcomputers." <u>Academic Therapy</u> 19, (January 1984): 285-291.

6.A.568   Grady, David. "A Hard Look At The World Of Educational Computing." <u>Personal Computing</u> 6, 8(August 1982): 40-44.

6.A.569   Gress, Eileen K. "A Computer-Literacy Module For The Junior
           High School." Arithmetic Teacher 29, 7(March 1982): 46-49.

6.A.570   Gring, Stephen R. "Introducing Computer Literacy."
           Educational Leadership 40, 1(October 1982): 62.

6.A.571   Guthrie, John T. "Research: One Computer Literacy Skill."
           Journal of Reading 24, 5(February 1981): 458-460.

6.A.572   Haeckel, S.H. "Ladder To Computer Literacy." Advocate
           (Florida) 12, (January 1986): 6.

6.A.573   Haggerty, Terry. Developing Microcomputer Literacy: A Guide
           For Sport, Physical Education, & Recreation Managers.
           Champaign, Illinois: Stipes Publishing Co., 1985.

6.A.574   Haigh, Roger W. "Planning For Computer Literacy." Journal of
           Higher Education 56, 2(March-April 1985): 161-171.

6.A.575   Hall-Sheehy, James. Computer Basics For Human Resource
           Professionals. New York: John Wiley & Sons, Inc., 1986.

6.A.576   Halpern, Noemi. "Artificial Intelligence and The Education of
           The Learning Disabled." Journal of Learning Disability 17,
           2(February 1984): 118-120.

6.A.577   Hankin, Edward K., et al. The Development of Pre-Vocational
           Education Literacy Courses For Use With Computer Assisted
           Instruction of Disadvantaged Youths and Adults. Final Report.
           Tallahassee, Florida: Florida State University, 1967. ED 024 763

6.A.578   Hansen, Thomas P., et al. "What Teachers Think Every High
           School Graduate Should Know About Computers." School
           Science and Mathematics 81, 6(October 1981): 467-472.

6.A.579   Hanson, Charles D. "Computer Literacy in an Academic Library:
           Technological Hit or Myth?" Community & Junior College
           Libraries 3, 1(Fall 1984): 3-11.

6.A.580   Harper, Dennis O., and Stewart, James H. Run: Computer
           Education, 2nd Edition. Pacific Grove, California: Brooks-Cole
           Publishing, Co., 1985.

6.A.581   Hartsuijker, Ard P. ""Curriculum Development of Computer and Information Literacy in the Netherlands." Education and Computing 2, 1(1986): 89-93.

6.A.582   Harvey, Brian. "Stop Saying 'Computer Literacy'!" Classroom Computer News 3, 6(May-June 1983): 56-57.

6.A.583   Harvey, W.B. "The Impact of Computers on Education and The Widening Income Gap." Journal of Educational Technology Systems 15, 1(1986-1987): 53-60.

6.A.584   Healy, Patricia, and Schilmoeller, Gary L. "Parent Attitudes Toward Computer Use by Young Children." Research in Rural Education 2, 4(Spring 1985): 135-140.

6.A.585   Heermann, Barry. "Strategies for Adult Computer Learning." New Directions For Continuing Education, 29(March 1986): 5-15.

6.A.586   Helms, Susan. "The Computer as a Tool: Basic For a University-Wide Computer Literacy Course." Technological Horizons in Education 13, 2(September 1985): 104-106.

6.A.587   Hentrel, Bobbie K., & Harper, Linda. Computers In Education: A Guide For Educators. Ann Arbor, Michigan: University of Michigan Press, 1985.

6.A.588   Hernandez, A.P. "Microcomputer Literacy For Law Enforcers." The Police Chief 53, (May 1986): 36-37.

6.A.589   Herron, R. "The Born Again Computer." Journal of Physical Education, Recreation and Dance 54, (November/December 1983): 11.

6.A.590   Hertsgaard, Doris M., et al. "An Approach to Faculty Microcomputer Literacy." Journal of Computers in Mathematics and Science Teaching 5, 2(Winter 1985-1986): 29-31.

6.A.591   "High Technology and Computers in Teacher Education." Journal of Teacher Education 34, (September/October 1983): 2-12.

6.A.592   Hind, Jim. "Computer Programming With Infants and Juniors." Gifted Education International 2, 2(1984): 129-133.

6.A.593   Hirsch, Rudolph E. Computer Literacy For Middle Management. Englewood Cliffs, New Jersey: Prentice-Hall, Inc., 1948.

6.A.594   Hirschbuhl, K. "Need For Computer Literacy and Computer Applications in The Nation's Classrooms." Journal of Educational Technology Systems 9, 3(1980-1981): 183-191.

6.A.595   Hoffman, I. "When Computer Literacy Metamorphosis is Complete." Electronic Education 4, (November/December 1984): 18.

6.A.596   Hofstetter, Fred T. Computer Literacy For Musicians. Englewood Cliffs, New Jersey: Prentice-Hall, Inc., 1988.

6.A.597   Hopping, Lorraine. "States To Watch. Tennessee: A Four-Point Computer Literacy Requirement Plan." Electronic Learning 2, 7(April 1983): 42-44.

6.A.598   Horn, Carin E., and Collins, Carroll L. Com-Lit: Computer Literacy For Kids. Lexington, Massachusetts: D.C. Heath, Inc., 1984.

6.A.599   Horton, Forest Woody, Jr. "Information Literacy vs. Computer Literacy." Bulletin of the American Society for Information Science 9, 4(April 1983): 14-16.

6.A.600   Howe, S.F. "After Computer Literacy." Media & Methods 20, (January 1984): 27.

6.A.601   Howell, N.B. and Cox, D.W. "Faculty Computer Literacy." AEDS Journal 19, (Summer 1986): 287-294.

6.A.602   Hubbard, Guy. "Computer Literacy and The Art Program." Art Education 38, 2(March 1985); 15-18.

6.A.603   Hunka, Steve. "CAI Developments in Canada." Technilogical Horizons in Education 8, 1(January 1981): 57-59.

6.A.604   Hunter, Beverly. My Students Use Computers: A Guide For Computer Literacy In The K-8 Curriculum. Englewood Cliffs, New Jersey: Reston, 1983.

6.A.605   Hunter, B. "Computer Literacy in Grades K-8" Journal of Educational Technology Systems 10, 1(1982-1982): 59-66.

6.A.606   Hunter, Beverly, et al. "Computer Literacy in The K-8
           Curriculum." Phi Delta Kappan 65, 2(October 1983): 115-118.

6.A.607   Hunter, James. "Make Your Students Computer Literate."
           Business Education Forum 38, 8(April-May 1984): 45-50.

6.A.608   Huntington, J.F. "Computer Comments; Computer Literacy;
           Selected Courseware." Educational Technology 22, (October
           1982): 34-35.

6.A.609   Hyson, Marion C., and Eyman, Alice. "Approaches To
           Computer Literacy in Early Childhood Teacher Education."
           Young Children 41, 6(September 1986): 54-59.

6.A.610   Ide, Nancy M. "Computers and The Humanities Courses:
           Philosophical Bases and Approach." Computers and The
           Humanities 21, 4(October-December 1987): 209-215.

6.A.611   Inskeep, James E., Jr. "Computer Literacy: What It Is and Why
           We Need It." Curriculum Review 21, 2(May 1982): 138-141.

6.A.612   "Introduction Of Computer Science Into Soviet Secondary
           Education (Symposium), The." Soviet Education 28,
           (August/September 1986): 5-229.

6.A.613   Jackson, William K., et al. "Computer Awareness and Use at a
           Research University." Journal of Educational Technology
           Systems 13, 1(1984-1985): 47-56.

6.A.614   Jay, T.B. "Computerphobia: What To Do About It?"
           Educational Technology 21, (January 1981): 47-48.

6.A.615   Jeffcoat, M.K., et al. "Computer Education for Dental Students."
           Journal of Dental Education 50, 5(May 1986): 260-263.

6.A.616   Jenkins, Nancy. "Computer Literacy Training . . . An Effective
           Model For One District." Journal of Staff Development 4,
           2(November 1983): 42-50.

6.A.617   Jensh, Ronald P., and Veloski, J. Jan. "Program for Increasing
           Use of Computers in Medical Education." Journal of Medical
           Education 61, 2(February 1986): 137-139.

6.A.618   John, David G. "Computer-Assisted Instruction in German."
           Canadian Modern Language Review 41, 1(October 1984): 53-62.

6.A.619   Johnson, David C. "Computer Literacy - What Is It?"
           Mathematics Teacher 73, 2(February 1980): 91-96.

6.A.620   Johnson, J.E. "Computer Literacy: A Necessity, Not a Luxury."
           Business Education Forum 41, (December 1986): 12-13.

6.A.621   Johnson, Marvin L. "Computer Literacy at The Community
           College - A Way to Start." Mathematics and Computer
           Education 18, 2(Spring 1984): 89-92.

6.A.622   Johnson, Mildred Fitzgerald. "Computer Literacy: What Is It?"
           Business Education Forum 35, 3(December 1980): 18-22.

6.A.623   Johnson, Richard R. "Computer Literacy: A Longer View."
           EDUCOM 18, 3(Fall-Winter 1984): 3-4, 8.

6.A.624   Jones, Philip R., and Stratford, Brian, "The Elaboration of
           Blissymbols." Early Child Development and Care 27, 1(1987):
           107-137.

6.A.625   Jones, Warren, et al Computer Literacy: Programming,
           Problem-Solving, Projects On The Apple. Englewood Cliffs,
           New Jersey: Reston, 1983.

6.A.626   Judy, R.W. and Lommel, J.M. "The New Soviet Computer
           Literacy Campaign." Educational Communication and
           Technology 34, (Summer 1986): 108-123.

6.A.627   Julian, A.A. "Witness: North Carolina." Community and
           Junior College Journal 53, (May 1983): 47.

6.A.628   Kagan, D., and Pietron, L.R. "Cognitive Level and Achievement
           In Computer Literacy." The Journal of Psychology 121, (July
           1987): 317-327.

6.A.629   Kalmar, I. "Computer Literacy as Myth: A Critique of The
           Computer Literacy Credo." Educational Technology 26,
           (November 1986): 19-24.

6.A.630   Kay, A. "Computer as Palette and Model Builder." Learning
           (Belmont, California)11, (March 1983): 46.

6.A.631   Kearsley, G., et al. "Two Decades of Computer Based Instruction
           Projects: What Have We Learned?" Technological Horizons in
           Education 10, 3(January 1983): 90-94.

6.A.632   Keeling, Roger. "Tomorrow's Teachers - Yesterday's
           Technology? NUT Education Review 2, 1(Spring 1988): 34-38.

6.A.633   Kern, Alfred. "GOTO Poetry." Perspectives in Computing:
           Applications in The Academic and Scientific Community 3,
           3(October 1983): 44-52.

6.A.634   Kerr, Stephen T. "Soviet Applications of Microcomputers in
           Education: Developments in Research and Practice During the
           Gorbachev Era." Journal of Educational Computing Research 3,
           1(1987): 1-17.

6.A.635   Killian, Joyce E. "Fostering Computer Competence in Schools."
           Educational Leadership 42, 4(December-January 1984-1985): 81-
           83.

6.A.636   "K-8 Computer Literacy Curriculum." Computing Teacher 10,
           7(March 1983): 7-10.

6.A.637   King, Kenneth M. "Evolution of the Concept of Computer
           Literacy." EDUCOM Bulletin 20, 3(Fall 1985): 18-21.

6.A.638   Kinzer, Charles K. "A 5 Part Categorization For Use of
           Microcomputers in Reading Classrooms. Journal of Reading 30,
           3(December 1986): 226-232.

6.A.639   Kirchner, Alice M. "One State's Approach to Computer
           Literacy." Technological Horizons in Education 8, 4(May 1981):
           43-44.

6.A.640   Kitch, Dale. "Computer Literacy: The Fourth Basic Skill?"
           Business Education Form 35, 2(November 1980): 22-23.

6.A.641   Klassen, D. "Computer Literacy Revisited." AEDS Journal 17,
           (Fall/Winter 1983): 41-48.

6.A.642   Klassen, Daniel. "Computer Literacy: What It Is And How To
           Get It." School Business Affairs 49, 5(May 1983): 44-45.

6.A.643   Knapper, Christopher K., and Wills, Barry L. "Teaching
           Computing Across The Curriculum: A Canadian Viewpoint."
           Technological Horizons in Education 11, 4(January 1984): 98-
           102.

6.A.644   Kow, Khoo Goh. "Potentials of Computer Assisted Learning in
           Malaysian Schools." Journal of Science and Mathematic
           Education in Southeast Asia 5, 2(December 1982): 19-21.

6.A.645   Kypferberg, Natalie. "End-Users: How Are They Doing? A Librarian Interviews Six 'Do-It-Yourself' Searchers." Online 10, 2(March 1986): 24-28.

6.A.646   Lacina, Lorna J. "Computer Equity in Public Education." Education 104, 2(Winter 1983): 128-130.

6.A.647   Lambrecht, Judith C. "New Microcomputer Teaching Competencies." Balance Sheet 63, 5(March 1982): 233-236, 278.

6.A.648   Landry, Michael. "Algebra and The Computer." Mathematics Teacher 73, 9(December 1980): 663-667.

6.A.649   Lange, Mary. "Using The Turtle Tot Robot To Enhance Logo For The Hearing Impaired." American Annals of the Deaf 130, 5(November 1985): 377-382.

6.A.650   Langlois, Lyle. Dare To Be Computer Literate. Beaverton, Oregon: Dilithium Press, 1984.

6.A.651   Lanza, Leonard G. "Elementary School Computer Literacy: A Case Study of Success." Educational Computer 3, 2(March-April 1983): 14-15.

6.A.652   Larson, Arthur. "The Availability and Use of Computer Instructional Resources in Secondary Education, 1969-1983." Journal of Business Education 60, 2(November 1984): 60-62.

6.A.653   Lee, Jinn-Bao. "A Curriculum Model for Computer Literacy In Taiwan." Ph.D. dissertation, Texas A & M University, 1982. 43/03-A, p.702.

6.A.654   Lee, Marjorie W. "The Match: Learning Styles of Black Children and Microcomputer Programming." Journal of Negro Education 55, 1(Winter 1986): 78-90.

6.A.655   Leone, G.J., and Overfield, K. "Computer Literacy Myth." Business Education Forum 37, (November 1982): 3-5.

6.A.656   Lesgold, A.M. "Preparing Children for a Computer-Rich World." Educational Leadership 43, (March 1986): 7-11.

6.A.657   Levin, Dan. "Educational Computing: The Global View." Electronic Learning 4, 4(January 1985): 76.

6.A.658   Levin, Dan. "Everybody Wants 'Computer Literacy', So Maybe
           We Should Know What It Means." American School Board
           Journal 170, 3(March 1983): 25-28.

6.A.659   Lewis, Linda H. "Evaluators Not Designers: Another Aspect of
           Computer Literacy." Computers in the Schools 1, 2(Summer
           1984): 59-69.

6.A.660   Liao, Thomas T. "Microcomputers: Tools for Developing
           Technological Literacy." Weaver of Information and
           Perspectives on Technological Literacy 1, 2(Spring 1983): 13.

6.A.661   Lichty, Donald, and Laubacher, Marilyn R. "Computer Literacy:
           Where to Begin? And Microcomputers: Some Basic Resources."
           Perspectives For Teachers of the Hearing Impaired 2,
           1(September 1983): 10-13.

6.A.662   Lipkin, John. "Computer Equity and Computer Educators
           (You)." Computing Teacher 11, 8(April 1984): 19-21.

6.A.663   Lipkin, John P. "Equity in Computer Education." Educational
           Leadership 41, 1(September 1983): 26.

6.A.664   Lockard, James. "Computers Blossom at a Small School in
           Iowa." Instructional Innovator 25, 6(September 1980): 25, 48.

6.A.665   Locker, N. "Computer Illiteracy?" Delta Kappa Gamma Bulletin
           53, (Fall 1986): 25-26.

6.A.666   Lockheed, Marlaine. "Trends in Educational Computing:
           Decreasing Interest and the Changing Focus of Instruction."
           Educational Researcher 15, 5(May 1986): 21-26.

6.A.667   Lockheed, Marlaine E., et al. "Determinants of Microcomputer
           Literacy in High School Students." Journal of Educational
           Computing Research 1, 1(1985): 81-96.

6.A.668   Lombardi, John V. Computer Literacy: The Basic Concepts &
           Language. Bloomington, Indiana: Indiana University Press,
           1983.

6.A.669   Longstreet, William S., and Sorant, Peter E. "Computer Literacy-
           Definition?" Educational Horizons 63, 3(Spring 1985): 117-120

6.A.670   Loop, L. "ComputerTown, USA!" Instructional Innovator 27,
           (February 1982): 22-23.

6.A.671   Lopez, Antonio M., Jr. "Computer Literacy For Teachers: High
           School and University Cooperation." Educational Technology
           21, 6(June 1981): 15-18.

6.A.672   Lovell, P. "Staff Development For Computer Literacy."
           Educational Technology 23, (March 1983): 18-19.

6.A.673   Lowe, Dennis W. "Designing and Implementing a Computer
           Literacy Course in a Graduate Clinical/Counseling Psychology
           Program." Teaching of Psychology 14, 1(February 1987): 26-29.

6.A.674   Luehrmann, Arthur. "School of the Future School of the Past.
           Adopting Microcomputers in Ways That Will and Won't
           Work." Peabody Journal of Education 62, 2(Winter 1985): 42-51.

6.A.675   Luehrmann, Arthur. "Computer Literacy - What Should It Be?"
           Mathematics Teacher 74, 9(December 1981): 682-686.

6.A.676   Luehrmann, Arthur, and Peckham, H. Computer Literacy
           Survival Kit: For The Apple II, IIe Family of Computers. New
           York: McGraw-Hill, Inc., 1984.

6.A.677   Luehrmann, Arthur, and Peckham, H. Computer Literacy: A
           Hands-on Approach. New York: McGraw-Hill, Inc., 1983.

6.A.678   Luehrmann, Arthur, and Spain T. "The Best Way To Teach
           Computer Literacy." Electronic Learning 3, 7(April 1984): 38-44.

           Examines the concept - and goal - of teaching computer literacy.
           Questions the feasibility of the K-12 computer literacy approach.
           Analyzes the reasons why the K-12 approach fails. Explores the
           way around the traps of the K-12 approach. Identifies the
           formula for the teaching of computer literacy as the "beachhead
           approach." Discusses the aspects of said approach. Concludes
           with suggestions for the steps to follow after the "beachhead
           approach" has been implemented.

6.A.679   Lykos, Peter. "Lyons Township High School Has 236 Personal
           Computers." Computers in Chemical Education Newsletter 5,
           4(December 1982): 2.

6.A.680   "Lyons Township High School, The." Electronic Learning 2,
           1(September 1982): 28-30.

6.A.681   MacKinnon, C.F. "Computer Literacy and The Future: Is It
            Possible To Prevent The Computer From Doing Our Thinking
            For Us?" Educational Technology 20, (December 1980): 33-34.

6.A.682   Maclay, Connie M., and Askov, Eunice N. "Computer-Aided
            Instruction For Mom and Dad." Issues in Science and
            Technology 4, 1(Fall 1987): 88-91.

6.A.683   Magarrell, J. "Computer Literacy Gaining Place in
            Undergraduate Curriculum." Chronicle of Higher Education 24,
            (April 21, 1982): 1.

6.A.684   Many, Wesley, and Friker, Walter. Building Computer Literacy:
            Levels A Through I. Wheeling, Illinois: National School
            Services, 1985.

6.A.685   Marchionini, Gary, et al. "Centering on Computers: From
            Awareness to Literacy." Journal of Staff Development 4,
            2(November 1983): 59-68.

6.A.686   Marshall, Joe, and Pfeifer, Jerilyn K. "Computer Literacy for
            Teacher Education." Phi Delta Kappan 66, 3(November 1984):
            219.

6.A.687   Marshall, John E. "Computer Literacy and Prospective Teachers:
            A 'Minds-On' Experience." Action in Teacher Education 5,
            4(Winter 1983-1984): 35-41.

6.A.688   Martin, C. Dianne, and Heller, Rachelle S. "Computer Literacy
            for Teachers." Educational Leadership 40, 1(October 1982): 46-47.

6.A.689   Martin, C. Dianne, and Heller, Rachelle S. "Presenting
            Computer Literacy For The B.C. Generation at The Smithsonian
            Institution." Technological Horizons in Education 11, 4(January
            1984): 125-126.

6.A.690   Martin, Elaine Russo. "Computers in Teacher Education."
            Journal of Teacher Education 34, 5(September-October 1983): 58-
            60.

6.A.691   Martin, M. "Computer Literacy: The Issue Revisited."
            Community, Technical, and Junior College Journal 58,
            (October/November 1987): 7.

6.A.692   Marvin, Carolyn, and Winther, Mark. "Computer-Ease: A
           Twentieth-Century Literacy Emergent." Journal of
           Communication 33, 1(Winter 1983): 92-108.

6.A.693   Masland, Andrew T. "Cultural Influences on Academic
           Computing: Implications For Liberal Education." Liberal
           Education 70, 1(Spring 1984): 83-90.

6.A.694   Mathews, W.M., and Winkle, L.W. "Microliteracy, School
           Administrators and Survival." Compact 15, (Fall 1981): 22-23.

6.A.695   Mathieson, Coris A. "Computers: From Confusion To
           Collaboration." Educational Leadership 40, 2(November 1982):
           13-15.

6.A.696   Maughan, G., Jr. "Computer Literacy in The Middle School."
           Man/Society/Technology a Journal of Industrial Arts Education
           42, (September/October 1982): 28-30.

6.A.697   McCann, S.K., and Keleman, E.J. "Micro-Computers: New
           Directions and Methods For The Preparation of Special
           Education Personnel." Teacher Education and Special Education
           7, (Summer 1984): 178-184.

6.A.698   McClain, Martha B. "Electrifying Art in the Elementary School."
           School Administrator 42, 10(November 1985): 11.

6.A.699   McDonald, Clement J. "Computer Technology and Continuing
           Medical Education: A Scenario for The Future." MOBIUS
           (Technology and The Future of Continuing Education 3, 2(April
           1983): 7-12.

6.A.700   McGee, P. "Computer Studies at GCSE: The Applications
           Approach." Computer Education, 54 (November 1986): 5-6.

6.A.701   McKay, Alan B., et al. "Computer Literacy: A Strategy For
           Change." American Journal of Pharmaceutical Education 52,
           1(Spring 1988): 36-41.

6.A.702   McMeen, G.R. "Developing Computer Literacy Workshops For
           College Faculty." Educational Technology 24, (April 1984): 25-
           29.

6.A.703   Mechling, Kenneth, et al. "Pennsylvania's Innovative
            Computer Education Program." Technological Horizons in
            Education 15, 3(October 1987): 93-96.

6.A.704   Menosky, Joseph A. "Computer Literacy and The Press."
            Teachers College Record 85, 4(Summer 1984): 615-621.

6.A.705   Michayluk, J.O. "LOGO: More Than a Decade Later." British
            Journal of Educational Technology 17, 1(January 1986): 35-41.

6.A.706   Miller, Inabeth, "How Schools Become Computer Literate: And
            Guidelines on How To Evaluate Educational Software." Popular
            Computing 3, 13(October 1984): 26-28.

6.A.707   "Mini-Issue: Art and Computers" Art Education 36, 3(May
            1983): 6-21.

6.A.708   "Mission: Define Computer Literacy. The Illinois-Wisconsin
            ISACA Computer Coordinators' Committee on Computer
            Literacy Report (May 1985)." Computing Teacher 13,
            3(November 1985): 14-15.

6.A.709   "Mitterand Seeks Computer Literacy For Third World."
            Chronicle of Higher Education 28, (April 4, 1984): 29-30.

6.A.710   Molnar, A.R. "Coming of Computer Literacy: Are We Prepared
            For It?" Educational Technology 21, (January 1981): 26-28.

6.A.711   Molnar, Andrew R. "The Next Great Crisis in American
            Education: Computer Literacy." Journal of Educational
            Technology Systems 7, 3(1978-1979): 275-285.

6.A.712   Molnar, Andrew R. "The Next Great Crisis in American
            Education: Computer Literacy." AEDS Journal 12 1(Fall 1978):
            11-20.

6.A.713   Molnar, Andrew R., and Babb, Patricia W. "The Electronic Age
            Challenges Education." Appalachia 16, 2(November-December
            1982): 1-7.

6.A.714   Montanus, Mark. Computer Literacy: Beginning. Dubuque,
            Iowa: Kendall/Hunt Publishing Co., 1986.

6.A.715   Montanus, Mark. Computer Literacy: Intermediate. Dubuque,
            Iowa: Kendall/Hunt Publishing Co., 1986.

6.A.716   Moont, Sue. "Computer Literacy: An Archeological View."
            Educational Computing Organization of Ontario 7, 2(September
            1986): 14-17.

6.A.717   Moursund, David. BASIC Programming For Computer Literacy.
            McGraw-Hill, Inc., 1978.

6.A.718   Moynes, Riley E. "Megatrends and Education's Future."
            Education Canada 24, 3(Fall 1984): 4-8.

6.A.719   Muller, James H. "Learning Must Be More Than Computer
            Literacy: Logo and The Computer." NASSP Bulletin 70,
            489(April 1986): 36-40.

6.A.720   Murphy, Susanne. "Of Greased Pigs and Moving Targets:
            Computer Education in The Fast Track," Journal of Staff
            Development 4, 2(November 1983): 35-41.

6.A.721   Nakhlek, M.B. "Overview of Microcomputers in the Secondary
            Science Curriculum, An." Journal of Computers in
            Mathematics and Science Teaching 3,(Fall 1983): 13-21

6.A.722   Nansen, Craig. "Teaching Computer Use - Not Programming.
            An Outline For A Five-Session Course." Electronic Learning 2,
            3(November-December 1982): 24,31.

6.A.723   Nave, Gary, and Browning, Philip. "Preparing Rehabilitation
            Leaders For The Computer Age." Rehabilitation Counseling
            Bulletin 26, 5(May 1983): 364-367.

6.A.724   Neal, W. G. "Beyond Computer Literacy: Information Literacy."
            Business Education Forum 42, (December 1987): 14-15.

6.A.725   Neibauer, Alan. "The Computer Literacy Myth." Technological
            Horizons in Education 12, 6(February 1985): 88-90.

6.A.726   Neights, G.; Hirshberg, P.; and Trippett, B.L. "3 Successful
            Programs in Computer Literacy." Instructional Innovator 26,
            (September 1981): 26-31.

6.A.727   Nelson, Charles A. "Evaluating a Computer Literacy Program."
            Journal of Developmental & Remedial Education 6, Special
            Issue (1983): 16-17, 28.

6.A.728   Nelson, Phillip, and Waack, William. "The Status of
            Computer/Literacy-Assisted Instruction Awareness as a Factor in
            Classroom Instruction and Teacher Selection." Educational
            Technology 25, 10(October 1985): 23-26.

6.A.729   Neufeld, H.H. "Reading, Writing and Algorithms; Computer
            Literacy in the Schools." Yearbook (Claremont Reading
            Conference) 46, (1982): 133-138.

6.A.730   Neuwirth, Erich. "Programming Languages or Generic Software
            Tools, For Beginners' Courses in Computer Literacy?"
            Education and Computing 3, 3-4(1987): 265-268.

6.A.731   Newman, Anne. "Computer Training Helps Appalachians
            Compete." Appalachia 17, 3-4(January-April 1984): 20-26.

6.A.732   Newman, Michael E., and Henderson, Janet L. "Teacher and
            Employer Perceptions of Computer Skills Needed by Secondary
            Agribusiness Students." Journal of the American Association of
            Teacher Educators in Agriculture 28, 2(Summer 1987): 50.

6.A.733   Nielsen, L.L. "Computer Literacy: A Hands-on Approach."
            (Computer Program Review). Curriculum Review 23,
            (February 1984): 44-45.

6.A.734   Noble, Douglas. "Computer Literacy and Ideology." Teachers
            College Record 85, 4(Summer 1984): 602-614.

6.A.735   Novy, Helen Jean. "A Student-Centered Approach to The
            Computer." Momentum 14, 2(May 1983): 35-37.

6.A.736   Nummela, Renata M. "Computer Literacy: What It's All
            About." Computer News 3, 2(November-December 1982): 19-
            21, 23.

6.A.737   Oakley, J., ed. Computers In Education: Issues and Applications.
            Broadway, Australia: Computer Education Group of New South
            Wales, 1985.

6.A.738   Oakman, Robert L. "Perspectives on Teaching Computing in
            The Humanities." Computers and The Humanities 21,
            4(October-December 1987): 227-233.

6.A.739   O'Connor, Vincent F. "When Computer Meets Kid in Middle
            School Math." Classroom Computer News 2, 4(March-April
            1982): 60-61.

6.A.740   O'Donnell, H. "Beyond Computer Literacy: ERIC/RCS."
            (Report). Journal of Reading 27, (October 1983): 78-80.

6.A.741   O'Donnell, H. "Computer Literacy: ERIC/RCS." (Report). The
            Reading Teacher 35, (January 1982): 490-494. (February 1982): 614-
            617.

6.A.742   O'Donnell, Holly. "Computer Literacy, Part II: Classroom
            Applications." Reading Teacher 35, 5(February 1982): 614-617.

6.A.743   O'Donnell, Holly. "ERIC/RCS: Computer Literacy, Part I: An
            Overview." Reading Teacher 34, 4(January 1982): 490-494.

6.A.744   OHanian, S. "What Does It Take To Be A Good Computer
            Teacher?" Learning (Belmont, California) 12, (March 1984): 30-
            33.

6.A.745   Ohmann, Richard. "Literacy, Technology, and Monopoly
            Capital." College English 47, 7(November 1985): 675-689.

6.A.746   Olson, D.R. "Computers as Tools of The Intellect." Educational
            Research 14, (May 1985): 5-8.

6.A.747   Oman, Paul W., and Willson, Debra. "Paradigm for K-8
            Computer Curriculum Design." Technological Horizons in
            Education 14, 2(September 1986): 82-88.

6.A.748   "One-year Shot at K-12 Computer Literacy, A." Electronic
            Learning 3, (May/June 1984): 43.

6.A.749   Ordman, E.T. "Impact of Computers: a Syllabus, The."
            Yearbook (National Council of Teachers of Mathematics) 1984,
            (1984): 30-34.

6.A.750   Orr, William T., Jr., et al. "Committed to Computers." Florida
            Vocational Journal 7, 4(February-March 1982): 8-16.

6.A.751   Ossman, Marian R. "Information Sources on Computer
            Literacy." Microcomputers for Information Management: An
            International Journal for Library and Information Services 1,
            2(June 1984): 155-158.

6.A.752   Oswalt, B. "Capstone Course Ensures Computer Literacy."
            Business Education Forum 39, (October 1984): 13-15.

6.A.753   Owen, Richard. "Soviets Aim To Put Desk-Top Computers into All of Nations School and Colleges." Chronicle of Higher Education 29, 21(February 6, 1985): 38.

6.A.754   Papagiannis, George J., and Milton, Sande. "Computer Literacy For Development: an Evolving Metaphor." Prospects 17, 3(1987): 355-366.

6.A.755   Parks, Peggy L., et al. "Faculty and Students Perceptions of Computer Applications in Nursing." Journal of Professional Nursing 2, 2(March-April 1986): 104-113.

6.A.756   Patterson, J.H. "Computers and Low-Achievers: Looking Beyond Drill and Practice." Electronic Education 6, (February 1987): 38.

6.A.757   Peelle, Howard. Computer Metaphors: Approaches To Computer Literacy. Eugene, Oregon: International Council For Computers In Education, 1984.

6.A.758   Peele, Howard A. "Computer Metaphors: Approaches to Computer Literacy For Educators." Weaver of Information and Perspectives on Technological Literacy 1, 2(Spring 1983): 10-11.

6.A.759   "Pennsylvania: Improving Schools through Technology." Classroom Computer News 3, 5(April 1983): 25.

6.A.760   Penrod, James, and Hughes, Nancy. "Computer Literacy: Synopsis of an Institute." CAUSE/EFFECT 6, 6(November 1983): 3-7.

6.A.761   Penrod, James I. "Information Technology Literacy: Initiatives at Pepperdine University." EDUCOM 18, 2(Summer 1983): 11-15.

6.A.762   Peters, Judy, and Smith, Richard A. "How Do You Rate?" American School and University 56, 6(February 1984): 71.

6.A.763   Pickert, Sarah M., and Hunter, Beverly. "Redefining 'Literacy'." Momentum 14, 3(September 1983): 7-9.

6.A.764   Piele, Linda J., et al. "Teaching Microcomputer Literacy: New Roles For Academic Librarians." College and Research Libraries 47, 4(July 1986): 374-378.

6.A.765   Piemonte, C. "Can We Legislate Computer Literacy?" Curriculum Review 24, (March/April 1985): 42.

6.A.766   Pipho, Chris. "The Computer Literacy Dilemma in The Public Schools." Educational Horizons 63, 3(Spring 1985): 100-103.

6.A.767   Plomp, Tjeerd, and Carleer, Gerrit. "Towards a Strategy for The Introduction of Information and Computer Literacy (ICL) Courses." Computers and Education II, 1(1987): 53-62.

6.A.768   Polansky, Daniel W. "The American School For The Deaf Computer Literacy Program." American Annals of The Deaf 130, 5(November 1985): 392-396.

6.A.769   Pollack, Maxine, and Stapleton, Ross Alan. "Why Ivan Can't Compute." High Technology 6, 2(February 1986): 42-45.

6.A.770   Porter, J.B. "Newest Literacy - The Computer." Tennessee School Boards Bulletin 34, (January-February 1983): 19.

6.A.771   Potter, Tom. "A Model For The Development of Computer In-Service Educational Programs." Journal of Computers in Mathematics and Science Teaching 5, 4(Summer 1986): 33-36.

6.A.772   Priest, Simon. "Teaching Microcomputer Applications in Physical Education." Journal of Physical Education, Recreation & Dance 58, 6(August 1987): 18-20.

6.A.773   Pritchard, William H., Jr., and Spicer, Donald Z. "The Vassar Computer Literacy Program." EDUCOM 18, 2(Summer 1983): 2-4, 32.

6.A.774   Pumo, B.J. "Future is Now: Preparing The Blind and Visually Impaired For Employment in the Computer Age, The." Journal of Visual Impairment & Blindness 78, (March 1984): 122-123.

6.A.775   Radin, Stephen, and Greenberg, Harold M. Computer Literacy For School Administrators. Lexington, Massachusetts: Lexington Books, 1983.

6.A.776   Rakovic, Gloria. "Brooklyn High School Dedicated To High-Technology Learning." Technological Horizons in Education 14, 7(March 1987): 58-60.

6.A.777   Randhawa, Bikkar S., and Hunt, Dennis. "Computers and
           Computer Literacy in Contemporary Psychological, Socio-
           Economic and Educational Context." AEDS Journal 17, 3(Spring
           1984): 1-13.

6.A.778   Rankin, R. "Business Educators Teach Computer Literacy to
           General Populace." Business Education Forum 37, (May 1983):
           5.

6.A.779   Rappoport, S. "Literacy and Computers." Library Journal 110
           (October 1, 1985): 74-75.

6.A.780   Rawitsch, Don G. "Minnesota's Statewide Push For Computer
           Literacy." Instructional Innovator 27, 2(February 1982): 34-35.

6.A.781   Ray, John R., and Malo, George E. "Computing in Tennessee."
           Tennessee Education 13, 2(Fall 1983): 12-23.

6.A.782   "Readers' Survey Results: What is Computer Literacy?"
           Classroom Computer Learning 6, 6(March 1986): 53.

6.A.783   Reide, Anne M. BASIC Computer Literacy. Manteno, Illinois:
           Basic Computer Literacy, Inc., 1984.

6.A.784   Reiss, Levi. Computer Literacy. Boston: PWS Kent Publishing
           Co., 1984.

6.A.785   Richman, Ellen. The Random House of Computer Literacy.
           New York: Random House, 1984.

6.A.786   Richman, Ellen. Spotlight On Computer Literacy. New York:
           Random House, 1982.

6.A.787   Riedl, Richard. "Computer Communication Problems: How To
           Teach Your Students To Overcome Them." School Library
           Media Activities Monthly 3, 4(December 1986): 50.

6.A.788   Roblyer, M.D., and Castine, W.H. "Instructional Computing
           Project Uses 'Multiplier Effect" To Train Florida Teachers."
           Technological Horizons in Education 14, 6(February 1987): 63-
           67.

6.A.789   Rodrigues, Raymond J. "Computer Program Models For
           Teacher Education." Action in Teacher Education 5, 4(Winter
           1983-1984): 15-21.

6.A.790   Root, Bud, et al. "Microcomputers in a Small Rural Junior High? You Bet!" NASSP Bulletin 68, 472(May 1984): 35-37.

6.A.791   Roth, Audrey J. "How To Become an Instant Computer Expert." Teaching English in The Two-Year College 13, 1(Febuary 1986):20-24.

6.A.792   Rothstein, Samuel, and Elgarten, Gerald H. "Teaching Junior High Students to Be Computer Literate." NASSP Bulletin 67, 463 (May 1983): 119-121.

6.A.793   Rotter, Joseph C., ed. "Special Issue on Computers." Elementary School Guidance and Counseling 18, 1(October 1983): 5-63.

6.A.794   Rude-Parkins, Carolyn. "Computer Literacy Through School District-University Collaboration." Journal of Staff Development 4, 2(November 1983): 69-79.

6.A.795   Ruhter, J.A. "Computer Literacy: An Emerging Endeavor." Lutheran Education 121, (September/October 1985): 22-27.

6.A.796   Rundall, Richard A. "A Child's Problem: Which Computer?" Clearing House 59, 4(December 1985): 174-175.

6.A.797   Ruthven, K. "Computer Literacy and The Curriculum." British Journal of Educational Studies 32, (June 1984): 134-147.

6.A.798   Sadowski, Barbara R. "A Model For Preparing Teachers To Teach With The Microcomputer." Arithmetic Teacher 30, 6(February 1983): 24-25, 62-63.

6.A.799   St. Clair-Atkinson, June. Help With Computer Literacy. Boston: Houghton Mifflin Co., n.d.

6.A.800   Sanders, Jo Shuchat. "Making The Computer Neuter." Computing Teacher 12, 7(April 1985): 23-27.

6.A.801   Santinelli, P. "Beeb Gets Over Its Boob." Times Higher Education Supplement 490, (March 26, 1982): 10.

6.A.802   Scalzitti, J. "Added Dimensions To Literacy." Arithmetic Teacher 32, (September 1984): 14-15.

6.A.803   Scheffler, I. "Computers At School?" Teachers College Record 87, (Summer 1986): 513-528.

6.A.804   Schradar, Vincent E. "The Computer in Education - Are We Over Our Heads?" NASSP Bulletin 68, 472 (May 1984): 38-42.

6.A.805   Schrum, Lynne. "Introducing Teachers To Telecommunication: California's (ESTTI)." Technological Horizons in Education 15, 8(April 1988): 85-89.

6.A.806   Schug, Mark C., and Kepner, Harry S., Jr. "Helping Students Deal With Computer Issues in Social Studies." Georgia Social Science Journal 16, 1(Winter 1985): 5-15.

6.A.807   Schwartz, Ruth. "Computers and The Arts." College Teaching 34, 1(Winter 1986): 11-16.

6.A.808   Seidel, Robert J., ed. Computer Literacy: Issues & Directions For 1985. San Diego, California: Academic Press, Inc., 1982.

6.A.809   Seim, D.N. "Computer Literacy: a Beginning." Lutheran Education 118, (November/December 1982): 64-71.

6.A.810   Selfe, C.L. "The Humanization of Computers: Forget Technology, Remember Literacy." English Journal 77, (October 1988): 69-71.

6.A.811   Senter, J. "Computer Technology and Education." Educational Forum 46, (Fall 1981): 55-64.

6.A.812   Sharma, S. "Learners' Cognitive Styles and Psychological Types as Intervening Variables Influencing Performance in Computer Science Courses." Journal of Educational Technology Systems 15, 4(1986-1987): 391-399.

6.A.813   Sharon, Dan, et al. "The ORT Open Tech Robotics and Automation Literacy Course." Programmed Learning and Educational Technology 24, 3(August 1987): 200-210.

6.A.814   Sherwook, Robert D., et al. "Developing Computer Literacy and Compentency For Preservice and Inservice Teachers." Journal of Computers in Mathematics and Science Teaching 1, 2(Winter 1981) 23-24.

6.A.815   Shore, B. "Does Computer Literacy Need an Update?" Journal of Business Education 59, (May 1984): 328-331.

6.A.816   Siegfried, Pat. "Computers and Children: Problems and Possibilities." Top of the News 39, 3(Spring 1983): 241-246.

6.A.817   Simon, Herbert A. "Computers in Education: Realizing The Potential." American Education 19, 10(December 1983): 17-23.

6.A.818   Sive, M.R. "Balanced View of Computers." Curriculum Review 21, (May 1982): 129-130.

6.A.819   Slesnick, Twila. "Creative Play: An Alternative Use of The Computer in Education." Simulation and Games 14, 1(March 1983): 11-19.

6.A.820   Smith, D.J., and Sage, M.W. "Computer Literacy and The Education/Training Interface." Computers and Education 7, 4(1983): 227-234.

6.A.821   Smith, Sara Dawn, and Smith, William D. "Hardware/Software and Hard Times: Educational Computing and Curriculum Change." Action in Teacher Education 5, 4(Winter 1983-1984): 27-34.

6.A.822   Sopp, Nancy Parks. "Do You Really Need a Children's Data Base?" Computing Teacher 13, 3(November 1985): 43-45.

6.A.823   Southall, George A. "Integrating Computer Literacy and Software Usage into Core Special Education Teacher-Training Programs." Journal of Reading, Writing, and Learning Disabilities International 1, 2(Winter 1985): 147-155.

6.A.824   Spain, Tom. "A School That Markets Its Own Resources." Electronic Learning 3, 6(March 1984): 34.

6.A.825   Spencer, Donald. An Introduction To Computers: Developing Computer Literacy. Columbus, Ohio: Merrill Publishing Co., 1983.

6.A.826   Spero, Samuel. "Let Them Have Micros: An Approach to Computer Literacy For Teachers." Technological Horizons in Education 10, 1(September 1982): 127-129.

6.A.827   Spresser, Diane M. "Topics in Computer Literacy as Elements of Two Introductory College Mathematics Courses." Journal of Computers in Mathematics and Science Teaching 6, 1(Fall 1986): 28-30.

6.A.828   "States With Computer Literacy Requirements." Electronic Learning 5, (October 1985): 28-29.

6.A.829   Steele, K.J., et al. "Using Microcomputer-Assisted Mathematics
           Instruction To Develop Computer Literacy." School Science and
           Mathematics 84, (February 1984): 119-124.

6.A.830   Steele, K.J., et al. "Effect of Microcomputer Assisted Instruction
           Upon The Computer Literacy of High Ability Students." Gifted
           Chico Quarterly 26, (Fall 1982): 162-164.

6.A.831   Steen, L.A. "The Cant of Computer Literacy." UMAP Journal 5,
           4(1984): 515-517.

6.A.832   Stephenson, Bette, and deLandsheere, Gilbert. "Excerpts From
           The International Conference on Education and New
           Information Technologies." Peabody Journal of Education 62,
           2(Winter 1985): 75-92.

6.A.833   Stevens, D.J. "Computers, Curriculum, and Careful Planning."
           Educational Technology 21, (November 1981): 21-24.

6.A.834   Stevens, Dorothy J. "Educator's Perception of Computers in
           Education: 1979 and 1981." AEDS Journal 16, 1(Fall 1982): 1-15.

6.A.835   Stickles, Mary. "Girls, Minorities and Low Income Students:
           Are They Getting Computer Time?" PTA Today 13, 6(April
           1988): 10-11.

6.A.836   Stocker, H.R., et al. "Microcomputer Applications in Business
           Education Programs." Business Education Forum 37, (March
           1983): 30-32.

6.A.837   Storey, Patrick B. "The Future of Computers in Continuing
           Medical Education." MOBIUS 3, 4(October 1983): 56-63.

6.A.838   Strehlo, Kevin, ed. "The Electronic Schoolhouse Graduates
           Better Thinkers." Personal Computing 7, 9(September 1983):
           66-67, 69, 71-72, 74, 196.

6.A.839   Streibel, M.J., and Garhart, C. "Beyond Computer Literacy."
           T.H.E. Journal 12, (June 1985): 69-73.

6.A.840   Streibel, Michael J. "Visual Literacy, Television Literacy, and
           Computer Literacy: Some Parallels and a Synthesis" Journal of
           Visual/Verbal Languaging 5, 2(Fall 1985): 5-14.

6.A.841   Strong, Gary E., and Gibson, Liz. "Adult Computer Literacy: The
           California State Library Commitment." Microcomputers For

Information Management: An International Journal for Library and Information Services 1, 2(June 1984): 143-153.

6.A.842   Sugarman, M.N. "Microcomputer Literacy Important in Vocational Teacher Education." School Shop 44, (April 1985): 29.

6.A.843   Swett, Sheila. "Cross-Cultural Computing." Electronic Learning 5, 4(January 1986): 73.

6.A.844   Szekely, Beatrice Beach, ed. "The Introduction of Computer Science into Soviet Secondary Education." Soviet Education 28, 10-11 (August-September 1986): 5-229.

6.A.845   Taffee, Stephen J., and Keogh, Andrew. "Dead Ends on the Road to Computer Literacy." Action in Teachers Education 5, 4(Winter 1983-1984): 43-48.

6.A.846   Talbert, Roy, Jr.,. "Myths and Symbols of Information Technology." CAUSE/EFFECT 7, 4(July 1984): 16-19.

6.A.847   Tan, Leslie E. "Computers in Pre-School Education." Early Child Development and Care 19, 4(1985): 319-336.

6.A.848   Tannenbaum, Robert S. "How Should We Teach Computing To Humanists?" Computers and The Hunamities 21, 4(October-December 1987): 217-225.

6.A.849   Tannenbaum, Robert S., and Rahn, B.J. "Computer Literacy For Undergraduate Humanities and Social Sciences Majors." Collegiate Microcomputer 3, 2(May 1985): 169-178.

6.A.850   Targ, Joan. "Computer Tutors: An Innovative Approach to Computer Literacy. Part II: A Role Model - From the Selection Process to Implementation." Educational Computer 1, 2(July-August 1981): 20-22, 24.

6.A.851   Targ, Joan. "Computer Tutors: An Innovative Approach to Computer Literacy. Part I: The Early Stages." Educational Computer Magazine 1, 1(May-June 1981): 8-10.

6.A.852   Tashner, John H., ed. Computer Literacy For Teachers: Issues, Questions & Concerns. Phoeniz, Arizona: Oryx Press, 1984.

6.A.853   Terry, Charles. "A Computer Literate Middle School." Middle
           School Journal 14, 3(May 1983): 25-27.

6.A.854   The, Lee. "Gee Whiz, These Computing Kids!" Personal
           Computing 6, 12(December 1982): 58-61, 64-67.

6.A.855   The, Lee. "Squaring Off Over Computer Literacy." Personal
           Computing 6, 9(September 1982): 58-64, 69-72.

6.A.856   "This We Believe About Computer Literacy." Business
           Education Forum 39, (October 1984): 9-10.

6.A.857   Thompson, S.J. "Integrating Computer Literacy Into The
           Curriculum." Yearbook (National Council of Teachers of
           Mathematics) 1982: 35-49.

6.A.858   Thorne, Michael. "The Legacy of The Microelectronics
           Education Programme," British Journal of Educational
           Technology 18, 3(October 1987): 165-181.

6.A.859   Thornton, L. Jay. "Microcomputer Literature and Special Needs
           Students. Ascertaining Whether Literacy Requirements Pose
           Real or Artificial Barriers." Journal For Vocational Special
           Needs Education 6, 3(Spring 1984): 20.

6.A.860   Thrush, J. Ann P., and Thrush, Randolph S. "Microcomputers
           in Foreign Language Instruction." Modern Language Journal
           68, !(Spring 1984): 21-26.

6.A.861   Tobin, Catherine D. "Developing Computer Literacy."
           Arithmetic Teacher 30, 6(February 1983): 22-23, 60.

6.A.862   Tobin, Laurence. "Faculty Training in Computers and
           Competition: Warnings and Recommendations." College
           Composition and Communication 38, 2(May 1987): 195-198.

6.A.863   Traberman, Tama. "Using Interactive Computer Techniques to
           Develop Global Understanding." Computing Teacher 11,
           2(September 1983): 43-50.

6.A.864   Trainor, Timothy N. Computer Literacy: Concepts &
           Application. Santa Cruz, California: Mitchell Publishing, Inc.,
           1984.

6.A.865   Troutner, J. "Computer Careers and History." The Journal of
           Computers in Mathematics and Science Teaching 5, (Summer
           1986): 13-14.

6.A.866   Troutner, J. "Teaching Computer Ethics." The Journal of
           Computers in Mathematics and Science Teaching 5, (Spring
           1986): 11-12.

6.A.867   Troutner, J.J. "Helping Teach Computer Literacy." Educational
           Computer Magazine 3, (September 1983): 30.

6.A.868   Trumbull, Deborah J. "Games Children Play: A Cautionary
           Tale." Educational Leadership 43, 6(March 1986): 18-21.

6.A.869   Turkel, Susan B., and Chapline, Elaine Burns. "A Computer
           Literacy Program For Prospective Elementary School Teachers."
           Journal of Computers in Mathematics and Science Teaching 4,
           1(Fall 1984): 24-28.

6.A.870   Turner, J.A. "Familiarity With New Technology Breeds
           Changes in Computer Literacy Courses." Chronicle of Higher
           Education 33, (July 22, 1987): 9.

6.A.871   Turner, J.A. "Ohio State Eyes Computer Literacy: Who Needs
           It? Who Should Teach It?" Chronicle of Higher Education 27,
           (January 11, 1984): 1.

6.A.872   Turner, Judith Axler. "Familiarity With New Technology
           Breeds Changes in Computer-Literacy Courses." Chronicle of
           Higher Education 33, 45(July 22, 1987): 12.

6.A.873   Van Dusseldorp, Ralph. "A Successful Boostrap Program For
           Infusion of Computer Competencies into a School of Education
           Curriculum." AEDS Journal 17, 4(Summer 1984): 9-13.

6.A.874   VanLoan, Charles F. "Computer Science and The Liberal Arts
           Student." Educational Forum 45, 1(November 1980): 29-42.

6.A.875   Via, Nancy. "Computer Literacy: The Message Is The Medium."
           Classroom Computer News 3, 6(May-June 1983): 42-45.

6.A.876   Wall, Roger. "A Museum Approach To Computer Learning."
           Science and Children 23, 4(January 1986): 11-13.

6.A.877   Wallace, Danny P., and Boyce, Bert R. "Computer Technology and Interdisciplinary Efforts: A Discussion and Model Program." Journal of Education For Library and Information Science 27, 3(Winter 1987): 158-168.

6.A.878   Wangberg, E.G. "An Interactive, Language Experience Based Microcomputer Approach To Reduce Adult Illiteracy." Lifelong Learning 9, (February 1986): 8-12.

6.A.879   Wascura, Robert. "Model For Computer Novices: New York School District Uses Cupertino Concept To Build Computer Program." Thrust For Educational Leadership 16, 5(February-March 1987): 16-17.

6.A.880   Watson, E.D. "When Computer Literacy Becomes Multidimensional." Electronic Education 4, (January 1985): 40.

6.A.881   Watt, D.H. "Computer Literacy: What Should Schools Do About It?" Instructor 91, (October 1981): 85-87.

6.A.882   Watt, Dan. "The Feds Are Coming! Computer Education Could Be a Hot Federal Issue in an Election Year." Popular Computing 3, 8(June 1984): 94.

6.A.883   Watt, Dan. "Neighborhood Computer Centers." Popular Computing 3, 7(May 1984): 94.

6.A.884   Watt, Daniel. "Should Children Be Computer Programmers?" Popular Computing 1, 11(September 1982): 130-133.

6.A.885   Waugh, Michael. "Should Computers Be in Our Classrooms?" Science Activities 19, 3(September-October 1982): 4-11.

6.A.886   Wayrik, John J. "A Short Presentation in 'Computer Literacy' Using Programmable Calculators." Calculators/Computers Magazine 2, 7(November-December 1978): 9-11.

6.A.887   Webster, Staten W., and Webster, Linda S. "Computer Literacy or Competency?" Teacher Education Quarterly 12, 2(Spring 1985): 1-7.

6.A.888   Wedman, John, and Heller, Marvin. "Concerns of Teachers About Educational Computing." AEDS Journal 18, 1(Fall 1984): 31-40.

6.A.889   Wedman, John, and Heller, Marvin. "Transformations: How To Fit Computer Literacy into Your Curriculum." Curriculum Review 22, 1(February 1983): 33-34.

6.A.890   Wedman, J.F., and Strathe, M. "Faculty Development in Technology: A Model For Higher Education." Educational Technology 25, (February 1985): 15-19.

6.A.891   West, Christopher, and Lloyd, Jo. Course In Computer Literacy: "You and The Computer." N.P. : E. Arnold, 1984.

6.A.892   Weyer, Stephen A. "Computers For Communication." Childhood Education 59, 4(March-April 1983): 232-236.

6.A.893   "What is Computer Literacy?" Classroom Computer Learning 6, (March 1986): 53.

6.A.894   Wholeben, Brent E. "Structuring The Undergraduate Computer Literacy Curriculum For 4th Year Teacher Education Majors." Collegiate Microcomputer 3, 2(May 1985): 179-187.

6.A.895   "Why Be A Computer Literate?" Thrust 10, (January/February 1981): 25-27.

6.A.896   Wilson, K.G. "The Minicourse Approach To Teaching Computer Literacy." Education Digest 52, (September 1986): 44-45.

6.A.897   Wilson, Kara Gae. "Literacy Lab Mini-Courses Maximize The Curriculum." NASSP Bulletin 70, 489(April 1986): 25-27.

6.A.898   Wilson, Kara Gae. "English Teachers: Keys To Computer Literacy." English Journal 70, 5(September 1981): 50-53.

6.A.899   Winner, Alice-Ann. "Computer Literacy in The Elementary School: An Argument For Change From Within." AEDS Journal 16, 3(Spring 1983): 153-165.

6.A.900   Wortman, Alexandra, and Hable, Mary P. BASIC Computer Literacy For Beginners. Manteno, Illinois: Basic Computer Literacy. Inc., 1984.

6.A.901   Wright, Jane Perryman, and McNair, Rita Hadley. "Computer Literacy: Curriculum Transformation or Addition?" Contemporary Education 55, 4(Summer 1984): 233-236.

6.A.902   Wright, June L., and Church, Marilyn J. "The Evolution of An
           Effective Home-School Microcomputer Connection." Education
           and Computing 2, 1(1986): 67-74.

6.A.903   Young, D.R. "Computer Technology and Its Application To
           Teaching Training Programs." Canadian Vocational Journal 23,
           1(May 1987): 2-5.

6.A.904   Young, Marsha. "Faculty Computer Workshops: A Faculty
           Becoming Computer Literate." American Annals of The Deaf
           130, 5(November 1985): 347-353.

6.A.905   Yucha, Carolyn, and Reigeluth, Charles M. "The Use of
           Computers in Nursing Education, Practice and Administration."
           Computers and Education 7, 4(1983): 223-226.

6.A.906   Yuen, Steve Chi-Yin. "The Challenge of Microcomputer
           Technology to Vocational Education." Journal of Studies in
           Technical Careers 10, 1(Winter 1988): 49-59.

6.A.907   Zucker, Andrew. "Computers in Education: National Policy in
           The USA." European Journal of Education 17, 4(1982): 395-410.

B.   B.B.C. COMPUTER LITERACY PROJECT

6.B.908   Dane, N.P. Learning To Use The BBC Microcomputer: A Gower
           Read-Out Publication. Brookfield, Vermont: Gower Publishing
           Company, 1982.

6.B.909   Hall, D. "Screen Tests For Computer Literacy: BBC's Computer
           Project." Times Educational Supplement 3385, (May 8, 1981): 36.

6.B.910   Makins, V. "Thieves Came Down From The Mountains." (BBC
           Computer Literacy Project in Belmont School, London). Times
           Educational Supplement 3427, (March 5, 1982): 36.

6.B.911   Megarry, J. "Digital Awareness." (BBC Computer Literacy
           Project: Great Britain). Times Educational Supplement 3427,
           (March 5, 1982): 34.

6.B.912   Radcliffe, J. "Computer Literacy Worldwide." Media in
           Education and Development 17, (March 1984): 5-8.

6.B.913   Radcliffe, J. "British Programme Teaches Computer Literacy in U.S. (The Computer Programme)." Community and Junior College Journal 53, (May 1983): 46.

6.B.914   Salkeld, Bob. "BBC Computer Literacy Project." Media in Education and Development 15, 2(June 1982): 67-70.

6.B.915   Salkeld, Robert. "BBC Computer Literacy Project." Convergence 15, 4(1982): 20-25.

C.   BIBLIOGRAPHIES

6.C.916   Browne, M. Patricia. "Microcomputers and Early Childhood: Summer Reading and Viewing." Early Childhood Education 19, 2(Summer 1986): 33-34.

6.C.917   Bruwelheide, Janis H. "Teacher Competencies For Microcomputer Use in The Classroom: A Literature Review." Educational Technology 22, 10(October 1982): 29-31.

6.C.918   Hanlon, Heather, and Roland, Craig. "Artists, Educators, and Microcomputers: An Annotated Bibliography of Software and Publications." Art Education 36, 4(July 1983): 22-27.

6.C.919   Mandell, P.L. "Computer Literacy, Languages, and Careers." School Library Journal 28, (April 1982): 19-22.

6.C.920   Schullstrom, F.Z., and Mertz, M.P. "Computer Revolution: Implications For Education." English Journal 71, (December 1982): 60-62.

6.C.921   Smith, Richard L. "Bibliography: Computer Literacy For Teachers." Journal of Computers in Mathematics and Science Teaching 2, 1(Fall 1982): 43-45.

6.C.922   Smith, Richard L. "Bibliography: Computers in Elementary Education." Journal of Computers in Mathematics and Science Teaching 2, 2(Winter 1982): 44-45.

D.   COMPUTER APTITUDE, LITERACY AND INTEREST PROFILE

6.D.923   Allen, Judy Edwards, et al. "Gender Equity in Computer Education." <u>AEDS Monitor</u> 24, 7-8(January-February 1986): 10-23, 26.

6.D.924   Anderson, Ronald E., et al. "Inequities in Opportunities For Computer Literacy." <u>Computing Teacher</u> 11, 8(April 1984): 10-12.

6.D.925   Arndt, Stephen, et al. "Students' Attitudes Toward Computers." <u>Computers and The Social Sciences</u> 1, 3-4(July-December 1985): 181-190.

6.D.926   Billings, Karen, and Maursund, David. <u>Are You Computer Literate?</u> Beaverton, Oregon: Dilithium Press, 1979.

6.D.927   Bostock, Stephen J., et al. "The Effects of Learning Environment and Gender on The Attainment of Computer Literacy." <u>Studies in The Education of Adults</u> 19, 1(April 1987): 37-45.

6.D.928   Bresnitz, Eddy A, et al. "A Survey of Computer Literacy Among Medical Students." <u>Journal of Medical Education</u> 61, 5(May 1986): 410-412.

6.D.929   Coffin, Gregory C. "Minimum Computer Knowledge For Elementary Principals." <u>Journal of Computers in Mathematics and Science Teaching</u> 5, 4(Summer 1986): 37-39.

6.D.930   Culley, Lorraine. "Girls, Boys and Computers." <u>Educational Studies</u> 14, 1(1988): 3-8.

6.D.931   Durndell, A., et al. "A Survey of Attitudes To, Knowledge About and Experience of Computers." <u>Computers and Education</u> 11, 3(1987): 167-175.

6.D.932   Elkins, R.R. "Computer Illiterate, and Proud of It." <u>Community, Technical, and Junior College Journal</u> 56, (October/November 1985): 28-31.

6.D.933   Fusselman, Kay. "Do Computer Skills Mean Higher Pay, Better Jobs?" <u>Secretary</u> 46, 6(June-July 1986): 20-23.

6.D.934   Gable, R.S., et al. "Is There an Aptitude For Learning About Computers?" <u>Yearbook</u> (Claremont Reading Conference) (1985): 101-106.

6.D.935   Griswold, Philip A. "Differences Between Education and
            Business Majors in Their Attitudes About Computers." AEDS
            Journal 18, 3(Spring 1985): 131-138.

6.D.936   Griswold, Philip A. "Computer Awareness and Attitudes of
            Prospective Rural Teachers." Rural Educator 5, 3(Spring 1984):
            11-15.

6.D.937   Hattie, John, and Fitzgerald, Donald. "Sex Differences in
            Attitudes: Achievement and Use of Computers." Australian
            Journal of Education 31, 1(April 1987): 3-26.

6.D.938   Hearne, J.D., and Lasley, J. "The Relationship Between
            Achievement Factors and Gender-Specific Computer Aptitude
            Among Junior High School Students." Education (Chula Vista,
            California) 106, (Fall 1985): 81-87.

6.D.939   Hearne, J. Dixon, et al. "Predicting Mathematics Achievement
            Computer Aptitude in Junior High Students." Educational
            Research Quarterly 10, 4 (1986-1987): 18-24.

6.D.940   Hoffman, Charles. "Access and Equity: Computers for
            Everyone." Technological Horizons in Education 12, 9(May
            1985): 72-74.

6.D.941   Johnson, James P. "Can Computers Close The Educational
            Equity Gap?" Perspectives. The Civil Rights Quarterly 14,
            3(Fall 1982): 20-25.

6.D.942   Lenkway, P. "Minimum Student Performance Standards in
            Computer Literacy: Florida's New State Law." T.H.E. Journal
            13, (May 1986): 74-77.

6.D.943   Levinson, E.M. "A Review of The Computer Aptitude, Literacy,
            and Interest Profile (CALIP)." The Journal of Counseling and
            Development 64, (June 1986): 658-659.

6.D.944   Lockheed, Marlaine E., and Frakt, Steven B. "Sex Equity:
            Increasing Girls' Use of Computers." Computing Teacher 11,
            8(April 1984): 16-18.

6.D.945   Loyd, Brenda H., and Gressard, Clarice. "The Effects of Sex, Age,
            and Computer Experience on Computer Attitudes," AEDS
            Journal 18, 2(Winter 1984): 67-77.

6.D.946   Marshall, Joh C. "Computer Attitudes and Knowledge in Rural Settings." Research in Rural Education 2, 4(Spring 1985): 155-158.

6.D.947   McCoy, L.T. "Computer Literacy is Real Literacy." English Journal 72, (October 1983): 27.

6.D.948   McDonald, Glenda, and Hollaway, William H. "Computer Awareness: Teaching Different Age Groups." NASSP Bulletin 66, 455(September 1982): 92-98.

6.D.949   Morgenson, Donald F. "There's More To Knowledge Than Computer Literacy." Ontario Mathematics Gazette 25, 1(September 1986): 22-24.

6.D.950   Pantiel, Mindy, and Peterson, Becky. "Are Your Teachers Ready for Computers?" Principal 64, 4(March 1985): 44-46.

6.D.951   Powell, William. "Database: A Learning Tool and a Vocational Competence." Journal of Education For Business 63, 4(January 1988): 168-171.

6.D.952   Schubert, Jane G. "Gender Equity in Computer Learning." Theory into Practice 25, 4(Autumn 1986): 267-275.

6.D.953   Stevens, Dorothy Jo. "How Educators Perceive Computers in the Classroom." AEDS Journal 13, 3(Spring 1980): 221-232.

6.D.954   Tuttle, Mark S. "What Should a Computer-Literate Physician Know? How Should He or She Come to Know It?" MOBIUS 3, 4(October 1983): 43-52.

6.D.955   Voogt, Joke. "Computer Literacy in Secondary Education: The Performance and Engagement of Girls." Computers and Education 11, 4(1987): 305-312.

6.D.956   Whiteside, Custer. "Developing Sex Equite Awareness in Computer Literacy Courses." Action in Teacher Education 8, 1(Spring 1986): 45-49.

6.D.957   Whitfield, David. "Attitudes and Literacy of College Instructors and High School Seniors Regarding The Use of Microcomputers In Education." Ed.D. dissertation, University of San Francisco, 1983. 45/01-A, p.49.

6.D.958   Widmer, Connie, and Parker, Janet. "Computerphobia: Causes and Cures." Action in Teacher Education 5, 4(Winter 1983-1984): 23-25.

6.D.959   Winer, J.L., et al. "Women, Education, Mathematics, and Computers: an Instance of Vocational Incongruence." Journal of Employment Counseling 20, (March 1983): 12-18.

6.D.960   Woodrow, Janice E.J. "Educators' Attitudes and Predispositions Towards Computers." Journal of Computers in Mathematics and Science Teaching 6, 3(Spring 1987): 27-37.

E.   TESTS AND SCALES

6.E.961   Brady, H. "Do We Really Need A National Computer Assessment Test?" Classroom Computer Learning 6, (October 1985): 7.

6.E.962   Burns, B. and Gerguson, E. "A Developmental Study of Children's Computer-Aptitude and Knowledge About Computer Technology." Early Child Development and Care 32, 1-4(1988): 7-22.

6.E.963   Cassel, R.N., and Cassel, S.L. "Cassel Computer Literacy Test (CMLRTC)." Journal of Instructional Psychology 11 (March 1984): 3-9

6.E.964   Cheng, T.T., et al. "A Validation Study of The Computer Literacy Examination: Cognitive Aspect." AEDS Journal 18, (Spring 1985): 139-152.

6.E.965   Dologite, D.G. "Measuring Microcomputer Literacy." Journal of Educational Technology Systems 16, 1(1987-1988): 29-43.

6.E.966   Eastman, S.T. and Krendl, K.A. "Computers and Gender: Differential Effects of Electronic Search on Students' Achievement and Attitudes." Journal of Research and Development in Education 20, (Spring 1987): 41-48.

6.E.967   Ellsworth, Randy, and Bowman, Barbara E. "A Beliefs About Computers' Scale Based on Ahl's Questionaire Items." Computing Teacher 10, 4(December 1982): 32-34.

6.E.968   Feldman, P., and Uhlig, G.E. "Comparing The Computer
             Literacy For Freshman and Senior College Army ROTC Students
             (Use of Cassel Computer Literacy Test)." College Student Journal
             18, (Fall 1984): 257-260.

6.E.969   Gabriel, Roy M. "Assessing Computer Literacy: A Validated
             Instrument and Empirical Results." AEDS Journal 18, 3(Spring
             1985): 153-171.

6.E.970   Geisert, G. "Scope-and-Sequence for Computer Literacy." Early
             Years 14, (March 1984): 14-15.

6.E.971   Grover, S.C. "Level of Planning Skill as a Predictor of Variations
             in Computer Competency Among Intellectually Gifted and Non-
             Gifted Children." The Journal of Educational Research 80,
             (January/February 1987): 173-180.

6.E.972   Helft, B.L. and Levine, L.H. "Computer Terminology:
             Familiarity vs. Understanding." Journal of Educational
             Technology Systems 14, 3(1985-1986): 203-216.

6.E.973   Hofman, R.J. "Microcomputers, Evaluation, Literacy: Will The
             Teacher Survive?" Journal of Learning Disabilities 15,
             (June/July 1982): 370-372.

6.E.974   Jackson, L.M., and Yamanaka, E. "Measuring Women's
             Attitudes, Goals, and Literacy Toward Computers and Advanced
             Technology." Educational Technology 25, (February 1985): 12-
             14.

6.E.975   Lockheed, Marlaine E. Computer Literacy: Definition & Survey
             Items For Assessment In Schools. Washington, D.C.:
             Government Printing Office, 1983.

6.E.976   Montague, E.C., and King, R.A. "Which Computer
             Compentencies Are Most Needed By School Managers? A
             Comparison of The Views of Computer Experts and School
             Principals." Educational Technology 25, (March 1985): 25-30.

6.E.977   Senn, Peter R. "Six Checklists to Prepare Your Classroom For
             Technology." Social Education 47, 5(May 1983): 317-320.

6.E.978   Simonson, Michael R., et al. "Development of a Standardized
             Test of Computer Literacy and a Computer Anxiety Index."
             Journal of Educational Computing Research 3, 2(1987): 231-247.

6.E.979   Smith, S.D. "Relationship of Computer Attitudes To Sex, Grade-Level, and Teacher Influence (Use of Minnesota Computer Awareness and Literacy Test)." Education 106, (Spring 1986): 338-344.

6.E.980   Spencer, Donald D. Computer Literacy Test Questions. Ormond Beach, Florida: Camelot Publishing Co., 1983.

6.E.981   Stananought, J., and Stananought, D. Computer Literacy Flash Cards. N.P.: Sanda Press, 1986.

6.E.982   Swadener, M. and Hannafin, M.J. "Gender Similarities and Differences in Sixth Graders' Attitudes Toward Computers: An Exploratory Study (Use of Computer Literacy and Awareness Assessment Instrument)." Educational Technology 27, (January 1987): 37-42.

6.E.983   Van Dusseldorp, R. "A Successful Bootstrap Program For Infusion of Computer Compentencies into a School of Education Curriculum." AEDS Journal 17, (Summer 1984): 9-13.

6.E.984   Zemke, Ron. Computer Literacy Needs Assessment: A Trainer's Guide. N.P.: Addison-Wesley, 1985.

6.E.985   Ziegler, E.W., et al. "A Preliminary Comparison of Applications Oriented Microcomputer Training and Traditional Microcomputer Awareness Training." International Journal of Instructional Media 11, 4(1983-1984): 285-288.

F.   TEXTBOOKS AND MATERIALS

6.F.986   Birch, Alison. "Monsters, Purple Penguins, and Fun with Words: An Introduction To Logo List Processing." Classroom Computer Learning 8, 5(February 1988): 54-57.

6.F.987   Black, Steve, and Mele, Tom. "Our Mobile Microcomputer Labs Stretch Resources and Ease Scheduling." American School Board Journal 175, 5(May 1988): 41.

6.F.988   Bosch, K.A. "A Microcomputer Literacy Training Model For School Administrators." Journal of Research on Computing In Education 20, (Summer 1988): 331-338.

6.F.989   Brecher, Deborah L. The Women's Computer Literacy
              Handbook. New York: NAL, 1985.

6.F.990   Burke, Walter. Computers In The Classroom . . . What Shall I
              Do? A Guide. New York: Garland Publishing, 1986.

6.F.991   Cavanaugh, Ann. The Computer Primer. Monroe, New York:
              Trillium Press, 1983.

6.F.992   Cloke, C., et al. Basic Guide To Computer Literacy. Cambridge:
              Hobsons Press, 1984.

6.F.993   Computer Literacy Made Easy: A Programmed Primer. N.P.:
              n.p., 1985.

6.F.994   "Cover to Cover - Evaluating The New Computer Literacy
              Texts." Classroom Computer Learning 6, (February 1986): 53.

6.F.995   Curran, Susan, and Curnow, Ray. Overcoming Computer
              Illiteracy: A Friendly Introduction To Computers. New York:
              Penguin Books, Inc., 1984.

6.F.996   Dale, R. "Secondary Computer Literacy Programs." Quest, 41
              (October 1986): 46-47.

6.F.997   Hobart, R.D., et al. "Teaching Computer Literacy With Freeware
              and Shareware." T.H.E. Journal 15, (May 1988): 78-81.

6.F.998   Lathrop, Ann. "Recommended Books For Elementary and
              Junior High School Library Media Centers." Educational
              Computer 2, 6(November-December 1982): 30-31, 62.

6.F.999   Sanscin, John. The Incredible Shrinking Computer: A Guide To
              Computer Literacy. Bedford, Massachusetts: Digital Press, 1984.

6.F.1000   Thompson, C.J., and Friske, J.S. "Programming: Impact On
              Computer Literacy Training For Teachers." Journal Of Research
              On Computing In Education 20, (Summer 1988): 367-374.

6.F.1001   Troutner, Joanne. "Hi-Quality, Hi-Tech Books." Classroom
              Computer Learning 7, 6(March 1987): 43-46.

6.F.1002   Turner, J.A. "New Computer-Literacy Textbook Reads Like a
              Science-Fiction Novel." Chronicle of Higher Education 31,
              (October 2, 1985): 32.

6.F.1003   Walsh, Vincent. Computer Literacy: A Beginner's Guide. London: Macmillan Publishers, Ltd., 1984.

6.F.1004   Weal, Elizabeth. "Does The Manual Measure Up?" Popular Computing 2, 9(July 1983): 166, 169.

6.F.1005   Westley, J. "How Texas Made History With The New Literacy Texts." Classroom Computer Learning 6, (February 1986): 50-52.

6.F.1006   Westley, J.E. "Textbooks Go High-Tech." Classroom Computer Learning 5, (January 1985): 42-45.

6.F.1007   Winkler, K.J. "Interest in Computer Literacy Sets Off Big Textbook Boom." Chronicle of Higher Education 25, (September 8, 1982): 1.

G.   RESEARCH

6.G.1008   Anderson, Ronald E. "Females Surpass Males in Computer Problem Solving: Findings From The Minnesota Computer Literacy Assessment." Journal of Educational Computing Research 3, 1(1987): 39-51.

6.G.1009   Banks, David. "Adult Classes in Computing - A Survey." Adult Education (London) 56, 1(June 1983): 6-10.

6.G.1010   Battista, Michael T., and Krockover, Gerald H. "The Effects of Computer Use in Science and Mathematics Education Upon The Computer Literacy of Preservice Elementary Teachers." Journal of Research in Science Teaching 21, 1(January 1984): 39-46.

6.G.1011   Battista, Michael T., and Steele, Kathleen J. "The Effect of Computer-Assisted and Computer Programming Instruction On The Computer Literacy of High Ability Fifth Grade Students." School Science and Mathematics 84, 8(December): 649-658.

6.G.1012   Berghel, Hall. "Computer Literacy Programs: The Effects of the Large-Class Setting on Student Performance." Collegiate Microcomputer 4, 1(February 1986): 69-81.

6.G.1013   Bruwelheide, Janis H. "Computer Literacy: A Current Review of The Literature." Rural Educator 5, 3(Spring 1984): 6-10.

6.G.1014   Burns, Barbara, and Ferguson, Elizabeth. "A Developmental Study of Children's Computer-Attitude and Knowledge About Computer Technology." Early Child Development and Care 32, 1-4(1988): 7-22.

6.G.1015   Christensen, Carol A., and Cosden, Merith A. "The Relationship Between Special Education Placement and Instruction in Computer Literacy Skills." Journal of Educational Computing Research 2, 3(1986): 299-306.

6.G.1016   Computer Education: A Catalog of Projects Sponsored By The United States Department of Education. Washington, D.C.: Government Printing Office, 1984.

6.G.1017   Datta, Kamal. "Computer Education In Indian Secondary Schools: A Survey of Class." Prospects 17, 4(1987): 581-586.

6.G.1018   Divoky, D. "Finding Ways To Change The Classroom; IBM's PALS Targets Illiteracy [Principles of The Alphabet Literacy System]." Classroom Computer Learning 8, (April 1988): 38-40.

6.G.1019   Dologite, D.G. "Measuring Microcomputer Literacy." Journal of Educational Technology Systems 16, 1(1987-1988): 29-43.

6.G.1020   D'Onofrio, Marianne J., and Slama, Mark E. "An Investigation of The Computer Literacy Resulting From The Use of Microcomputers in High School Accounting Classes." Delta Pi Epsilon Journal 25, 4(October 1983): 143-154.

6.G.1021   Gabriel, Roy M. "Computer Literacy Assessment and Validation: Empirical Relationships at Both Student and School Levels." Journal of Educational Computing Research 1, 4(1985): 415-425.

6.G.1022   Gelder, Amanda, and Maggs, Alex. "Direct Instruction Microcomputing in Primary Schools: Manipulation of Critical Instructional Variables." Research in Science and Technological Education 1, 2(9183): 221-238.

6.G.1023   Gressard, Clarice P., and Loyd, Brenda H. "An Investigation of The Effects of Math Anziety and Sex on Computer Attitudes." School Science and Mathematics 87, 2(February 1987): 125-135.

6.G.1024   Guthrie, John T. "Research: One Computer Literacy Skill," Journal of Reading 24, 5(February 1981): 458-460.

6.G.1025   Hahn, J.S. "An Exploratory Study of The Relationship Between Learner Cognitive Styles and Three Different Teaching Methods Used to Teach Computer Literacy With The Pittsburgh Information Retrievel System (PIRETS)." International Journal of Instructional Media 11, 2(1983-1984): 147-158.

6.G.1026   Hearne, J.D., et al. "Computer Aptitude: An Investigation of Differences Among Junior High Students With Learning Disabilities and Their Non-Learning Disabled Peers." Journal of Learning Disabilities 21, (October 1988): 489-492.

6.G.1027   Helms, Susan. "Faculty Microcomputer Usage: Results of a Training Workshop and Follow-Up Study." Journal of Education For Business 62, 4(January 1987): 149-152.

6.G.1028   Hill, T., et al. "Roll of Efficacy Expectations In Predicting The Decision To Use Advanced Technologies: The Case of Computers." Journal of Applied Psychology 72, (May 1987): 307-313.

6.G.1029   Johnson, Jerry. "Research and The Decision-Making Process." Computing Teacher 11, 6(February 1984): 67.

6.G.1030   Johnson, Marvin L. "Computer Literacy and Computer Science and Their Relationship to Mathematics." Mathematics and Computer Education 20, 3(Fall 1986): 150-154.

6.G.1031   Kagan, Dona M. "Learning How To Program or Use Computers: A Review of Six Applied Studies." Educational Technology 28, 3(March 1988): 49-51.

6.G.1032   Kaplan, Irene Petzinger, and Andritz, Mary H. "Incorporation of Online Literature Searching Into The Didactic and Experiential Curriculum For BS Pharmacy Students." Journal of Pharmaceutical Education 51, 4(Winter 1987): 424-426.

6.G.1033   Kazlauskas, Edward John, and McCrady, Jacqueline C. "Microcomputer Training Approaches: Review and Evaluation Criteria." Microcomputers For Information Management: An International Journal For Library and Information Services 2, 2(June 1985): 91-101.

6.G.1034   Kearsley, G., et al. "Computer Literacy in Business and Industry: Three Examples Using Microcomputers." Educational Technology 2, (July 1982): 9-14.

6.G.1035   Kollerbaur, Anita. "Computers in Swedish Schools: Experience, Research and Problems." Technological Horizons in Education 10, 3(January 1983): 79-86.

6.G.1036   Koohang, Alex A. "Effects of Age, Gender, College Status, and Computer Experience on Attitudes Toward Library Computer Systems(LCS)." Library and Information Science Research 8, 4(October-December 1986): 349-353.

6.G.1037   Larson, A. "The Availability and Use of Computer Instructional Resources in Secondary Education, 1969-1983." Journal of Business Education 60, (November 1984): 60-62.

6.G.1038   Lawton, Johnny, and Gerschner, Vera T. "A Review of The Literature on Attitudes Towards Computers and Computerized Instruction." Journal of Research and Development in Education 16, 1(Fall 1982): 50-55.

6.G.1039   Lee, Jo Ann. "The Effects of Past Computer Experience on Computerized Aptitude Test Performance." Educational and Psychological Measurement 46, 3(Autumn 1986): 727-733.

6.G.1040   Madsen, Jane M., and Sebastiani, Lee Ann. "The Effect of Computer Literacy Instruction On Teachers' Knowledge of and Attitudes Toward Microcomputers." Journal of Computer-Based Instruction 14, 2(Spring 1987): 68-72.

6.G.1041   Massey, Tom K. Jr., and Engelbrecht, James W. "Empirical Effects of Selected Antecedent Computer Literacy Skills on Computer Orientation of College Students." Computers and Education 11, 3(1987): 177-180.

6.G.1042   Miura, I.T. "The Relationship Computer Self-Efficacy Expectations To Computer Interest and Course Enrollment In College." Sex Roles 16, (March 1987): 303-311.

6.G.1043   Moon, Y.S., et al. "Statistical Analysis of The Characteristics of The Secondary School Computer Studies' Students in Hong Kong." AEDS Journal 19, (Winter/Spring 1986): 162-167.

6.G.1044   Morris, R.C. and Meyer, E. "Assessing Microcomputer Competencies For The Elementary Teacher: An Indepth Study of Illinois Schools." Early Child Development and Care 32, 1-2(1988): 101-118.

6.G.1045   Mruk, Christopher J. "Teaching Adult Learners Basic Computer
            Skills: A New Look at Age, Sex, and Motivational Factors."
            Collegiate Microcomputer 5, 3(August 1987): 294-300.

6.G.1046   Norris, Cathleen A., and Lumsden, D. Barry. "Evaluating Do-It-
            Yourself Computer Inservice Training Packages: Methodology
            and Some Findings." Computing Teacher 11, 6(February 1984):
            65-66.

6.G.1047   Samuels, Melvin H., and Holtzapple-Toxey, Lisa. "Perceived
            Needs of School Administrators For Computer Training: A
            Study." Computers in the Schools 4, 2(Summer 1987): 71-78.

6.G.1048   Schmidt, B. June, et al. "Current Considerations For Preparing
            Business Teachers. NABTE Bulletin 110." Business Education
            Forum 42, 6(March 1988): 25-34.

6.G.1049   Simpson, Nan. "A Research Study of School Computer Use."
            Educational Computer 3, 4(July-August 1983): 15-16, 37.

6.G.1050   Steele, Kathleen J., et al. "The Effect of Microcomputer Assisted
            Instruction Upon The Computer Literacy of High Ability
            Students." Gifted Child Quarterly 26, 4(Fall 1982): 162-164.

6.G.1051   Steele, Kathleen J., et al. "The Effect of Microcomputer-Assisted
            Instruction on The Computer Literacy of Fifth Grade Students."
            Journal of Educational Research 76, 5(May-June 1983): 298-301.

6.G.1052   Suydam, Marilyn N. "What Research Says: Microcomputers
            and Mathematics Instruction." School Science and Mathematics
            84, 4(April 1984): 337-343.

6.G.1053   Terry, Margaret S., and Ziegler, Edward W. "Instructional
            Methodology, Computer Literacy and Problem Solving Among
            Gifted and Talented Students." Creative Child and Adult
            Quarterly 12, 2(Summer 1987): 124-128.

6.G.1054   Tweeten, B. "A Model Program To Improve Computer Literacy
            of Business Teachers." Business Education Forum 42, (March
            1988): 25-27.

6.G.1055   Vesilind, P. Aarne. "Using Needs Assessment To Ensure The
            Quality of Corporate Computer Training." Technological
            Horizons in Education 15, 7(March 1988): 86-89.

6.G.1056   Wesley, Beth Eddinger, et al. "Locus of Control and Acquisition of Computer Literacy." Journal of Computer-Based Instruction 12, 1(Winter 1985): 12-16.

6.G.1057   Whitfield, D., and Bishop, L.A. "Attitude and Literacy of College Instructors and High School Seniors Regarding The Use of Microcomputers in Education." High School Journal 69, (February/March 1986): 228-237.

6.G.1058   Williams, Frederick, et al. "Children's Attitudes Toward Small Computers: A Preliminary Study." Educational Communication and Technology: A Journal of Theory, Research, and Development 31, 1(Spring 1983): 3-7.

6.G.1059   Winer, J.L. "Computer Science Literacy Training For Educators: A Case Study." Journal of Computers in Mathematics and Science Teaching 7, (Spring 1988): 26-29.

7

Correctional Facilities
and Illiteracy

7.1060   Amoroso, Henry C., Jr. "Commentary: Conversations With a
           New Literate." Journal of Reading 29, 6(March 1986): 484-488.

7.1061   A Reading Needs Assessment Handbook For Correctional
           Educators. Washington, D.C.: American Bar Association, 1974.
           ED 114 814.

7.1062   Black, S. "Assessing Adult Literacy Needs In A Prison Context.
           Austrailian Journal of Adult Education 24, 2(July 1984): 21-26.

7.1063   Bochtler, Stanley E. "Reading Goes To Jail - - and Sends A Word
           To All." Journal of Reading 17, 7(April 1974): 527-530.

7.1064   Brennan, M. Doing Language: An Account of a Developing
           Teacher Project Tackling Issues of Literacy and Incarceration.
           Wagga Wagga, NSW, Australia: Riverina College of Advanced
           Education, Literacy Centre, 1984.

7.1065   Brennan, M., and Brennan R.E. Literacy and Learning - The
           Human Factor: A Report To The Criminology Research Council
           of The Australian Institute of Criminology On The Literacy
           Needs and Abilities of Prison Inmates. Wagga Wagga, Australia:
           Riverina College of Advanced Education, 1984.

7.1066   Call For Papers. Correctional Education Association
           International Conference (39th, Philadelphia, Pennsylvania,
           July 1-4, 1984). N.P.: n.p., 1984. ED 270 572.

7.1067   Chenault, P. "Correctional Institutions Helping The
           Functionally Illiterate." ALA Bulletin 58, (October 1964): 804-809.

7.1068   Cortright, R.W. "Inmate Illiteracy." Journal of Reading 8,
           (January 1965): 163-167.

7.1069   Daiglish, C. "Basic Education for Offenders." International
          Journal of Offender Therapy and Comparative Criminology 23,
          3(1979): 240-243.

7.1070   Dalglish, Carol, "Illiteracy and The Offender." Adult Education
          56, 1(June 1983): 23-26.

7.1071   Davidson, Howard H. "Meaningful Literacy in Prison?
          Problems and Possibilities." Journal of Correctional Education
          39, 2(June 1988): 76-81

7.1072   Eckenrode, C.J. "Librarian Plays The Central Role; Correctional
          Institutions." ALA Bulletin 58, (October 1964): 810-811.

7.1073   Food Stamps. Learning Packet No. 2. Washington, D.C.:
          American Bar Association, 1975. ED 109 640.

7.1074   Gold, Patricia Cohen, and Horn, Pamela L. "Achievement in
          Reading, Verbal Language, Listening Comprehension and Locus
          of Control of Adult Illiterates in a Volunteer Tutorial Project."
          Perceptual and Motor Skills 54, 3, Part 2 (June 1982): 1243-1250.

7.1075   Gold, Patricia Cohen, and Horn, Pamela L. "Intelligence and
          Achievement of Adult Illiterates in a Tutorial Project: A
          Preliminary Analysis." Journal of Clinical Psychology 39,
          1(January 1983): 107-113.

7.1076   Griggs, Mildred, and Oppert, Judy. "Teachers Behind Bars."
          Adult Leadership 23, 4(October 1974): 112-114.

7.1077   Harding, Lowry W., and Burr, James B. "Men In The Armed
          Forces, A Serviceman's Reader." Madison, Wisconsin: Armed
          Forces Institute, 1966. ED 012 837..

7.1078   Helgeson, Marc E., and Hisama, T. "Teaching Basic Reading
          Skills in Incarcerated Non-Readers: The Brickwall Analogy and
          a Multi-Modality Approach." Journal of Correctional Education
          33, 4(December 1982): 25-28.

7.1079   Henney, Robert Lee. "Reading Instruction By A Phonic Method
          For Functionally Illiterate Adults At The Indiana Reformatory."
          Ph.D. dissertation, Indiana University, 1964. 25/05, p.2812.

7.1080   Holmes, Mary Ellen. "Teaching Convicts To Read in Colonial
          Australia." Australian Journal of Reading 6, 2(June 1983): 86-87.

7.1081   Job Application. Learning Packet No. 1 Washington, D.C.:
          American Bar Association, 1975. ED 109 641.

7.1082   Littlefield, John F., ed. "Call For Papers." International
          Correctional Education Conference (40th, Atlanta, Georgia, July
          14-17, 1985). N.P.: Correctional Education Association, 1985. ED
          270 573.

7.1083   Loeffler, Cynthia A., and Martin, Thomas C. The Functional
          Illiterate: Is Correctional Education Doing Its Job? Huntsville,
          Texas: Marloe Research, 1982. ED 218 454.

7.1084   Lucas, G.S. Volunteer Community Based Organizations Behind
          Walls: A Sensible Approach To The Adult Illiteracy Problem
          (An Evolutionary/Historical Review). N.P.: n.p., 1985. ED 263
          310.

7.1085   Marlin, Dale. "Reading and Rehabilitation: Literacy Volunteers
          of America in Corrections." Journal of Correctional Education
          39, 3(September 1988): 135-136.

7.1086   Martyn, P. "Literacy Development Project For Incarcerated
          Students." Literacy Link, 12(Winter 1982): 26-30.

7.1087   Metcalf, Richard Jay. "A Study To Compare The Effectiveness of
          a Programmed Linguistic Spelling Kit With Traditional Methods
          of Teaching Spelling To Functionally Illiterate Adults In
          Correctional Institutions." Ph.D. dissertation, The Florida State
          University, 1971. 32/11-A, p. 6083.

7.1088   Moke, Paul, and Holloway, Jarrell. "Post-Secondary Correctional
          Education: Issues of Functional Illiteracy." Journal of
          Correctional Education 37, 1(March 1986): 18-22.

7.1089   Norris, W. "Writing on The Prison Wall" Times Higher
          Education Supplement 694, (February 21, 1986): 9.

7.1090   Palfrey, Colin. "Remedial Education and The Adult Offender."
          Howard Journal 14, (1974): 78-85.

7.1091   Potential of Correctional School District Organizations
          Coordination Bulletin No. 22. Washington, D.C.: American Bar
          Association, 1973. ED 114 821.

7.1092   Project READ (Reading Efficiency and Delinquency), Annual Report 1976-1977. Washington, D.C.: Department of Justice, 1977. ED 136 226.

7.1093   Ruchlis, Hy. Guidelines To Education of Nonreaders. Brooklyn, New York: Book-Lab, Inc., 1973. ED 080 954.

7.1094   Sainz, Jo-Ann, and Biggins, Catherine. Literacy: A Tool For Assisting The Hispanic Inmate. Bronx, New York: Fordham University, 1979. ED 179 948.

7.1095   Smith, Edwin H. "Adult Basic Education: Some Spin-off For Culturally Deprived Youth Education." Indian Journal of Adult Education 32, 9(September 1971): 15-17.

7.1096   Special Answers For Special Needs. A Guide To Available 310 Resources. Washington, D.C.: Office of Vocational and Adult Education, 1986. ED 271 572.

7.1097   Stewart, C.W. "Illiteracy As A Factor In The Crime Situation." National Education Association Prodeedings 1932: 52-7.

7.1098   Swartz, Linda Kay. "Teaching an Illiterate Prisoner." Academic Therapy 21, 4(March 1986) 433-440.

          Presents a case history of the process by which a prisoner was taught to read. Stresses the importance of modalites in the process of learning to read. Briefly reviews the research on modality studies. Examines what did not work, deciding what should work, and prescribing what should work. Discusses the assessment of what had been prescribed.

7.1099   Thomas, Audrey M. "Funtional Literacy for Inmates." Learning 3, 3(1981): 8-10.

7.1100   Tinkle, Jimmy Lasister. "A Study of Two Teaching Schedules of Teaching Functionally Illiterate Adults To Read at The Indiana State Penal Farm." Ed. D. dissertation, Indiana University, 1973. 34/08-A, p. 4682.

7.1101   "Va. Gov. Seeks Teacher Volunteers for His Prison Literacy Program." VEA News (Virginia) 28, (September 1986): 3.

8

Cultural Literacy

8.1102   Anderson, Albert A., and Anderson, Lieselotte Z. "The Error of Expectations: Cultural Literacy in The Twenty-First Century." ADFL Bulletin 15, 2(November 1983): 19-22.

8.1103   Anson, Chris M. "Book Lists, Cultural Literacy, and The Stagnation of Discourse." English Journal 77, 2(February 1988): 14-18.

8.1104   Bizzell, Patricia. "Arguing About Literacy." College English 50, 2(February 1988): 141-153.

8.1105   "Cultural Literacy." Special Issue. English Journal 77, 5(September 1988).

8.1106   Culture and Literacy, The Problems and The Promise. N.P.: n.p., 1979.

8.1107   Downing, John. "Cultural Priorities and The Acquisition of Literacy." International Review of Education 19, (1973): 345-354.

8.1108   Edwards, Audrey T. "Cultural Literacy: What Are Our Goals? English Journal 73, 4(April 1984): 71-72.

8.1109   Eisner, Elliot. "Mind as Cultural Achievement." Educational Leadership 38, 6(March 1981): 466-471.

8.1110   El-Gabalawy, Saad. "Illiteracy and The Disintegration of Culture." ATA Magazine 57, 2(January 1977): 31-33.

8.1111   Greene, Brenda M. "A Cross-Cultural Approach To Literacy: The Immigrant Experience." English Journal 77, 5(September 1988): 45-48.

8.1112   Greene, Maxine. "Toward Possibility: Expanding The Range of
          Literacy." English Education 18, 4(December 1986): 231-243.

8.1113   Hartwell, Patrick, "Creating a Literate Environment in
          Freshman English: Why and How." Rhetoric Review 6, 1(Fall
          1987): 4-20.

8.1114   Hirsch, E.D. "Restoring Cultural Literacy in The Early Grades."
          Educational Leadership 43, (December 1987/January 1988): 63-70.

8.1115   Hirsch, E.D., Jr. Cultural Literacy. Boston: Houghton Mifflin
          Company, 1987.

          Presentation of the notion of a command of a common
          knowledge, referred to as cultural literacy. Reviews both literacy
          and cultural literacy. Discusses the decline of literate knowledge,
          the nature, use and decline of cultural literacy. Presents research
          on background knowledge in reading. Also explores the dual
          phenomena of national language and national culture.
          Examines the relationship between cultural literacy and the
          American school. Concludes with a definition of the contents of
          cultural literacy, and a preliminary list of what literate
          Americans know.

8.1116   Hirsch, E.D., Jr. "Cultural Literacy Does Not Mean a List of
          Works." ADE Bulletin, 84 (Fall 1986): 1-3.

8.1117   Hirsch, E.D., Jr. "'Cultural Literacy' Doesn't Mean 'Core
          Curriculum'"." English Journal, 74, 6(October 1985): 47-49.

8.1118   Hirsch, E.D., Jr. "Cultural Literacy." American Scholar 52,
          (Spring 1983): 159-169.

8.1119   Hirsch, E.D., Jr. "Culture and Literacy." Journal of Basic Writing
          3, 1(Fall-Winter 1980): 27-47.

8.1120   Hirsch, E.D., Jr., et al. Dictionary of Cultural Literacy, The.
          Boston: Houghton Mifflin Company, 1988.

          Comprehensive guide which lists common cultural knowledge.
          Subtitled, "What Every American Needs To Know." Contains
          twenty-three sections. Each section is alphabetically arranged.
          Sections cover subjects such as "The Bible," "Idioms," "Fine
          Arts," "World Politics," "Earth Sciences," and "Technology."
          Also contains chapters on "The Theory Behind The Dictionary,"

and "How To Use This Dictionary." Includes pictures, maps, charts, and an index.

8.1121   Jacobs, William Jay. "Cultural Literacy: That All May Be Guardians. A Bulletin Special." NASSP Bulletin 72, 510(October 1988): 54-64.

8.1122   Johnson, Michael L. "Hell Is The Place We Don't Know We're In: The Control-Dictions of Cultural Literacy, Strong Reading and Poetry." College English 50, 3(March 1988): 309-317.

8.1123   McMillen, Liz. "Scholar Decries Cultural Illiteracy in America." Chronicle of Higher Education 33, 32(April 22, 1987): 3.

8.1124   Newmann, F.M. "Another View of Cultural Literacy: Go For Depth." Social Education 52, (October 1988): 432+.

8.1125   Spooner, Michael. "ERIC/RCS U.S. Cultural Literacy Debate." Journal of Reading 30, 8(May 1987): 734-737.

8.1126   Swaffar, J.K. "Reading and Cultural Literacy." Journal of General Education 38, 2(1986): 70-84.

8.1127   Tucker, Edward F.J., ed. Culture and Literacy, The Problem and The Promise: Proceedings of a Conference Held On The Campus of Lenoir-Rhyne College, Hickory, North Carolina, October 1978. Ann Arbor, Michigan: n.p., 1979.

8.1128   Warnock, John. "Reply to Hirsch's Comment on 'Cultural Literacy: A Worm in The Bud?'" ADE Bulletin, 84(Fall 1986): 4-5.

8.1129   Worsham, Toni. "From Cultural Literacy To Cultural Thoughtfulness." Educational Leadership 46, 1(September 1988): 20-21.

9

Economics of Illiteracy

9.1130   Alphabetisation et Development; le Role de L'alphabetisation
           Fonctionelle Dans Le Developpement Economique et La
           Modernisation. Paris: Anthropos, 1973.

9.1131   Bendick, M., Jr. "Literacy of Welfare Client." Social Service
           Review 52, (March 1978): 56-68.

9.1132   Blaug, Mark. "Literacy and Economic Development." School
           Review 74, 4(Winter 1966) n.p. ED 016 174.

9.1133   Cipolla, Carlo M. Literacy and Development In The West.
           Baltimore, Maryland: Penguin Books, 1969.

9.1134   Duggan, Paula. "Literacy in a Global Economy." SERAmerica,
           (Winter 1988): 16, 26, 28.

9.1135   Duke, Chris. "Adult Education and Poverty: What Are The
           Connections?" Convergence 16, 1(1983): 76-83.

           Examines the question of whether adult education reduces
           poverty. Reports that studies fail to prove that adult education
           either reduces poverty or is important to its reduction.
           Continues to state that there is evidence that adult education is
           important to both the reduction of poverty, and the removal of
           its causes as long as certain conditions are met. Reviews the
           quality of life as a dependent variable. Also discusses factors
           such as power and politics of the government, the values of the
           people, and the organization and dynamics of adult education
           agencies.

9.1136   Educational Development and Education For Socio-Economic
            Development. Teheran: International Institute For Adult
            Literacy Methods, 1971.

9.1137   Faidley, Ray A. "Economic Illiteracy - The Silent Subversive."
            Balance Sheet 58, 4(December 1976 - January 1977): 174-175.

9.1138   Harman, David. "Illiteracy, Poverty and Racism: Their
            Interconnexion." Literacy Work 7, 2(Summer 1978): 11-20.

9.1139   Lagarde, J.-P., and Vigier, C. Alphabetisation et Insertion
            Linguistique des Traviilleurs Etrangers (Literacy Education and
            Linguistic Adaptation of Foreign Laborers). Melanges
            Pedagogiques, 1974. Nancy, France: Nancy University, 1974. ED
            148 114.

9.1140   "Literacy In Industrialized Countries." Convergence 20, 2(1987):
            1-29.

9.1141   "Literacy is Economic." Journal of Reading 23, (October 1979):
            60-62.

9.1142   Lloyd, R. Grann. "Functional Literacy and/or Minimum
            Competency Testing in The Nation's Schools as a Prerequisite
            To Receiving a High School Diploma: Some Economic
            Implications." Negro Education Review 31, 1(January 1980): 3-16.

9.1143   Meister, Albert. Alphabetisation et Developpement. N.P.: n.p.,
            1973.

9.1144   Norris, W. "Illiteracy May Force Reagan's Hand In Budget."
            Times Higher Education Supplement 737, 7(December 19, 1986):
            7.

9.1145   Phillips, Herbert Moore. Literacy and Development. Paris:
            UNESCO, 1970.

9.1146   Puxley, L. "Poverty, Illiteracy." Arcturus 3, January 1974): 23-27.

9.1147   Qutub, I.Y., and Mansour, R.F. Illiteracy as an Impediment To
            Production: An Investigation." Indian Journal of Adult
            Education 34, 2(February 1973): 7-10, 16-20.

9.1148   "Research: Literacy Is Economic." Journal of Reading 23,
            1(October 1979): 60-62.

9.1149   Villaume, John Michael. Literacy and The Adoption of
          Agricultural Innovations. N.P.: n.p., 1978.

9.1150   Weber, Robert E. "A Dollar and Cents Look at Reading Failure."
          Reading Newsreport 5, 7(May-June 1971): 26-29.

9.1151   West, E.G. "Literacy and The Industrial Revolution." The
          Economic History Review 31, S2(August 1978): 369-383.

9.1152   Wilson, Vernon C. The Social and Economic Implications of
          Programs In Basic Literacy. N.P.: n.p., 1977.

10

Evaluation of Literacy

10.1153 Accardo, P., et al. "Literacy Achievement Ratio: Predicting Long Term Outcome of Dyslexic Readers." Reading Improvement 22, 1(Spring 1985): 73-77.

Evaluation of mature reading ability of fifteen severe dyslexics, nine years after they were initially evaluated. Results indicated that all subjects still demonstrated significant delays in reading ability. Discusses the results in relation to a prognosis of limited literacy acquisition in severely dyslexic children.

10.1154 Ahmed, Mushtaq. "Time Factor In The Attainment of Literacy Skills." Indian Journal of Adult Education 32, 4(June 1971): 3-4, 20

10.1155 Anders, P.L. "Tests of Functional Literacy: Test Review." Journal of Reading 24, (April 1981): 612-619.

10.1156 Bhola, H.S. "Making Evaluation Operational In Functional Literacy Programs." Literacy Discussion 4, 4(December 1973): 457-493.

10.1157 Bhola, H.S., ed. Evaluating Functional Literacy. Teheran: International Institute For Adult Literacy Methods, 1979. ED 169 498.

10.1158 Bhola, H.S. Evaluation Planning, Evaluation Management, and Utilization of Evaluation Results Within Adult Literacy Campaigns, Programs and Projects (With Implications For Adult Basic Education and Nonformal Education Programs in General). A Working Paper. Bonn: German Foundation For International Development, 1982. ED 221 759.

10.1159   Bormuth, John R. "Reading Literacy: Its Definition and Assessment." Reading Research Quarterly 9, 1(Fall 1973-1974): 7-66.

10.1160   Boyd, R.D. "Model For The Analysis of Motivation." Adult Education 16, (Autumn 1965): 24-33.

10.1161   Branscomb, Lewis M. "Support For Reviews and Data Evaluation." Science 187, 4177(February 1975): 603.

10.1162   Brown, Barbara E. Identifying Inservice Topics For Volunteer Literacy Tutors. N.P.: n.p., 1981. ED 209 506.

10.1163   Comprehensive Evaluation Project. Final Report. Washington, D.C.: Office of Education, 1969. ED 037 571.

10.1164   Couvert, Roger. The Evaluation of Literacy Programmes: A Practical Guide. New York: Unipub, 1979. ED 179 922.

10.1165   Development of The Brief Test of Literacy. National Center For Health Statistics, Series 2, No. 27. Rockville, Maryland: Department of Health, Education, and Welfare, 1968. ED 113 693.

10.1166   Diack, Junter. "A Way Of Measuring Literacy." New Society 27, (January 24, 1974): 191-192.

10.1167   "Document of The Month: A Literacy Test." Social Education 42, (January 1978): 32-33.

10.1168   Draper, James A. "Evaluation; an Investment In Learning." Literacy Discussion 5, 3(Fall 1974): 441-469.

10.1169   Effect of Basic Literacy Training on Test Scores. Washington, D.C.: U.S. Department of Labor, 1969. ED 057 169.

10.1170   Evaluation of Literacy Programmes: A Practical Guide. London: UNESCO, H.M.S.O., 1979.

10.1171   "Field Test and Evaluation Of Selected Adult Basic Education Systems." New York: Greenleigh Associates, Inc., 1966. ED 011 090.

10.1172   Fisher, D.L. "Funtional Literacy Tests: A Model of Question-Answering and an Analysis of Efforts." Reading Research Quarterly 16, 3(1981): 418-448.

10.1173   Gadway, Charles J., and Wilson, H.A. A Handbook of The Mini-
            Assessment of Functional Literacy - 1974 and 1975; Functional
            Literacy Basic Reading Performance. Denver: National
            Assessment of Educational Progress, 1976. ED 134 951.

10.1174   Gaillard, Theodore Lee, Jr. "Test Scores and Literacy: Declining
            Verbal Skills - Prickly Pear of the 70's." Independent School
            Bulletin 35, 1(October 1975): 41-42.

10.1175   Guidelines For The Collection of Statistics On Literacy
            Programmes. Preliminary Manual. Paris: UNESCO, 1979. ED
            190 998.

10.1176   Haemmerli, A. "Some Observations of the Methodological
            Nature Concerning The Evaluation of The Experimental World
            Literacy Programme." Convergence 5, 1(1972): 66-70.

10.1177   Hayes, Larry Wayne. "An Opinion Survey of Teachers Using
            An Easy-To-Read Newspaper In The Classroom For New
            Literates." M.A.J. Thesis, Syracuse University, 1970. ED 037 602.

10.1178   Holtmann, A.G. Cost-Benefit Analysis In Adult Literacy
            Programmes. Paris: UNESCO, 1970. ED 052 437.

10.1179   Inventory of Readiness For Literacy. Phase 2: Auditory
            Discrimination. Albany, New York: New York State Education
            Department, Bureau of Continuing Education Curriculum
            Development, 1972. ED 073 355.

10.1180   Johnson, Deborah Wilcox. "Evaluation of Library Literacy
            Projects." Library Trends 35, 2(Fall 1986): 311-326.

10.1181   Johnston, Peter. "Teachers as Evaluation Experts." Reading
            Teacher 40, 8(April 1987): 744-748.

10.1182   Johnson, Raymond L., et al. "Measurement and Classification of
            Teacher Attitudes Toward Adult Illiterates." N.D. ED 011 631.

10.1183   Karlsen, Bjorn. "Methods of Large Scale Literacy Assessment."
            Literacy Discussion 4, 3(September 1973): 158-171.

10.1184   Kedney, Robert J. "Assessing Adult Literacy Projects." Scottish
            Journal of Adult Education 2, 3(Autumn 1976): 13-18.

10.1185   Kirsch, Irwin S. "Construct Validity of Functional Reading Tests." Journal of Educational Measurement 17, 2(Summer 1980): 81-93.

10.1186   Kills, M. "Defining Literacy Through Measurement: Problems, Issues and Curricular Concerns." Yearbook (Claremont Reading Conference) 46, (1982): 153-158.

10.1187   Lichtman, Marilyn. "The Development and Validation of R/EAL, an Instrument To Assess Functional Literacy." Journal of Reading Behavior 6, 2(July 1974): 167-182.

10.1188   Lichtman, Marilyn. The Development and Validation of R/EAL, an Instrument To Assess Functional Literacy. Washington, D.C.: Catholic University of America, 1973. ED 081 811.

10.1189   McDonald, T.F., and Moorman, J. "Criterion Referenced Testing for Functional Literacy: Phoenix Union High School System, Arizona." Journal of Reading 17, (February 1974): 363-366.

10.1190   McDonald, Thomas F. "Pro: Minimal Competency Testing as Viewed From The Front Line." Journal of Reading 22, 1(October 1978): 13-15.

10.1191   Monroe, Margaret E. "The Evolution of Literacy Programs in The Context of Library Adult Education." Library Trends 35, 2(Fall 1986): 197-205.

10.1192   Moore, Susan. "Literacy and Standards." English in Australia, 51(March 1980): 21-25.

10.1193   Murph, D., and McCormick, S. "Evaluation of an Instructional Program Designed to Teach Minimally Literate Juvenile Delinquents To Read Road Signs." Education and Treatment of Children 8, (Spring 1985): 133-151.

10.1194   Nafziger, Dean H., et al. Tests of Functional Adult Literacy: An Evaluation of Currently Available Instruments. Portland, Oregon 8: Northwest Regional Educational Lab, 1975. ED 109 265.

10.1195   Niemi, J.A., and Anderson, D. "Remedial Adult Education - An Analytical Review of Evaluation Research." Continuous Learning 8, (March - April 1969): 90-94.

10.1196   O'Donnell, Dennis H. "Assessment Within Schools: A Study In
           One Country." Educational Research 24, 1(November 1981): 43-
           48.

10.1197   O'Donnell, Michael P., and Wood, Margo. "Adult Learning
           Problems: A Critique of The London Procedure." Adult Literacy
           and Basic Education 5, 4(Winter 1981): 243-250.

10.1198   Plog, S.C. "Literacy Index For The Mailbag." Journal of Applied
           Psychology 50, (February 1966): 86-91.

10.1199   Routh, Donald K., and Rettig, Kathryn. "The Mailbag Literacy
           Index In A Clinical Population: Relation To Education, Income,
           Occupation, and Social Class." Educational and Psychological
           Measurement 29, 2(Summer 1969): 485-488.

10.1200   Saksena, H.P. "Evaluation of The Experimental Literacy
           Program." Convergence 1, (September 1968): 74-79.

10.1201   Serling, Albert M. "The Measurement of Public Literacy."
           College Board Review, 114(Winter 1979-1980): 26-29.

10.1202   Soper, John C., and Brenneke, Judith Staley. "The Test of
           Economic Literacy and an Evaluation of The DEEP System."
           Journal of Economic Education 12, 2(Summer 1981): 1-14.

10.1203   Third Meeting Of The Panel For Evaluation Of Experimental
           Literacy Projects. Final Report. Paris: UNESCO, 1970. ED 051
           483.

10.1204   Van Til, W. "What To Expect If Your Legislature Orders Literacy
           Testing." Phi Delta Kappan 59, (April 1978): 556-557.

10.1205   Vaugrante, Christiane. Techniques For Analysing Changes In
           Literacy Rates and In The Number Of Illiterates. Dakar:
           UNESCO Regional Office For Education in Africa, 1970.

10.1206   Wiemann, John M. "Needed Research and Training in
           Speaking and Listening Literacy." Communication Education
           27, 4(November 1978): 310-315.

10.1207   Wood, Freddie. The Evaluation of Functional Literacy Projects
           UNESCO Workshop. London: London University, Institute of
           Education, 1969. ED 044 577.

11

Functional Illiteracy

11.1208   Adiseshiah, Malcolm S. "Raising Literacy Standards - What
           Standards - And For Whom." Indian Journal of Adult
           Education 35, 9(September 1974): 45-47.

11.1209   Adiseshiah, Malcolm S. "Literacy's Functionality To The Fight
           For Social Justice." Convergence 8, 4(1975): 23-28.

11.1210   "Adult Functional Illiteracy: A Pervasive Problem." Catholic
           Library World 55, 3(October 1983): 117-121.

11.1211   Allen, James E., Jr. "The Right To Read: Education's New
           National Priority." American School Board Journal 157,
           4(October 1969): 25-27.

11.1212   Allen, James E., Jr. "The Right To Read - - Target For The 70's."
           School and Society 98, 2323(February 1970): 82-84.

11.1213   Anders, Patricia L. "Test Reviews: Tests of Functional Literacy."
           Journal of Reading 24, 7(April 1981): 612-619.

           Reviews Five Commercially available tests of functional literacy.
           Tests reviewed are: 1.) Reading/Everyday Activities in Life
           (R/EAL); 2.) Performance Assessment In Reading (PAIR); 3.)
           Senior High Assessment of Reading Performance (SHARP); 4.)
           Life Skills (Reading); and 5.) Minimal Essentials Test (MET).
           Concludes with a discussion regarding the broader concerns
           involved with functional literacy.

11.1214   Anderson, Lorin W., and Anderson, Jo Craig. "Functional
           Literacy Tests: A Case of Anticipatory Validity?" Educational
           Evaluation and Policy Analysis 3, 2(March-April 1981): 51-55.

11.1215   Ayrer, J.E. "Problems in The Development of a Test of
           Functional Literacy." Journal of Reading 20, (May 1977): 697-
           705.

11.1216   Bellahsene, C. Practical Guide To Functional Literacy; A
           Method of Training For Development. Paris: UNESCO, 1973.

11.1217   Berman, Bennett H. "Training The Hard To Train: The
           Functional Illiterate." NSPI Journal 18, 7(September 1979): 7-10.

11.1218   Bhola, H.S. "The Methods and The Materials of Functional
           Literacy." Literacy Discussion 1, 4(Autumn 1970): 31-72.

11.1219   Bonanni, C. "Functional Literacy Methodology and Its
           Implications For The Broader Field of Adult Education." Indian
           Journal of Adult Education 33, 9(September 1972): 3-8, 20.

11.1220   Brand, Eugen. "Functional Illiteracy In Industrialized
           Countries." Prospects 17, 2(1987): 201-211.

11.1221   Cassidy, Jack. "High School Graduation: Exit Competencies?"
           Journal of Reading 21, 5(February 1978): 398-402.

11.1222   Chatterjee, B.B. "Functional Literacy For Family Planning In
           Tribal Areas." Indian Journal of Adult Education 31, 1(January
           1970): 12-12. 16.

11.1223   Chosson, Jean-Francois. "Functional Illiteracy and Vocational
           Training For Young People in Rural France." Prospects 17,
           2(1987): 241-250.

11.1224   Ciancio, Jean. "Literacy: The Basic Skill," Vocational Education
           Journal 63, 2(March 1988): 41-42.

           Discussion regarding the author's perception that literacy is a
           overarching basic skill. Reviews the role that functional literacy
           plays in every day life. Specifically examines the extent that
           functional literacy plays in the job environment. Presents a
           number of programs designed to increase functional literacy.
           Briefly discusses the nationwide assault on functional illiteracy.

11.1225   Cohen, Royce. "Citizen Power - - Partners For Literacy."
           American Education 6, 5(June 1970): 36.

11.1226   Corbett, Edward P.J. "The Demands For and of Literacy."
           English Quarterly 15, 3(October 1982): 5-13.

11.1227   Cotten, A.M. "Shall We Segregate The Functionally Illiterate?"
           Community and Junior College Journal 49, (April 1979): 14-18;
           Reply Roueche, J.E., and Armes, N.R. 50, (March 1980): 21-24.

11.1228   Cotterell, Arthur. "Functional Literacy: A World Perspective on
           Reading." Technical Journal 11, 7(October 1973): 18-19, 23.

11.1229   Courtenay, Bradley C., et al. "Functional Literacy Among The
           Elderly: Where We Are (n't)." Educational Gerontology 8,
           4(July-August 1982): 339-352.

11.1230   Cripwell, Kenneth R. "Towards A Training In Film
           Appreciation For Semi-Literates." Teacher Education 8,
           (February 1968): 239-246.

11.1231   Danckwortt, D. "Neve Ansatze Fur Funktionale
           Apohabetisierung." International Review of Education 21,
           (1975): 111-114.

11.1232   Davis, Robbie G. "Needed: Functional Literacy Skills Curricula
           and Tests." Educational Technology 17, 3(March 1977): 52-54.

11.1233   Experiment In Motivating Functional Illiterates To Learn. Final
           Report. N.P.: Tuskagee Institute, School of Applied Sciences,
           1969. ED 039 442.

11.1234   Farnen, Russell F., Jr. "How Others See What's Beyond
           Tomorrow: A Political Scientist Reacts to 'Beyond Tomorrow -
           What?'" Educational Horizons 50, 1(Fall 1971): 13-14.

11.1235   Final Report. International Symposium on Functional Literacy
           In The Context of Adult Education, Berlin, 1973. N.P.: n.p.,
           1974.

11.1236   Fisher, Donald L. "Functional Literacy Tests: A Model of
           Question-Answering and an Analysis of Errors." Reading
           Research Quarterly 16, 3(1981): 418-448.

11.1237   Fitzgerald, Gisela G. "Functional Literacy: Right or Obligation?"
           Journal of Reading 28, 3(December 1984): 196-199.

11.1238   Fry, Edward. "Graphical Literacy." Journal of Reading 24,
           5(February 1981): 383-390.

11.1239   "Functional Illiterate." New Jersey Education Association
           Review 48, 2(September 1974): 14.

11.1240   "Functional Illiterates." OECTA Review 1, 6(March 1976): 20.

11.1241   Functional Literacy: A Method of Training For Development. Paris: UNESCO, 1970. ED 051 485.

11.1242   Functional Literacy and Co-operatives. ICA Seminar on Functional Literacy and Cooperatives, Ibadan, Nigeria, 1975. N.P.: n.p., 1975.

11.1243   "Functional Literacy As A Factor In Development." Indian Journal of Adult Education 31, 9(September 1970): 9-12.

11.1244   "Functional Literacy in The Context of Adult Education," Convergence 6, 3 & 4(1973): 64-66.

11.1245   Functional Literacy. N.P.: UNESCO, 1970.

11.1246   "Functional Literacy; Pilot Projects." Times Educational Supplement 2645, (January 28, 1966): 235.

11.1247   Functional Literacy: Why and How. Paris: UNESCO, 1970.

11.1248   Giordano, G. "Instructional Implications of Functional and Critical Reading." Reading Improvement 13, (Winter 1976): 204-206.

11.1249   Guide Pratique d'alphabetisation Fonctionnelle. N.P.: n.p., 1972.

11.1250   Guthrie, John T. "Research: Functional Reading: One or Many." Journal of Reading 22, 7(April 1979): 648-650.

11.1251   Harman, David. "Illiteracy: An Overview." Harvard Educational Review 40, 2(May 1970): 226-243.

11.1252   Hiatt, Peter, and Drennan, Henry T., eds. Public Library Services For The Functionally Illiterate; A Survey of Practice. Chicago: Public Library Association, 1967.

11.1253   Hill, Barry. "The Making of Adult Illiterates." Times Educational Supplement 2942(October 8, 1971): 5.

11.1254   International Day For Functional Literacy. International Day For Functional Literacy, Turin, 1968. N.P.: n.p., 1969.

11.1255   International Day For Functional Literacy. Geneva: World Federation of Trade Unions, 1969.

11.1256   Jamieson, G.H. "Instructional Innovation: a Field Study in
           Functional Literacy." in Aspects of Educational Technology,
           Volume 8, Communication and Learning, pp. 345-352. Edited by
           Jon Baggaley, G. Harry Jamieson and Harry Marchant. London:
           Pitman, 1975.

11.1257   Joynes, Yvonne D., et al. "Teaching Reading Disabled Students
           to Read and Complete Employment Applications." Journal of
           Reading 23, 8(May 1980): 709-714.

11.1258   Karunaratne, Garvin. "Developing a Functional Literacy
           Programme." Literacy Work 5, 4(Winter 1976-1977): 45-51, 53, 54.

11.1259   Kazemek, Francis E. "Functional Literacy Is Not Enough: Adult
           Literacy as a Developmental Process." Journal of Reading 28,
           4(January 1985): 332-335.

11.1260   Keenan, Donna, et al. "Oral Drivers' Test: Solution to a Lifelong
           Learning Problem." Lifelong Learning 5, 7(March 1982): 6-8.

11.1261   Kelly, Leonard P. "Survival Literacy: Teaching Reading To
           Those With A 'Need To Know.'" Journal of Reading 17,
           5(February 1974): 352-355.

11.1262   Kimball, James C. "Career Interest Search: Reaching
           Functionally Illiterate Adults." Wisconsin Vocational Educator
           12, 3(Fall 1988): 12.

11.1263   King, Kenneth J. "Research on Literacy and Work Among The
           Rural Poor." Indian Journal of Adult Education 41, 1-2(January-
           February 1980): 15-23.

11.1264   Kirsch, Irwin, and Guthrie, John T. "The Concept and
           Measurement of Functional Literacy." Reading Research
           Quarterly 13, 4(1977-1978): 485-507.

11.1265   Lankshear, Colin. "Review Article - Humanizing Functional
           Literacy: Beyond Utilitarian Necessity." Educational Theory 36,
           4(Fall 1986): 375-387.

11.1266   Lathen, Levi. An Analysis of Schooling, Literacy, and
           Functional Literacy of Urban and Suburban Eight Grade
           Students. N.P.: n.p., 1976.

11.1267   Leven, C.S. "One Pragmatist Looks Back: Some Views On Functional Literacy Programmes." Literacy Discussion 2, 3(Summer 1971): 111-119.

11.1268   Levine, K. "Functional Literacy: Found Illusions and False Economies." Harvard Educational Review 52, (August 1982): 249-266.

11.1269   Lewis, D.M. "Certifying Functional Literacy: Compentency Testing and Implications For Due Process and Equal Educational Opportunity." Journal of Law & Education 8, (April 1979): 145-183.

11.1270   Lindberg, Wayne, and Hoffman, Terrye. "Reading, Writing, and Documentation and Managing The Development of User Documentation." Data Training 6, 11(October 1987): 24-29.

11.1271   Linn, Reid J., et al. "Communication Skills of Learning Disabled Adolescents." B.C. Journal of Special Education 11, 4(1987): 301-312.

11.1272   Long, F. "Library and The Functional Illiterate in Cleveland." ALA Bulletin 60, (June 1966): 637-638.

11.1273   Mason, H. "Fundamental Education and Functional Literacy - Problems and Possibilities." Convergence 6, 3 and 4(1973): 55-63.

11.1274   McBeath, Neil. "Some Techniques for Improving Reading Aloud in EAL." Spoken English 19, 1(January 1986): 25-29.

11.1275   Merrill, M.H. "A Helping Hand: Educational Programs For The Functionally Illiterate." Lifelong Learning 11, (May 1988): 25-27.

11.1276   Murph, Debra, and McCormick, Sandra. "Evaluation of an Instructional Program Designed to Teach Minimally Literate Juvenile Deliquents to Read Road Signs." Education and Treatment of Children 8, 2(Spring 1985): 133-155.

11.1277   O'Donnell, H. "Striving for Functional Literacy in The Job Market: ERIC/RCS (Report)." Journal of Reading 29, (October 1985): 74-76.

11.1278   Omaggio, Alice C. "Using Games and Interaction Activities for The Development of Functional Proficiency in a Second Language." Canadian Modern Language Review 38, 3(Spring 1982): 517-546.

11.1279   O'Neill, Wayne. "Properly Literate." Harvard Educational
            Review 40, 2(May 1970): 260-263.

11.1280   Otto, Wayne. "Research: My Father, My Self." Journal of
            Reading 29, 5(February 1986): 476-478.

11.1281   Otto, Wayne. "Research: Reading on The Far Side." Journal of
            Reading 31, 1(October 1987): 64-67.

11.1282   Parke, T.H. "Realism and Artificiality in Language Teaching."
            Modern Languages 66, 4(December 1985): 263-267.

11.1283   Paul, Michael. "Reading After Survival Literacy: Language
            Immersion and an Idea From Confucius." Journal of Reading
            29, 5(February 1986): 423-427.

11.1284   Practical Guide To Functional Literacy: A Method of Training
            For Development. Lanham, Maryland: Bernan - Unipub, 1973.

11.1285   Pratt, Sidney. "ESL/Literacy: A Beginning." TESL Talk 13,
            3(Summer 1982): 96-103.

11.1286   Rahnema, Majid. "From Functional Literacy to Lifelong
            Education." Prospect 2, 3(Autumn 1972): 321-333.

11.1287   Rivera, William M. "The Politics of Literacy." Community
            College Review 4, 1(Summer 1976): 65-70.

11.1288   Rizza, Peter J., and Walker-Hunter, Peggy. "New Technology
            Solves an Old Problem: Functional Illiteracy." Audiovisual
            Instruction 24, 1(January 1979): 22-23, 63.

11.1289   Rupley, William H., and Gwinn, Paula B. "Reading in the Real
            World." Reading World 18, 2(December 1978): 117-122.

11.1290   Ryan, Anne. "Functional Literacy and Language Demands on
            Apprentices." Australian Journal of Reading 2, 4(November
            1979): 211-219.

11.1291   Saksena, H.P. "Framework For Analysis of Functional Literacy."
            Literacy Discussion 1, 4(Autumn 1970): 7-30.

11.1292   Scheier, Elaine. "An Experimental Study Designed To Test The
            Relative Effectiveness of A Multi-Media Instructional System."
            Paper presented at the National Seminar on Adult Education,
            Toronto, Ontario, 1969. ED 026 611.

11.1293   Shaw, E.C. "An Institution For Functional Literacy: Literacy House." Literacy Discussion 2, 1(Winter 1971): 83-92.

11.1294   Smith, Lawrence L. "Literacy: Definitions and Implications." Language Arts 54, 2(February 1977): 135-138.

11.1295   Taylor, Nancy, and Waynant, Priscilla Pilson. "Reading Logs Reflect Students' Real World Reading Needs." Reading Teacher 32, 1(October 1978): 7-9.

11.1296   Taylor, Paul G. "Competency-Based Adult Education: Toward a Functional Definition." Adult Literacy and Basic Education 2, 3(Fall 1978): 146-157.

11.1297   Tierney, R.J., and Rogers, T. "Functional Literacy in School Settings." Theory into Practice 25, (Spring 1986): 124-127.

11.1298   Unoh, Solomon Ogbodum. "On Teaching Reading and Writing For Functional Literacy." Reading Horizons 17, 2(Winter 1977): 110-117.

11.1299   Valentine, Thomas. "Adult Functional Literacy as a Goal of Instruction." Adult Education Quarterly 36, 2(Winter 1986): 108-113.

11.1300   Voyat, Gilbert. "Minimizing The Problems of Functional Illiteracy." Record 72, 2(December 1970): 171-186.

11.1301   Walters, Keith, et al. "Formal and Functional Approaches to Literacy." Language Arts 64, 8(December 1987): 855-868.

11.1302   Wangberg, Elaine G. "A Microcomputer Approach to Developing Functional Literacy among Adolescents and Adults." Computers in the Schools 2, 4(Winter 1985-1986): 123-128.

11.1303   Warsh, Herman Enoch. "Behavior Modification of Adult Illiterates and Functional Illiterates Who Learned To Read." Ed.D. dissertation, Wayne State University, 31/03-A, p. 1002.

11.1304   Welch, Jennifer S. Promoting The Necessity To Read: A Guide For Instructors of The Disabled Reader In The Teaching of Survival Reading. North Billings, Montana: Alpine Publishing Company, 1980. ED 193 624.

11.1305   Zepezaver, F.S. "I Promoted a Functional Illiterate." <u>Education Digest</u> 46, (October 1980): 14-16.

12

Functional Reading

12.1306   Adiseshiah, Malcolm S. "Functionalities of Literacy." <u>Prospects</u> 6, (1976): 83-91.

12.1307   Allington, R.L., and Walmsley, S. A. "Functional Competence in Reading Among The Urban Aged." <u>Journal of Reading</u> 23, (March 1980): 494-497.

12.1308   "Basic Reading Materials - A Description." <u>Canadian Library Journal</u> 37, 4(August 1980): 247-248.

12.1309   Brock, Christine. "Breaking The Failure Barrier." <u>Australian Journal of Reading</u> 6, 3(August 1983): 105-107.

12.1310   Burnett, Richard W. "Basic Reading Inventory, Form A (and) Adult Basic Reading Inventory, Form A., Manual of Directions (and) Technical Report No. 1, Basic Reading Inventory." Bensenville, Illinois: Scholastic Testing Service, 1966. ED 019 548

12.1311   Caliver, Ambrose. <u>Fundamental Education, The What, How, Where, and Why of It</u>. Washington, D.C.: U.S. Office of Education, 1958.

12.1312   Carrison, Muriel Paskin. "On Reading: Ritual or Right?" <u>Intellect</u> 101, 2350(Summer 1973): 513-515.

12.1313   Cassidy, Jack, and Vukelich, Carol. "Survival Reading for Parents and Kids: A Parent Education Program." <u>Reading Teacher</u> 31, 6(March 1978): 638-641.

12.1314   Cole, Fannie T. "Functional Reading Techniques." <u>Education For The Disadvantaged Child</u> 2, 4(Fall 1974): 11-13.

12.1315   Duane, Michael. "Speech and Reading." English in Education
           4, 3(Autumn 1970): 63-73.

12.1316   Eisner, Elliott W. What It Means to Read. Edmonton:
           University of Alberta, Department of Elementary Education,
           1985.

12.1317   Fader, Daniel. "Getting Them to Use Their Reading." English in
           Education 4, 3(Autumn 1970): 59-62.

12.1318   Farr, Roger C. Reading. N.P.: n.p., 1986.

12.1319   Fishman, Andrea R. "Literacy and Cultural Context: A Lesson
           From the Amish." Language Arts 64, 8(December 1987): 842-854.

           Reviews the relationship between literacy and the Amish
           cultural context. Discusses the role and extent of reading and
           writing within an Amish cultural context. Examines literacy as a
           force and a power in the Amish world. Compares Amish
           literacy and mainstream school literacy. Concludes with a
           discussion of the issues for mainstream curriculum and
           instruction in literacy.

12.1320   Fletcher, Donna, and Abood, Doris. "An Analysis of The
           Readability of Product Warning Labels: Implications For
           Curriculum Development For Persons With Moderate and
           Severe Mental Retardation." Education and Training in Mental
           Retardation 23, 3(September 1988): 224-227.

12.1321   Folk, Mary C., and Campbell, Jack. "Teaching Functional
           Reading to The TMR." Education and Training of The Mentally
           Retarded 13, 3(October 1978): 322-326.

12.1322   Gambrell, Linda B., and Cleland, Craig J. "Minimum
           Compentency Testing: Guidelines For Functional Reading
           Programs." Journal of Reading 25, 4(January 1982): 342-344.

12.1323   Ganopole, Selina J. "The Fundamental Reading Competencies
           Test." Journal of Educational Measurement 17, 1(Spring 1980):
           71-74.

12.1324   Giordano, Gerard. "Instructional Implications of Functional and
           Critical Reading." Reading Improvement 13, 4(Winter 1976):
           204-206.

12.1325   Guthrie, John T. "Research Views: Apologia For Ethnography of Literacy in The Community." Reading Teacher 34, 1(October 1980): 118-121.

12.1326   Harrison, Alton, Jr., et al. "Declining Reading Scores: So What?" Illinois School Research and Development 16, 1(Fall 1979): 7-11.

12.1327   Heath, Shirley. "The Functions and Uses of Literacy." Journal of Communication 30, 1(Winter 1980): 123-133.

12.1328   Henderson, Kathy. "Reading Through The Screen." Times Educational Supplement 3131, (May 30, 1975): 18.

12.1329   Hogan, Robert F., and Judy, Stephen. "The 'Back to Basics' Controversy." Media and Methods 13, 1(September 1976): 17-18, 54-56.

12.1330   Hunter, Dianne. "Editorial Comment: Enlarging The Perspective Whole Teacher, Whole Student, Whole Reading." Reading Horizons 19, 3(Spring 1979): 190-192.

12.1331   Huus, Helen. "Developmental Reading: An International Challenge." Paper presented at the Third International Reading Association World Congress on Reading, Sydney, Australia, 1970. ED 046 645.

12.1332   "Improving Literacy Level is Crucial: NAEP." Phi Delta Kappan 68, (May 1987): 711.

12.1333   Jennings, Frank G. "Please Make Words Make Sense." School Guidance Worker 32, 6(July 1977): 45-47.

12.1334   Juhasz, Anne McCreary, and Wilson, Leslie R. "Should Students Be Well Read or Should They Read Well?" NASSP Bulletin 70, 488(March 1986): 78-83.

12.1335   Kidd, J. Roby. Functional Literacy and International Development, A Study of Canadian Capability To Assist With The World Campaign To Eradicate Illiteracy. Toronto: Ontario Institute For Studies In Education, 1967. ED 015 364.

12.1336   Kolers, Paul A. "Reading and Knowing." Canadian Journal of Psychology 33, 2(June 1979): 106-117.

12.1337   Latham, W., and Parry, O. "Functional Reading and The
           Schools: A Progress Report." Journal of Research in Reading 3,
           2(September 1980): 140-149.

12.1338   Lelong, Donald, and Shirley, Robert. "Teaching Functional
           Reading Skills to Speach Impaired Adults with Special Needs."
           B.C. Journal of Special Education 8, 2(1984): 149-155.

12.1339   "Literacy Skills." Curriculum Review 27, (September/October
           1987): 12-36.

12.1340   Luke, Allan. "Functional Literacy In The Classroom."
           Australian Journal of Reading 11, 1(March 1988): 4-10.

12.1341   Madge, C. "Some Aspects of Mass Literacy." British Journal of
           Educational Studies 4, (November 1955): 3-14.

12.1342   Malmquist, Eve. Developing Reading Ability - A Worldwide
           Challenge. N.P.: n.p., 1981.

12.1343   McCabe, James J., Jr. "Reading and The American High School."
           Community Review 6, 1(Fall 1985): 33-40.

12.1344   McGee, Donna. "Reading Skills for Basic Literacy." TESL Talk 9,
           1(Winter 1978): 53-58.

12.1345   McNally, Joseph, and Murray, William. Keywords to Literacy
           and The Teaching of Reading. N.P.: Teacher Publishing
           Company, 1984.

12.1346   Memory, David M. "Preparing Students in Survival Reading:
           The Content Area Operation." Clearing House 56, 8(April
           1983): 349-353.

12.1347   Mitzel, M.A. "Functional Reading Word List for Adults." Adult
           Education 16, (Winter 1966): 67-69.

12.1348   Moore, David W. "Laura Zirbes and Progressive Reading
           Instruction." Elementary School Journal 86, 5(May 1986): 663-672.

12.1349   Moorehead, Caroline. "Left! Right! Quick Read!" Times
           Educational Supplement 2920, (May 7, 1971): 1020.

12.1350   Mountford, John. "Some Psycholinguistic Components of
           Initial Standard Literacy." Journal of Typographical Research 4,
           4(Autumn 1970): 295-306.

12.1351   Negin, Gary A., and Krugler, Dee. "Essential Literacy Skills For
            Functioning In An Urban Community." Journal of Reading 24,
            2(November 1980): 109-115.

            Discusses functional literacy in relation to minimal competency
            standards. Attempts to define functional literacy for Milwaukee,
            Wisconsin. Examines the types of materials which must be
            understood to achieve a functional literacy capacity. Analyzes
            the readability of said materials. Provides a master list of
            vocabulary and skills needed for functional literacy.

12.1352   "Open To Suggestion." Journal of Reading 24, 5(February 1981):
            430-432.

12.1353   Otto, W. "Reading on The Far Side." Journal of Reading 31,
            (October 1987): 64-67.

12.1354   Otto, Wayne, and Ford, David. "Teaching Adults To Read."
            1967. ED 014 680.

12.1355   Pyrczak, Fred. "Effects of Abbreviations on Comprehension of
            Classified Employment Advertisements." Journal of Reading
            24, 3(December 1980): 249-252.

12.1356   Pyrczak, Fred. "Knowledge of Abbreviations Used in Classified
            Advertisements On Employment Opportunities." Journal of
            Reading 21, 6(March 1978): 493-497.

12.1357   Readence, John E., and Moore, David. "Coping with Minimal
            Reading Requirements: Suggestions For The Reading Teacher."
            Reading World 19, 2(December 1979): 139-148.

12.1358   "Reading." Times Educational Supplement 3343, (July 11, 1980):
            33-40.

12.1359   Reis, Ron. "A Curriculum For Real Life Reading Skills."
            Journal of Reading 21, 3(December 1977): 208-211.

12.1360   Showell, Romola. "Reading Instructions." Reading 12, 2(July
            1978): 30-38.

12.1361   Smith, Edwin H. "Meeting The Literacy Needs of
            Undereducated Youth and Adults: What Can and Should Be
            Done In The 1970's." Journal of Reading Behavior 2, 4(Winter
            1970): 306-313.

12.1362   Taggart, Robert, et al. "Basic Skills: The Sine Qua Non." Youth and Society 19, 1(September 1987): 3-21.

12.1363   Vacca, Richard T. "The Reading - Career Education Connection." Reading Horizons 18, 2(Winter 1978): 138-141.

12.1364   Vacca, Richard T. "The Development of a Functional Reading Strategy: Implications For Content Area Instruction." Journal of Educational Research 69, 3(November 1975): 108-112.

12.1365   Vandermeulen, Kenneth. "Reading in The Secondary School." Reading Horizons 13, 3(Spring 1973): 140-144.

12.1366   Venn, Grant, et al. A Comprehensive Plan For Solution of The Functionally Illiterate Problem, A Report of The Present, A Plan For The Future. Washington, D.C.: Management Technology, Inc., 1968. ED 019 603

12.1367   Vergara, Robert. "Introduction To Folk Media." Media and Adult Learning 8, 2(Spring 1986): 3-10.

12.1368   Walmsley, Sean A. "On The Purpose and Content of Secondary Reading Programs: An Educational Ideological Perspective." Curriculum Inquiry 11, 1(Spring 1981): 73-93.

12.1369   Watson, Dorothy J. "In College and In Trouble - With Reading." Reading Manitoba 2, 2(February 1982): 11-18.

12.1370   Watts, Janet. "Reading Is The Key." Times Educational Supplement 2781, (September 6, 1968): 403.

12.1371   Weber, Robert E. "A Dollar and Cents Look at Reading Failure." Reading Newsreport 5, 7(May-June 1971): 26-29.

12.1372   Williams, Joanna. "Reading Instruction Today." American Psychologist 34, 10(October 1979): 917-922.

13

Graphic Literacy

13.1373   Conroy, Michael T. "Project Bookmark: Reading and Graphic
           Arts." Journal of Reading 15, 1(October 1971): 60-61.

13.1374   Sofo, F. "Graphic Literacy: Part II. A Recent Study." Vocational
           Aspects of Education (UK) 38, 101(December 1986): 81-84.

13.1375   Sofo, Francesco. "Graphic Literacy: Part I. A Review of the
           Literature." Vocational Aspects of Education (UK) 1374,
           98(December 1985): 107-113.

14

History of Literacy

14.1376   Adamson, John W. Illiterate Anglo-Saxon & Other Essays On Education, Medieval & Modern. N.P.: n.p., 1946.

14.1377   Aldrich, Richard. "Literacy, Illiteracy, Semi-Literacy and Marriage Registers." History of Education Society Bulletin, 22(Autumn 1978): 2-6.

14.1378   Arnove, Robert F., and Graff, Harvey J. "National Literacy Campaigns: Historical and Comparative Lessons." Phi Delta Kappan 69, 3(November 1987): 202-206.

14.1379   Baumann, Gerd, ed. The Written Word: Literacy In Transition. New York: Oxford University Press, 1986.

14.1380   Bauml, F.H. "Varieties and Consequences of Medieval Literacy and Illiteracy." Speculum 55, (April 1980): 237-265.

14.1381   Best, E.E., Jr. "Literate Roman Soldier." The Classical Journal 62, (December 1966): 122-127.

14.1382   Brinkley, S.G. "Growth of School Attendance and Literacy In The United States Since 1840." Journal of Experimental Education 26, (September 1957): 51-66.

14.1383   Burns, A. "Athenian Literacy in The Fifth Century B.C." Journal of The History of Ideas 42, (July/September 1981): 371-387.

14.1384   Cartledge, P. "Literacy in The Spartan Oligarchy." The Journal of Hellenic Studies 98, (1978): 25-37.

14.1385   Casteleyn, Mary. History of Literacy and Libraries in Ireland:
           The Long Traced Pedigree. N.P.: Gower Publishing Company,
           1984.

14.1386   Clanchy, M.T. From Memory To Written Record, England, 1066-
           1307 N.P.: n.p., 1979.

14.1387   Clifford, Geraldine Joncich. "Buch and Lesen: Historical
           Perspectives on Literacy and Schooling." Review of Educational
           Research 54, 4(Winter 1984): 472-500.

           Discusses the changing meanings of literacy. Explains the ways
           of estimating and measuring literacy, the concept of functional
           literacy, the issue of literacy as thinking, and the extending of
           literacy to other fields. Surveys the development of literacy.
           Includes discussions on biblical, civic, and economic literacy.
           Explores the relationship between universal literacy and
           universal schooling. Also presents some examples of attempts
           to elevate the school literacy standard.

14.1388   Comprone, Joseph. "An Ongian Perspective on the History of
           Literacy: Psychological Context and Today's College Student
           Writer." Rhetoric Review 4, 2(January 1986): 138-148.

14.1389   Cook, Wanda Dauksza. "A History of Adult Literacy Education
           In The United States." Ed.D. dissertation, The Florida State
           University, 1971. 33/02-A, p. 5440.

14.1390   Coss, P.R. "Aspects of Cultural Diffusion in Medieval England:
           The Early Romances Local Society and Robin Hood." Past and
           Present, 108(August 1985): 35-79.

14.1391   Cressy, D. "Levels of Illiteracy in England, 1530-1730." Historical
           Journal 20, (March 1977): 1-23.

14.1392   Cressy, David. Literacy and The Social Order: Reading and
           Writing In Tudor and Stuart England. Cambridge: Cambridge
           University Press, 1980.

14.1393   De Evlis, Marilyn Davis. The Idelogy of Literacy In Nineteenth
           Century American Prose. N.P.: n.p., 1983.

14.1394   Donald, James. "How Illiteracy Became a Problem (and Literacy
           Stopped Being One)." Journal of Education 165, 1(Winter 1983):
           35-52.

14.1395   Engs, Robert F. "Historical Perspectives on The Problem of Black
            Literacy." Educational Horizons 66, 1(Fall 1987): 13-17.

14.1396   Franklin, S. "Literacy and Documentation In Early Medieval
            Russia." Speculum, 60(January 1985): 1-38.

14.1397   Galbraith, Vivian Hunter. Literacy of Mediaeval English Kings.
            London: n.p., n.d.

14.1398   Galenson, D. "Literacy and The Social Origins of Some Early
            Americans." The Historical Journal 22, (March 1979): 75-91.

14.1399   Galenson, D.W. "Literacy and Age In Preindustrial England:
            Quantitative Evidence and Implications." Economic
            Development and Cultural Change 29, (July 1981): 813-829.

14.1400   Gallman, R.E. "Changes In The Level of Literacy In A New
            Community of Early America." Journal of Economic History 48,
            (September 1988): 567-582.

14.1401   Gawthrop, R. and Strauss, G. "Protestantism and Literacy in
            Early Modern Germany." Past and Present, 104(August 1984):
            31-55.

14.1402   Goody, Jack, ed. Literacy In Traditional Societies. Cambridge:
            Cambridge University Press, 1968.

14.1403   Goody, Jack The Logic of Writing & The Organization of Society.
            New York: Cambridge University Press, n.d.

14.1404   Gordon, Cyrus H. "The Alphabet." New York University
            Education Quarterly 5, 4(Summer 1974): 11-15.

14.1405   Graff, Harvey J. The Legacies of Literacy: Continuities &
            Contradictions In Western Culture & Society. Bloomington:
            Indiana University Press, 1987.

14.1406   Graff, Harvey J. "The History of Literacy: Toward The Third
            Generation." Interchange 17, 2(Summer 1986): 122-134.

14.1407   Graff, Harvey J. "The Legacies of Literacy." Journal of
            Communication 32, 1(Winter 1982): 12-26.

14.1408   Graff, Harvey J. "On Literacy in The Renaissance: Review and
            Reflections." History of Education 12, 2(June 1983): 69-85

14.1409   Graff, Harvey J. Literacy Myth: Literacy and Social Structure In
            The 19th Century City. London: Academic Press, 1979.

14.1410   Graff, H.J. "Pauperism, Misery, and Vice: Illiteracy and
            Criminality In The Nineteenth Century." Social History 11,
            (Winter 1977): 245-268.

14.1411   Graff, H.J. "Literacy In History." History of Education Quarterly
            15, (Winter 1975): 467-474.

14.1412   Gratton, J.M. "Aspects of Literacy and 19th Century Society: The
            Environs of Liverpool." Journal of Educational Administration
            and History 17, 2(July 1985): 13-29.

14.1413   Guss, D.M. "Keeping It Oral: A Yekuana Ethnology." American
            Ethnologist 13, (August 1986): 413-429.

14.1414   Hallager, E. "The Inscribed Stirrup Jars: Implications For Late
            Minoan IIIB Crete." American Journal of Archaeology 91,
            (April 1987): 171-190.

14.1415   Harrop, Sylvia A. "Adult Education and Literacy: The
            Importance of Post-school Education For Literacy Levels in The
            Eighteenth and Nineteenth Centuries." History of Education 13,
            3(September 1984): 191-205.

14.1416   Hatley, Victor A. "Literacy at Northampton, 1761-1900: Further
            Interim Figures." Northamptonshire Past and Present 5, (1974):
            84.

14.1417   Havelock, E.A. "Preliteracy of The Greeks." New Literacy
            History 8, (Spring 1977): 521-534.

14.1418   Havelock, Eric A. "The Coming of Literate Communication To
            Western Culture." Journal of Communication 30, 1(Winter
            1980): 90-98.

14.1419   Havelock, Eric A. Origins of Western Literacy. Four Lectures
            Delivered At The Ontario Institute For Studies in Education,
            Toronto, March 25-28, 1974. Monograph Series No. 14. Toronto:
            Ontario Institute For Studies In Education, 1976. ED 157 053.

14.1420   Havelock, Eric A., and Hershbell, Jackson P., eds
            Communication Arts In The Ancient World. New York:
            Hastings House, Publishers, Inc., 1978. ED 161 108.

14.1421   Hayes, T.W. "Nicholas of Cusa and Popular Literacy in
           Seventeenth-Century England." Studies in Philology 84,
           (Winter 1987): 80-94.

14.1422   Herman, Patricia A. Southern Blacks: Accounts of Learning To
           Read Before 1861. N.P.: n.p., 1983. ED 246 394.

14.1423   Hibler, Richard W. "Martin Luther, The Educator." Educational
           Forum 49, 3(Spring 1985): 297-305.

14.1424   History of The Adult Education Act, A. Washington, D.C.:
           National Advisory Council on Adult Education, 1980. ED 245
           098.

14.1425   Hollis, Karyn. Literacy In Ancient Greece: The Evidence From
           History and Archaeology. N.P.: n.p., 1977. ED 253 866.

14.1426   Houston, R. "Literacy and Society In The West, 1500-1850."
           Social History 8, (October 1983): 269-293.

14.1427   Houston, R.A. Illiteracy and Society In Scotland and Northern
           England 1600-1800: Scottish Literacy and The Scottish Identity.
           Cambridge: Cambridge University Press, 1985.

14.1428   Houston, R.A. "Development of Literacy: Northern England,
           1640-1750." The Economic History Review 52 35, (May 1982):
           199-216.

14.1429   Illich, Ivan. "A Plea for Research on Lay Literacy." Interchange
           18, 1-2(Spring-Summer 1987): 23-31.

14.1430   Kaestle, Carl F. "Perspectives: Literacy and Mainstream Culture
           in American History." Language Arts 58, 2(February 1981): 207-
           217.

14.1431   Kaeuper, R. W. "Two Early Lists of Literates in England: 1334,
           1371." English Historical Review 99, (April 1984): 363-369.

14.1432   Kaston, Carren. The Community of The Book. N.P.: n.p., 1986.

14.1433   Laquer, Thomas. "The Cultural Origins of Popular Literacy in
           England, 1500-1850." Oxford Review of Education 2, (1976):
           255-275.

14.1434   Laqueur, T.W. "Literacy and Social Mobility in The Industrial
Revolution in England." Past & Present, 64(August 1974): 96-
112.

14.1435   Levine, D. "Illiteracy and Family Life During The First
Industrial Revolution." Journal of Social History 14, (Fall 1980):
25-44.

14.1436   Literacy In Historical Perspective. N.P.: n.p., 1983.

14.1437   Literacy In Traditional Societies. N.P.: n.p., 1975.

14.1438   Literacy, 1972-1976: Progress Achieved In Literacy Throughout
The World. Lanham, Maryland: Bernan-Unipub, 1980.

14.1439   Lockridge, Kenneth A. Literacy In Colonial New England; An
Enquiry Into The Social Context of Literacy In The Early Modern
West. New York: Norton, 1974.

14.1440   Long, Huey B. "Literacy in Early America: Some Observations."
Adult Literacy and Basic Education 3, 4(Winter 1980): 303-310.

14.1441   Lorenzetto, Anna. Lineamenti Storici e Teorici Dell'educazione
Permanente. N.P.: N.p., 1976.

14.1442   Lucas, G.R. "The Diffusion of Literacy in England and Wales In
The Nineteenth Century." Studies In Education 3. (July 1961):
240-248.

14.1443   MacMullen, R. "Epigraphic Habit in The Roman Empire."
American Journal of Philology 103, (Fall 1982): 233-246.

14.1444   Malmquist, Eve. "Readings That Made a Difference: Cooperating
in The Attack on Illiteracy." Journal of Reading 23, 5(February
1980): 392-396.

14.1445   Markoff, J. "Some Effects of Literacy In Eighteenth-Century
France." The Journal of Interdisciplinary History 17, (Autumn
1986): 311-333.

14.1446   Marvin, Carolyn. "Constructed and Reconstructed Discourse:
Inscription and Talk in The History of Literacy."
Communication Research: An International Quarterly 11,
4(October 1984): 563-594.

14.1447   Melton, J.V.H. "From Image to Word: Cultural Reform and
           The Rise of Literate Culture in Eighteenth-Century Austria."
           The Journal of Modern History 58, (March 1986): 95-124.

14.1448   Mitch, D. "Underinvestment In Literacy? The Potential
           Contribution of Government Involvement In Elementary
           Education To Economic Growth In Nineteenth-Century
           England." Journal of Economic History 44, (June 1984): 557-566.

14.1449   Mitch, D. "Spread of Literacy In Nineteenth-Century England."
           The Journal of Economic History 43, (March 1983): 287-288, 291-
           293.

14.1450   Mitch, David Franklin. "The Spread of Literacy In Nineteenth-
           Century England." Ph.D. dissertation, The University of
           Chicago, 1982. 43/06-A. p. 1856.

14.1451   Model, J. "Expansion of State Education: Two New Views."
           Journal of Urban History 8, (February 1982): 197-205.

14.1452   Monaghan, E.J. "Literacy Instruction and Gender In Colonial
           New England." American Quarterly 40, (March 1988): 18-41.

14.1453   Moran, Jo Ann Hoeppner. The Growth of English Schooling,
           1340-1548. N.P.: n.p., 1985.

14.1454   Murphy, K. "Illiterates' Progress: The Descent Into Literacy in
           Huckleberry Finn." Texas Studies in Literature and Language,
           26 (Winter 1984): 363-387.

14.1455   Myers, Miles. "Shifting Standards of Literacy - The Teacher's
           Catch-22." English Journal 73, 4(April 1984): 26-32.

14.1456   Ong, W.J. "Orality, Literacy, and Medieval Textualization."
           New Literary History, 16(Autumn 1984): 1-12.

14.1457   Pattison, Robert. On Literacy: Politics of The Word From
           Homer To The Age of Rock. New York: Oxford University
           Press, 1983.

14.1458   Pearpoint, Jack C. "Frontier College: Literacy Education Since
           1899." Prospects 17, 2(1987): 277-286.

14.1459   Rachal, J.R. "Gutenberg, Literacy, and The Ancient Arts of
           Memory." Adult Education Quarterly 38, (Spring 1988): 125-
           135.

14.1460   Rachal, John R. "Measuring English and American Historical
             Literacy: A Review of Methodological Approaches."
             International Journal of Lifelong Education 6, 3(July-September
             1987): 185-198.

14.1461   Rappaport, J. "Mythic Images, Historical Thought, and Printed
             Texts: The Paez and The Written Word." Journal of
             Anthropological Research 43, (Spring 1987): 43-61.

14.1462   Resnick, Daniel P., ed Literacy In Historical Perspective.
             Washington, D.C.: Government Printing Office, 1983. ED 237
             942.

14.1463   Resnick, Daniel P., and Resnick, Lauren B. "The Nature of
             Literacy: An Historical Exploration." Harvard Educational
             Review 47, 3(1977): 370-385.

14.1464   Schatz, Albert. "The Reading Problem in School: How It Began
             and How It Ended." Journal of Reading 18, 8(May 1975): 602-
             605.

14.1465   Schneider, J.S. "Extent of Illiteracy in Oxyrhynchus and Its
             Environs During The Late Third Century A.D." Classical
             Journal 28, (June 1933): 670-74.

14.1466   Shahidullah, Kazi. Literacy In Mid-Nineteenth Century. N.P.:
             n.p., 1984.

14.1467   Smith, Alan. "Private Schools and Schoolmasters in The
             Diocese of Lichfield and Coventry in The Seventeenth Century."
             History of Education 5, 2(June 1976): 117-126.

14.1468   Smout, T.C. "Born Again At Cambuslans: New Evidence on
             Popular Religion and Literacy in Eighteenth-Century Scotland."
             Past and Present, 97 (November 1982): 114-127.

14.1469   Soltow, L., and Stevens, E. "Economic Aspects of School
             Participation in Mid-Nineteenth-Century United States."
             Journal of Interdisciplinary History 8, (August 1977): 221-243.

14.1470   Stedman, L.C. and Kaestle, C.F. "Literacy and Reading
             Performance In The United States from 1880 to The Present."
             Reading Research Quarterly 22, (Winter 1987): 8-46.

14.1471   Stevens, W.B. Education, Literacy & Society: Eighteen Thirty to
             Eighteen Seventy, The Geography of Diversity in Provincial

England. Wolfeboro, New Hampshire: Longwood Publishing Group, Inc., 1987.

14.1472   Stephens, W.B. "Male and Female Adult Illiteracy in 17th-Century Cornwall." Journal of Educational Administration and History 9, 2(July 1977): 1-7.

14.1473   Stephens, W.B. "Illiteracy in Devon During The Industrial Revolution 1754-1844." Journal of Educational Administration and History 8, 1(January 1976): 1-5.

14.1474   Stock, B. "Medieval Literacy, Linguistic Theory, and Social Organization." New Literary History 16, (Autumn 1984): 13-29.

14.1475   Stone, Lawrence. "Literacy and Education in England, 1640-1900." Past and Present 42, (February 1969): 69-139.

14.1476   Suhor, Charles. "ERIC/RCS Report: Understanding Literacy - An Overview." Language Arts 64, 6(October 1987): 59-63.

14.1477   Thomas, Joy. Sequoyah and The Cherokee Syllabary. N.P.: n.p., 1972. ED 266 886.

14.1478   Treadgold, W.T. "Revival of Byzantine Learning and The Revival of Byzantine State." The American Historical Review 84, (December 1979): 1245-1266.

14.1479   Treitler, L. "Oral, Written, and Literate Process in The Transmission of Medieval Music." Speculum 56, (July 1981): 471-491.

14.1480   Turner, R.V. "Miles Literatus in Twelfth and Thirteenth-Century England: How Rare a Phenomenon?" American Historical Review 83, (Ocatober 1978): 928-945.

14.1481   Ullman, B.L. "Illiteracy In The Roman Empire." Classical Journal 29, (November 1933): 127-8.

14.1482   Vale, Malcolm Graham Allan. Piety, Charity, and Literacy Among The Yorkshire Gentry, 1370-1480. York: St. Anthony's Press, 1976.

14.1483   Vann, R.T. "Literacy in Seventeenth-Century England: Some Hearth-Tax Evidence." Journal of Interdisciplinary History 5, (Autumn 1974): 287-293.

14.1484   Varnum, Robin. "From Crisis to Crisis: The Evolution Toward Higher Standards of Literacy in The United States." Rhetoric Society Quarterly 16, 3(Summer 1986): 145-165.

14.1485   Verner, C. "Education of Adult Illiterates: An Historical Footnote." English Quarterly 2, (January 1969): 65-70.

14.1486   Verner, Coolie. "Illiteracy and Poverty." Literacy Discussion 5, 2(Summer 1974): 303-313.

14.1487   Verner, Coolie. Pole's History of Adult Schools. A Facsimile of The 1816 Edition With An Introduction and Bibliographic Notes. Washington, D.C.: Adult Education Association of The U.S.A., 1967. ED 047 276.

14.1488   Wald, K.D. "Visible Empire: The Ku Klux Klan as an Electoral Movement." Journal of Interdisciplinary History 11, (August 1980): 217-234.

14.1489   Watkins, Morris. Literacy, Bible Reading, and Church Growth Through The Ages. South Pasadena, California: William Carey Library, 1978.

14.1490   Webb, R.K. "Literacy Among The Working Classes In Nineteenth Century Scotland." Scottish Historical Review 33 (October 1954): 100-114.

14.1491   Wesling, D. "Writing as Power In The Slave Narrative of The Early Republic." Michigan Quarterly Review 26, (Summer 1987): 459-472.

14.1492   West, S. "Archilochus' Message-Stick." Classical Quarterly 38, 1(1988): 42-48.

14.1493   Zboray, R. J. "The Letter and The Fiction Reading Public in Antebellum America." Journal of American Culture 10, (Spring 1977): 27-34.

15

Illiteracy

15.1494   Adam, F. "La alfabetizacion en las zonas rurales." <u>Convergence</u>
1(September 1968): 37-45.

15.1495   Adiseshiah, M.S. "Place of Literacy in Education." <u>Convergence</u>
6, 1(1973): 9-14.

15.1496   Albani, Salvador. <u>Lingua Ortographia e Analfabetismo</u>. Sao
Paulo, Brazil: Lusitana Editora, 1969.

15.1497   <u>Alfabetizacion, Concientizacion, Educacion</u>. N.P.: Secretariado
Social Mexicano, 1972.

15.1498   Altus, W.D. "Relationship of Intelligence and Years of
Schooling When Literacy Is Held Constant." <u>Journal of
Consulting Psychology</u> 13, (October 1949): 375-376.

15.1499   Amberg, J. "Buck Stopped Here: Letter From a High School
English Teachers' Convention." <u>The American Scholar</u> 49,
(Summer 1980): 385-390.

15.1500   "Analphabetisme." (extrait de l'Unesco). <u>L'Ecole Ontarienne</u>
24, (May-June 1968): 219-221.

15.1501   Anderson, A.P. "The Eradication of Illiteracy." (World Congress
of Ministers of Education, Teheran, September 8-19, 1965).
<u>Information</u> 17 (January 1966): 3-6.

15.1502   Andrews, Alison. "'Illiterates' Record." <u>ATA Magazine</u> 57,
2(January 1977): 16-19.

15.1503   Aronowitz, Stanley. "Politics and Higher Education in The
1980's" <u>Journal of Education</u> 162, 3(Summer 1980): 40-59.

15.1504   Axam, John A. "The Library's Role in Eradicating Illiteracy." Catholic Library World 55, 3(October 1983): 122-123.

15.1505   Babb, V. "The Color Purple: Writing To Undo What Writing Has Done." Phylon 47, (June 1986): 107-116.

15.1506   Baergen, Peter. "Comma or The Camera?" ATA Magazine 57, 2(January 1977): 34-35.

15.1507   Baker-Smith, D. "Swords, Scripts and Sealing Wax." History Today 30, (February 1980): 51.

15.1508   Barnes, D.F. et al. "Rural Literacy and Agricultural Development: Cause or Effect?" Rural Sociology 47, (Summer 1982): 251-271.

15.1509   Beales, R.W., Jr. "Studying Literacy at The Community Level: A Research Note." Journal of Interdisciplinary History 9, (Summer 1978): 93-102.

15.1510   Beatty, W.W. "Half The World Can't Read." Phi Delta Kappan 37, (June 1956): 386-395.

15.1511   Berger, P.L. "Consciousness Raising: To Whom-by Whom?" Social Policy 5, (September 1974): 38-42.

15.1512   Bettelheim, B. "Janet and Mark & The New Illiteracy: Reading and The Emotions." Encounter 43, (November 1974): 15-23.

15.1513   Bhagwat, S.R. "Removal Of Illiteracy." Educational Review (China) 28, (October 1936): 273-280.

15.1514   Bhola, H.S. "Needed Research in Adult Literacy For Policy Makers and Planners." Adult Education 31, (Sprint 1981): 169-176.

15.1515   Bickel, R., and Milton, S. "The Social Circumstances of Illiteracy: Interpretation and Exchange in a Class-based Society." Urban Review 15, 4(1983): 203-215.

15.1516   "Big Lift For Illiterates." Life 42, (January 28, 1957): 47.

15.1517   Bittner, W.S. "Prevent Illiteracy." Child Welfare 23, (February 1929): 296-8.

15.1518   Boardman, G.C. "Literacy Has New Meanings." Wisconsin
            Journal of Education 89, (March 1957): 19.

15.1519   Borchardt, S.M. "Eradicate Illiteracy! Don't Conceal It."
            American Teacher 15, (October 1930): 14-16.

15.1520   Botstein, Leon. "Imitative Literacy." Partisan Review 48, 3(1981):
            399-408.

            Discusses both the crisis in literacy among the middle class,
            college-bound students and college graduates, and the
            catastrophe of illiteracy among the poor. Introduces the concept
            of imitative literacy wherein college-bound and college
            graduating students "become literate" by imitating different
            varieties of functional and economic English. Examines the
            social and political consequences of the new character of
            language and literacy. Concludes with a discussion of the
            possibility that an entire generation has become alienated from
            true literacy.

15.1521   Bouchard, A. "L'industrie du savoir ou les satellites de
            communication dans l'enseignment futur." Education et
            Societe 4, 7(November 1973): 18-19.

15.1522   Brock, A. "Battle Against Illiteracy: A UNESCO Survey."
            School & Society 98, (March 1979): 181.

15.1523   Brown, R. "Literacy: Not So Basic." Compact 15, (Fall 1981): 16-
            19.

15.1524   Browne, R.B. "Popular Culture: Medicine For Illiteracy and
            Associated Educational Ills." Journal of Popular Culture 21,
            (Winter 1987): 1-15.

15.1525   Brownstein, Michael. "Saving Grace." Learning 17, 8(April
            1988): 36-38.

15.1526   Calfee, R. "Literacy and Illiteracy: Teaching The Nonreader To
            Survive In The Modern World." Annals of Dyslexia 32, (1982):
            71-91.

15.1527   Caliver, A. "Illiteracy and Manpower Mobilization." School Life
            33, (June 1951): 131-133.

15.1528   "Cause and Cure of Illiteracy." Times Educational Supplement
            1846, (September 15, 1950): 707.

15.1529   Chall, J.S. "Literacy: Trends and Explanations." American
           Education 20, (November 1984): 16-22.

15.1530   Chase, F.S. "Higher Illiteracy." New York State Education 52,
           (December 1964): 5. School and Community 51, (December
           1964): 15.

15.1531   Chase, F.S. "In The Next Decade." Conference on Reading,
           University of Chicago (1961): 7-18.

15.1532   Cibrowski, L. "Coping With Student Illiteracy." Forecast for
           Home Economics 26, (November 1980): 29.

15.1533   Clanchy, John. "'The Higher Illiteracy': Some Personal
           Observations." English in Australia 37, (September 1977): 20-
           24, 41-47.

15.1534   Clark, R.M. "Significant Concepts for Analyzing How Home Life
           Affects Literacy Development." Yearbook (Claremont Reading
           Conference) 45, (1981): 34-41.

15.1535   Coles, G.S., and Coppel, L.A. "Literacy, CETA, and
           Unemployment: Coming up Empty." Urban Education 17,
           (July 1982): 199-212.

15.1536   Coles, G.S. et al. "Educational Therapy In A Community Mental
           Health Center." Community Mental Health Journal 16, (Spring
           1980): 79-89.

15.1537   Collinson, P. "Significance of Signatures." Times Literary
           Supplement, 4058 (January 9, 1981): 31.

15.1538   Commonwealth Education Conference, 3rd Report. Ottawa: n.p.
           1964.

15.1539   Cook, D.R.S. "Student Writings: It Is Dissolving Into The New
           Illiteracy." Skylark 11, 2(Winter 1975): 22-27.

15.1540   Coomaraswamy, A.K. "Bugbear of Literacy." Asia 44, (February
           1944): 52-57.

15.1541   Coons, John E. "Shanker Vouchers - Is The Genie Out?" Phi
           Delta Kappan 63, 4(December 1981): 255.

15.1542   Copeland, R. "Dance and The Decline of Literacy: Is There A
           Dark Side To The Boom?" Chronicle of Higher Education 34,
           (December 2, 1987): B1-2.

15.1543   Corbin, Richard K. Literacy, Literature, and The Disadvantaged.
           N.P.: n.p., 1964?

15.1544   Cortright, R.W. "Helpful Definitions; Terms Used by Literacy
           Workers." Adult Leadership 12, (December 1963): 184.

15.1545   Cortright, R.W. "War Against World Illiteracy." Overseas 2,
           (April 1963): 6-9.

15.1546   Cortright, R.W. "First University Literacy Center." School &
           Society 89, (April 22, 1961): 207-208.

15.1547   Cortright, R.W., and Kelley, D.L. "I'm Tired of Looking at Blank
           Signs." Texas Outlook 44, (June 1960): 14-15.

15.1548   Coughlin, E.K. "Literacy: 'Excitement' of New Field Attracts
           Scholars of Literature." Chronicle of Higher Education 29,
           (January 9, 1985): 1.

15.1549   Crichton, K.S. "Our Schools Are A Scandal." Colliers 117,
           (April 13, 1946): 32.

15.1550   Cunningham, P.M. "Are We a Nation of Illiterates?"
           Educational Leadership 44, (May 1987): 83.

15.1551   Curtis, Redmond. "A Plea for Literacy." ACT, 11(November
           1981): 7-10.

15.1552   Custance, A.C. "Education Toward Illiteracy?" Challenge in
           Educational Administration 13, 4(1975): 8-15.

15.1553   Dale, E. "Toward a Literate World." Edcuation Digest 30,
           (November 1964): 32-34.

15.1554   Dalglish, Carol. Illiteracy and The Offender. Cambridge:
           Huntington Publishers, 1982.

15.1555   Daniels, H., and Ledbetter, J.T. "Is There a Decline In Literacy?"
           English Journal 65, (September 1976): 16-20.

15.1556   Darville, Richard. "Framing Il/literacy In The Media." Learning
           (Canada) 5, 1(1988): 9-11.

15.1557   Dauster, Tania. <u>Analise Do Nivel Operatorio do Adulto Analfabeto</u>. N.P.: n.p., 1977.

15.1558   Davidoff, J.B. et al. "Information Extraction From Brief Verbal Displays: Half-field and Serial Position Effects For Children, Normal and Illiterate Adults." <u>British Journal of Psychology</u> 73, (February 1982): 29-39.

15.1559   "Decrease of Illiteracy." <u>School and Society</u> 34, (September 19, 1931): 394

15.1560   Deva, I. "Cultural Level of Unlettered Folk." <u>Diogenes</u>, 100(Winter 1977): 26-47.

15.1561   Deverell, A.F. "Future of Literacy." <u>Quary</u> 4, (November-December 1973): 2-4.

15.1562   Dow, S. "Century of Humane Archaeology." <u>Archaeology</u> 33, (May/June 1980): 42-51.

15.1563   Duckenfield, Mike. "Reports Reveal 'Alarming Illiteracy'". <u>Times Educational Supplement</u> 3154, (November 14, 1975): 14.

15.1564   Edington, A.B. "Mass Illiteracy: The Only Solution?" <u>Educational Television International</u> 4, 1(March 1970): 47-49.

15.1565   <u>Education For Better Living; The Role of The School In Community Improvement</u>. Washington, D.C.: Office of Education, 1957.

15.1566   Ellison, E.J. "He Leads Millions Out of The Dark." <u>Saturday Evening Post</u> 226, (April 17, 1954): 32-33.

15.1567   Epstein, J. "Why Madame Bovary Couldn't Make Love in The Concrete." <u>Commentary</u> 71, (February 1981): 42-47.

15.1568   Ewing, Guy. "On Not Seeing Words: Illiteracy and Language." <u>Interchange</u> 18, 1-2(Spring-Summer 1987): 89-96.

15.1569   Fargo, G., and Vincente, A. "Power of Literacy: Applied to Traditional Birth Attendants, Saulteaux-Cree Indians and Hawaiian Children." <u>Yearbook</u> (Claremont Reading Conference) 45, (1981): 166-172.

15.1570   Farley, B.M. "Our Lost Legions." <u>Journal of The National Education Association</u> 31, (September 1942): 178.

15.1571   Farr, Roger C. Reading: Trends and Challenges. Washington,
           D.C.: National Education Association, 1981.

15.1572   Farrell, E. "Vice/Vise of Standardized Testing: National
           Depreciation by Quantification." Language Arts 54, (May 1977):
           486-490.

15.1573   Farrell, T.J. "Literacy, The Basics, and All That Jazz." College
           English 38, (January 1977): 443-459.

15.1574   Ferguson, C.A. "Literacy In A Hunting-Gathering Society: The
           Case of The Diyari." Journal of Anthropological Research 43,
           (Fall 1987): 223-237.

15.1575   Ferriman, Annabel. "A Land Rich From Oil Where Most
           Cannot Read." Times Educational Supplement 3138, (July 25,
           1975): 9.

15.1576   "Fight Against Illiteracy." International Bureau of Education
           Bulletin 10, (2nd Quarter 1936): 75.

15.1577   Fingeret, A. "Social Network: A New Perspective On
           Independence And Illiterate Adults." Adult Education Quarterly
           33, (Spring 1983): 133-146.

15.1578   Fisher, E.A. "Illiteracy In Context." Prospects 12, 2(1982): 155-
           162.

15.1579   Flory, S. "Who Read Herodotus' Histories?" American Journal
           of Philology 101, (Spring 1980): 12-28.

15.1580   Forest, S.S. "Non-readers Need Not Apply." School and
           Community 66, (December 1979): 10-11.

15.1581   Frake, C.O. "Did Literacy Cause The Great Cognitive Divide?"
           American Ethnologist 10, (May 1983): 368-371.

15.1582   Freedman, M. "Those Futile Attempts To Legislate Literacy."
           Chronicle of Higher Education 27, (February 1, 1984): 80.

15.1583   Freedman, M. "For Students, Looking and Listening Ought To
           Be As Edifying As Reading." Chronicle of Higher Education 25,
           (October 17, 1982): 29.

15.1584   Freire, Paulo. Acao Cultural Para a Liberdade e Outros Escritos.
           Rio de Janeiro: n.p., 1979.

15.1585   Freire, Paulo. Acao Cultural para a Liberdade e Outros Escritos.
           Rio de Janeiro: Paz e Terra, 1976.

15.1586   French, J.L. "Rural Community Modernization, Inequality and
           Local Political Involvements." Social Science Quarterly 60,
           (December 1979): 401-417.

15.1587   Fuglesang, Andreas. Communication With Illiterates. N.P.:
           n.p., 1969.

15.1588   Furter, Pierre. De La Lucha Contra el Analfabetismo al
           Desarrollo Cultural. Caracas: Fondo Editorial Comun, 1978.

15.1589   Galtung, Johan. Literacy, Education and Schooling - For What?
           Oslo: Universitetet i Oslo, Professoratet i Konflikt-og
           Fredsforskning, 1977.

15.1590   Galtung, Johan. "Literacy, Education and Schooling - For
           What?" Convergence 8, 4(1975): 39-50.

15.1591   Gates, H.L. "James Gronniosaw and The Trope of The Talking
           Book." Southern Review 22, (April 1986): 252-272.

15.1592   Gates, H.L. "Editor's Introduction: Writing "Race" and The
           Difference It Makes." Critical Inquiry, 12, (Autumn 1985): 1-20.

15.1593   Ginzberg, E., and Bray, D.W. Uneducated. New York: Columbia
           University Press, 1953.

15.1594   Giroux, Henry A. "Mass Culture and The Rise of The New
           Illiteracy: Implications for Reading." Interchange 10,
           4(1979/1980): 89-98

15.1595   Gold, P.C. and Johnson, J.A. "Entry Level Achievement
           Characteristics of Youth and Adults Reading Below Fifth Grade
           Equivalent: A Preliminary Profile and Analysis." Psychological
           Reports 50, (June Part 1 1982): 1011-1019.

15.1596   Goldthwait, John T. "The Sub-Literate College Student."
           Educational Forum 47, 2(Winter 1983): 199-207.

15.1597   Gonzalves, S.J. "Ethnicity and The Politics of Literacy: A Ten
           Year Look At Livingston College." Journal of Ethnic Studies 11,
           (Summer 1983): 107-118.

15.1598   Goodhall, P.E. "'He Is Illiterate Who Is Less Literate Than
            Someone Else Says He Ought To Be.'" ATA Magazine 57,
            2(January 1977): 27-30.

15.1599   Goodwin, S.W. "Educational Triage? The Churches and
            Illiteracy." Christianity and Crisis 36, (July 19, 1976): 170-172.

15.1600   Goody, John Rankin. The Domestication of The Savage Mind.
            New York: Cambridge University Press, 1977.

15.1601   Gould, Sir R. "World is Our Classroom - Why Not?" Teacher's
            Magazine 50, (March 1970): 34-42.

15.1602   Graff, H.J. "Literacy in Literature and in Life: An Early
            Twentieth-Century Example." History of Education Quarterly
            23, (Fall 1983): 279-296.

15.1603   Graff, H.J. "Legacies of Literacy." Journal of Communication 32,
            (Winter 1982): 12-26.

15.1604   Graff, Harvey J. "Exaggerated Estimates of Reading and Writing
            as Means of Education (1867). by W.B. Hodgson." History of
            Education Quarterly 26, 3(Fall 1986): 377-393.

15.1605   Gray, W.S. "Fundamental Education For All Peoples."
            Elementary School Journal 48, (May 1984): 464-466.

15.1606   Green, D.H. "The Reception of Hartmann's Works: Listening,
            Reading, or Both?" Modern Language Review 81, (April 1986):
            357-368.

15.1607   Greene, M. "Literacy For What?" Phi Delta Kappan 63,
            (January 1982): 326-329.

15.1608   Griffin, E. "Universal Literacy in The Development Decade."
            International Journal of Adult and Youth Education 14, 4(1962):
            200-204.

15.1609   Gudschinsky, Sarah Caroline. A Manual of Literacy For
            Preliterate Peoples. Ukarumpa, Papua New Guinea: Summer
            Institute of Linguistics, 1973.

15.1610   Guss, D.M. "Keeping It Oral: A Yekuana Ethnology." American
            Ethnologist 13, (August 1986): 413-429.

15.1611   Guthrie, J.T. "Equilibrium of Literacy." Journal of Reading 26, (April 1983): 668-670.

15.1612   Guthrie, J.T. "Being Literate." Journal of Reading 22, (February 1979): 450-452.

15.1613   Guthrie, J.T., and Kirsch, I.S. "The Emergent Perspective on Literacy." Phi Delta Kappan 65, (January 1984): 351-355.

15.1614   Hagerman, B.P. "Skill Support For The Poor Reader." Synoptic 14, (Spring 1974): 7-14.

15.1615   Hardaway, Francine. "It Isn't The Medium. It's The Message." Community College Frontiers 8, 1(Fall 1979): 39-42.

15.1616   Hargreaves, David. "On The Move." Educational Broadcasting International 10, (June 1977): 77-78.

15.1617   Harman, David. Community Fundamental Education. N.P.: n.p., 1974.

15.1618   Harmon, D. "Illiteracy: An Overview." Harvard Education Review 40, (May 1970): 226-243.

15.1619   Harvey, C.C. "Challenge To High Schools." Journal of Education 125, (November 1942): 247-248.

15.1620   Haste, Hans. ABC För En Battre Värld. Stockholm: Folket i Bilds Förlag, 1957.

15.1621   Hayes, Woody. "The Average, The Poor and The Illiterate." Canadian Quill 12, 2(December 1982): 3-6.

15.1622   "He Has Taught 60 Million People To Read." Texas Outlook 36, (February 1952): 6-7.

15.1623   Henneberg, S. "What Do You Mean, You Can't Read?" English Journal 75, (January 1986): 53-55.

15.1624   Henquet, P. "L'Unesco et l'elimination de l'analphabetisme." Convergence 1, (September 1968): 8-18.

15.1625   Heymann, C.L. "Half The World Is Illiterate." United Nations World 5, (October 1951): 25-27.

15.1626   Hicks, F.R. "Second Call For Pupils; Giving Illiterates Another
           Chance." Nation's Schools 18, (November 1936): 33-34.

15.1627   Higonnet, P. "Reading, Writing and Revolution." Times
           Literary Supplement 3993, (October 13, 1978): 1153-1154.

15.1628   Hildreth, G. "World Literacy and Education." School & Society
           89, (November 4, 1961): 371-372.

15.1629   Hill, H.H., and Cherry, R. "No Brand New Illiterates." Nation's
           Schools 22, (October 1938): 29-30.

15.1630   "How Can We Reduce Illiteracy? Radio Script." Education For
           Victory 3, (January 20, 1945): 22-26.

15.1631   Hrychuk, Bill. "Other Side of Silence." ATA Magazine 57,
           2(January 1977): 4-8.

15.1632   Hudson, V.O. "Shelve The Classics For The Duration?"
           Virginia Journal of Education 36, (April 1943): 303-304.

15.1633   "Hughes, A.G. "Illiteracy: A Symptom of Fundamental
           Backwardness." Journal of Education (London) 81, (October
           1949): 564.

15.1634   Hurst, Antony. "Hope For Illiterates." Times Educational
           Supplement 2652, (March 18, 1966): 835.

15.1635   "Illiteracy, A World Problem." Journal of The National
           Education Association 39, (December 1950): 648.

15.1636   "Illiteracy: Let's Wipe It Out!" Tennessee Teacher 40, (January
           1973): 23.

15.1637   "Illiterate Millions." Times Educational Supplement 1951,
           (September 19, 1952): 767.

15.1638   "International Literacy Day Awards." School & Society 99,
           (January 1971): 9.

15.1639   "International Symposuim For Literacy: Declaration of
           Persepolis." Convergence 8, 4(1975): 5-7.

15.1640   Isenberg, J., and Jacob, E. "Literacy and Symbolic Play: A Review
           of The Literature." Childhood Education 59, (March/April
           1983): 272-274.

15.1641   "Is Reading Important?" USA Today 108, (April 1980): 15-16.

15.1642   Jeffries, Charles. Illiteracy, A World Problem. London: Pall Mall Press, Ltd., 1967. ED 018 758.

15.1643   Kallen, Denis. "Failure and Under-Achievement In Education: The New Illiterates." Prospects 17, 2(1987): 213-222.

15.1644   Kandel, I.L. "New Illiteracy." School & Society 72, (November 25, 1950): 348.

15.1645   Kandel, I.L. "Salvation Through Literacy" School & Society 64, (December 7, 1946): 396.

15.1646   Kerr, Jack. "Presidential Address: The Control of Change," School Science Review 58, 205 (June 1977): 625-634.

15.1647   Kidd, J.R. "Literacy Around The World." Canadian National Commission For UNESCO Bulletin 10, (October 1967): 1-3.

15.1648   Kidd, James Robbins. Whilst Time Is Burning: A Report On Education For Development. Ottawa: International Development Research Centre, 1974.

15.1649   Kilgore, H.M. "Literacy and The National Welfare." School Life 34, (March 1952): 90-91.

15.1650   Kingston, A. J. "Does Literacy Really Enhance The Lives of The Elderly?" Reading World 20, (March 1981): 169-172.

15.1651   Kirland, Ralph A. "Literacy and Beyond." Query 7, 1(February 1977): 18-21.

15.1652   Knappert, J. "State of Our Knowledge of African Languages." Linguistics, 124(March 15, 1974): 71-89.

15.1653   Knight, M.F. "Education Of The Masses." Christian Science Monitor Weekly Magazine Section, (September 14, 1946): 7.

15.1654   Knight, Roberta, et al. "Views From Some Teachers of The 'Illiterates'." ATA Magazine 57, 2(January 1977): 20-23.

15.1655   Kochman, T. "Orality and Literacy As Factors of Black and White Communicative Behavior." Linguistics,136 (September 15, 1974): 91-115.

15.1656   Kozol, J. "Dehumanizing The Humanities." Chronicle of
           Higher Education 30, (March 13, 1985): 88.

15.1657   Krapp, JoAnn Vergona. "Teaching Research Skills: A Critical-
           Thinking Approach." School Library Journal 34, 5(January
           1988): 32-35.

15.1658   Lang, B. "Preliteracy, Postliteracy, and The Cunning of History."
           Journal of Reading 26, (April 1983): 581-585.

15.1659   Lange, B. "World Literacy's Vital Signs." (ERIC/RCS Report) 25,
           (December 1981): 278-282.

15.1660   La Prensa Se Pronuncia; la Alfabetizacion: el Gran Reto
           Historico. La Paz: Ministerio de Educacion, 1970.

15.1661   Larrick, Nancy. "Illiteracy Starts Too Soon." Phi Delta Kappan
           69, 3(November 1987): 184-189.

15.1662   Laubach, F.C. "I Remember." Phi Delta Kappan 32, (May 1951):
           378-381.

15.1663   Laubach, F.C. "World Is Learning To Read." International
           Journal of Religious Education 26, (February 1950): 5-6.

15.1664   Laubach, F.C. Teaching The World To Read. New York:
           Friendship Press, 1947.

15.1665   Laubach, F.C. Silent Billion Speak. New York: Friendship Press,
           1943.

15.1666   Laubach, Frank Charles. Forty Years With The Silent Billion.
           N.P.: n.p., 1970.

15.1667   Laubach, Frank Charles. Toward World Literacy, The Each One
           Teach One Way. N.P.; n.p., 1960.

15.1668   Leblanc, Daniel A. "A Film About Illiteracy." Meqnews 62,
           (December 1981): 16.

15.1669   Lerner, Barbara. "Vouchers For Literacy: Second Chance
           Legislation." Phi Delta kappan 63, 4(December 1981): 252-255.

15.1670   Lestage, Andre. Literacy and Illiteracy. N.P.: n.p., 1982.

15.1671   Levine, K. "Illiteracy and The Information Explosion." Media In Education and Development 16, (March 1983): 17-19.

15.1672   Levinger, Larry. "The Human Side of Illiteracy." English Journal 67, 8(November 1978): 26-29.

15.1673   Lewis, A.C. "Reading The Writing on The Wall." Phi Delta Kappan 69, (March 1988): 468-469.

15.1674   Lewis, M.M. "Importance of Illiteracy." London: Harrap, 1953.

15.1675   Limage, Leslie J. "Illiteracy In Industrialized Countries: A Sociological Commentary." Prospects 10, 2(1980): 141-158.

15.1676   Lipson, Alice M. "Can Illiteracy Be Prevented?" Academic Therapy 21, 5(May 1986): 591-597.

15.1677   "Liquidation of Illiteracy." International Bureau of Education Bulletin 10, (2nd Quarter 1936): 71.

15.1678   "Literacy and Ideology." Journal of Education 165, (Winter 1983): 5-129.

15.1679   "Literacy Drive Transformed; Three-year Pilot Schemes Mooted." Times Educational Supplement 2553, (April 24, 1964): 1061.

15.1680   "Looking At Problem Of Illiteracy." School Life 35, (October 1951): 11.

15.1681   Lyons, Gene. "The Higher Illiteracy." Harpers 253, (September 1976): 33-40.

15.1682   Mace, Jane. "Blaming The Victim." Times Educational Supplement 3131, (May 30, 1975): 18.

15.1683   MacKenzie, L.L. "Service To Inmates And Staff." ALA Bulletin 58, (October 1964): 809.

15.1684   Maheu, R. "Struggle Against Illiteracy." Information 13, (April 1965): 26-28.

15.1685   Maheu, R. "Abolition of Illiteracy." School & Society 90, (April 7, 1962): 155.

15.1686   Malmquist, E. "Cooperating inThe Attack On Illiteracy: Works of Helen M. Robinson And William S. Gray." Journal of Reading 23, (February 1980): 392-396.

15.1687   Mandler, J.M. et al. "Cross-Cultural Invariance In Story Recall." Child Development 51, (March 1980): 19-26.

15.1688   Manley, W. "Facing The Public (Causes of Illiteracy)." Wilson Library Bulletin 62, (February 1988): 64-65.

15.1689   Mashiter, T. J. "The Illiterate." Spectator 182, (June 3, 1949): 752.

15.1690   Mason, David E. Reaching The Silent Billion; The Opportunity of Literacy Missions. Grand Rapids, Michigan: Zondervan Publishing House, 1967.

15.1691   Mason, David E. Apostle To The Illiterates; Chapters In The Life of Frank C. Laubach. Grand Rapids, Michigan: Zondervan Publishing House, 1966.

15.1692   Mathies, Lorraine. "Citings on The Educational Horizon." Educational Horizons 55, 4(Summer 1977): 210-211.

15.1693   Maynes, M.J. "Schooling and Hegemony." Journal of Interdisciplinary History 13, (Winter 1983): 515-520.

15.1694   Mazzetti, Roberto. Alfabeto e Societa. N.P.: n.p., 1963.

15.1695   M'Bow, A.M. "International Literacy." Journal of Reading 22, (March 1979): 498-500.

15.1696   McEvoy, T.P. "Each One Teach One." Readers Digest 45, (September 1944): 44-48.

15.1697   Melo, Orlando Ferreira de. A Alfabetizacao No Curso Primario E Outros Estudos. Rio de Janeiro: n.p., 1958.

15.1698   Messon, B. "Who Stole The Body Out of English? Reflections on Skills For The Seventies." Skylark 12, (Fall 1975): 23-26.

15.1699   Meyer, Ziona, ed. Learning Never Ends; Proceedings. Tel Aviv: Achduth Co-op. Press, 1965.

15.1700   Muir, Pearl. "Visionaries Have Fallen Silent." ATA Magazine 57, 2(January 1977): 24-26.

15.1701   Muller, Joseph. "Illiteracy: No Field For Fast Results."
           Convergence 17, 3(1984): 43-45.

15.1702   Neuman, Susan B. "Rethinking The Censorship Issue." English
           Journal 75, 5(September 1986): 46-50.

15.1703   New Educational Media In Action - Case Studies For Planners
           III. Paris: UNESCO, 1967. ED 018 986.

15.1704   "New Readers Begin Here." Economist 254, (February 22, 1975):
           15-16.

15.1705   "New Shape of Illiteracy." Human Ecology Forum 10, (Fall
           1979): 25.

15.1706   "Not So Illiterate After All." Mental Hygiene 26, (October 1942):
           675-677.

15.1707   Norris, B. "Illiteracy Test Shows The Writing On The Wall."
           Times Educational Supplement 3644, (May 2, 1986): 17.

15.1708   O'Grady, Carolyn. "Illiteracy Campaign Begins - Now Read on . .
           ." Times Educational Supplement 3150, (October 17, 1975): 11.

15.1709   "One-Man Literacy Crusade." Life 26, (April 11, 1949): 74.

15.1710   Orata, P.T. "Paradox of Ignorance." School and Society 71,
           (June 10, 1950): 356-358.

15.1711   "Origins of Illiteracy." Times Educational Supplement 2183,
           (March 22, 1957): 382.

15.1712   Paiva, Vanilda Pereira. Paulo Freire e o Nacionalismo-
           Desenvolvimentista. Rio de Janeiro: Edicoes UFC, 1980.

15.1713   Powell, W.R. "Levels of Literacy." Journal of Reading 20,
           (March 1977): 488-492.

15.1714   Proceedings of The International Literacy Day Conference,
           Washington, D.C., September 8, 1978. Washington, D.C.:
           National Endowment For The Humanities, 1978.

15.1715   Read, M.H. "Dr. Frank Laubach, Literacy's Tireless Advocate."
           Times Educational Supplement 2207, (September 6, 1957): 1171.

15.1716   Reece, B.C. "High Cost of Illiteracy." School Life 34, (May 1952):
           115-116.

15.1717   "Research in Comparative Education; Literacy and Education for
           Adults." International Bureau of Education Bulletin 38, 3rd
           Quarter (1964): 150-152.

15.1718   Richardson, R.C. "How are Students Learning." Change 17,
           (May/June 1985): 42-49.

15.1719   "Rise in World Illiteracy." School & Society 93, (December 25,
           1965): 492.

15.1720   Roberts, Don. "Tomorrow's Illiterates." Library Trends 20,
           2(October 1971): 297-307.

15.1721   Rogers, C.S., and Wolfle, J.A. "Foundations For Literacy a
           Building Blocks Model." Young Children 36, (January 1981): 26-
           32.

15.1722   Rossman, M.H. "Recruiting Illiterates Via The Media." Adult
           Leadership 23, (January 1975): 223-224

15.1723   Rothenberg, J.G. "English Errors of Slow Learners." English
           Journal 32, (December 1943): 551-556.

15.1724   Roueche, S.D. "Literacy Development: Community College
           Task of The '80's." Community College Frontiers 9, (Winter
           1981): 41-45.

15.1725   Russell, W.F. "Shortages In Education In The Midst of Plenty."
           Teachers College Record 44, (November 1942): 75-83.

15.1726   Rytkheu, Y. "Leaping Over The Centuries." Soviet Literature,
           1(1978): 133-139.

15.1727   Sanghi, V. "My Revived Native Land." Soviet Literature,
           12(1977): 140-141.

15.1728   Scott, Jack. "Community Colleges: Vital Link in National
           Defense." Community Services Catalyst 18, 2(Spring 1988): 3-5.

15.1729   Scribner, S., and Cole, M. "Literacy Without Schooling: Testing
           For Intellectual Effects." Harvard Education Review 48,
           (November 1978): 448-461.

15.1730   Seidenfeld, M.A. "Illiteracy - Fact and Fiction." School & Society 58, (October 23, 1943): 330-332.

15.1731   Seidenfeld, M.A. "Care and Treatment of Language Deficiencies." In Handbook of Applied Psychology Volume 2, pp. 400-404. Edited by D.H. Fryer and E.R. Henry. N.P.: n.p., n.d.

15.1732   Serling, A.M. "Measurement of Public Literacy." College Board Review 114 (Winter 1979-1980): 26-29.

15.1733   Shack, S.F. "Tomorrow's Teacher - More Than a Craftsman." Manitoba Teacher 45, (March-April 1967): 9-11.

15.1734   "Shah of Iran Appeals To UN To Fight Illiteracy." School & Society 93, (December 11, 1965): 470.

15.1735   Shannon, L.W. "Underdeveloped Areas and Their Influence on Personal Development." The Journal of Negro Education 30, 4(Fall 1961): 386-395.

15.1736   Sheldon, W.D. "Literacy: A World Problem." International Reading Association Conference Papers 14, (1970): 291-297.

15.1737   Shenkman, H. "Reversing The Literacy Decline By Controlling The Electronic Demons." Educational Leadership 42, (February 1985): 26-29.

15.1738   Sisco, B. "Undereducated: Myth or Reality, The." Lifelong Learning 6, (April 1983): 14-15.

15.1739   Smalley, Frank Albert. Silent Ambassador; The Power of The Printed Page. London: United Society For Christian Literature, 1954.

15.1740   Smith, J.P. "Race and Human Capital." The American Economic Review 74, (September 1984): 685-698.

15.1741   Smith, L.L. "Literacy: Definitions and Implications." Language Arts 54, (February 1977): 135-138.

15.1742   Snowsell, Frank. "Literacy, Exams and Other Myths." B.C. Teacher 56, 3(January-February 1977): 102-103.

15.1743   Sochor, E. "International Campaign Against Illiteracy; World Congress of Ministers of Education on The Eradication of Illiteracy." School & Society 94, (February 5, 1966): 76.

15.1744   Sopher, D.E. "Temporal Disparity As A Measure of Change."
            Professional Geographer 31, (November 1979): 377-381.

15.1745   Southgate, Vera. "Backlash Against Illiteracy." Times
            Educational Supplement 2966, (March 24, 1972): 4.

15.1746   Spencer, Margaret. "Place of Literature in Literacy: 'Dip a Finger
            Into Fafnir'." English Quarterly 9, 4(Winter 1976-1977): 1-10.

15.1747   Spolsky, B. "Sociolinguistics 'of Literacy, Bilingual Education,
            and TESOL." TESOL Quarterly 16, (June 1982): 141-151.

15.1748   Stanley, M. "Literacy: The Crisis of a Conventional Wisdom."
            Convergence 6, 1(1973): 62-77.

15.1749   Stein, N.L., ed. "The Development of Literacy in The American
            Schools." (Symposium). American Journal of Education 93,
            (November 1984): 1-199.

15.1750   Stewart, C. "Challenge of Illiteracy." Illinois Teacher 19,
            (October 1930): 49.

15.1751   Strang, R.M. "Contribution of The Psychology of Reading To
            International Cooperation." School & Society 67, (January 31,
            1948): 65-68.

15.1752   "Symposium International pour L'aphabetisation: Declaration
            de Persepolis." Convergence 8, 4(1975): 8-10.

15.1753   Tenth Anniversary of The International Literacy Day, 8
            September 1975. National Committee For World Literacy
            Programme, Iran. Tehran: The Committee, 1975.

15.1754   Thant. "Toward World Literacy." School & Society 99,
            (Summer 1971): 282-283.

15.1755   Totten, W.F. "Conquering Illiteracy: A Responsibility of The
            Entire Society." American Secondary Education 7, (September
            1977): 28-31.

15.1756   Turner, S. "Illiteracy is on The Increase." Times Educational
            Supplement 2985, (August 4, 1972): 17.

15.1757   "UNESCO's Adult Literacy Program." School & Society 93,
            (January 9, 1965): 4.

15.1758   "UNESCO Seminar On Illiteracy." School & Society 70,
           (September 10, 1949): 172.

15.1759   "Urban and Rural Illiteracy." School & Society 32, (August 9,
           1930): 202.

15.1760   Vance, N.S. "Court Reinstates Lawsuit Against U. of Michigan
           By Illiterate Athlete Who Suffered Breakdown." Chronicle of
           Higher Education 26, (June 15, 1983): 17.

15.1761   Waldrep, Tom. "A New Model For Writing Centers.: Teaching
           English in The Two-Year College 8, 3(Spring 1982): 201-205.

15.1762   Walker, John. "Arguments Over Test . . . An Irrelevant Tempest
           In A Literary Teapot." ATA Magazine 57, 2(January 1977): 10-
           12.

15.1763   Wambach, Michel. "L'enseignement d'une langue (non-
           maternelle ou maternelle) aux apprenants en difficulte et aux
           enfants issues de milieux socialement de favorises."
           International Review of Education 32, 2(1986): 175-190.

15.1764   Wangoola, Paul. "The Political Economy of Illiteracy: A Global
           Analysis of Myth and Reality About its Eradication." Education
           With Production 3, 1(1984): 51-69.

15.1765   "War Against Ignorance." Times Educational Supplement 2496,
           (March 22, 1963): 574-575.

15.1766   "Wasteland: United States." Time 61, (March 30, 1953): 39.

15.1767   Watkins, B.T. "Scholars Increasingly Concerned About
           Deterioration of Literacy." Chronicle of Higher Education 21,
           (February 2, 1981): 3-4.

15.1768   Weeks, A.D. "Strange Ailment." Education 56, (February 1936):
           355-358.

15.1769   Weigl, E. "Zur Schriftsprache, Ihrem Erwerb und Ihren
           Alexisch-Agraphischen Storungen." Linguistics, 154-155 (June
           15, 1975): 137-160.

15.1770   "Will Industry Fill The Gap?" Economist 257, (November 1,
           1975): 31-32.

15.1771   Williams, J.D. "Literacy Crisis: A Time For Reevaluation."
College Board Review 119, (Spring 1981): 20-21.

15.1772   Witty, P.A. "Unfinished Business In Education." (In National
Congress of Parents and Teachers. Proceedings, 1946. pp. 25-29.).

15.1773   Witty, P.A. "Conquest of Illiteracy." School & Society 62, (July 7,
1945): 1-3.

15.1774   Witty, P.A., and Van Buskirk, G.M. "Beam In The Eye."
Childhood Education 21, (October 1944): 80-85.

15.1775   Wolf, Maryanne, et al., eds. Thought and Language/Language &
Reading. Cambridge, Massachusetts: Harvard Educational
Review, 1980.

15.1776   Wolfthal, M. "Reading Scores Revisited." Phi Delta Kappan 62,
(May 1981): 662-663.

15.1777   Woodring, P. "Let's Go Back To The Dictionary Definition:
Illiteracy is The Inability To Read and Write." Chronicle of
Higher Education 33, (May 6, 1987): 48.

15.1778   "World Problem of Illiteracy." Education Digest 38, (October
1972): 30-31.

15.1779   "World Problem of Illiteracy." NEA Research Bulletin 50, (May
1972): 53-58.

15.1780   Yesner, Seymour. "The Basics and The Basic Value of Human
Beings." English Journal 67, 1(January 1978): 15-17.

15.1781   Zirinsky, D. "Facing Our Own Literacy Crisis." English Journal
76, (December 1987): 61-62.

16

Illiterate Adults

16.1782   Altus, W.D., and Mahler, C.A. "Significance of Verbal Aptitude
           In The Type of Occupation Pursued By Illiterates" Journal of
           Applied Psychology 30, (April 1946): 155-160.

16.1783   Baumann, James F. "Coping With Reading Disability: Portrait
           of an Adult Disabled Reader." Journal of Reading 27, 6(March
           1984): 530-535.

16.1784   Becker, John T. "Language Experience Approach In A Job Corps
           Reading Lab." Journal of Reading 13, 4(January 1970): 281-284,
           319-321.

16.1785   Belz, Elaine. "Educational Therapy: A Model For The
           Treatment of Functionally Illiterate Adults." Adult Education
           Quarterly 35, 2(Winter 1984): 96-104.

16.1786   Bristow, Page Simpson, and Leslie, Lauren. "Indicators of
           Reading Difficulty: Discrimination Between Instructional - and
           Frustration - Range Performance of Functionally Illiterate
           Adults." Reading Research Quarterly 23, 2(Spring 1988): 200-
           218.

           Study to examine the validity of (1) accuracy in oral reading
           performance, and (2) comprehension as indicators to measure
           and ascertain difficulty in the learning to read process of
           functionally illiterate adults. Reviews the use of other indicators
           of difficulty such as (1) reading rate; (2) miscue quality; (3) self-
           correction; and (4) subjective ratings of difficulty. Asks the
           additional question of what variables are the best indicators of
           difficulty.

16.1787   Brown, Don A. "Variables Predictive of Success In Learning To Read." International Reading Association Conference Proceedings, Part 1, 13, (April 1968): 794-797.

16.1788   Brown, Don, and Newman, Annabel. "Attitudes of Materials and Educational Programs." Paper presented at the National Reading Conference, Tampa, Florida, 1967. ED 015 855.

16.1789   Burt, C.L. "Education of Illiterate Adults." British Journal of Educational Psychology 15, (February 1945): 20-27.

16.1790   Caldwell, Robert M. "Designing Effective Computer-Based Education To Teach Reading To Nonliterate Adults." Journal of Instructional Development 3, 4(Summer 1980): 16-18, 224.

16.1791   Carner, Richard L. "The Adult Dyslexic - - Dilemma and Challenge." International Reading Association Conference Proceedings, Part 3, 13, (April 1968): 22-28.

16.1792   Cass, Angelica Watson. "The Role of Television In Reaching Illiterate Adults With A Literacy Program Series." Ed.D. dissertation, Columbia University, 1969. 31/02-A, p 602.

16.1793   Clabby, John F., and Belz, Elaine Jacob. "Psychological Barriers to Learning: Approach Using Group Treatment." Small Group Behavior 16, 4(November 1985): 525-533.

16.1794   Cortright, Richard W. "A Study of Literacy Voter Tests." A paper prepared for the Workshop to Increase and Improve University teaching Training Programs In Adult Basic Education, 1969. ED 029 218.

16.1795   Cotterell, Arthur. "Adult Illiteracy - an Urgent Problem." Education & Training 17, (January/February 1975): 7-8.

16.1796   Cotton, Dorothy F. "CEP: Challenge To The New Education." Freedomways 9, 1(Winter 1969): 66-70.

16.1797   de Avila, Marcia. "Illiterate Adults and Readers: Their Exchange System." Adult Literacy and Basic Education 7, 3(1983): 117-128.

16.1798   Derbyshire, R.L. "Sociology of Exclusion: Implications For Teaching Adult Illiterates." Adult Education 17, (Autumn 1966): 3-11.

16.1799   Diehl, W.A., and Mikulecky, L. "Nature of Reading at Work."
           (Functional Reading Skills). Journal of Reading 24, (December
           1980): 221-227.

16.1800   Draper, James A. "Adult Illiteracy In Industrialized Countries:
           An International Focus." ASPBAE Courier, 43(July 1988): 4-7.

16.1801   Dymock, Darryl. "Adult Illiteracy In Perspective." Australian
           Journal of Reading 6, 3(August 1983): 108-116.

16.1802   Fagan, William T. "Concepts of Reading and Writing Among
           Low-Literate Adults." Reading Research and Instruction 27,
           4(Summer 1988): 47-60.

16.1803   Fingeret, Arlene. "Social Network: A New Perspective on
           Independence and Illiterate Adults." Adult Education Quarterly
           33, 3(Spring 1983): 133-146.

16.1804   Fitzgerald, L.A. "Programs For The Adult Illiterate in Selected
           Areas." Conference on Reading. University of Pittsburgh.
           Report 22, (1966): 162-167.

16.1805   Furter, Pierre. "Adult Education: Its Clients." Prospect 2,
           3(Autumn 1972): 314-320.

16.1806   Gilbert, Eleanor. "Attracting The Adult Illiterate." Canadian
           Library Journal 37, 4(August 1980): 271-272.

16.1807   Gold, Patricia Cohen, and Johnson, John A. "Prediction of
           Achievement in Reading, Self-Esteem, Auding, and Verbal
           Language by Adult Illiterates in a Psychoeducational Tutorial
           Program." Journal of Clinical Psychology 38, 3(July 1982): 513-
           522.

16.1808   Goodman, Ruth. "Motivating The ABE Student - Wilmington
           Project." Adult Leadership 17, 8(February 1969): 355-356.

16.1809   Hastings, Dorothy M.H. "Significant Assets of Effective Teachers
           of Adult Reading." Paper presented at International Reading
           Association Conference, Boston, Massachusetts, 1968. ED 025
           374.

16.1810   Hayes, Elisabeth R., and Darkenwald, Gordon G. "Participation
           In Basic Education: Deterents for Low-Literate Adults." Studies
           In The Education of Adults 20, 1(April 1988): 16-28.

16.1811   Hildick, E. W. "Reading Material For Illiterate Adults." Forward Trends In The Education of Backward Children 1, (July 1957): 109-112.

16.1812   Hill, Barry and Moorehead, Caroline. "The Making of Adult Illiterates." Times Educational Supplement 2941, (October 1, 1971): 4-5.

16.1813   Hinds, Lillian Ruth. "An Evaluation of Words In Color or Morphologico-Algebraic Approach to Teaching Reading To Functionally Illiterate Adults." Ph.D. dissertation, Case Western Reserve University, 1966. 28/08-A, p. 2973.

16.1814   Hunter, C.S., and Harman, D. "Dealing With Adult Illiteracy." USA Today 108, (December 1979): 8-9.

16.1815   Hutchison, L.F. "Relationship Between Expressed Interests and Reading Achievement in Functionally Illiterate Adults." Reading Improvement 15, (Fall 9178): 203-207.

16.1816   "Illiterate Adults and Readers: Their Exchange System." Adult Literacy and Basic Education 7, 3(1983): 117-128.

16.1817   Kamm, Margaret. "Adult Illiterates." Adult Education 40, (January 1968): 290-293.

16.1818   Keefe, Donald, and Meyer, Valerie. "Profiles of and Instructional Strategies For Adult Disabled Readers." Journal of Reading 31, 7 (April 1988): 614-619.

16.1819   Kerley, Richard. "The Adult Illiterate - Some Recent Research." Scottish Journal of Adult Education 2, 1(Autumn 1975): 9-14.

16.1820   Kozol, J. "Dehumanizing The Humanities: Scholars and Adult Illiteracy." Education Digest 51, (December 1985): 6-9.

Note: There are no citations with the numbers 1821 through 1920.

16.1921   Lasisi, M.J. "Influence of Reading Time and Reading Rate on Liberal and Interpretative Comprehension, The." Reading Improvement 20, (Fall 1983): 209-223.

16.1922   "Library and Adult Illiteracy: Symposium." Wilson Library Bulletin 40, (September 1965): 40-83.

16.1923   Long, Fern. Reading Centers Project. Final Report. Cleveland, Ohio: Cleveland Public Library, Adult Education Department, 1967. ED 023 430.

16.1924   MacDonald, B. "Libraries and Literacy Activities; Exerpts From Report of The Sutdy of Services To Adult Illiterates." Wilson Library Bulletin 40, (September 1965): 48-50.

16.1925   MacDonald, Bernice. Literacy Activities In Public Libraries, A Report of A Study of Services To Adult Illiterates. Chicago: American Library Association, 1966. ED 010 855.

16.1926   Mace, Jane. "Blaming The Victim." Times Educational Supplement (London) 3131, (1975): 18-19.

16.1927   Malicky, Grace, and Norman, Charles A. "Reading Strategies of Adult Illiterates." Journal of Reading 25, 8(May 1982): 731-735.

16.1928   Maxwell, G.L. "Federal Aid For The Education of Adult Illiterates." National Education Association Proceedings 1942: 92.

16.1929   McCallan, Norma J. "What State Libraries Can Do To Eliminate Illiteracy." Catholic Library World 52, 2(September 1980): 71-74.

16.1930   Morris, Joyce. "The Problem of Adult Illiteracy." Books, 18 and 19 (Spring and Summer 1975): 47-54.

16.1931   Munns, Kenneth L. "Why Can't Johnny's Parents Read?" Reading Improvement 19, 2(Summer 1982): 144-148.

16.1932   Norris, B. "Adult Illiteracy: Movement But No Action Yet From Bennett." Times Educational Supplement 3625, (December 20, 1985): 10.

16.1933   O'Connor, Aleda. "Illiterate Adult's Second Chance." Reporter 7, 5(February 1982): 22-24.

16.1934   Olsen, J.T. "Instructional Materials for Functionally Illiterate Adults." Phi Delta Kappan 46, (May 1965): 450-452.

16.1935   Rigg, Pat, and Taylor, Liz. "A Twenty-One-Year-Old Begins to Read." English Journal 68, 3(March 1979): 52-56.

16.1936   Risman, Ann. "Adult Illiterate Students." Studies in Adult Education 7, (October 1975): 142-149.

16.1937   Sarkisian, Ellen. "Now I Know What The Story is About." English Education 8, 2(Winter 1977): 95-102.

16.1938   Sawford-Hanger, Barrie. "Curing The Grownup Illiterate."
           Times Educational Supplement 2890, (October 9, 1970): 23.

16.1939   Schneiderman, P. "Active Reading Techniques System (ARTS):
           A Method For Instruction of Functionally Illiterate Adults."
           Urban Education 13, (July 1985): 195-202.

16.1940   Smith, James L. "Motivating The Illiterate Adult." Adult
           Leadership 23, 11(May 1975): 342-344.

16.1941   Staples, Peter, and Gardner, John. "Illiterates Anonymous."
           Teacher 22, 2(January 12, 1973): 3.

16.1942   Stevens, Larry P., and Piland, William E. "Adult Illiteracy and
           The Role of The Community College." Community College
           Review 15, 3(Winter 1987): 48-54.

16.1943   Studebaker, J.W. "Our Lost Legions." Adult Education Bulletin
           7, (October 1942): 8-13.

16.1944   "UNESCO Plan to Cut Adult Literacy." School & Society 90.
           (November 3, 1962): 369.

16.1945   Veri, Clive C. "A Bill of Rights For Functionally Illiterate
           Adults." Adult Leadership 22, 5(November 1973): 164-168.

16.1946   Versluys, J.D.N. "Why Do You Want To Read?" Prospects 2,
           2(Summer 1972): 202-205.

16.1947   Wangberg, Elaine G. "An Interactive, Language Experience
           Based Microcomputer Approach to Reduce Adult Illiteracy."
           Lifelong Learning 9, 5(February 1986): 8-12.

16.1948   Williams, Paul. "Now Teachers Are Training Tutors For The
           Illiteracy Battle." Teacher 27, 6(August 8, 1975): 3.

16.1949   Wolf, Evelyn, and Havanagh, Catherine. "Adult Illiteracy: A
           Public Library Responds." Catholic Library World 55, 3(October
           1983): 125-128.

16.1950   Wood, J. "Teaching The Illiterate Adult." Oregon Education 44,
           (March 1970): 9.

17

Job Literacy

17.1951   Adams, Roy J. "The Functionally Illiterate Worker and Public Policy." TESL Talk 13, 4(Fall 1982): 9-16.

17.1952   Auten, Anne. "ERIC/RCS: The Challenge: Job Literacy in The 1980's" Journal of Reading 23, 8(May 1980): 750-754.

17.1953   Chang, Kathryn L. "Occupational Literacy: Án Overview." Lifelong Learning 11, 1(September 1987): 19-22.

17.1954   Cornell, R. "Characteristics of Effective Occupational Literacy Programs." Journal of Reading 31, (April 1988): 654-656.

17.1955   Drotning, John E., et al. Jobs, Education, and Training; Research of A Project Combining On-The-Job and Literacy Training For The Disadvantaged. Buffalo, New York: State University of New York at Buffalo, Department of Industrial Relations, 1969. ED 030 823.

17.1956   Edgerton, H.A., and Blum, M.L. "Technique To Determine Illiteracy-Literacy Requirements of Jobs." Personnel and Guidance Journal 32, (May 1954): 524-527.

17.1957   Faigley, Lester, and Miller, Thomas P. "What We Learn From Writing on The Job." College English 44, 6(October 1982): 555-569.

17.1958   "Functional Literacy and Language Demands on Apprentices." Australian Journal of Reading 2, 4(November 1979): 211-219.

17.1959   Given, Naomi. "A Report From The Field: Literacy in Eight New Jersy Corporations." Teaching English in the Two-Year College 9, 1(Fall 1982): 57-60.

17.1960   Greenfield, Stuart. The Human Capital Model and American Youths: The Role of Schooling, Experience and Functional Literacy. Final Report, August 1, 1979 to September 30, 1980. Washington, D.C.: National Institute of Education, 1980. ED 195 772.

17.1961   Gupta, N.R. "Work Based Literacy - The Banwasi Sewa Ashram Project." Indian Journal of Adult Education 34, 1(January 1973): 2-4.

17.1962   Hannan, R., and Learmont, J. Relationships Among Apprentices' Backgrounds, Literacy Levels and Numeracy Skills. Hawthorn, Australia: Swinburne Technical College, 1980.

17.1963   Horne, G. Porter. Functional Job Literacy: Implications For Instruction. Wellesley, Massachusetts: Commonwealth Center For High Technology/Education, 1979.

17.1964   Hull, William L., and Sechler, Judith A. Adult Literacy: Skills For The American Work Force. Research and Development Series No. 265B. Columbus, Ohio: Ohio State University, 1987. ED 284 980.

17.1965   Inter-Agency Meeting On Work-Oriented Literacy. Final Report. Paris: UNESCO, 1971. ED 051 484.

17.1966   Kallaus, Norman F. "Developing Office Literacy." Business Education Forum 42, 2(November 1987): 14-15.

17.1967   Kirsch, Irwin, and Guthrie, John. Reading Practices of Adults In One High Technology Company. Reading Competencies and Practices. Technical Report #6. Newark, Delaware: International Reading Association, 1983. ED 265 512.

17.1968   Kirsch, Irwin, and Guthrie, John. Case Studies of Reading In A High Technology Corporation. Reading Competencies and Practices. Technical Report #2. Newark, Delaware: International Reading Association, 1982. ED 265 509.

17.1969   Kokes, Loralyn B. "Reading Program Helps Employees Step Ahead." Journal of Reading 20, 5(February 1977): 364-367.

17.1970   Lee, Chris. "Literacy Training: A Hidden Need." Training 23, 9(September 1986): 64-68, 71-72.

17.1971   McFann, Howard H. "HumRRO Research and Project 100,000."
           Paper presented at American Psychological Association
           Convention, Miami, Florida, 1970. ED 050 314.

17.1972   Mealyea, R. "Apprentice Literacy - 'Reading': The Role of The
           Trade Teacher." Human Resource Management Australia 19,
           3(November 1981): 45-55.

17.1973   Mealyea, R. Reading: The Role of The Trade Teacher,
           Apprentice Literacy. Melbourne: Education Department, 1981.

17.1974   Mealyea, R.J. Readability: Concept and Measurement;
           Apprentices and Literacy. Melbourne: Education Department,
           Technical Schools Division, 1979.

17.1975   Meyers, Gertrude S. "Written Language Skills and Job
           Opportunity: A Model For The High School Curriculum."
           Illinois Schools Journal 58, 3(Fall 1978): 3-12.

17.1976   Mikulecky, Larry. "Preparing Students For Workplace Literacy
           Demands." Journal of Reading 28, 3(December 1984): 253-257.

17.1977   Mikulecky, Larry. "Job Literacy: The Relationship Between
           School Preparations and Workplace Actuality." Reading
           Research Quarterly 17, 3(1982): 400-419.

17.1978   Mikulechy, Larry. "The Mismatch Between School Training and
           Job Literacy Demands." Vocational Guidance Quarterly 30,
           2(December 1981): 174-180.

           Study examining the literacy skills required in the workplace
           and those found in the schools. Results indicate that the literacy
           demands and competencies asked of a worker are greater than
           those asked of students in school. Stresses that the findings can
           help job counselors and personnel directors design appropriate
           training programs. Argues that job preparation should be one
           goal of the school curriculum.

17.1979   Mikulecky, Larry, and Diehl, William. "Reading For Vocational
           Literacy." VocEd 58, 5(August 1983): 34-35.

17.1980   Mikulecky, Larry, and Diehl, William. Job Literacy: A Study of
           Literacy Demands, Attitudes, and Strategies In A Cross Section of
           Occupations. Bloomington, Indiana: Indiana University, 1980.
           ED 189 313.

17.1981   Mikulecky, Larry, and Diehl, William. Literacy Requirements in
           Business and Industry. Washington, D.C.: National Institute of
           Education, 1979. ED 186 867.

17.1982   Mikulecky, Larry, and Diehl, William. National Literacy
           Comissions and Functional Literacy: A Status Report. N.P.:
           n.p., 1978. ED 188 117.

17.1983   Murphy, Brian P. "Changes in The Workplace: Preparing
           Workers For Continuing Employability." Journal of Industrial
           Teacher Education 23, 1(Fall 1985): 19-25.

17.1984   Nasution, Amir H. Functional-Literacy: A Method of
           Vocational Training For Farmers-Workers: International
           Literacy Day, 1972. Ibadan, Nigeria: Ibadan University, Institute
           of African Adult Education, 1972. ED 065 776.

17.1985   Noe, Katherine Schlick. "Technical Reading Technique: A
           Briefcase Reading Strategy." Journal of Reading 27, 3(December
           1983): 234-237.

17.1986   O'Donnell, Holly. "ERIC/RCS: Striving For Functional Literacy
           in The Job Market." Journal of Reading 29, 1(October 1985): 74-
           76.

17.1987   Park, Rosemarie J. "Overcoming The Illiteracy Barrier."
           Training and Development Journal 38, 3(March 1984): 77-80.

17.1988   Robinson, Sandra Faye. "Literacy Training In The Workplace: A
           Case Study of Two Utility Companies (Basic Skills, Remedial, Job
           Training)." Ed.D. dissertation, The American University, 1986.
           47/05-A, p. 1574.

17.1989   Rush, R. Timothy. "Job Skills: Basic Literacy and Related
           Competencies." Adult Literacy and Basic Education 9, 1(1985):
           35-44.

17.1990   Rush, R. Timothy, et al. Occupational Literacy Education.
           Newark, Delaware: International Reading Association, 1986.

17.1991   Saunders, J.M., and Smith, C.J. The Croydon Park College
           Intervention Programme: A Report On The Introduction and
           Continuing Development of An Intervention Programme For
           Academically 'At Risk' Apprentices at Croydon Park College.
           Adelaide, Australia: Department of Further Education, 1979.

17.1992   Seifert, Mary. "Research: Reading on The Job." Journal of
           Reading 22, 4(January 1979): 360-362.

17.1993   Sticht, Thomas G., and Kern, Richard P. "Project Realistic:
           Determining Literacy Demands of Jobs." Journal of Reading
           Behavior 2, 3(Summer 1970): 191-212.

17.1994   Sticht, Thomas G., and Mickulecky, Larry. Job-Related Basic
           Skills: Cases and Conclusions. Washington, D.C.: National
           Institute of Education, 1984. ED 246 312.

17.1995   Submission To Standing Committee on Education Inquiry: The
           Effectiveness of Australian Schools In Preparing Young People
           For The Work Force, With Particular Emphasis on Literacy and
           Numeracy. Mount Gambier, Australia: South East Community
           College, 1979.

17.1996   Torrence, David R., and Torrence, Jo Ann. "Training in The
           Face of Illiteracy." Training and Development Journal 41,
           8(August 1987): 44-48.

18

Literacy

18.1997   Acquisition of Literacy, The. N.P.: n.p., 1986.

18.1998   Adiseshiah, Malcolm S. "Literacy's Functionality To The Fight For Social Justice." Convergence 8, 4(1975): 23-27.

18.1999   Adler, Sol, ed. Cultural Language Differences: Their Educational & Clinical - Professional Implications. Springfield, Illinois: Charles C. Thomas, Publisher, 1985.

18.2000   "After Tokyo." Convergence 4, 4(1972): n.p.

18.2001   Agee, Jane M. "The Realities of College Composition Courses." English Journal 66, 8(November 1977): 58-60.

18.2002   Allen, James E., Jr. "Ther Right To Read - Target For The 70's." Journal of Reading 13, 2(November 1969): 95-101.

18.2003   Allen, Lee E. "Beyond Basics: JH/MS Idea Factory." English Journal 67, 4(April 1978): 84-86.

18.2004   Allen, Sheilan, and Matheson, Joyce. "The Two Faces of Literacy." Paper presented at The Annual Meeting of the International Reading Association, Transmountain Regional Conference. Vancouver: n.p., 1977. ED 154 351.

18.2005   Amoroso, H.C., Jr., "Conversations With A New Literate." Journal of Reading 29, (March 1986): 484-488.

18.2006   Anson, Brian. "Grand Design That Should Go Back To The Drawing Board." Times Educational Supplement 441, (April 17, 1981): 10-11.

18.2007   "Apocalypse Now." College Canada 5, 3(March 1980): 4-5.

18.2008   Aristides. "Marboro County." American Scholar 46, 4(Autumn 1977): 432-440.

18.2009   Arnett, John. "The Importance of Being Literate." Adult Education 60, 4(March 1988): 341-343.

18.2010   Aronowitz, Stanley. "Toward Redefining Literacy." Social Policy 12, 2(September-October 1981): 53-55.

18.2011   Aston, M. "Lollardy and Literacy." History 62, (October 1977): 347-371.

18.2012   Atwell, Nancie. "Writing and Reading Literature From The Inside Out." Language Arts 61, 3(March 1984): 240-252.

18.2013   Baijens, J.M. "Equipment: A New Tool." Literacy Discussion 1, 2(Spring 1970): 73-75.

18.2014   Baker, Gwendolyn Calvert. "Recognition of Our Culturally Pluralistic Society and Multicultural Education in Our Schools." Education and Society 1, 1(Spring 1988): 23-24, 26-28.

18.2015   Banks, James A. "Education, Citizenship, and Cultural Options." Education and Society 1, 1(Spring 1988): 19-22.

18.2016   Barbour, Thomas. The Road To Nowhere. N.P.: n.p., 1979.

18.2017   Barclay, D.J., ed. Notes On The Future of Education. Volume II, Issue 1, Fall 1970. Syracuse, New York: Educational Policy Research Center, 1970. ED 046 681.

18.2018   Bastian, Ann, et al. "Choosing Equality: The Case For Democratic Schooling." Social Policy 15, 4(Spring 1985): 34-51.

18.2019   Baucom, Kenneth L. The ABC's of Literacy: Lessons From Linguistics. Amersham: Hutton For The International Institute For Adult Literacy Methods, 1978.

18.2020   Behavior Modification. N.P.: International Symposium on Behavior Modification, 8th, Caracas, 1978, 1981.

18.2021   Belanger, Paul. "Lire et ecrire: Un droit." l'ICEA 4, 2(December 1980): 9.

18.2022   Bellonde, Guy. "Literacy for What?" CASME Journal 1, 2(February/March 1981): 21-25.

18.2023   Bennett, Adrian T. "Discourses of Power The Dialectics of Understanding, The Power of Literacy." Journal of Education 165, 1(Winter 1983): 53-74.

18.2024   Benschoten, J.A. "Just To Read and Write!" World's Work 59, (December 1930): 77-80.

18.2025   Berg, P.C. "Who Is Literate?" Compact 13, (Summer 1979): 11-13.

18.2026   Berggen, Carol, and Berggen, Lars. The Literacy Process: A Practice In Domestication or Liberation. London: Writers and Readers Publishing Cooperative, 1975.

18.2027   Berland, Jody, and McGee, Diane. "The Literacy Crisis: Beyond Banality and 'Basics' and Down To Business." This Magazine 12, 1(March 1978): 12-14.

18.2028   Berman, Bennett H. "Training for Invisibility." NSPI Journal 19, 3(April 1980): 16-18, 21.

18.2029   Beswick, Joan. "Language and The Hearing Impaired Student." A.C.E.H.I. Journal 10, 3(Winter 1984): 149-156.

18.2030   Bhola, H.S. "Destined For Literacy." Educational Horizons 66, 1(Fall 1987): 9-12.

18.2031   Bhola, H.S. The Promise of Literacy. N.P.: n.p., 1983.

18.2032   Bhola, Herbans S. "Why Literacy Can't Wait: Issues For The 1980's" Convergence 14, 1(1981): 6-23.

18.2033   Biggs, Bernice Prince. "Literacy and Higher Education." Phi Delta Kappan 52, 8(April 1971): 476-478.

18.2034   Bizzell, P. "Arguing About Literacy." College English 50, (February 1988): 141-153.

18.2035   Blau, S. "Literacy Crisis." Center Magazine 14, (January/February 1981): 38-39.

18.2036   Blau, Sherican D. "Commentary: Literacy As A Form Of Courage." Journal of Reading 25, 2(November 1981): 101-105.

18.2037   Boomer, G. Fair Dinkum Teaching and Learning: Reflections on Literacy and Power. Upper Montclair, New Jersey: Boynton/Cook, 1985.

18.2038   Boomer, Garth. "Literacy, Power, and The Community." Language Arts 61, 6(October 1984): 575-584.

18.2039   Bormuth, J.R. "Reading Literacy: Its Definition and Assessment." Reading Research Quarterly 9(1973): 7-66.

18.2040   Bormuth, John R. "Value and Volume of Literacy." Visible Language 12, 2(Spring 1978): 118-161.

18.2041   Botel, Morton. "Book Commentary: Becoming a Nation of Readers: A Review." Reading Teacher 39, 3(December 1985): 260-262.

18.2042   Bou, I. Rodriguez. "Pointers On Literacy." School & Society 77, (January 10, 1953): 19-22.

18.2043   Bourgeois, Denis. "La boite a lettres ou l'absurdite d'alphabetiser des jeunes de 20 ans." Apprentissage et socialization en piste 8, 3(September 1985): 55-57.

18.2044   Bowers, J. "Mass Literacy: A World Problem." Visual Education (August/September 1972): 78-82.

18.2045   Bowers, John. "Literacy and The Media: An Overview." MED: Media in Education and Development 16, 1(March 1983): 2-4.

18.2046   Boyd, Robert D. The Psychological and Mythmaking Phenomena In Visual Symbolization of Adult Illiterates. Report From The Adult Re-education Project. Madison, Wisconsin: University of Wisconsin, Research and Development Center For Cognitive Learning, 1969. ED 034 962.

18.2047   Boyer, Ernest L. "The Time Has Come - School Reform: Completing The Course." NASSP Bulletin 72, 504 (January 1988): 61-68.

18.2048   Boyer, Ernest L. "Communication: Message Senders and Receivers." Communication Education 27, 4(November 1978): 271-276.

18.2049   Brickman, W.W. "Literacy Is Not Enough." School & Society 78, (November 28, 1953): 171-172.

18.2050   Brock, Christine. "Breaking The Failure Barrier." Australian
           Journal of Reading 6, 3(August 1983): 105-107.

18.2051   Brodkey, Linda. "Topics of Literacy." Journal of Education 168,
           2(1986): 47-54.

18.2052   Brooks, Ellen J. Learning To Read and Write: The Role of
           Language Acquisition & Aesthetic Development. New York:
           Garland Publishing, 1986.

18.2053   Brown, David L., and Briggs, L.D. "Collaborative Learning :
           Bridging The Gap Between Reading and Writing." Reading
           Improvement 24, 4(Winter 1987): 278-281.

18.2054   Brown, Rexford. Contributions of The National Assessment To
           Understanding The Problems of Literacy and Equity. Denver,
           Colorado: Education Commission of The States, 1980. ED 192
           294.

18.2055   Bruder, I. "Ed Schools: Literacy Requirements Stagnant, But
           More Offer Degrees." Electronic Learning 7, (April 1988): 18-19.

18.2056   Bruner, Jerome S. "Pre-Convention Spotlight." Journal of
           Reading 15, 5(February 1972): 328-329.

18.2057   Bruss, Neal, and Macedo, Donaldo P. "A Conversation With
           Paulo Freire At The University of Massachusetts at Boston."
           Journal of Education 166, 3(Fall 1984): 215-225.

18.2058   Buchanan, D.W. "Two Visions of Literacy." English Quarterly
           10, 2(Summer 1977): 73-75.

18.2059   Bulcock, Jeffrey W., and Beebe, Mona, Jo "Some Common
           Causes of Literacy and Numeracy." Canadian Journal of
           Education 6, 3(1981): 19-44.

18.2060   Bundy, Robert F. "Coming Changes in Learning, Leisure, and
           Literacy." Momentum 13, 1(February 1982): 15-17.

18.2061   Burnett, David, and Whatley, A., eds. Language and Literacy:
           The Public Library Role - Conference Proceedings. Birmingham,
           England: Library Association, 1981.

18.2062   Burrows, Julie, and Prescott, Lynda. "Reading Skills: The Key
           To Successful Study." Adult Education (London) 59, 4(March
           1987): 310-316.

18.2063   Butterfield, K.L. "Toward A Literate Rural World." Journal of
           Adult Education 4, (October 1932): 383-8.

18.2064   Cairns, Len. "From Teaching Skills to Seeking Sense."
           Australian Journal of Reading 8, 2(June 1985): 71-76.

18.2065   Caldwell, Bettye M. "Bi-Directionality in Education."
           Educational Forum 50, 3(Spring 1986): 295-297.

18.2066   Calfee, Robert C. "The School as a Context For Assessment of
           Literacy." Reading Teacher 40, 8(April 1987): 738-743.

18.2067   Cameron, Ralph F., et al. "Aphasia and Literacy." British
           Journal of Disorders of Communication 6, 2(October 1971): 161-
           163.

18.2068   Campaine, B.M. "New Literacy." Daedalus 112, (Winter 1983):
           129-142.

18.2069   Campbell, Roald F. "Reading Achievement and Public Policy."
           Journal of Reading 21, 8(May 1978): 685-687.

18.2070   Carnovsky, L. "Toward World Literacy." Wilson Library
           Bulletin 39, (June 1965): 887-895.

18.2071   Cashdan, Asher. Literacy. New York: Basil Blackwell, Inc.,
           1985.

18.2072   Cassidy, Jack, and Shanahan, Timothy. "Survival Skills: Some
           Considerations." Journal of Reading 23, 2(November 1979):
           136-140.

18.2073   Castell, Suzanne De., ed Literacy, Society and Schooling: A
           Reader. Cambridge: Cambridge University Press, 1986.

18.2074   Chall, Jeanne S. "Literacy: Trends and Explanations." American
           Education 20, 9(November 1984): 16-22.

18.2075   Chambers, Aidan. "The Making of a Literary Reader." Horn
           Book Magazine 51, 3(June 1975): 301-310.

18.2076   Christianson, P. "Chaucer's Literacy." Chaucer Review 11, (Fall
           1986): 112-127.

18.2077   Ciancio, J. "Literacy: The Basic Skill." Vocational Education
           Journal 63, (March 1988): 41-42.

18.2078   Clark, R.A. "Definitions of Literacy: Implications for Policy and Proctice." Adult Literacy and Basic Education 8, 3(1984): 133-146.

18.2079   Coleman, Elizabeth. "On Redefining The Baccalaureate Degree." Nursing and Health Care 7, 4(April 1986): 192-196.

18.2080   Collins, Patrick M. "Toward Dramatic Literacy: A Position Paper." Children's Theatre Review 34, 4(October 1985): 3-6.

18.2081   Comprehending Oral and Written Language. N.P.: n.p., 1987.

18.2082   Cook, David R.S. "Student Writing: It Is Dissolving Into The New Literacy." English Quarterly 8, 3(Fall 1975): 33-40.

18.2083   Copperman, Paul. "The Decline of Literacy." Journal of Communication 30, 1(Winter 1980): 113-122.

18.2084   Corbett, Edward P.J. "The Demands For And Of Literacy." English Quarterly 15, 3(October 1982): 5-13.

18.2085   Corder, Reginald. "Project III: The Information Base For Reading." Reading Teacher 25, 2(November 1971): 154-156.

18.2086   Couder, Bruno. Maintenant Lire n'est plus un probleme pour moi. N.P.: n.p., 1983.

18.2087   Cowan, George M. The Word That Kindles. N.P.: n.p., 1979.

18.2088   Cox, Vivian Elaine Lewis. "Reciprocal Oracy/Literacy Recognition Skills In The Language Production of Language Experience Approach Students." Ed.D. dissertation, The University of Arizona, 1971. 32/06A, p. 2905

18.2089   "Crisis in Literacy." Center Magazine 13, (November 1980): 54-61.

18.2090   Crosby, Muriel. "Reading and Literacy In The Education of The Disadvantaged." Reading Teacher 19(October 1965): 18-22.

18.2091   Crowther, Shirley. "Language and Literature for Life." British Journal of Language Teaching 24, 1(Spring 1986): 46-52, 55.

18.2092   Cunningham, Clifford. "Breakthrough To Literacy." Reading 5, 1(March 1971): 23-30.

18.2093   Dahile, Hallvard. "University Professor Looks At The Literacy Issue." ATA Magazine 57, 4(April 1977): 40-42.

18.2094   Dale, Edgar. "Things To Come: The New Literacy." Theory Into Practice 9, 2(April 1970): 131-138.

18.2095   Dauzat, Sam V., and Dauzat, JoAnn. "Literacy: In Quest Of A Definition." Adult Literacy and Basic Education 1, 1(Spring 1977): 1-5.

18.2096   DeCastell, Suzanne, et al., eds. Literacy, Society, and Schooling. New York: Cambridge University Press, 1986.

18.2097   DeCastell, Suzanne, et al. "On Defining Literacy." Canadian Journal of Education 6, 3(1981): 7-18.

18.2098   Deford, Diane E. "Literacy: Reading, Writing and Other Essentials." Language Arts 58, 6(September 1981): 652-658.

18.2099   DeJesus, Susan E. Bangs. "Literacy and The Home: A True Story." Language Arts 62, 8(December 1985): 845-847.

18.2100   Devereux, Bill. "A Remarkable Enterprise." Special Education: Forward Trends 6, 1(March 1979): 30-32.

18.2101   Dewar, Diana. "Now Read On." Education Guardian, (February 17, 1981): 11.

18.2102   Discourses In Reading and Linguistics. N.P.: n.p., 1984.

18.2103   Douglass, Malcolm P., ed. Claremont Reading Conference Forty-Forth Yearbook: Reading: A Humanizing Experience; Proceedings of The Claremont Reading Conference (47th, Claremont, California, January 18-19, 1980). Claremont, California: Claremont Graduate School, 1980. ED 191 010.

18.2104   Douglass, Malcolm P., ed. Claremont Reading Conference 41st Yearbook: All Things Considered . . .;Proceedings of The Claremont Reading Conference (44th, Claremont, California, January 1977). Claremont, California: Claremont Graduate School, 1977. ED 170 719.

18.2105   Dudley-Marling, C.C. and Phodes L.K. "Pragmatics and Literacy." Language, Speech, and Hearing Services in Schools 18,(January 1987): 41-52.

18.2106   Dumont, Bernard. "After Literacy, Teaching: Paradoxes of Post-Literacy Work." Prospects: Quarterly Review of Education 9, 2(1979): 145-158.

18.2107   Dunning, Stephen. "The Public and English Teachers: An Adversary Relationship." English Journal 64, 6(September 1975): 9.

18.2108   Early, Katherine. "Late Blooming Is Better Than No Blooming At All." Journal of Developmental and Remedial Education 7, 2(Winter 1984): 20-21.

18.2109   Edwards, Bruce L. A Rhetoric of Reading. N.P.: n.p., 1986.

18.2110   Egan, Kieran. "Literacy and The Oral Foundations of Education." Harvard Educational Review 57, 4(November 1987): 445-472.

18.2111   Eisenberg, Leon. "Reading Retardation: I. Psychiatric and Sociologic Aspects." Pediatrics 37, 2(February 1966): n.p. ED 034 651.

18.2112   Eisner, Elliot W. "The Celebration of Thinking." National Forum: Phi Kappa Phi Journal 68, 2(Spring 1988): 30-33.

18.2113   Eldridge, Carlton. "Braille Literacy and Higher Education." Education of The Visually Handicapped II, 1(Spring 1979): 8-12.

18.2114   Elerian, Abdullah Firky. "Programmed Learning: A Study In Literacy." Programmed Learning and Educational Technology 15, 1(February 1978): 69-78.

18.2115   Elgin, S.H. "Reading Literacy Crisis." Change 10, (November 1978): 10-11.

18.2116   Elsasser, Nan, and John-Steiner, Vera P. "An Interactionist Approach To Advancing Literacy." Harvard Educational Review 47, 3(1977): 355-369.

18.2117   Emergent Literacy. N.P.: n.p., 1986.

18.2118   Enos, Theresa. "Concentric Circles of Identification: Writing About Writing." Teaching English in The Two-Year College 13, 2(May 1986): 98-100.

18.2119   "Environmental Study." Literacy Discussion 1, 4(Autumn 1970): 73-102.

18.2120   Epstein, Donald B. Community Colleges and Literacy. New York: Andrew W. Mellon Foundation, 1978. ED 158 817.

18.2121   Erikson, Frederick. "School Literacy, Reasoning, and Civility: An Anthropologist's Perspective." Review of Educational Research 54, 4(Winter 1984): 525-546.

18.2122   Experimental World Literacy Programme. N.P.: n.p., 1976.

18.2123   Family Life and Literacy. Tehran: International Institute For Adult Literacy Methods, 1972.

18.2124   Farr, Roger. "IRA's Silver Anniversary 1980: 25 Years of Accomplishment in Reading." Reading Teacher 33, 8(May 1980): 904-906.

18.2125   Farr, Roger. Reading. N.P.: n.p., 1981.

18.2126   Farrell, Thomas J. "Literacy, The Basics, and All That Jazz.' College English 38, 5(January 1977): 443-459.

18.2127   Farrell, Thomas J. "Open Admissions, Orality, and Literacy." Journal of Youth and Adolescence 3, 3(September 1974): 247-260.

18.2128   Feitelson, Dina, ed. Mother Tongue or Second Language? Newark, Delaware: International Reading Association, 1979.

18.2129   Ferreiro, Emilia. Proceso de Alfabetizacion, La Alfabetizacion en Proceso. N.P.: n.p., 1986.

18.2130   Fielden, John S., and Dulek, Ronald E. What Do Ya Mean I Can't Write? Englewood Cliffs, New Jersey: Prentice-Hall, Inc., 1983.

18.2131   "First IRA Literacy Award 1979." Journal of Reading 23, 5(February 1980): 397-400.

18.2132   Flores, Barbara M., and Garcia, Erninda A. "A Collaborative Learning and Teaching Experience Using Journal Writing." NABE: The Journal for The National Association For Bilingual Education 8, 2(Winter 1984): 67-83.

18.2133   Fobes, John E. "A Turning Point For Literacy: The Changing Response of The World Community." Prospects 6, (1976): 121-126.

18.2134   Foden, Frank. "Literacy in Further Education." Liberal Education, 33-34 (1978): 12-19.

18.2135   Forbes, Jack E. "Some Thoughts on 'Minimal Competencies.'" Mathematics Teacher 71, 2(February 1978): 94-100.

18.2136   Forest, Marsha. "Quoi de neuf dens le monde de l'education?" Deficience Mentale 33, 2(Spring 1983): 46-48.

18.2137   France, M.G., and Meeks, J. W. "Parents Who Can't Read: What Schools Can Do." Education Digest 53, (April 1988): 46-49.

18.2138   Freire, Paulo. Literacy. N.P.: n.p., 1987.

18.2139   Freire, Paulo. The Politics of Education. N.P.: n.p., 1985.

18.2140   Freire, Paulo. "Literacy and The Possible Dream." Prospects 6, (1976): 68-71.

18.2141   Freire, Paulo, and Macedo, Donaldo. Literacy: Reading The Word & The World. South Hadley, Massachusetts: Gergin & Garvey, 1987.

18.2142   Fugelsang, Andreas, and Chandler, Dale. "The Leap To Literacy." Convergence 19, 1(1986): 48-52.

18.2143   Furter, Pierre. "Contribution A L'Etude De L'analphabetisme." International Review of Education 11,(1965): 267-284.

18.2144   Gadsby, David. "Dinosaurs and Roundabouts." School Librarian 24, (June 1976): 101-108.

18.2145   Gardner, John. "The Literacy Bogy." Education & Training 14, (March 1972): 92-93.

18.2146   Garforth, Chris. "Who Do You Think You're Talking To?" MED: Media In Education and Development 16, 1(March 1983): 9-12.

18.2147   Gates, H.L. "Editor's Introduction: Writing 'Race' and The Difference It Makes." Critical Inquiry 12, (Autumn 1985): 1-20 Discussion 13, (Autumn 1986): 197-200, 203-210.

18.2148   Gates, H.L. "James Gronniosaw and The Trope of The Talking Book." Southern Review 22, (April 1986): 252-272.

18.2149   Gibson, Walker." Writing Programs and The Department of English." ADE Bulletin, 60(February 1979): 19-22.

18.2150   Gilham, Bruce, ed. The Language of School Subjects. Portsmouth, New Hampshire: Heinemann Educational Books, Inc., 1986.

18.2151   Gillete, Arthur. "Youth, Literacy and Participation." International Review of Education 31, 4(1985): 373-396.

18.2152   Gilmore, Perry. "'Gimme Room': School Resistance, Attitudes, and Access to Literacy." Journal of Education 167, 1(1985): 111-128.

18.2153   Giroux, Henry A. "Literacy and The Pedagogy of Voice and Political Empowerment." Educational Theory 38, 1(Winter1988): 61-75.

18.2154   Giroux, Henry A. "Mass Culture and The Rise of The New Illiteracy: Implications For Reading." Interchange on Educational Policy 10, 4(1979-1980): 89-98.

18.2155   Glaser, Susan M., and Searfoss, Lyndon W. Reading Diagnosis & Instruction: A C-A-L-M Approach. Englewood Cliffs, New Jersey: Prentice-Hall, Inc., 1988.

18.2156   Goelman, Hillel, et al., eds. Awakening To Literacy. Portsmouth, New Hampshire: Heinemann Educational Books, Inc., 1984.

18.2157   Good, A. "Noting The Decline of Literacy and Birth Rates." Times Educational Supplement 3542, (May 18, 1984): 17.

18.2158   Goodman, Kenneth S. "Commentary: On Being Literate in an Age of Information." Journal of Reading 28, 5(February 1985): 388-392.

18.2159   Goodman, Kenneth S. "Growing into Literacy." Prospects 15, 1(1985): 57-65.

18.2160   "Good News on World Literacy Rate." Texas Outlook 55, (November 1971): 62.

18.2161   Goody, Jack, ed. The Domestication of The Savage Mind. New
            York: Cambridge University Press, 1977.

18.2162   Gopinathan, S. "Unfinished Agenda For The 80's: Report On
            International Commitment To Literacy." Reading Teacher 35,
            4(January 1982): 430-432.

            Reviews the international involvement in the promotion of
            literacy. Provides a background analysis of organization and
            institutional efforts to promote reading. Examines international
            literacy efforts occurring in the 1980's. Also explores literacy
            efforts of developing nations. Concludes with a discussion of
            the future of international literacy promotion.

18.2163   Graff, H.J. "Legacies of Literacy." Journal of Communication 32,
            (Winter 1982): 12-26.

18.2164   Graff, H.J. "Literacy Past and Present: Critical Approaches in The
            Literacy/Society Relationship." Interchange 9, 2(1978-1979): 1-21.

18.2165   Graff, Harvey J. "Breaking The Bounds of Literacy: A Response
            to Willinsky." Interchange 15, 4(1984): 53-57.

18.2166   Graff, Harvey J., ed. Literacy and Social Development In The
            West: A Reader. Cambridge: Cambridge University Press, 1982.

18.2167   Graham, P.A. "Literacy: A Goal For Secondary Schools."
            Daedalus 110, (Summer 1981): 19-34.

18.2168   Graham, P.A. "Whither Equality of Educational Opportunity?"
            Daedalus 109, (Summer 1980): 115-132.

18.2169   Green, D.H. "The Reception of Hartmann's Works: Listening,
            Reading, or Both?" Modern Language Review 81, (April 1986):
            357-368.

18.2170   Greene, Maxine. "Literacy For What?" Phi Delta Kappan 63,
            5(January 1982): 326-329.

18.2171   Gregor, Alexander. "Humanism: A Definition of Literacy."
            Journal of Educational Thought 15, 3(December 1981): 202-208.

18.2172   Gribble, Helen. "'J For Giraffe' Spells Fear." Australian Journal
            of Reading 6, 3(August 1983): 137-143.

18.2173   Grigsby, J.L. "Remnants of Chretien's Aesthetics In The Early Perceval Continuations And The Incipient Triumph of Writing." Romance Philology 41, (May 1988): 379-393.

18.2174   Grimond, J. Literacy. Oxford: Oxford University Press, 1972.

18.2175   Grosso, Lia D.J. Alfabetizando. Rio de Janeiro: J. Olympio, 1969.

18.2176   Grundin, Hans U. "A Commission of Selective Readers: A Critique of 'Becoming a Nation of Readers'." Reading Teacher 39, 3(December 1985): 262-266.

18.2177   Gudschinsky, Sarah Caroline. Literacy: The Growing Influence of Linguistics. The Hague: Mauton, 1976.

18.2178   Gumperz, Jenny Cook, ed. Social Construction of Literacy. Cambridge: Cambridge University Press, 1986.

18.2179   Guthrie, J.T. "Equilibrium of Literacy." Journal of Reading 26, (April 1983): 668-670.

18.2180   Guthrie, John T., and Kirsch, Irwin S. "The Emergent Perspective on Literacy." Phi Delta Kappan 65, 5(January 1984): 351-355.

18.2181   Haddad, Chafica. "Celebration of International Literacy Day To Promote Peace." International Understanding at School, Special Supplement 1(1986): 15-22.

18.2182   Haile, H.G. "Luther and Literacy." PMLA 91, (October 1976): 816-828.

18.2183   Hall, Nigel. "Reading About 'Reading'." Reading Horizons 25, 2(Winter 1985): 103-106.

18.2184   Harker, W. John. "Teaching a Joyful Literacy." English Quarterly 13, 4(Winter 1980-1981): 29-40.

18.2185   Harper, A.W.J. "Literacy Problem." Alberta Modern Language Journal 15, 1(Fall 1976): 4-5.

18.2186   Harste, Jerome C., et al. "Examining Our Assumptions: A Transactional View of Literacy and Learning." Research in The Teaching of English 18, 1(February 1984): 84-108.

18.2187   Hartcup, Adeline. "Learning On Site." Times Educational
           Supplement 3160, (December 26, 1975): 10.

18.2188   Hartman, Geoffrey H. "The Humanist Alternative." ADE
           Bulletin, 62(September-November 1979): 39-41.

18.2189   Hartoonian, H. Michael. "The Courage To Be Literate And
           Free." Social Studies 73, 1(January-February 1982): 37-40.

18.2190   Haussman, Fay. "Literacy Drives On." Times Higher Education
           Supplement 80, (April 27, 1973): 9

18.2191   Hautecoeur, Jean-Paul. "Developpement inegal et sous-
           developpement sectoriel de l'aphabetisation." Grain de Sel
           numero special, (May 1979): 12-16.

18.2192   Hautecoeur, Jean-Paul. "Resume des propositions de
           development." Update, numero special (May 1979): 2.

18.2193   Hautecoeur, Jean-Paul. "Alphabetisation: Quelques Questions."
           Grain de Sel 2, 1(October 1978): 22-27.

18.2194   Hautecoeur, Jean-Paul, ed. Alpha 82. Quebec: Ministere de
           l'education, 1982.

18.2195   Haydon, C. "Lessons From Literacy; Summary Of Two Reports."
           Times Educational Supplement 3300, (September 29, 1978): 10.

18.2196   Heath, S.B. "Oral and Literate Traditions." International Social
           Science Journal 36, 1(1984): 41-57.

18.2197   Heath, Shirley Brice. "The Functions And Uses Of Literacy."
           Journal of Communication 30, 1(Winter 1980): 123-133.

18.2198   Heinen, H. "Ulrich von Lichtenstein: Homo (IL) Litteratus or
           Poet/Performer?" Journal of English and Germanic Philogy 83,
           (April 1984): 159-172.

18.2199   Heins, Ethel L. "From Reading To Literacy." Today's Education
           69, 2(April-May 1980): 41, 44-46.

18.2200   Henderson, Robert P. "View From The Corporate Sector."
           American Education 18, 7(August-September 1982): 35-37.

18.2201   Hentoff, N. "Greatest Consumer Fraud Of All." Social Policy 8,
           (November 1977): 83-86.

18.2202   Herrick, Michael J. "Beyond Literacy: Style." English Quarterly
           11, 4(Winter 1978/1979): 9-18.

18.2203   Hill, R.T. "Making The People Literate." School & Society 35,
           (April 9, 1932): 488-92.

18.2204   Hillerich, Robert L. "Toward an Assessable Definition of
           Literacy." English Journal 65, 2(February 1976): 50-55.

           Explores the concept of literacy. Examines various existing
           definitions of literacy. Attempts to design a definition of literacy
           which will serve as a vehicle of its assessment in the population.
           Calls for the need for clarification of the term, "literacy."
           Provides an educational, sociological and economic view of
           literacy. Concludes with some thoughts on the assessment of
           literacy.

18.2205   Hoggart, Richard. Uses of Literacy. London: Peregrine Books,
           1984.

18.2206   Holdaway, Don. Stability & Change in Literacy Learning.
           Portsmouth, New Hampshire: Heinemann Educational Books,
           Inc., 1984.

18.2207   Holdaway, Don. The Foundations of Literacy. N.P.: n.p., 1979.

18.2208   Hornsby, Beve. "Predicting Reading Failure In A Speech And
           Language Defective Population." Links 6, 2(Spring 1981): 31-36.

18.2209   Hoyles, Martin, ed. The Politics of Literacy. London: Writers
           and Readers Publishing Cooperative, 1977.

18.2210   Hrychuk, Bill. "Feedback: Literacy and The Stupidity Crisis."
           ATA Magazine 58, 1(November 1977): 9-11.

18.2211   Huck, Charlotte S. "No Wider Than The Heart Is Wide." In
           Using Literature & Poetry Affectively, pp 26-36. Edited by Jon E.
           Shapiro. Newark, Delaware: International Reading Association,
           1979.

18.2212   Hulcoop, John. "University Expectations: Like Ordering Filet in
           McDonald's?" B.C. English Teacher Journal 20, 1(Winter 1979):
           27-29.

18.2213   Iannaccone, Lawrence. "Reviewing The Reviews on Literacy and Reasoning: Some Selected Themes and References." Review of Educational Research 54, 4(Winter 1984): 682-688.

18.2214   Illiteracy and Human Rights. N.P.: n.p., 1968.

18.2215   Isenberg, Joan, and Jacob, Evelyn. "Literacy and Symbolic Play: A Review of The Literature." Childhood Education 59, 4(March-April 1983): 272-276.

18.2216   Issues In Literacy. N.P.: n.p., 1985.

18.2217   Jamison, Cy. "Inter-Office Memo: To Ed Lynas, Editor, Courier. From Cy Jamison." Educational Courier 48, 3(January 1978): 12-13.

18.2218   Janko, Edmond. "Diminished Literacy: The Clear and Present Danger." College Board Review, 120(Summer 1981): 13, 28-29.

18.2219   Jeffery, J., and Maginn, C. Who Needs Literacy Provisions? London: Macmillan Educational, 1979.

18.2220   Jobbins, D. "Need Fo A More Literate Workforce." Times Higher Education Supplement 499, (May 28, 1982): 10.

18.2221   Johns, Jerry L., ed. Literacy For Diverse Learners: Promoting Reading Growth At All Levels. Newark, Delaware: International Reading Association, 1974. ED 097 630.

18.2222   Johnson, Terry D. Literacy Through Literature. N.P.: n.p., 1987.

18.2223   Jolliffe, B. "Creative Literacy in The Secondary School." Journal of Applied Educational Studies 4, 2(Winter 1975): 37-44.

18.2224   Jones, F. Noel. "Literacy Symposium: A Local Authority Scheme - An Appraisal." Adult Education (London) 47, (January 1975): 285-296.

18.2225   Karpen, James L. The Digitized Word. N.P.: n.p., 1985.

18.2226   Keiser, John H. "Social Conversation: Presidents as Educators." Improving College and University Teaching 28, 3(Summer 1980): 107-109.

18.2227   Kidd, J. R. Whilst Time Is Burning. N.P.: n.p., 1974.

18.2228   King, Kenneth. "Research On Literacy and Work Among The
           Rural Poor." Convergence 12, 3(1979): 32-41.

18.2229   Kirkman, A.J. "Words, Words, Words." Training Officer 5,
           4(April 1969): 107-110.

18.2230   Klopfer, Leopold E., and Weber, Victor L., Jr. IPI Science: A
           Teaching Revolution In The Making, Reprint 51. Pittsburgh,
           Pennsylvania: University of Pittsburg, Learning Research and
           Development Center, 1969. ED 040 045.

18.2231   Knight, Patrick. "Literacy Scheme Under Fire." Times
           Educational Supplement 3144, (September 5, 1975): 15.

18.2232   Kohn, Sherwood Davidson. "In The Wintertime, Snakes
           Carbonate." National Elementary Principal 57, 4(June 1978): 14-
           19.

18.2233   Kort, Melissa Sue. "The Politics of Literacy: Issues Facing A
           Two-Year College." Teaching English In The Two Year College
           14, 3(October 1987): 174-180.

18.2234   Kottmeyer, William. Except After C. N.P.: n.p., 1988.

18.2235   Kuykendall, Carol. "Grammar and Composition: Myths and
           Realities." English Journal 64, 9(December 1975): 6-7.

18.2236   "Language Arts Ads Aimed At Students." Journal of Reading
           23, 2(November 1979): 154-155.

18.2237   Language, Communication, and Education. N.P.: n.p., 1987.

18.2238   Language, Literacy, and Culture. N.P.: n.p., 1987.

18.2239   Language, Communication, & Education. N.P.: n.p., 1987.

18.2240   Lamham, R.A. Literacy and The Survival of Humanism.
           London: Yale University Press, 1983.

18.2241   Laperriere, Micheline, and Wagner, Serge. L'aphabetisation; a
           repenser. Quebec: La Carrefour deducation populaire juillet,
           1980.

18.2242   Lapointe, A.E. "Is There Really A National Literacy Crisis?"
           Curriculum Review 27, (September/October 1987): 12-15.

18.2243   LaRocque, Geraldine E. "Literacy in The Two-Year College English Class." Teaching English in The Two-Year College 1, 3(Spring 1975): 133-139.

18.2244   Larudee, Faze. "Creative Reading For World Literacy." Literacy Discussion 3, 3-4(September-December 1972): 428-451.

18.2245   Laubach, F.C. "Literacy As A Base For World Peace." Phi Delta Kappan 33, (October 1951): 84-86.

18.2246   Laubach, Frank Charles. Forty Years With The Silent Billion; Adventuring In Literacy. Old Tappan, New Jersey: F.H. Revell Co., 1970.

18.2247   Laubach, Frank Charles. How To Teach One and Win One For Christ. Christ's Plan For Winning The World. Grand Rapids, Michigan: Zondervan Publishing, 1964.

18.2248   Laubach, Frank Charles. Thirty Years With The Silent Billion; Adventuring In Literacy. Westwood, New Jersey: Revell, 1959, 1960.

18.2249   Laubach, Frank Charles, How To Make The World Literate; The Each One Teach One Way. Syracuse, New York: n.p., 1957.

18.2250   Laubach Frank C., and Laubach, Robert S. Toward World Literacy; The Each One Teach One Way. Syracuse, New York: Syracuse University Press, 1960.

18.2251   Laurita, Raymond E. Solving The Literacy Mystery. Yorktown Heights, New York: Leonardo Press, 1983.

18.2252   Lazarus, Ruth. "Reflections on Creating a 'Literate Environment'." Convergence 15, 3(1982): 67-72.

18.2253   Lazere, D. "Literacy and Mass Media: The Political Implications." New Literacy History 18, (Winter 1987): 237-255.

18.2254   Learning Never Ends. International Seminar On Workers and Adult Education. 2d, Jerusalem, 1964. N.P.: n.p., 1965.

18.2255   Learning Strategies For Post-Literacy and Continuing Education. N.P.: n.p., 1985.

18.2256   Ledson, Sidney. "On The Conditions For Quick Literacy." Moccasin Telegraph 21, (Fall/Winter 1978): 18-21.

18.2257   Lee, G.R. and Kezis, M. "Societal Literacy and The Status Of The Aged." International Journal of Aging and Human Development 12, 3(1980/1981): 221-234.

18.2258   Leibowitz, Arnold H. "English Literacy: Legal Sanction For Discrimination." Notre Dame Lawyer 45, 1(1969): 7-67. ED 040 378.

18.2259   Lieb-Brilhart, Barbara. "What If Johnny Could Read and Write? . . . Another Look At The Literacy Issue." Communication Education 26, 3(September 1977): 251-253.

18.2260   Le Monde de l'aphabetisation: Politiques, Recherche et action. Ottawa: Centre de recherches pour le developpement international, 1983.

18.2261   Lestage, Andre. Literacy & Illiteracy. Lanham, Maryland: Bernan-Unipub, 1982.

18.2262   Levine, Ken. "Illiteracy and The Information Explosion." MED: Media in Education and Development 16, 1(March 1983): 17-19.

18.2263   Levine, Kenneth. Social Context of Literacy. London: Routledge and Kegan Paul, 1986.

18.2264   Lewis, A. "Defining The Issues." Momentum 19, (April 1988): 6-9.

18.2265   Lewis, A.C. "Reading The Writing On The Wall." Phi Delta Kappan 69, (March 1988): 468-469.

18.2266   Lindsey, Alfred J. "Freshman Composition: A Misadventure in Higher Education." English Education 7, 2(Winter 1976): 112-120.

18.2267   Linguistics And Literacy. N.P.: Delaware Symposium on Language Studies, University of Delaware, 1982.

18.2268   Lingusitics And Literacy. N.P.: n.p., 1972.

18.2269   "Literacy (Symposium)." Phi Delta Kappan 69, (November 1987): 184-207.

18.2270   "Literacy. (Symposium)." Educational Horizons 66, (Fall 1987): 7-48.

18.2271   Literacy. N.P.: n.p., 1986.

18.2272   "Literacy." Language Arts 62, (October 1985): 593-630.

18.2273   Literacy 1972-1976. N.P.: n.p., 1980.

18.2274   "Literacy and Learning: The Facts." UN Chronicle 20, (Fall 1983): 64.

18.2275   Literacy and Revolution. N.P.: n.p., 1980.

18.2276   Literacy and Schooling. N.P.: n.p., 1987.

18.2277   "Literacy and World Population." Population Bulletin 30, 2(1975): 2-29.

18.2278   Literacy As A Human Problem. N.P.: n.p., 1982.

18.2279   "Literacy Controversy: A Brief Look Across The Country." ATA Magazine 57, 2(January 1977): 14-15.

18.2280   "Literacy For All By The Year 2000: Udaipur Literacy Declaration." Convergence 14, 4(1981): 7-9.

18.2281   Literacy For Life. N.P.: n.p., 1983.

18.2282   Literacy, Language and Learning. N.P.: n.p., 1985.

18.2283   "Literacy Must Be Expanded." Oklahoma Education 13, (February 1984): 9.

18.2284   "Literacy, Progress and Projects (World Congress of Ministers of Education, Teheran, September 1965 sponsored by Unesco)." Australian Teacher 42 (December 1966): 13-20.

18.2285   "Literacy Progress: 1965-1975." Literacy Work 4, 5/6(1975): 25-38.

18.2286   Literacy Seminar, Karachi, 1968. Report. N.P.: n.p., 1968.

18.2287   "Literacy '78 A Success At Grant MacEwan C.C." College Canada 4, 1(January 1979): 19.

18.2288   Literacy, Society and Schooling. N.P.: n.p., 1986.

18.2289   "Literacy: The News Is Still Bad." American Teacher 71, (February 1987): 20.

18.2290   Literacy Today. New Delhi: Literacy International Committee, n.d.

18.2291   Loughlin, Catherine E. Supporting Literacy. N.P.: n.p., 1987.

18.2292   Lubin, Bernard, et al. "Comparison of Self-Administered and Examiner-Administered Depression Adjective Check List." Journal of Consulting and Clinical Psychology 46, 3(June 1978): 584-585.

18.2293   Luke, Allan, and Ward, Geoff. "Literacy, Cognition and The Cultural Conventions of Text: An Interview with David Olson." Australian Journal of Reading 11, 2(June 1988): 105-114.

18.2294   Lund, Peter. "The Right To Literacy." Reading 7, 2(June 1973): 21-26.

18.2295   Lyman, Helen Huguenor. Literacy And The Nation's Libraries. N.P.: American Library Association, 1978.

18.2296   "MacArthur Fund Backs Programs To Boost Literacy." Chronicle of Higher Education 33, (March 4, 1987): 27.

18.2297   MacDonald, Monica, and Crick, Philip. "The Literacy Issue." Liberal Education, 33+34(1978): 37-46.

18.2298   Mace, Jane. "Watch Your Language: The Politics of Literacy Now." Red Letters, 12: 2-12.

18.2299   Madge, C.H. "Some Aspects of Mass Literacy." British Journal of Educational Studies 4, (November 1955): 3-14.

18.2300   Mahmood, Zahid. "Literacy and The Chronic Psychiatric Patient." Bulletin of The British Psychological Society 36, (January 1983): 6-8.

18.2301   Mahy, Joyce. "Toward Literacy: A Language Development Programme." Viewpoint 9, 4(Winter 1976): 8-12.

18.2302   Martin, Larry G. "Adult High School Noncompleters: Toward a Typology of Phychosocial Development." Adult Literacy and Basic Education 8, 1(1984): 1-20.

18.2303   Martinez, Armando. "Literacy Through Democratization of Education." Harvard Educational Review 40, 2(May 1970): 280-282.

18.2304   Mattleman, M.S., and Gaige, M. "Literacy." Media Methods 24, (January/February 1988): 9-10.

18.2305   Maxwell, Madeline. "Some Functions and Uses of Literacy in the Deaf Community." Language in Society 14, 2(June 1985): 205-221.

18.2306   Mayer, Steven E. Guidelines For Effective Adult Literacy Programs. Minneapolis, Minnesota: Rainbow Research, Inc., 1984. ED 268 332.

18.2307   M'Bow, Amadou-Mahtar. "Bombs or Literacy." New Era 61, 4(July/August 1980): 131-132.

18.2308   McCall, Daniel F. "Literacy and Social Structure." History of Education Quarterly 11, 1(Spring 1971): 85-92.

18.2309   McConaghy, T.W. "Literacy Crisis: A Myth or Reality." ATA Magazine 57, 2(January 1977): 3.

18.2310   McCracken, Hugh Thomas. "Guidelines for Establishing Literacy Projects Utilizing Agencies In A University And A Rural Community." Ph.D. dissertation, University of Illinois at Urbana, 1971. 32/02-A, p. 722.

18.2311   McDonald, Roderick. "The Road To Literacy." OSSTF Forum 4, 2(March 1978): 87-88.

18.2312   McGeeney, Patrick. "Bernstein On Compensatory Education." English in Education 4, 3(Autumn 1970): 78-94.

18.2313   McKague, T.R. "The Many Faces of Literacy." Query 12, 4(Winter 1982): 6-12.

18.2314   McLuhan, Marshall. "The Brain and The Media: The 'Western' Hemisphere." Journal of Communication 28, 4(Fall 1978): 54-60.

18.2315   McVicar, John. "Why Should Joggers Read?" B.C. English Teacher Journal 19, 1(Summer 1978): 8-12.

18.2316   Meyer, Barbara. "Education and Patterns of Communication in a Situation of Restricted Literacy." Scottish Educational Review 14, 1(May 1982): 23-30.

18.2317   Mickelson, Norma I., and Forester, Anne. "Lanugage Variation
             and Literacy." Canadian Journal of Native Education 6,
             3(Spring 1979): 1-2.

18.2318   Miller, C.L. "Orality Through Literacy: Mande Verbal Art After
             The Letter." Southern Review 23, (January 1987): 84-105.

18.2319   Milligan, Barbara. "Literate at Last - You 'Can' Teach an Old
             Dog." Australian Journal of Reading 5, 1(March 1982): 24-29.

18.2320   Morris, Joan. "The Counsellor and The Problem of The More
             Literate Student." School Guidance Worker 32, 6(July 1977): 42-
             44.

18.2321   Morrison, T.R. "Literacy Redefined." Education Manitoba 10,
             6(February 1984): 12-14.

18.2322   Mossenson, David. "Improving Literacy: A Role For Society As
             Well As Schools." Australian Journal of Reading 3, 1(March
             1980): 31-34.

18.2323   Motta, J., and Riley, K. Breakthrough To Literacy. Reading,
             Massachusetts: Addison-Wesley Publishing Co., Inc., 1981.

18.2324   Moynes, Riley E. "Megatrends and Education's Future."
             Education Canada 24, 3(Fall 1984): 4-8.

18.2325   Mullikin, Thomas Owen. "Nonrural Schools As Measured By
             The Testing For Essential Learning and Literacy Skills." Ed.D.
             dissertation, Temple University, 1987. 48/04A, p. 888.

18.2326   Murphy, James J., et al. The Rhetorical Tradition and Modern
             Writing. New York: Modern Language Association of America,
             1982.

18.2327   Narain, Raj. Education For Literacy; Its Nature, Function, and
             Dynamics. Allahabad: n.p., 1958.

18.2328   Narain, Raj. "Education For Literacy." Ph.D. dissertation,
             Columbia University, 1958. X 1958. p. 46.

18.2329   Nelson, Sally Todd. "Literacy and The Aims of Community
             Colleges." Journal of The ACCC, Association of Canadian
             Community Colleges 3, 3(Autumn 1979): 115-140.

18.2330   Nespor, Jan. "The Construction of School Knowledge: A Case Study." Journal of Education 169, 2(1987): 34-54.

18.2331   Neuburg, Victor E. Literacy and Society. London: Woburn Press, 1971.

18.2332   Neuburg, Victor E. "Popular Education and Literacy." Local Population Studies Magazine 4, (Spring 1970): 51-55.

18.2333   "New Literacies: Close Encounters of Many Kinds." Medium 20, 2(Summer 1979): 28-29.

18.2334   Newton, Eunice Shaed. "Multilingual Impediments To Universal Literacy." Reading Teacher 26, 4(January 1973): 362-366.

18.2335   Notes on Literacy. N.P.: n.p., 1979.

18.2336   Norman, Charles, and Malicky, Grace. "Literacy as a Social Phenomenon: Implication For Instruction." Lifelong Learning 9, 7(May 1986): 12-15.

18.2337   Nystrom, C., "Literacy As Deviance." Etc. 44, (Summer 1987): 111-115.

18.2338   O'Donnell, Holly. "ERIC/RCS: Reading and The Vocational Education Student." Journal of Reading 25, 5(February 1982): 474-478.

18.2339   Oliver, Hugh. "A Literate Person is First and Foremost an Articulate Person . . ." Interchange 7, 4(1976-1977): 32-38.

18.2340   Olson, David R. "McLuhan: Preface to Literacy." Journal of Communication 31, 3(Summer 1981): 136-143.

18.2341   Olson, David R. "On The Language and Authority of Textbooks." Journal of Communication 30, 1(Winter 1980): 186-196.

18.2342   Olson, David R. "From Utterance to Text: The Bias of Language is Speech and Writing." Harvard Educational Review 47, 3(1977): 257-281.

18.2343   Olson, David R., and Torrance, Nancy. "Language, Literacy, and Mental States." Discourse Processes 16, 2(April-June 1987): 157-168.

18.2344   Olson, David R., et al. Literacy, Language and Learning: The
           Nature and Consequences of Reading and Writing. Cambridge:
           Cambridge University Press, 1985.

18.2345   O'Neill, Julie. "Literacy Symposium: The Failures of Literacy
           Schemes." Adult Education (London) 47, (March 1975): 347-
           363.

18.2346   Ong, Walter J. "Writing is a Humanizing Technology." ADE
           Bulletin, 74(Spring 1983): 13-16.

18.2347   Ong, Walter J. "Literacy and Orality in Our Times." Journal of
           Communication 30, 1(Winter 1980): 197-204.

18.2348   Ong, Walter J. "Literacy and Orality in Our Times." ADE
           Bulletin 58, 1-7(September 1978): n.p.

18.2349   Onset of Literacy, The. N.P.: n.p., 1986.

18.2350   "Open To Suggestion." Journal of Reading 26, 4(January 1983):
           360-362.

18.2351   Oral Language Competence and The Development of Literacy:
           Final Report. Toronto, Ontario: Ontario Institute for Studies in
           Education, 1978.

18.2352   Oxenham, John. Literacy: Writing, Reading, and Social
           Organization. London: Routledge & Kegan Paul, 1980.

18.2353   Paiva, Vanilda Pereira. Paulo Freire e o Nacionalismo -
           Desenvolvimentista. N.P.: n.p., 1980.

18.2354   Palmer, William S. "Reading, Writing, and The Realm of
           Reason." Phi Delta Kappan 52, 8(April 1971): 473-475.

18.2355   Parker, Robert P. "Literacy And The English Teacher." English
           In Australia, 39(February 1977): 5-22.

18.2356   Pauly, John J. "The Uses of Tone: On Rereading Richard
           Hoggart." Critical Studies in Mass Communication 3, 1(March
           1986): 102-106.

18.2357   Pearce, John. "Literacy is Not Enough." Cambridge Journal of
           Education 2, (Michaelmas 1972); 150-160.

18.2358   Pearpoint, Jack C. "Le driot de Lire: Essentiel a la vie en communaute." La Revue Canadienne de la deficience mentale 34, 4(Autumn 1984): 37-42.

18.2359   Perschy, Margaret. "A Student Approach To The Problem (Of Literacy)." Canadian Library Journal 37, 4(August 1980): 251-252.

18.2360   Phillips, C.J.; Stott, D.H.; and Birrell, Heather V. "The Effects of Learning Style on Progress Towards Literacy and Numeracy." Educational Review 39, 1(1987): 31-40.

18.2361   Pica, Teresa. "Communicative Competence and Literacy." Reading Research and Instruction 27, 3(Spring 1988): 1-15.

18.2362   Pickert, Sarah M., and Hunter, Beverly. "Redefining 'Literacy'." Momentum 14, 3(September 1983): 7-9.

18.2363   Pilkington, Gwen. "Our Lost Legacy of Learning - Can It Be Recovered?" School Guidance Worker 32, 6(July 1977): 37-41.

18.2364   Pitman, James. "Oracy and Literacy." Literacy Discussion 3, 3-4(September - December 1972): 319-336.

18.2365   Plaut, Rabbi W. Gunther. "Making It In School - Making It In Life." School Guidance Worker 32, 6(July 1977): 34-35.

18.2366   Plevnik, Danko. "Reading - The Most Important Concern For A University." Journal of Reading 24, 7(April 1981): 568-572.

18.2367   Politics of Literacy, The. N.P.: n.p., 1977.

18.2368   Postman, Neil. "The Politics of Reading." Harvard Educational Review 40, 2(May 1970): 244-252.

18.2369   Postman, Neil, et al. "The New Literacy." Grade Teacher 88, 7(March 1971): 26-52.

18.2370   Powell, William R. "Levels of Literacy." Journal of Reading 20, 6(March 1977): 488-492.

18.2371   Proceedings of The International Literacy Day Conference, Washington, D.C., September 8, 1978. Washington, D.C.: International Day Conference, 1978.

18.2372   Pullen, Alan D. "Thresholds of Literacy." English in Education 1, 1(Spring 1967): 45-48.

18.2373   Pulte, W. "A Note on Kickapoo Literacy." International Journal of American Linguistics 49, (October 1983): 437-438.

18.2374   Rachal, John R. "Gutenberg, Literacy, and The Ancient Arts of Memory." Adult Education Quarterly 38, 3(Spring 1988): 125-135.

18.2375   Rahnema, Majid. "Literacy: To Read The Word or The World?" Prospects 6, (1976): 72-82.

18.2376   Rankin, David. "A Rhetorical Problem For Rhetoricians." College Composition and Communication 29, 3(October 1978): 280-284.

18.2377   Rasinski, T.V. "The Role of Interest, Purpose, and Choice in Early Literacy." Reading Teacher 41, (January 1988): 396-400.

18.2378   Raymond, James C., ed. Literacy As A Human Problem. University, Alabama: University of Alabama Press, 1982.

18.2379   Read M. "Dr. Frank Laubach: Literacy's Tireless Advocate." Times Educational Supplement 2207, (September 6, 1957): 1171.

18.2380   Ready, W. "Death of Literacy." Educational Courier 45, (March 1975): 17-18.

18.2381   Report. Literacy Seminar, Karachi, 1968. N.P.: n.p., 1968.

18.2382   Right To Learn, The. Toronto: International Council For Adult Education, 1985.

18.2383   Rigg, Pat, and Kazemek, Francis E. "A Last Chance at Literacy: Real World Reading Comes To Job Corps Camp." Journal of Reading 27, 4(January 1984): 328-333.

18.2384   Risman, A.M. "Skills of Literacy." Coombe Lodge Reports 9, 11(1976): 359-363.

18.2385   Rivinus, Edward M. "Test Scores and Literacy: Back to Basics?" Independent School Bulletin 35, 1(October 1975): 43-44.

18.2386   Roberts, Helen M. Champion of The Silent Billion; The Story of
           Frank C. Laubach, Apostle of Literacy. St. Paul, Minnesota:
           Macalester Park Publishing Co., 1961.

18.2387   Robinson, Brent. "Media in Educational Research: Are The
           New Electronic Media A Threat To Literacy or A Challenge For
           The Literate?" British Journal of Educational Technology 16,
           1(January 1985): 42-59.

18.2388   Robinson, Jay L. "Literacy in The Department of English."
           College English 47, 5(September 1985): 428-498.

18.2389   Rodgers, S. "Orality, Literacy, and Batak Concepts of Marriage
           Alliance." Journal of Anthropological Research 40, (Fall 1984):
           433-450.

18.2390   Rogers, Will. The Illiterate Digest. Detroit, Michigan: Gale
           Research Company, 1975.

18.2391   Rose, Shirley K. Promises and Power. N.P.: n.p., 1984.

18.2392   Roth, Rita. "Schooling, Literacy Acquisition, and Cultural
           Transmission." Journal of Education 166, 3(Fall 1984): 291-308.

           Examines the relationship between schooling and the
           acquisition of literacy, and the impact that this relationship has
           on cultural transmission. Presents various views of literacy.
           Discusses and defines literacy as reading. Also explores the
           parallel between said definition of reading literacy, and three
           social science research orientations. Concludes with an analysis
           of cultural transmission and literacy acquisition.

18.2393   Roucek, Joseph S. "The Role of Literacy and Illiteracy In Social
           Change." International Review of Education 13, (1967): 483-
           491.

18.2394   Roueche, Suanne D. "Literacy Development: Community
           College Task of The '80's." Community College Frontiers 9,
           2(Winter 1981): 41-45.

18.2395   Schickedanz, Judith, and Sullivan, Maureen. "Mom, What Does
           U-F-F Spell?" Language Arts 61, 1(January 1984): 7-17.

18.2396   Schieffelin, Bambi, and Gilmore, Perry. The Acquisition of
           Literacy: Ethrographic Perspectives. Norwood, New Jersey:
           Ablex Publishing Corporation, 1986.

18.2397   Scott, B.A. "The Decline of Literacy and Liberal Learning."
           Journal of Education 168, 1(1986): 105-116.

18.2398   Scribner, Sylvia, and Cole, Michael. Psychology of Literacy.
           London: Harvard University Press, 1981.

18.2399   "Second Annual IRA Literacy Award." Journal of Reading 24,
           6(March 1981): 528-531.

18.2400   Seranne, Evelyn M. "Commentary: The Trouble With
           Shakespeare." Journal of Reading 22, 6(March 1979): 490-491.

18.2401   Sgouris, Katherine. "Literacy: An Integral Part of The
           Typewriting Curriculum." Balance Sheet 66, 1(September -
           October 1984): 35-38.

18.2402   Shack, Sybil. "Higher Literacy? Whose? Theirs? Ours?" School
           Guidance Worker 32, 6(July-August 1977): 20-26.

18.2403   "Shall We Close The Schools?" School & Society 38,
           (November 4, 1933): 601.

18.2404   Shantz, Marie. ". . . With Grace and Clarity." OSSTF Forum 5,
           1(February 1979): 33-34.

18.2405   Sharma, C. "Experiments In Literacy." World Association For
           Adult Education Bulletin 2d 21, (May 1940): 13-17.

18.2406   Shearer, John. "Education For The Down-And-In." Technical
           Journal 1, 8(November 1973): 12-13.

18.2407   Sheils, Merrill. "What Do Diplomas Mean?" Newsweek 91,
           2(January 9, 1978): 65-66.

18.2408   "Save The English Language?" U.S. News & World Report 84,
           16(April 24, 1978): 75.

18.2409   Shenkman, Harriet. "Reversing The Literacy Decline by
           Controlling The Electronic Demons." Educational Leadership
           42, 5(February 1985): 26-29.

           Argues that the proliferation of electronic games and devices
           consume substantial amounts of a teenager's time, thus keeping
           them from developing their minds. Discusses the nature,
           content, and extent of said electronic bombardment. Concludes
           with an examination of negative effects vs. positive potential.

18.2410   Shenkman, Harriet. "Reading - The Perfect Scapegoat."
           Educational Forum 49, 1(Fall 1984): 81-90.

18.2411   Shreefter, R. and Luttrell, W., "Relevant Education: Literacy at
           Work." Southern Exposure 14, No. 5/6 (1986): 57-60.

18.2412   Shuy, Roger W. "Holistic View Of Language." Research in The
           Teaching of English 15, 2(May 1981): 101-111.

18.2413   Sinclair, Anne. "Some Recent Trends in The Study of Language
           Development." International Journal of Behavioral
           Development 5, 4(December 1982): 413-431.

18.2414   Singler, J.V. "The Psychology of Literacy." Language 59,
           (December 1983): 893-901.

18.2415   Sledd, Andrew. "Readin' not Riotin': The Politics of Literacy
           (Essay)." College English 50, 5(September 1988): 495-508.

18.2416   Sloan, Glenna Davis. "Commentary: Developing Literacy
           Through Literature." Reading Teacher 34, 2(November 1980):
           132-136.

18.2417   Smith, Frank. Joining The Literacy Club. N.P.: n.p., 1988.

18.2418   Smith, Frank. Essays Into Literacy. Portsmouth, New
           Hampshire: Heinemann Educational Books, Inc. 1983.

18.2419   Smith, James V. "Reading, Writing and Reification." Scottish
           Educational Review 13, 1(May 1981): 25-35.

18.2420   Smith, K.J. "The Concept of Language and Literacy For The
           Teacher." New Education 1, 2(1979): 52-56.

18.2421   Smith, Virginia B. "Keynote Address." Journal of Basic Writing
           3, 1(Fall-Winter 1980): 19-26.

18.2422   Social Construction of Literacy, The. N.P.: n.p., 1986.

18.2423   Sola, Michele, and Bennett, Adrian T. "The Struggle For Voice:
           Narrative, Literacy, and Consciousness in an East Harlem
           School." Journal of Education 167, 1(1985): 88-110.

18.2424   Sooby, Andrew. "The Politics of Literacy." English in Australia,
           43(March 1978): 43-53.

18.2425   Southgate, Vera. "Literacy At All Levels." In Literacy At All Levels: Proceedings Of The Eighth Annual Study Converence of The United Kingdom Reading Association. Mancherster, 1971. London: Ward Lock Educational 1972, p. 9-20.

18.2426   Spencer, Margaret. "Place of Literature In Literacy: Dip a Finger Into Fafnir." Skylark 13, 4(Summer 1977): 10-15.

18.2427   Spencer, Margaret. "The Place of Literature in Literacy: 'Dip a Finger into Fafnir'." English Quarterly 9, 4(Winter 1976-1977): 1-9.

18.2428   Stevens, Edward W. Literacy, Law & Social Order. Dekalb, Illinois: Northern Illinois University Press, 1987.

18.2429   Stevens, John H. "Is There a Literate In The House?" Teacher Education, 11(October 1977): 4-14.

18.2430   Stewart, Peter M. "Literacy Problems in Technical Colleges: A Report." Vocational Aspect of Education 28, (August 1976): 51-53.

18.2431   Stewig, John Warren. "Alphabet Books: A Neglected Genre." Language Arts 55, 1(January 1988): 6-11.

18.2432   Sticht, Thomas G. "Developing Literacy and Learning Strategies in Organizational Settings." In Cognitive and Affective Learning Strategies, pp. 275-307. Edited by Harold F. O'Neil, Jr. and Charles D. Spielberger. New York: Academic Press, 1979.

18.2433   Sticht, Thomas G. "Dialogue: The Development of Literacy." Curriculum Inquiry 8, 4(Winter 1978): 341-351.

18.2434   Stigler, George J. "The Case, If Any, For Economic Literacy." Journal of Economic Education 14, 3(Summer 1983): 60-66.

18.2435   Stiller, R. "Why Literacy May Survive?" Etc. 39, (Winter 1982): 328-331.

18.2436   Stinson, R.H. "Operation Literacy." Field Development Newsletter 14, 2(November 1983): 1-7.

18.2437   Stott, D.H. "A Bridge To Literacy." Forward Trends 5, (Spring 1961): 105-109.

18.2438   Stowell, Pat. "Literacy Symposium: The Problems and Rewards
             of a College-Based Literacy Scheme." Adult Education (London)
             47, (January 1975): 285-296.

18.2439   Street, Brian. "Literacy and Ideology." Red Letters, 12 : 13-21.

18.2440   Strenski, Ellen. "Anti-'Subjectivity': A Thesis and Criteria for
             Texts." Teaching English in The Two Year College 6, 2(Winter
             1980): 121-128.

18.2441   Stubbs, Michael. Language & Literacy: The Sociolinguistics of
             Reading and Writing. New York: Methuen, Inc., 1980.

18.2442   Student Research Papers In Literacy & Education. Ukarumpa,
             Papua New Guinea: Summer Institute of Linguistics, 1976.

18.2443   Suhor, C. "ERIC/RCS Report: Understanding Literacy - An
             Overview." Language Arts 64, (October 1987): 659-663.

18.2444   Sulzby, Elizabeth, and Otto, Beverly. "Text Asan Object of
             Metalinguistic Knowledge A Study in Literacy Development."
             First Language 3, Part 3, 9(1982): 181-199.

18.2445   "Summary of Activities of European Affiliates." Journal of
             Reading 18, 5(February 1975): 360-362.

18.2446   Summary of Information Received Concerning The Celebration
             of International Literacy Day In 1980. N.P.: n.p., 1982?

18.2447   Taber, Sylvia Read. "ERIC/RCS: Current Definitions of
             Literacy." Journal of Reading 30, 5(February 1987): 458-461.

18.2448   Tannen, D. "The Commingling Of Orality And Literacy In
             Giving A Paper At A Scholarly Conference." American Speech
             63, (Spring 1988): 34-43.

18.2449   Taylor, Denny. Family Literacy. N.P.: n.p., 1983.

18.2450   Teaching Profession And The World-wide Literacy Programme,
             A Handbook For Leaders of WCOTP Affiliated Organizations.
             N.P.: World Confederation of Organizations of The Teaching
             Profession, 1967. ED 012 880.

18.2451   Tenth Anniversary of The International Literacy Day, 8
             September 1975. N.P.: n.p., 1975.

18.2452   Thant, U. "Toward World Literacy." School and Society 99, 2334 (Summer 1971): 282-283.

18.2453   "This We Believe About The Role of Business Education in The Comprehensive High School." Business Education Forum 40, 1(October 1985): 7.

18.2454   Thomas, Susan. "Reading For Pleasure." Times Educational Supplement 3495, (June 24, 1983): 42.

18.2455   Thompson, Keith P. "Communication and Evaluation." OCLEA, Ontario Council For Leadership in Educational Administration 16, (Summer 1979): 15-19.

18.2456   Thought & Language/Language & Reading. N.P.: n.p., 1980.

18.2457   Tickell, Gerry. "Literacy and Transition." English In Australia, 56 (July 1981): 3-9.

18.2458   "To Improve Literacy, First Educate The Public And Its Decision Makers, NCTE Commissions Say." Skylark 21, 1(Fall 1984): 12-14.

18.2459   Totton, S.J. "What Kind of Literacy?" School Guidance Worker 32, 6(July 1977): 15-19.

18.2460   Tovey, Duane R., and Kerber, James E., eds Roles In Literacy Learning: A New Perspective. Newark, Delaware: International Reading Association, 1986. ED 264 535.

18.2461   Toward A New Understanding of Literacy. N.P.: n.p., 1986.

18.2462   Traugott, Elizabeth Closs. "Literacy and Language Change: The Special Case of Speech Act Verbs." Interchange 18, 1-2(Spring-Summer 1987): 32-47.

18.2463   Troyka, Lynn Quitman. "Perspectives on Legacies and Literacy in The 1980's." College Composition and Communication 33, 3(October 1982): 252-262.

18.2464   Trueba, H.T. "The Forms, Functions and Values of Literacy: Reading For Survival In a Barrio as a Student." NABE Journal 9, (Fall 1984): 21-39.

18.2465   Tuinman, Jaap. "The Future of Literacy." Prime Areas 24, 3(Spring 1982): 5-6.

18.2466   Tuinman, Jaap. "'Reach For The Top': Stone Age Mentality."
          B.C. English Teacher Journal 19, 1(Summer 1978): 13-15.

18.2467   "Turning Point For Literacy, A." Literacy Work 6, 2(Summer
          1977): 1-10.

18.2468   Turning Point For Literacy, A. N.P.: International Symposium
          For Literacy, Perspolis, 1975.

18.2469   Tuttleton, J.W. "Literacy At The Barricades." Commentary 84,
          (July 1987): 45-48.

18.2470   Tway, Eileen. "The Resource Center: Critical Literacy."
          Language Arts 65, 6(October 1988): 592-597.

18.2471   Valgardson, William. "Years of The Disabled." B.C. English
          Teacher Journal 25, 1(Winter 1982): 14-16.

18.2472   Vance, Doug. "Research Update: Literacy - - Hoax or Hope?"
          Wisconsin State Reading Assocation Journal 25(October 1980):
          24-27.

18.2473   Vaugrante, Christiane. L'anlyse de l'evolution de
          l'analphabetisme dans les pays en voie de developpement.
          Dakar: Bureau Regional Pour l'education en Afrique, 1968.

18.2474   Versluys, J.D.N. "Why Do You Want To Read?" Prospects 2,
          2(Summer 1972): 202-205.

18.2475   Vyas, V.S. "Factors Influencing The Level of Literacy In Rural
          Areas." Artha-Vilnas 3, 1(1967): 15-23.

18.2476   Wagner, D.A., ed. The Future of Literacy In A Changing World.
          Oxford: Pergamon, 1987.

18.2477   Wagschal, P.H. "Literacy in The Electronic Age." Educational
          Technology 27, (June 1987): 5-9.

18.2478   Wagschal, P.H. "Illiterates With Doctorates: The Future of
          Education In Electronic Age." Futurist 12, (August 1978): 243-
          244.

18.2479   Wales, M.B., et al. "The Road To Literacy." National Froebel
          Foundation Bulletin 107, (August 1957): 15-17.

18.2480   Walker, B., et al. "Calling The Question on Literacy." Journal of Reading 30, (April 1987): 652-653.

18.2481   Walker, Laurie. "Literacy For Life." Highway One 4, 3(Fall 1981): 14-17.

18.2482   Wambach, Michel. "L'Enseignement d'une Langue (Non-maternelle ou maternelle) aux Apprenants en Difficulte et aux Enfants Issues de Mil Lieux Socialement de Favorises." International Review of Education 32, 2(1986): 175-190.

18.2483   Watson, Gladys. "The Right To Learn - A Development Priority." Canadian Library Journal 42, 4(August 1985): 197-201.

18.2484   Weinstein, Gail. "Literacy and Second Language Acquisition: Issues and Perspectives." TESOL Quarterly 18, 3(September 1984): 471-484.

18.2485   Wells, Gordon. "Creating Communities For Literacy Development." Australian Journal of Reading 11, 2(June 1988): 84-94.

18.2486   Wendell, Margaret M. Bootstrap Literature: Preliterate Societies Do It Themselves. Newark, Delaware: International Reading Association, 1982.

18.2487   Wenqing, Zhao. "Comprehensive Continuing Education Only Way To Build On Literacy." Convergence 17, 3(1984): 18-23.

18.2488   Wesner, Marlene, and Wesner, Miles E. Johnny Can Read! (& Spell & Write). Idabel, Oklahoma: Diversity Press, 1986.

18.2489   Weston, V.C.H. "Language Through School, College and Life." Liberal Education, 33 & 34 (1978): 31-36.

18.2490   Wharton, Clifton R., Jr. "The New Darwinism of Basic Learning." Change 11, 8(November-December 1979): 38-41.

18.2491   Wick, Tom. "The Pursuit of Universal Literacy." Journal of Communication 30, 1(Winter 1980): 107-112.

18.2492   Wicks, Katherine E. "Literacy In An Age Of Future Shock: The Improvement Of Language Skills Among Senior High School Students." School Guidance Worker 31, 4(March 1976): 14-22.

18.2493   Wilkinson, Andrew. "The Concept of Oracy." English Journal 59, 1(January 1970): 71-77.

18.2494   Williams, J.D. "The Literacy Crisis: A Time For Reevaluation." College Board Review, 119 (March 1981): 20-21, 28-29.

18.2495   Willinsky, John. The Writer in The Teacher." Language Arts 61, 6(October 1984): 585-591.

18.2496   Willinsky, John M. "The Bounds of Literacy." Interchange 15, 4(1984): 40-52.

18.2497   Willinsky, John M. "Literacy Unbound: A Response to Graff." Interchange 15, 3(1984): 58-62.

18.2498   Winchester, Ian. "Literacy and Intellect." Interchange 18, 1-2(Spring-Summer 1987): 23-31.

18.2499   Winchester, Ian. "Back To Basics: The Centrality of Literacy, Numeracy, and Good Manners in Western Cultural Survival." Teacher Education 16, (April 1980): 31-40.

18.2500   Winterowd, W. Ross. "The Paradox of The Humanities." ADE Bulletin, 64(May 1980): 1-3.

18.2501   Witty, P.A. "Some Suggestions For Vocabulary Development In Public Schools." Educational Administration and Supervision 31, (May 1945): 271-282.

18.2502   Wolf, Thomas. "Reading Reconsidered." Harvard Educational Review 47, 3(1977): 411-429.

18.2503   Wolff, U. "Who Needs Literacy?" Africa Report 20, (July 1975): 50-53.

18.2504   Woolsey, D.P., and Burton, F.R. "Blending Literary and Informational Ways of Knowing." Language Arts 63, (March 1980): 273-280.

18.2505   Workman, Brooke. "The Writing 'Crisis'." Today's Education 68, 3(September-October 1979): 29-31.

18.2506   World Conference Literacy and Society; Proceedings. Roma: Ente Nazionale Per Le Biblioteche Popolari e Scolastiche, 1963.

18.2507   World Directory of Literacy Organizations. N.P.: n.p., 1973?

18.2508   World of Literacy, The. N.P.: International Council For Adult Education, 1979.

18.2509   Wray, David. "Censorship and Literacy." Reading 22, 2(July 1988): 137-142.

18.2510   Wray, Virginia F. "Back To Basics: Which One?" National Forum: Phi Kappa Phi Journal 65, 4(Fall 1985): 7-10.

18.2511   Writing. N.P.: n.p., 1981.

18.2512   Wrolstad, Merald, and Fisher, Dennis F., ed. Towards A New Understanding of Literacy. London: Praeger, 1986.

18.2513   Wynne, D.R. "Literacy Symposium: Communication Skills Programme." Adult Education (London) 47, (March 1975): 347-363.

18.2514   Young, Peter, and Tyre, Colin. Dyslexia or Illiteracy? Realizing The Right To Read. New York: Taylor & Francis, Inc., 1983.

18.2515   Yule, Valerie. "The Design of Spelling To Match Needs and Abilities." Harvard Educational Review 56, 3(August 1986): 278-297.

19

Literacy and Children

19.2516   Avery, Carol S. "First Grade Thinkers Becoming Literate."
           Language Arts 64, 6(October 1987): 611-618.

           Case study of a class of first grade students observed from
           February through June. Chronicles the process and components
           by which these children become more literate. Discusses writing
           for learning and thinking across the curriculum. Provides
           examples of said activities. Concludes with a discussion of the
           notion of a literate community, the components of a literate
           environment, and the role of the teacher.

19.2517   Awakening To Literacy. N.P.: University of Victoria
           Symposium on Children's Response To A Literate
           Environment, 1984.

19.2518   Baynham, Mike. "Mother Tongue Materials and Second
           Language Literacy." ELT Journal 37, 4(October 1983): 312-318.

19.2519   Beardsley, Linda V., and Marecek-Zeman, Miriam. "Making
           Connections: Facilitating Literacy in Young Children."
           Childhood Education 63, 3(February 1987): 159-166.

19.2520   Bentley, Roy. "Images of Perfection? The Role of The Early
           Childhood Teacher in The Improvement of Literacy."
           Viewpoint 9, 4(Winter 1976): 1-2.

19.2521   Bessemer, David W., and Spencer, Mary L. Functional Literacy
           In Schoolchildren. Definition and Criteria of Test Selection.
           Berkeley, California: Pacific Training and Technical Assistance
           Corporation, 1975. ED 169 135.

19.2522   Biggs, Shirley A., and Bruder, Mary N. "Adult Memories of
           Early Reading Experiences." Educational Horizons 66, 1(Fall
           1987): 34-37.

19.2523   Bouffler, C. "What's In a Scribble: A Brief Study of a Child's
           Literacy Development." Early Childhood Bulletin 6, 2(1982):
           40-44.

19.2524   Brailsford, Anne. "Kindergarten Readers In Progress." Reading-
           Canada-Lecture 4, 2(Summer 1986): 113-122.

19.2525   Brown, Mac H., et al. "Shared Book Experiences in
           Kindergarten: Helping Children Come To Literacy." Early
           Childhood Research Quarterly 1, 4(December 1986): 397-405.

19.2526   ·Brown, Mac H., et al. "Kindergarten Children Coming to
           Literacy." Educational Leadership 44, 3(November 1986): 54-56.

19.2527   Chall, Jeanne, and Snow, Catherine. Families and Literacy: The
           Contribution of Out-of-School Experiences To Children's
           Acquisition of Literacy. Final Report. Cambridge,
           Massachusetts: Harvard University Graduate School of
           Education, 1982. ED 234 345.

19.2528   Children and Learning. N.P.: n.p., 1984.

19.2529   Clancy, S. "Concepts of Literacy Through Literature." Primary
           Journal, 2(1985): 6-9.

19.2530   Cohen, Rachel. "Early Reading: The State of The Problem."
           Prospects 15, 1(1985): 41-48.

19.2531   Cook, Valerie J. "The Influences of Home and Family on the
           Development of Literacy in Children." School Psychology
           Review 9, 4(Fall 1980): 369-373.

19.2532   Dolley, Diane, and Wheldall, Kevin. "Developing Functional
           Language With Young Children From English-Speaking and
           Punjabi-Speaking Home Backgrounds: Incidental Teaching and
           Contingent Access To Materials." Educational Psychology 8,
           1 & 2(1988): 101-116.

19.2533   Downing, J., et al. "Cultural Differences in Children's Concepts
           of Reading and Writing." British Journal of Educational
           Psychology 45, (November 1975): 312-316.

19.2534   Duane, Michael. "Speech and Reading." English In Education
           4, 3(Fall 1970): 63-73.

19.2535   Dyson, Anne Haas. "Appreciate The Drawing And Dictating Of
           Young Children." Young Children 43, 3(March 1988): 25-32.

19.2536   Dyson, Anne Haas. "Emerging Alphabetic Literacy in School
           Contexts: Toward Defining The Gap Between School
           Curriculum and Child Mind." Written Communication 1,
           1(January 1984): 5-55.

19.2537   Early Childhood and Literacy Development Committee of The
           International Reading Association. "IRA Position Statement on
           Reading and Writing in Early Childhood." Reading Teacher 39,.
           8(April 1986): 822-824.

19.2538   Early Childhood and Literacy Development Committee of The
           International Reading Association. "Joint Statement on Literacy
           Development and Pre-First Grade." Reading Teacher 39,
           8(April 1986): 819-821.

19.2539   Edelsky, Carol, et al. "Hookin' 'Em In At The Start Of School In
           A 'Whole Language' Classroom." Anthropology and Education
           Quarterly 14, 4(Winter 1983): 257-281.

19.2540   Ferreiro, Emilia, and Teberosky, Ana. Literacy Before Schooling.
           London: Heinemann Educational, 1983.

19.2541   Fry, I.W. "Thel Eats Miss Smith: Teaching Illiterate Children of
           The Middle and Upper Primary Years." Polycom, 30(March
           1982): 22-24.

19.2542   Gillette, Arthur. Youth and Literacy: You've Got A Ticket To
           Ride. N.P.: n.p., 1972.

19.2543   Goodman, Y. "Language, Cognitive Development, and Reading
           Behavior." Yearbook (Claremont Reading Conference) 1983,
           (1983): 10-16.

19.2544   Graham, Marben Robert. "A Study of The Comparative
           Influence of Learning Writing Conventions Upon The
           Expressive Literacy of Average Ability Blue and White Collar
           Children." Ph.D dissertation, Michigan State University, 1971.
           32/06-A, p. 3153.

19.2545   Hall, Nigel. "When Do Children Learn To Read?" Reading 19, 2(July 1985): 57-70.

19.2546   Harris, Sharon. "Evaluation of a Curriculum to Support Literacy Growth in Young Children." Early Childhood Research Quarterly 1, 4(December 1986): 333-348.

19.2547   Haussler, Myna Matlin. "Transitions Into Literacy: A Psycholinguistic Analysis of Beginning Reading In Kindergarten and First Grade Children." Ph.D. dissertation, The University of Arizona, 1982. 43/03-A, p. 742.

19.2548   Haussman, Fay. "Literacy Drive Aims To Catch Them Young." Times Educational Supplement 3091, (August 23, 1974): 9.

19.2549   Holbrook, David. "Literacy For Backward Children." Guardian 25, (February 1961): 7.

19.2550   Hudelson, Sarah. "The Role of Native Language Literacy in The Education of Language Minority Children." Language Arts 64, 8(December 1987): 827-841.

19.2551   Hudelson, Sarah. "Kan Yu Ret an Rayt en Ingles: Children Become Literate in English as a Second Language.: TESOL Quarterly 18, 2(June 1984): 221-238.

19.2552   "It Ain't What You Do, It's The Way That You Do It: ILEA Research Into Children's Literacy/Inner London Education Authority." Times Educational Supplement, 3579, (July 15, 1988): 19.

19.2553   Janiuk, Dolores M., and Shanahan, Timothy. "Applying Adult Literacy Practices in Primary Grade Instruction." Reading Teacher 41, 9(May 1988): 880-886.

19.2554   Johnson, Tony W. "Philosophy For Children: An Antidote To Declining Literacy." Educational Forum 48, 2(Winter 1984): 235-241.

19.2555   Juel, Connie, et al. "Acquisition of Literacy: A Longitudinal Study of Children in First and Second Grade." Journal of Educational Psychology 78, 4(August 1986): 243-255.

19.2556   Juliebo, Moira, and Prins, Becky. "Evaluating Literacy Development in Kindergarten." Elements 16, 2(Spring 1985): 9-10.

19.2557   Juliebo, Moira F. "The Literacy World of Five Young Children."
           R-C-L, Reading - Canada - Lecture 3, 2(Summer 1985): 126-136.

19.2558   Juliebo, Moira Fraser. "The Literacy World of Five Young
           Children." Elements 17, 1(Fall 1985): 26.

19.2559   Kuipers, Joan, and Riccio, Mary Lou. "From Graphomania To
           Graphophobia and Halfway Back." Elementary English 52,
           2(February 1975): 216-220.

19.2560   Literacy Before Schooling. N.P.: University of Victoria
           Symposium on Children's Response To A Literate
           Environment, 1982.

19.2561   "Literacy Development and Pre-First Grade." Young Children
           41, 4(May 1986): 10-13.

19.2562   "Literacy Development and Pre-First Grade: A Joint Statement."
           Childhood Education 63, 2(December 1986): 110-111.

19.2563   Livingston, Sue. "An Alternative View of Education For Deaf
           Children: Part I." American Annals of The Deaf 131, 1(March
           1986): 21-25.

19.2564   Loughton, M. "Child From A Non-reading Home." Times
           Educational Supplement 2838, (October 10, 1969): 4.

19.2565   Mabey, Christine. "Black British Literacy: A Study of Reading
           Attainment of London Black Children From 8 to 15 Years."
           Educational Research 23, 2(February 1981): 83-95.

19.2566   Malicky, Grace. "The Literacy World of Five Young Children:
           Some Further Implication." R-C-L, Reading - Canada - Lecture
           3, 2(Summer 1985): 137-138.

19.2567   McKeown, Gerry, and Freebody, Peter. "The Language of
           Aboriginal and Non-Aboriginal Children and The Texts They
           Encounter in School." Australian Journal of Reading 11, 2(June
           1988): 115-126.

19.2568   McNamee, Gillian D., et al. "Cognition and Affect in Early
           Literacy Development." Early Child Development and Care 20,
           4(1985): 229-244.

19.2569   McVitty, W., ed. Children and Learning: Some Aspects and
           Issues. Sydney, Australia: Primary English Teaching
           Association, 1984.

19.2570   Meek, Margaret. "The Role of Reading In The Development of
           Children and Adolescents In Our Changing Societies." Bookbird
           11, 2(June 1973): 3-7.

19.2571   Parker, Robert P., and Davis, Francis A., eds. Developing
           Literacy: Young Children's Use of Language. Newark, Delaware:
           International Reading Association, 1983.

19.2572   Payton, Shirley, ed. Young Child's First Steps Towards Literacy:
           Developing Awareness of Print. Birmingham, England:
           University of Birmingham, 1984.

19.2573   Pikulski, John J. "Questions and Answers." Reading Teacher 42,
           1(October 1988): 76.

19.2574   Rasinski, Timothy V., and Deford, Diane E. "First Graders'
           Conception of Literacy: A Matter of Schooling." Theory Into
           Practice 27, 1(Winter 1988): 53-61.

19.2575   Richards, J. "It's All Right If Kids Can't Read." Journal of
           Learning Disabilities 14, (February 1981): 62-67.

19.2576   Riding, R.J., and Pugh, J.C. "Visual Performance and Reading in
           Seven and Eleven Year Old Children." Journal of Research in
           Reading 4, 1(February 1981): 17-28.

19.2577   Sampson, M.R., and Thomason, T. "Children's Mistakes in
           Reading: Should We Correct Them?" NABE Journal 9, (Fall
           1984): 1-2.

19.2578   Scifres, Jarvis W." Parents Teach Your Children To Meet
           Challenges." Reading Improvement 16, 4(Winter 1979): 332-333.

19.2579   Seitz, Victoria. "Literacy and The School Child: Some
           Perspectives From an Educated Country." Educational
           Evaluation and Policy Analysis 3, 6(November-December 1981):
           15-23.

19.2580   Snow, Catherine E. "Literacy and Language: Relationships
           During The Preschool Years." Harvard Educational Review 53,
           2(May 1983): 165-189.

19.2581   Special Issue. Primary Teaching Studies 3, 2(February 1988).

19.2582   Stewart, Janice Porterfield. "A Study of Kindergarten Children's Awareness of How They Are Learning To Read: Home and School Perspectives." Ph.D. dissertation, University of Illinois at Urbana-Champaign, 1986. 47/08A, p. 2976.

19.2583   Sticht, Thomas G. Literacy and Human Resources Development At Work: Investing In The Education Of Adults To Improve The Educability of Children. Professional Paper 2-83. Alexandria, Virginia: Human Resources Research Organization, 1983. ED 262 201.

19.2584   Stone, Julie. "Can't I Finish The Story?: Teaching Braille To Infants." British Journal of Visual Impairment 6, 2(Summer 1988): 51-53.

19.2585   Sulzby, Elizabeth. "Children's Emergent Reading of Favorite Storybooks: A Developmental Study." Reading Research Quarterly 20, 4(Summer 1985): 458-481.

19.2586   Taylor, Denny. "Children's Social Use of Print." Reading Teacher 36, 2(November 1982): 144-148.

19.2587   Taylor, Denny. "The Family and The Development of Literacy Skills and Values." Journal of Research in Reading 4, 2(September 1981): 92-103.

19.2588   Teale, W.H. "Preschoolers and Literacy: Some Insights From Research." Australian Journal of Reading 5, 3(August 1982): 153-162.

19.2589   Teale, William H. "Toward a Theory of How Children Learn To Read and Write Naturally." Language Arts 59, 6(September 1982): 555-570.

19.2590   Teale, William H., et al. "Assessing Young Children's Literacy Development." Reading Teacher 40, 8(April 1987): 772-777.

19.2591   Thonis, Eleanor Wall. Literacy For America's Spanish Speaking Children. Newark, Delaware: International Reading Association, 1976. ED 126 425.

19.2592   Vandenhazel, Bessel J. "Yes! Most Children Do Learn To Read And Write." Ontario Education 9, 3(May-June 1977): 13-15.

19.2593   Varenne, Herve, et al. "I Teach Him Everything He Learns In School": The Acquisition Of Literacy In Working Class Families. Final Report. New York: Columbia University, Teachers College, 1982. ED 227 452.

19.2594   Verhoeven, Ludo T. "Literacy In A Second Language Context: Teaching Immigrant Children To Read." Educational Review 39, 3(1987): 245-261.

19.2595   Vincent, Denis. "Assessment and Observation of Language Development: Some Neglected Aspects." Research Intelligence 3, 1(1977): 38-41.

19.2596   Wells, Gordon. "Some Antecedents of Early Educational Attainment." British Journal of Sociology of Education 2, 2(1981): 181-200.

19.2597   Wolf, Dennis Palmer, and Perry, Martha Davis. "Becoming Literate: Beyond Scribes and Clerks." Theory Into Practice 27, 1(Winter 1988): 44-52.

19.2598   Zabawski, Irene. "Survival Kit For Non-Reading Boys." Grade Teacher 86, 9(May-June 1969): 112-113.

19.2599   Zubrick, Ann. "Some Strategies For Developing Reflective Language In Year 1 Children." Child Language Teaching and Therapy 3, 3(1987): 251-258.

20

Literacy and Minorities

20.2600   Aptheker, H. "Literacy, The Negro and World War II." Journal of Negro Education 15, (October 1946): 595-602.

20.2601   Baratz, Joan C., and Shuy, Roger W., eds. Teaching Black Children To Read. Urban Language Series, Number 4. Washington, D.C.: Center For Applied Linguistics, 1969. ED 025 761.

20.2602   Berke, Norman Daniel. "An Investigation of Adult Negro Illiteracy: Prediction of Reading Achievement and Description of Educational Characteristics of a Sample of City Core Adult Negro Illiterates." Doctoral Dissertation, University of Michigan, Ann Arbor, 1967.

20.2603   Bliss, Barbara A. "Dyslexics as Library Users." Library Trends 35, 2(Fall 1986): 293-302.

20.2604   Bommelyn, Loren, et al. The Tolowa Language. N.P.: California State University- Humboldt, Arcata. Center For Community Development, 1972. ED 287 617.

20.2605   Brandt, Elizabeth A. "Native American Attitudes Toward Literacy and Recording in The Southwest." Journal of The Linguistic Association of The Southwest 4, 2(July 1981): 185-195.

20.2606   Brod, Rodney L., and McQuiston, John M. "American Indian Adult Education and Literacy: The First National Survey." Journal of American Indian Education 22, 2(January 1983): 1-16.

20.2607   Chase, F.S. "Attack On Functional Illiteracy Among Negro Adults." Elementary School Journal 47, (October 1946): 69-70.

20.2608   Cornelius, Janet. "'We Slipped and Learned to Read': Slave Accounts of The Literacy Process, 1830-1865." Phylon 44, 3(September 1985): 171-186.

20.2609   Diaz, Roberto Perez. "La Pedagogia en el Barrio. (The Pedagogy in the Barrio)." Agenda 7, 6(November/December 1977): 24-27.

20.2610   Faltis, Christian Jan. "Reading and Writing in Spanish For Bilingual College Students: What's Taught at School and What's Used in The Community." Bilingual Review II, 1(January-April 1984): 21-32.

20.2611   Fishman, Andrea R. "Reading, Writing, and Meaning: A Literacy Study Among The Amish." Ph.D. dissertation, University of Pennsylvania, 1984. 46/01-A, p. 91.

20.2612   Flores, J.M. "Minority Students in The Computer Age." Educational Technology 25, (February 1985): 42-43.

20.2613   "Florida Atlantic U. Establishes Indian Education Center." NUEA Spectator, (April-May 1971): 14-17.

20.2614   Gartland, Annette. "Gypsies Write Here." Voluntary Action II, (Summer 1982): 24-25.

20.2615   Gates, Henry Lewis, ed. Black Literature and Literacy Theory. London: Methuen, 1984.

20.2616   Gilliland, Hap. Gilliland General Purpose Learning Potential Examination For Inter-Cultural Evaluation of Learning Aptitude. Manual of Directions. Billings, Montana: Montana Council For Indian Education, 1970. ED 237 268.

20.2617   Gilmore, Perry. "Spelling 'Mississippi': Recontextualizing a Literacy-Related Speech Event." Anthropology and Education Quarterly 14, 4(Winter 1983): 235-255.

20.2618   Gonzales, Ricardo R., and Roll, Samuel. "Using The Computer To Develop Literacy." Equity and Choice 1, 3(Spring 1985): 25-32.

20.2619   Hall, Paul R., et al. Literacy and Education Among Adult Indians In Oklahoma. Volume I. Washington, D.C.: Office of Education, 1977. ED 138 381.

20.2620   Hall, Paul R., et al. Literacy and Education Among Adult
            Indians In Oklahoma. Volume II: Appendixes. Washington,
            D.C.: Office of Education, 1977. ED 138 382.

20.2621   Hall, Paul R., et al. Literacy and Education Among Adult
            Indians In Oklahoma. Volume III: Appendixes. Washington,
            D.C.: Office of Education, 1977. ED 138 383.

20.2622   Hartcyp, Adeline. "Learning on Site." Times Educational
            Supplement 3160, (December 26, 1975): 10.

20.2623   Hvitfeldt, Christina Gail. "Learning Language and Literacy: A
            Microethnographic Study of Hmong Classroom Behavior
            (Laotians In The United States)." Ph.D. dissertation, The
            University of Wisconsin, Madison, 1982. 43/10-A, p. 3186.

20.2624   Illiterate Immigrant Workers In Industrialized Countries.
            Teheran: International Institute For Adult Literacy Methods,
            1971.

20.2625   Johnson, Mary. "Literacy For Adult Immigrants." Manitoba
            Modern Language Bulletin 13, 3(Spring 1979): 15-17.

20.2626   Langley, Elizabeth G. "The Development of a Literacy Program
            Among The Navaho Indians. The Influence of Culture In
            Begining to Set Up a Literacy Program. A Proposal For
            Developing an English Literacy Program Among The Navaho
            Indians. With Reference to Present Motivations of The
            Navahos For Learning To Read." Ed., D. dissertation, New York
            University, 1956. 18/05, p. 1688.

20.2627   "Literacy: The Imperative." SERAmerica, (Summer 1987): 26.

20.2628   Long, Richard Matthew. "A Case Study: Five Illiterate Black
            Men In A Literate Society (Adult Learning)." Ed.D. dissertation,
            The George Washington University, 1985. 46/06-A, p. 1578.

20.2629   McEachern, William Ross. "Materials Development For Native
            Language Programs." Canadian Journal of Native Education 15,
            1(1988): 39-42.

20.2630   Munns, Roger. "A Full Time Course in Literacy and Numeracy
            For Unemployed Adults From Ethnic Minorities: A TOPS
            Preparatory Course in an Adult College." Adult Education
            (London) 49, (July 1976): 75-81.

20.2631   Origins: A History Based English Language Program For The
             Second-Phase Learner of Migrant Background." Australian
             Journal of Reading 4, 1(March 1981): 3-11.

20.2632   Pixton, William H. "A Contemporary Delimma: The Question
             of Standard English." College Composition and
             Communication 25, 4(October 1974): 247-253.

20.2633   "Plight of The American Indian." NJEA Review 43,
             4(December 1969): 44-45.

20.2634   Rigg, Pat. "Petra: Learning To Read At 45." Journal of
             Education 167, 1(1985): 129-139.

20.2635   Rigg, Pat. "'Desert Wind': A Fresh Breeze in Indian Education."
             Journal of Reading 28, 5(February 1985): 393-397.

             Discussion of the application of the Foxfire idea in the
             reservation high school in Tuba City, Arizona. Reviews the fact
             that more than six ethnic groups exist in the high school.
             Presents an overview of the attempt to implement the Foxfire
             idea as Desert Wind. Includes rationale, problems encountered,
             strategies, examples, topics chosen, and a discussion of the
             results of said implementation.

20.2636   Schwartz, Judith I. "Dialect Interference in The Attainment of
             Literacy." Journal of Reading 25, 5(February 1982): 440-446.

20.2637   Scollon, Ron, and Scollon, Suzanne B.K. Literacy As Interethnic
             Communication: An Athabaskan Case. Working Papers In
             Sociolinguistics, No.59. Washington, D.C.: National Institute of
             Education, 1979. ED 175 276.

20.2638   Smith, Valerie. Self-Discovery and Authority In Afro-American
             Narrative. N.P.: n.p., 1987.

20.2639   Spolsky, Bernard. The Situation of Navajo Literacy Projects.
             Navaho Reading Study Progress Report No. 17. Albuquerque,
             New Mexico: Bureau of Indian Affairs, 1972. ED 068 227.

20.2640   Spolsky, Bernard, and Holm, Wayne. Literacy In The
             Vernacular: The Case of Navajo. Navajo Reading Study,
             Progress Report No. 8. Albuquerque, New Mexico University,
             1971. ED 048 584.

20.2641   Stein, Annette S. "Analysis of Word Frequencies and Range In Spoken Language of Adult Black Illiterates." Ed.D. dissertation, State University of New York at Buffalo, 1971. 32/05-A, p. 2395.

20.2642   Torrey Jane W. "Illiteracy In The Ghetto." Harvard Educational Review 40, 2(May 1970): 253-259.

20.2643   Trueba, Henry T. "The Forms, Functions and Values of Literacy: Reading For Survival in a Barrio as a Student." NABE: The Journal for The National Association For Bilingual Education 9, 1(Fall 1984): 21-39.

20.2644   Wilde, Sandra J. "The Experience and Consequences of Literacy: A Case Study." Language Arts 56, 2(February 1979): 141-145.

20.2645   Wilhelm, Rowena. "Power of Immediate Positive Feedback." Perceptual and Motor Skills 30, 1(February 1970): 337-338.

20.2646   Wright, Peter Craig. "Literacy and Custom In A Ladino Peasant Community." Ed.D dissertation, Columbia University, 1967. 28/02-A, p. 412.

21

Literacy and Print

21.2647   Axtell, J. "The Power of Print in The Eastern Woodlands."
            William and Mary Quarterly 44, (April 1987): 300-309.

21.2648   Baker, Carolyn, and Freebody, Peter. "Possible Worlds and
            Possible People: Interpretive Challenges In Beginning School
            Reading Books." Australian Journal of Reading 11, 2(June
            1988): 95-104.

21.2649   Bernard, H.R. "The Power of Print: The Role of Literacy In
            Preserving Native Cultures." Human Organization 44, (Spring
            1985): 88-93.

21.2650   Brinkman, Heather, and Troy, Kathleen. "Getting Meaning Out
            of Print: The Beginning Adult ESL Literacy Class." TESL Talk
            14, 1-2 (Winter-Spring 1983): 119-128.

21.2651   Browne, R.B. "Popular Literature: A History and Guide From
            The Beginning of Printing To The Year 1897." Journal of
            Popular Culture 12, (Fall 1978): 368-371.

21.2652   Chandler, Carolyn Ebel. "Use The News: Press To Read:
            Literacy Now!" Journal of Reading 31, 8(May 1988): 746-748.

21.2653   Daniels, Harvey. "Literacy and The Popular Press: Fear and
            Loathing At The 'Chicago Tribune'." ETC: A Review of General
            Semantics 35, 3(September 1978): 284-293.

21.2654   Freeman, Evelyn B., and Sanders, Tobie. "The Social Meaning of
            Literacy: Writing Instruction and The Community." Language
            Arts 64, 6(October 1987): 641-645.

21.2655   Leader, Z. "Print and Post-Print." Times Literary Supplement
            4191 (July 29, 1983): 801.

21.2656   Leonard, Ann. "Developing Print Materials in Mexico For People Who Do Not Read." Educational Broadcasting International 13, 4(December 1980): 168-173.

21.2657   "Literacy and The Future of Print: Symposium." Journal of Communication 30, (Winter 1980): 89-204.

21.2658   Mattleman, M.S. and Gaige, M. "Newspapers and Adult Literacy: The Philadelphia Story." Journal of Reading 31, (October 1987): 68-69.

21.2659   Mitton, Roger. "Distance Education Research on Understanding Print." Convergence 10, 3(1977): 30-33.

21.2660   Moll, Luis C. "Writing as Communication: Creating Strategic Learning Environments For Students." Theory Into Practice 25, 2(Spring 1986): 103-108.

21.2661   Shannon, Patrick, and Samuels, Barbara G. "Developing an Understanding of Literacy Through Production of Pop-Up Books." Reading Horizons 25, 3(Spring 1985): 213-221.

           Argues that pop-up books are useful tools through which children not only develop their own literacy but also begin to understand the concept of the production of meaning. Provides a number of steps toward the development and understanding of literacy. Said steps include: (1) oral reading and analysis of pop-up books; (2) conversion of a picture book to a pop-up book; (3) the writing and rewriting of the text for a pop-up book; and (4) the production of an original pop-up book.

21.2662   Styles, Ken, and Cavanagh, Gary. "Three Stages in The Teaching of Writing." Ontario Education 10, 3(May/June 1978): 10-15.

21.2663   Taylor, Denny. "Translating Children's Everyday Uses of Print Into Classroom Practice." Language Arts 59, 6(September 1982): 546-549.

21.2664   Wells, C. Gordon. The Meaning Makers. N.P.: n.p., 1986.

21.2665   Zellermayer, M. "Writing and Thought: Comparing Hebrew and English." Etc., 42(Spring 1985): 72-77.

22

Literacy Classes

22.2666   Bloome, David. "Building Literacy and The Classroom Community." <u>Theory Into Practice</u> 25, 2(Spring 1986): 71-76.

Discusses the changing perception of the processes of reading and writing. Lists the aspects that the new conception of reading and writing emphasizes. States that literacy is a social process, and thus depends greatly on its community for its definition. Explores literacy and the nature of the classroom community; literacy across school, home, and work settings; and the building of literacy in the classroom.

22.2667   Bloome, David, ed. <u>Literacy and Schooling</u>. Norwood, New Jersey: Ablex Publishing Corporation, 1987.

22.2668   Bloome, D. and Golden, C. "Literacy Learning, Classroom Processes, and Race: A Microanalytic Study of Two Desegregated Classrooms." <u>Journal of Black Studies</u> 13, (December 1982): 207-226.

22.2669   Bourzeng, E. "Pour un Ensignement d'Anglais de Specialite aus Techniciens et aus Techniciens Superieurs (For The Teaching of English for Special Purposes to Technicians)." <u>Langues Modernes</u> 69, 2-3(1975): 155-160.

22.2670   Brennan, Mark. <u>Literacy and Learning, The Human Factor</u>. N.P.: n.p., 1984.

22.2671   Brick, Michael, and Sanchis Robert. "Literacy: Troubled Waters." <u>AV Guide: The Learning Magazine</u> 51, 9(September 1972): 8-11, 20-21.

22.2672   Evans, Peter J.A. "Grade 7 and 8 Writing Competencies
           Analyzed." Reporting Classroom Research 7, 2(March-April
           1978): 2-3.

22.2673   Harste, Jerome, and Stephens, Diane. "Literacy in the Secondary
           Special Education Classroom." Theory Into Practice 25, 2(Spring
           1986): 128-133.

22.2674   Holzman, Michael. "A Post-Freirean Model For Adult Literacy
           Education." College English 50, 2(February 1988): 177-189.

22.2675   McGee, Donna. "Reading Skills For Basic Literacy." TESL Talk
           9, 1(Winter 1978): 53-58.

23

Literacy Education

A.   GENERAL

23.A.2676   Adam, F. "Definicion de las Bondiones de una Politica Eficaz de
             la Educacion de los Adultos en la America Latina." <u>Convergence</u>
             2, 3(1969): 84-91.

23.A.2677   Adiseshiah, M.S. "Place of Literacy in Education." <u>Convergence</u>
             6, 1(9173): 9-14.

23.A.2678   "Adult Literacy in Industrialized Countries." (Report of an
             International Seminar). <u>Convergence</u> 15, 1(1982): 74-76.

23.A.2679   "After Tokyo." <u>Convergence</u> 5, 4(1972): 15-21.

23.A.2680   Allen, JoBeth. "Sarah Joins A Literate Community." <u>Language
             Arts</u> 63, 7(November 1986): 685-691.

23.A.2681   Allen, Virginia French. <u>Reading For Life</u>. N.P.: n.p., 1987.

23.A.2682   Alschuler, A., et al. "Collaborative Problem Solving As An Aim
             Of Education In A Democracy: The Social Literacy Project."
             <u>Journal of Applied Behavioral Science</u> 13, (July/August/
             September 1977): 315-326.

23.A.2683   Amberg, Jay. "The Buck Stopped Here: Letter From a High
             School English Teacher's Convention." <u>American Scholar</u> 49,
             3(Summer 1980): 385-390.

23.A.2684   Applebee, A.N., et al. "Learning To Be Literate: Reading,
             Writing, Reasoning," <u>The Education Digest</u> 53, (December
             1987): 6-8.

23.A.2685   Bell, M.S. "What Does Everyman Really Need From School
             Mathematics?" Mathematics Teacher 66, (March 1974): 196-202.

23.A.2686   Bell, T.H. "Toward A Learning Society." American Education
             20, (April 1984): 2-3.

23.A.2687   Berman, E.H. "Politics of Literacy and Educational Under-
             development in Kentucky." Comparative Education Review 22,
             (February 1978): 115-133.

23.A.2688   Berman R. "Stamping Out Illiteracy." Chronicle of Higher
             Education 17, (October 2, 1978): 72.

23.A.2689   Bernard, T.L. "World Illiteracy and International Develop-
             ment." Adult Leadership 16, (November 1967): 166-168.

23.A.2690   Bernick, M. "Illiteracy and Inner-city Unemployment (Job
             Training and Literacy Class Sponsored by San Francisco
             Renaissance)." Phi Delta Kappan 67, January 1986): 364-367.

23.A.2691   Bhola, H.S. "Why Literacy Can't Wait: Issues For The 1980's."
             Convergence 14, 1(1981): 6-23.

23.A.2692   Blakely, R.J. "Thistle." Adult Leadership 14, (April 1966): 322-325.

23.A.2693   Braddock, C. "Project 100,000." Phi Delta Kappan 48, (May
             1967): 425-428.

23.A.2694   Brain, J.J. "Role of The Volunteer." Adult Leadership 16, (June
             1967): 57.

23.A.2695   Brock, Paul. "Thunder Without Enlightening." English in
             Australia, 53 (September 1980): 44-49.

23.A.2696   Brownell, J.A. "Literacy and The Spectrum of Dialects."
             Yearbook (Claremont Reading Conference) 30, (1966): 48-55.

23.A.2697   "Call For Cash To Help Adult Literacy." Times Higher
             Education Supplement 487, (March 5, 1982): 6.

23.A.2698   Cairn, J.C. "The 1960's; A Decisive Decade For Literacy."
             Convergence 3, 2(1970): 11-18.

23.A.2699   Carr, W.G. "New Ideas in an Ancient Land." Today's Education
             59, (November 1970): 28-29.

23.A.2700   Carter, Ronald, and Burton, D. Literacy Text and Language
Study. London: Edward Arnold, 1982.

23.A.2701   Chall, J.S. "Literacy: Trends and Explanations." Educational
Researcher 12, (November 1983): 3-8.

23.A.2702   Chilcott, J.H. "Teaching Literacy in a Multi-cultural Society."
Yearbook (Claremont Reading Conference) 36, (1972): 20-24.

23.A.2703   Chumley, P.D., and Spille, H.A. "The Role of Postsecondary
Education Institutions in The U.S. Department of Education's
Adult Literacy Initiative." Innovative Higher Education 8,
(Spring/Summer 1984): 74-83.

23.A.2704   Cortright, R. "Another Simplified Spelling? English The New
Way." Reading Teacher 19, (April 1966): 508-511.

23.A.2705   Cortright, R.W. "Subject of Literacy Has Come of Age." Reading
Teacher 19, (October 1965): 9-13.

23.A.2706   Cortright, R.W. "Laubach Method." Wilson Library Bulletin 40,
(September 1965): 51-54.

23.A.2707   Cortright, R.W. "Professional Preparation in Literacy in
Education." Journal of Teacher Education 16, (September 1965):
290-293.

23.A.2708   Coulmas, Florian, ed. Linguistic Minorities and Literacy:
Language Policy Issues In Developing Countries. Hawthorne,
New York: Mouton, 1984.

23.A.2709   Crabtree, A.P. "War on Poverty." Adult Leadership 14,
(Sepbermber 1965): 105-6; 14(January 1966): 239.

23.A.2710   Datta, L.E. "Employment-Related Basic Skills." Yearbook
(National Society For The Study of Education) 1981, pt 2(1982):
140-168.

23.A.2711   Dean, N. "Students Help Illiterates." Times Educational
Supplement 2803, (February 7, 1969): 415.

23.A.2712   Dobinson, C.H. "Fundamental Education." British Journal of
Educational Studies 1, (May 1953): 121-130.

23.A.2713   Douglass, Malcolm P., ed. Claremont Reading Conference Forty-
Fifth Yearbook. Reading: What Is Basic? Proceedings of The

Claremont Reading Conference (48th, Claremont, California, January 16-17, 1981). Claremont, California: Claremont Graduate School, 1981. ED 205 909.

23.A.2714   Downing, J. "Cultural Priorities and The Acquisition of Literacy." International Review of Education 19, 3(1973): 345-355.

23.A.2715   Dumont, Bernard. "After Literacy Teaching: Paradoxes of Post-Literacy Work." Prospects 9, 2(1979): 145-158.

23.A.2716   "Editorial: Versions of Literacy." Use of English 38, 2(Spring 1987): 1-6.

23.A.2717   Eisner, E. "Mind As Cultural Achievement." Educational Leadership 38, (March 1981): 166-171.

23.A.2718   Elman, L. "Languages Key to Understanding." Advocate (Indiana) 11, (January-February 1983): 3.

23.A.2719   Elvin, L. "Fundamental Education." Institute of International Education News Bulletin 28, (October 1952): 10-13.

23.A.2720   Fennel, Jon, and Liveritte, Rudy. "Kuhn, Education, and the Grounds of Rationality." Educational Theory 29, 2(Spring 1979): 117-127.

23.A.2721   Finch, Hilary. "Sounds Ideas." Times Educational Supplement, 3267(January 20, 1978): 18-19.

23.A.2722   "First IRA Literacy Award 1979." Journal of Reading 23, (February 1980): 397-400.

23.A.2723   France, M.G. and Meeks, J.W. "Parents Who Can't Read: What The Schools Can Do." Journal of Reading 31, (December 1987): 222-227.

23.A.2724   "Functional Literacy in The Context of Adult Education." Convergence 6, 3-4 (1973): 64-66.

23.A.2725   Garman, Eric Thomas. "Economic Literacy of Prospective Business Education Teachers." Ed.D. dissertation, Texas Tech. University, 1969. 31/01-A, p. 264.

23.A.2726   Gillette, A. "Youth, Literacy, and Participation." International Review of Education 31, 4(1985): 373-395.

23.A.2727   Giroux, H.A. "Literacy and The Pedagogy of Voice and Political Empowerment." Educational Theory 38, (Winter 1988): 61-75.

23.A.2728   Goodman, K.S. "On Being Literate in an Age of Information." Journal of Reading 28, (February 1985): 388-392.

23.A.2729   Goodman, Kenneth S. "Acquiring Literacy is Natural: Who Skilled Cock Robin?" Theory Into Practice 16, 5(December 1977): 309-314.

23.A.2730   Greene, Maxine. "Toward Possibility: Expanding The Range of Literacy." English Education 18, 4(December 1986): 231-243.

23.A.2731   Gross, T.L. "Organic Teacher." Change 10, (June/July 1978): 37-39.

23.A.2732   Growing Through Literacy. Naremburn, N.S.W.: New South Wales. Department of Education, 1986.

23.A.2733   Guthrie, J.T. "Literacy and Thinking." Reading Teacher 31, (December 1977): 340-342.

23.A.2734   Guthrie, J.T. and Mosenthal, P.B. "Literacy as a Multidimensional: Locating Information and Reading Comprehension." Educational Psychologist 22, (Summer/Fall 1987): 279-297.

23.A.2735   Hildebrandt, W. "Some of the Roots of The Ideal of Universal Literacy." Reading Teacher 19, (October 1965): 4-8.

23.A.2736   Hoffman, M., and Morris, J., eds. "Forced to Champion The Cause of Literacy: Interview." Times Educational Supplement 3049, (November 2, 1973): 10.

23.A.2737   Holbrook, Hilary Taylor. "ERIC/RCS Report: Teachers Working With Parents." Language Arts 62, 8(December 1985): 897-901.

23.A.2738   Holdaway, Don. Stability and Change In Literacy Learning. N.P.: n.p., 1984.

23.A.2739   Holzman, M. "Teaching is Remembering." College English 46, (March 1984): 229-238.

23.A.2740   Holzman, Michael. "Opinion: The Social Context of Literacy Education." College English 48, 1(January 1986): 27-33.

23.A.2741   Ilsley, P.J. "Including Educationally Deprived Adults in The Planning of Literacy Programs." New Directions For Continuing Education 26, (1985): 33-42.

23.A.2742   "International Conference on Public Education; Recommendation No. 58 To The Ministries Of Education Concerning Literacy And Adult Education." 39, 3rd Quarter (1965): 195-204.

23.A.2743   International Consultative Liaison Committee For Literacy. (Second Session, Paris, 3-6 September 1968) Final Report. Paris: UNESCO, 1968. ED 028 367.

23.A.2744   "International Literacy Day; September 8." Times Educational Supplement 2729, (September 8, 1967): 387.

23.A.2745   Judy, Stephen. The ABCs of Literacy: A Guide For Parents and Educators. New York: Oxford University Press, 1979. ED 178 950.

23.A.2746   Kandel, I.L. "New Light On Fundamental Education." School & Society 73, (June 30, 1951): 411.

23.A.2747   Kempfer, H.H. "Manpower Through Literacy Education; State School Systems Can Create It." School Life 34, (October 1951): 1-2.

23.A.2748   Kliger, S. "Transformational-Generative Grammer and Literacy Education." Literacy Discussion 2, 3(Summer 1971): 135-149.

23.A.2749   Kocher, Margaret. "If You Care . . ." Elementary English 51, 4(April 1974): 483-487.

23.A.2750   Kozol, J. "How We Can Win: A Plan To Reach And Teach Twenty-Five Million Illiterate Adults." Wilson Library Bulletin 54, (June 1980): 640-642.

23.A.2751   Kretovics, Joseph R. "Critical Literacy: Challenging The Assumptions of Mainstream Educational Theory." Journal of Education 167, 2(1985): 50-62.

Analyzes the relationship between traditional educational theory and the acquisition of functional literacy skills. Contends that such a focus maintains the structural inequalities found in society. Argues that if the interests of society, democracy and justice are to be properly served, then the development of critical literacy - becoming critically literate - is important. Explores the notion of critical literacy, and what it would be like to live in such a society.

23.A.2752   Laubach, Frank C., and Laubach, Robert S. "The Role of The Volunteer Teacher." Harvard Educational Review 40, 2(May 1970): 277-279.

23.A.2753   Lazarus, R. "Reflections on Creating a Literate Environment." Convergence 15, 3(1982): 67-72.

23.A.2754   "Learning Them Literacy." Education & Training 20, 2(February 1978): 55, 57.

23.A.2755   "LEA's 'Self-imposed Ignorance'." Education 161, 22(June 3, 1983); 436.

23.A.2756   Lehr, Fran. "ERIC/RCS Report: Instructional Scaffolding." Language Arts 62, 6(October 1985): 667-672.

23.A.2757   "Literacy." (Symposium). Media In Education And Development 16, (March 1983): 2-20.

23.A.2758   "Literacy Awards For 1982." Convergence 16, 2(1983): 81-83.

23.A.2759   "Literacy Awards Honor Nation-wide Actions." (Conducted under the Auspices of Unesco). Convergence 13, 4(1980): 75-77.

23.A.2760   "Literacy Award Winners For 1972." Intellect 101, (December 1972): 150-151.

23.A.2761   "Literacy Education" - Special Issue of ASPBAE Journal (Asian-South Pacific Bureau of Adult Education) I, 2(November 1966): n.p.

23.A.2762   "Literacy For All By The Year 2000; The Udaipur Literacy Declaration." Convergence 14, 4(1981): 7-9.

23.A.2763   Literacy For Diverse Learners: Promoting Reading Growth At All Levels. Papers from the Eighteenth Annual Convention 1973. Newark, Delaware: International Reading Association, 1974.

23.A.2764   "Literacy: Reaching Special Groups." (Symposium). Delta Kappa Gamma Bulletin 51, (Winter/Spring 1985): 3-63.

23.A.2765   Luke, R.A. "Responsibility of The Teaching Profession For The
             Reduction of Mass Illiteracy." Reading Teacher 19, (October
             1965): 14-17.

23.A.2766   Lyman, Helen Huguenor. "Literacy Education as Library
             Community Service." Library Trends 28, 2(Fall 1979): 193-217.

23.A.2767   Lyon, N. "ABC of Literacy." New York State Education 55,
             (March 1968): 10-11.

23.A.2768   Mace, J. "Blaming The Victim: Attitudes to Literacy Tuition."
             Times Educational Supplement 3131, (May 30, 1975): 18-19.

23.A.2769   Malya, Simoni. "Traditional Oral Literature For Post-Literacy
             Reading Materials." Prospects 6, (1976): 98-102.

23.A.2770   Mason, H. "Fundamental Education and Functional Literacy:
             Problems and Possibilities." Convergence 6, 3-4(1973): 55-63.

23.A.2771   McGrath, E.J. "Schools For Survival." School Life 34, (April
             1952): 106.

23.A.2772   Meardy, W.H. "Challenge Not To Be Ignored, A." Community
             and Junior College Journal 54, (April 1984): 9.

23.A.2773   Medary, M. Each One Teach One. N.P.: Longmans, 1954.

23.A.2774   "Mobile Printing Units For Rural Communities." School &
             Society 96, (Summer 1968): 272.

23.A.2775   Monteith, M.K. "Paulo Freire's Literacy Method; ERIC/RCS
             Report." Journal of Reading 20, (April 1977): 628-629.

23.A.2776   Morioka, Kanji. "Readability and Listenability." In The Esthetics
             of Language, pp. 209-248. Edited by Endo Yoshimoto. Tokyo:
             Nakayama Shoten, 1958.

23.A.2777   Murphy, J.G. "Paulo Freire's Program For Adult Literacy."
             Forum of Education 36, 3(September 1977): 1-9.

23.A.2778   Muyoba, Godwin N. Literacy Workers' Guide: Some Selected
             Concepts. Lusaka: Department of Community Development,
             1972?

23.A.2779   Myers, M. "Shifting Standards of Literacy - The Teacher's
             Catch-22." English Journal 73, (April 1984): 26-32.

23.A.2780   Naas, N.   "New Development in Adult Education."   Conference
             on Reading. University of Pittsburgh, Report 22, (1966): 152-161.

23.A.2781   Nash, I.   "Literacy Grant May Bypass L.E.A.S."   Times
             Educational Supplement 3727, (December 4, 1987): 4.

23.A.2782   "New Style Literacy; Launching The Pilots."   Times Educational
             Supplement 2601, (March 26, 1965): 923.

23.A.2783   O'Hanlon, Anne. "Overuse Injury: Are Students At Risk?"
             Unicorn, Journal of the Australian College of Education. 12,
             2(May 1986): 124-127.

23.A.2784   Olsen, Turee. "ERIC/RCS: International Adult Education."
             Journal of Reading 16, 7(April 1973): 584-589.

23.A.2785   Orefice, Paolo. Educazione Permanente e Alfabetizzazione
             Funzionale. Roma: Ministero Rubblica Istruzione, 1970.

23.A.2786   Oxenham, John. Non-formal Education Approaches To
             Teaching Literacy. N.P.: n.p., 1975.

23.A.2787   Park, G. "Cultural Styles and the Achievement of Literacy."
             Yearbook (Claremont Reading Conference) 31, (1967): 27-33.

23.A.2788   Pratt, Sidney. "ESL/Literacy: A Beginning." TESL Talk 13,
             3(Summer 1982): 96-103.

23.A.2789   Rincon, Erminia, and Ray, Rose. "Bilingual Ethnic Teachers An
             Answer To Illiteracy An Drop-out Problems." Reading
             Improvement 11, 1(Spring 1974): 34-46.

23.A.2790   Robinson, D.W. "Schoolmaster McNamara." Phi Delta Kappan
             48, (October 1966): 49.

23.A.2791   Roucek, J.S. "Role of Literacy and Illiteracy in Social Change."
             International Review of Education 13, 4(1967): 483-491.

23.A.2792   Roueche, John E., et al. "Open Door or Revolving Door? Open
             Access and The Community College." Community, Junior and
             Technical College Journal 57, 5(April-May 1987): 22-26.

23.A.2793   Roueche, S.D., and Hudgens, A.G. "No Tunnel Vision Here."
             Community and Junior College Journal 59, (May 1980): 43-44.

23.A.2794   Ryan, L.V. "Vatican and UNESCO Link Efforts For World
Literacy." Adult Leadership 19, (October 1970): 120-123.

23.A.2795   Saindon, Jacqueline J., and Holt, Margaret E. "The Tragedy of
The Commons Revisited." Continuing Higher Education
Review 51, 3(Autumn 1987): 55-65.

23.A.2796   Sheldon, William D. "Reading Instruction In The 1970's For
Megalopolis or Center City." International Reading Association
Conference Proceedings, Part I, 13(April 1968): 41-46.

23.A.2797   Smith, Henry Lee, Jr. English Morphophonics: Implications For
The Teaching of Literacy. Monograph Number Ten. Syracuse,
New York: New York State English Council, 1968. ED 024 671.

23.A.2798   Smith, M. "Literature on Literacy." Media in Education And
Development 16, (March 1983): 20.

23.A.2799   Spache, George D. "The Research and Development Program
On Reading." Paper presented at the National Reading
Conference, St. Petersbury, Florida, 1970. ED 050 892.

23.A.2800   Stanley, Manfred. "Literacy: The Crisis of A Conventional
Wisdom." School Review 80, 3(May 1972): 373-408.

23.A.2801   Stark, John. "Rhetoric, Literacy and Citizenship." Rhetoric
Society Quarterly 16, 3(Summer 1986): 135-143.

23.A.2802   Stewart, David H. "Reading in English Departments." College
English 43, 8(December 1981): 818-823.

23.A.2803   "Struggle For Literacy, The." Wilson Quarterly 10, (Spring
1986): 94-133.

23.A.2804   Stubbs, Michael. Language and Literacy: The Sociolinguistics of
Reading and Writing. London: Routledge & Kegan Paul, 1980.

23.A.2805   Tedeschi, J.T., and Horai, J. "Tactics and Costs of Illiteracy War."
Educational Forum 31, (November 1966): 85-90.

23.A.2806   Tovey, Duane R., and Kerber, James E. Roles In Literacy
Learning: A New Perspective. Newark, Delaware:
International Reading Association, 1986.

23.A.2807   Tuman, Myron C. A Preface To Literacy: An Inquiry Into
Padagogy, Practice & Progress. Tuscaloosa, Alabama: University
of Alabama Press, 1987.

23.A.2808   Walshe, J. "World Literacy Effort Proposed." Times Educational
Supplement 3450, (August 13, 1982): 10.

23.A.2809   Watkins, B.T. "Colleges Seek Ways To Help Adults Who Can't
Read." Chronicle of Higher Education 25, (December 8, 1982): 8.

23.A.2810   Watts, J. "Reading The Key." Times Educational Supplement
2781, (September 6, 1968): 403.

23.A.2811   Webster, M. "Spreading The Written Word; UNESCO." Times
Educational Supplement 3211, (December 17, 1976): 10.

23.A.2812   Weimann, J.M. "Needed Research and Training in Speaking
and Listening Literacy." Communication Education 27,
(November 1978): 310-315.

23.A.2813   Whiteside, T. "Each One Teach One; Missionary Who Has
Helped 50,000,000 Learn To Read." Collier's 126, (August 5,
1950) 26-27.

23.A.2814   Wick, T. "Pursuit of Universal Literacy." Journal of
Communication 30, (Winter 1980): 107-112.

23.A.2815   Williams, Bill. "It Takes The Write Break." Access Magazine,
(September-October 1982): 13.

23.A.2816   Work, W. "Toward Comprehensive Communication Literacy:
ERIC Report." Communication Education 27, (November
1978): 336-342.

23.A.2817   Yesner, Seymour. "The Basics and the Basic Value of Human
Beings." English Journal 67, 1(January 1978): 15-17.

B.   COURSES OF STUDY

23.B.2818   Akamatsu, Carol Jane. "Instruction In Text Structure:
Metacognitive Strategy Instruction For Literacy Development In
Deaf Students." A.C.E.H.I. Journal 14, 1(1988): 13-32.

23.B.2819   Beauchesne, Jean-Marc. "Recreologie-L'Etude de L'Homme et du Loisir. (Recreology - The Study of Man and Leisure)." Convergence 2, 4(1969): 42-47.

23.B.2820   Bereiter, Carl, and Scardamalia, Marlene. "An Attainable Version of High Literacy: Approaches to Teaching Higher-Order Skills in Reading and Writing." Curriculum Inquiry 17, 1(Spring 1987): 9-30.

23.B.2821   Bertrand, Nancy Parks. A Descriptive Study Of Learning Literacy Skills In A Remedial Reading Classroom N.P.: n.p., 1984.

23.B.2822   Brown, Stephen, and Nathenson, Michael. "Designing Instructional Materials: Guesswork or Facts?" Distance Education 2, 1(March 1981): 7-22.

23.B.2823   Bullock, R.H. "Churches in a Literacy Program." International Journal of Religious Education 42, (May 1966): 18-19.

23.B.2824   Burron, Arni, and Santopietro, Kathy, comps. Course Outline Workshop II: Paraprofessional Training. Washington, D.C.: Office of Education, 1976. ED 124 887.

23.B.2825   Burron, Arni, and Santopietro, Kathy, comps. Course Outline Workshop III: Paraprofessional Training. Washington, D.C.: Office of Education, 1976. ED 124 888.

23.B.2826   Byron, William J. "Comprehensive Continuing Education The Only Way To Build on Literacy." Convergence 17, 3(1984): 18-22.

23.B.2827   Cain, Mary A. "Born To Read: Making A Reading Culture." Teacher 95, 5(January 1978): 64-66.

23.B.2828   Coffey, O.D. "Book 'em: No Read, No Release." Corrections Today 49, (June 1987): 116.

23.B.2829   "Conducting a Program of Basic Education With Adults." New York City. Board of Education. Curriculum Bulletins, 17 (1964-1965): 1-80.

23.B.2830   Corbet, Irene. "Literacy. 3. Towards Positive Remedial Treatment." Special Education 53, (Autumn 1964): 18-20.

23.B.2831   Corbet, Irene. "Literacy. 2. The Meaning and Application of Literacy." Special Education 53, (Summer 1964): 8-10.

23.B.2832   Corbet, Irene. "Literacy. 1. The Spread of Ability In The Schools." Special Education 53, (Spring 1964): 4-6, 26.

23.B.2833   Curtis, Krystyna J. "ABE and The Re-Education of Brain-Injured People." Adult Education (London) 59, 1(June 1986): 44-47.

23.B.2834   de Castell, Suzanne, and Luke, Allan. "Literacy Instruction: Technology and Technique." American Journal of Education 95, 3(May 1987): 413-440.

23.B.2835   De Faveri, Romayne. Curriculum Guide: ESL Instruction For Indochinese Refugees. Denver, Colorado: Spring Institute For International Studies, 1981. ED 215 556.

23.B.2836   De Lespinois, P. "Educating Foreign Illiterates In English." Modern Language Journal 42, (April 1958): 178-185.

23.B.2837   Fillion, Bryant. "Advice To The Curriculum Committee: Begin With The Three -cy's." English Journal 59, 8(November 1969): 1230-1232.

23.B.2838   Gibbons, Beryl. "Language and Literacy: An Investigation Into An LEA Instigated School-Focused In-Service Exercise." British Journal of In-Service Education 13, 2(Spring 1987): 90-94.

23.B.2839   Goddard, N.L. Literacy: Language, Experiences, Approaches. London: Macmillan Educational, 1974.

23.B.2840   Goldstein, Miriam B. The Teaching of Language In Our Schools: A MacMillan Guidebook For Parents. New York: The MacMillan Co., 1966. ED 024 689.

23.B.2841   Hemming, June, and Clifford, Lynne. "Caught or Taught? Some Implications For Literacy Development In A Shared-Reading Project." Education 3-13 16, 2(June 1988): 16-21.

23.B.2842   Howell, Olga M. "Never Too Late." Audiovisual Instruction 15, 3(March 1970): 81-82.

23.B.2843   Knott, Gladys. "Secondary School Contexts of Reading and Writing Instruction." Theory Into Practice 25, 2(Spring 1986): 77-83.

Discusses the current state of literacy development, and its facilitation, in the secondary school. Attempts to define the concept of literacy. Explores literacy development and secondary school students. Survey current practices of literacy development. Describes ways of facilitating literacy with secondary students. Also points out how to build a framework for literacy instruction. Included in said framework are the notions of classroom communication and instructional strategies.

23.B.2844   Lavallee, Marcel. "L'alphabetisation des personnes vivant avec un handicap mental." La Revue Canadienne de la deCicience Mentale 34, 3(Summer 1984): 22-32.

23.B.2845   Levinson, Melvin. "Literacy Without Reading." Media and Methods - Exploration In Education 8, 6(February 1972): 41-44, 63.

23.B.2846   Matiru, Barbara. "Training Literacy Teachers Through Distance Teaching." Bildung und Erziehung 36, 3(1983): 327-334.

23.B.2847   "New Literacy Package." Teacher 22, 6(November 23, 1983): 5.

23.B.2848   Park, Barbara. "Outdated Teaching Practices Hamper Literacy Development." Highway One 9, 2(Spring 1986): 67-70.

23.B.2849   Pearpoint, J.C. "Frontier College Literacy Education Since 1899." Prospects 17, 2(1987): 277-286.

23.B.2850   Ranard, Don, and Hazerson, Wayne. Teaching ESL To Illiterate Adults. Adult Education Series #9. Indo-Chinese Refugee Education Guides. Washington, D.C.: Center For Applied Linguistics, 1981. ED 197 628.

23.B.2851   Royston, Lloyd. A Curriculum And Methods Handbook for The Seasonally Employed Agricultural Workers' Program. Washington, D.C.: Office of Economic Opportunity, 1968.

23.B.2852   Santopietro, Kathy, and Coy, Joye Jenkins, comps. Course Outline Workshop I: Paraprofessional Training. Washington, D.C.: Office of Education, 1975. ED 124 886.

23.B.2853   Singh, Sohan. Learning To Read and Reading To Learn: An Approach To A System of Literacy Instruction. Teheran: International Institute For Adult Literacy Methods, 1976.

23.B.2854   Sloan, G.D. "Developing Literacy Through Literature." Reading Teacher 34, (November 1980): 132-136.

23.B.2855   Smith, Edwin H. Literacy Education For Adolescents and Adults: A Teacher's Resource Book. San Francisco: Boyd & Fraser Publishing Company, 1970. ED 036 776.

23.B.2856   "The Freire Method." Indian Journal of Adult Education 36, 6(June 1975): 17-18.

23.B.2857   Toward A Technological Breakthrough To Literacy. Brooklyn, New York: City University of New York, Brooklyn College, 1970. ED 046 620.

23.B.2858   Vinegrad M. Microteaching For Adult Literacy Skills With The PET Microprocessor. London: Kogan Page, 1983.

23.B.2859   Wood, W.R. "Community Responsibility For Literacy Education." School Life 34, (November 1951): 23.

C.   LIBRARY PARTICIPATION

23.C.2860   Albertus, Ursula. "The Role of Libraries In The Educational Literacy Programme: Library Services For New Literates." UNESCO Bulletin For Libraries 24, 4(July-August 1970): 201-204, 210.

23.C.2861   Axam, John A. "The Library's Role In Eradicating Illiteracy." Catholic Library World 55, 3(October 1983): 122-123.

23.C.2862   Cameron, J.R. "Librarian and a Redefinition of Literacy." Alberta School Library Review 10, (Winter 1973-1974): 6-9.

23.C.2863   Carter, Edward. Literacy. Libraries and Literacy. London: Library Association, 1969.

23.C.2864   Directory of Libraries, Information Centres and Projects In The Field of Literacy. Teheran: International Institute For Adult Literacy Methods, 1972.

23.C.2865   Directory of Libraries and Information Centres In The Field of Literacy. Teheran: International Institute For Adult Literacy Methods, 1973.

23.C.2866   Drennan, Henry. "Libraries and Literacy Education." Catholic Library World 52, 9(April 1981): 376-385.

23.C.2867   Fleming, Lois D. "The Role of the State Library Agency in the
             Battle for Literacy." Drexel Library Quarterly 14, 4(October 1978):
             65-72.

23.C.2868   Gerhardt, Stephen L. "Library Administered Remediation: One
             Program That Works." Community & Junior College Libraries
             4, 2(Winter 1985-1986): 41-44.

23.C.2869   Gillies, Laurey, et al. "Planning a Library-Based Program."
             Canadian Library Journal 37, 4(August 1980): 265-266.

23.C.2870   Johnson, Debra W., and Soule, Jennifer. Libraries & Literacy: A
             Planning Manual. Chicago: American Library Association, 1987.

23.C.2871   Koenke, K. "Libraries Take An Active Role In Literacy Training:
             ERIC/RCS (Report)." Reading Teacher 39, (May 1986): 940-943.

23.C.2872   Person, R.J., and Phifer, K.O. "Support For Literacy Education in
             Academic Libraries." College & Research Libraries 46, (March
             1985): 147-152.

23.C.2873   Phifer, Kenneth O., and Person, Ruth J. "The Role of
             Community College Libraries and Learning Resource Centers in
             Literacy Education." Community & Junior College Libraries 2,
             1(Fall 1983): 9-22.

23.C.2874   Smith, Ester Gottlieb. "The Literacy Education Gap: The
             Involvement of Public Libraries in Literacy Education." Library
             and Information Science Research 6, 1(January-March 1984):
             75-94.

23.C.2875   Strong, G. "Public Libraries and Literacy: A New Role To Play."
             Wilson Library Bulletin 59, (November 1984): 179-182.

23.C.2876   Thomas, Lucille C. "Librarians Can Make A Difference."
             Bookmark 44, 3(Spring 1986): 173-176.

23.C.2877   Weibel, Marguerite Crowley. The Library Literacy Connection.
             N.P.: n.p., 1984.

D.   RESEARCH

23.D.2878   Barnes, R.F. "Materials, Methods, and Programs For Literacy
             Education." Review of Educational Research 35, (June 1965):
             218-223.

23.D.2879   Bijou, Sidney W., and Ruiz, Roberto, eds. Behavior
             Modification: Contributions To Education. Hillsdale, New
             Jersey: L. Erlbaum Associates, 1981.

23.D.2880   Dudley-Marling, Curt. "The Role of SLP's in Literacy Learning."
             Journal of Childhood Communication Disorders 11, 1(Fall-
             Winter 1987): 81-90.

23.D.2881   Johnson, R.L., et al. "Attitude Changes Among Literacy Teachers
             Coincident With Training and Experience." Adult Education 18,
             (Winter 1968): 71-80.

23.D.2882   Juliebo, Moira Fraser. "To Mediate or Not To Mediate? That Is
             The Question." Language Arts 62, 8(December 1985): 848-856.

23.D.2883   Kierstead, J. "The Effects of a Single-task vs. a Multi-task
             Approach to Literacy: A Sociological View." Yearbook
             (Claremont Reading Conference) 1983, (1983): 100-109.

23.D.2884   Margo, R.A. "Educational Achievement In Segragated School
             Systems: The Effects of 'Separate-but-Equal.'" American
             Economic Review 76, (September 1986): 794-801.

23.D.2885   Miller, John W. "Ten Reform Reports That Can Change Your
             School." Principal 66, 2(November 1986): 26-28.

23.D.2886   Park, R.J. "Three Approaches To Improving Literacy Levels."
             Educational Horizons 66, (Fall 1987): 38-41.

23.D.2887   Reynolds, Richard J., et al. "Effect of Mode of Input On
             Ideational Fluency In Adult Training Groups." Journal of
             Reading Behavior 1, (Spring 1969): 53-63.

E.   TEACHING AIDS AND DEVICES/MATERIALS

23.E.2888   Amoroso, Henry C., Jr. "Organic Primers For Basic Literacy
             Instruction." Journal of Reading 28, 5(February 1985): 398-401.

23.E.2889   Audio Visual Aids And Some Aspects Of Literacy. Teheran:
International Institute For Adult Literacy Methods, 1971.

23.E.2890   Barbour, Thomas. The Road To Nowhere: A Play About
Illiteracy - Its Causes And Effects. New York: Plays For Living, A
Division Of The Family Service Association of America, 1979.

23.E.2891   Barnes, Robert F., and Hendrickson, Andrew. A Review And
Appraisal of Adult Literacy Materials and Programs. Columbus,
Ohio: Ohio State University Research Foundation, 1965.

23.E.2892   BCD Test Administrator's Manual. N.P.: n.p., 1982.

23.E.2893   Bhuiyan, A.A. Writers' Seminar On Preparation And
Production of Adult Literature, May 2-7, 1966. Comilla, East
Pakistan: East Pakistan Education Directorate, 1966.

23.E.2894   Bordman, Catherine I. Available Teaching Materials For
Undereducated English-Speaking Adults. Newark, New Jersey:
Newark Board of Education, 1968. ED 022 104.

23.E.2895   Brazziel, W.F. "Revolution In Materials For UnderEducated
Adults." Audiovisual Instruction 11, (April 1966): 254-256.

23.E.2896   Casey, Genevieve M., ed. Public Library Service To The Illiterate
Adult, Proceedings of A Seminar (March 9-11, 1972).
Washington, D.C.: Office of Education, 1972. ED 067 133.

23.E.2897   Cass, Angelica W. Basic Education For Adults: A Handbook For
Teachers, Teacher Trainers, and Leaders. Geneva: International
Institute For Labour Studies, 1971. ED 053 362.

23.E.2898   Colvin, Ruth J., and Root, Jane H. READ: Reading Evaluation
Adult Diagnosis. Syracuse, New York: Literacy Volunteers, Inc.,
1972. ED 078 236.

23.E.2899   Dames, J.J. Keyword Pictures For African Literacy Primers.
Nairobi, Kenya: Literacy Centre of Kenya, 1968.

23.E.2900   Federal Textbook on Citizenship. English and State Government. Home Study Course. Section 3 For Student. Revised
1973. Washington, D.C.: Department of Justice, 1973. ED 087
680.

23.E.2901   Federal Textbook On Citizenship. Our American Way of Life.
             Becoming A Citizen Series Book 1. Revised. Washington, D.C.:
             Department of Justice, 1974. ED 111 746.

23.E.2902   Gamapathy, K.R. Writing For Low Level Literates. N.P.:
             University of Agricultural Sciences, 1971.

23.E.2903   Gudschinsky, Sarah C. A Manual of Literacy For Preliterate
             Peoples. Dallas, Texas: Summer Institute of Linguistics, 1973.

23.E.2904   Heggart, P. "The Most Common Content Words For
             Instructional Purposes In Basic Literacy." Reading Education 3,
             2(Spring 1978): 5-14.

23.E.2905   Hollis, Jennie-Clyde, et. al., eds. Curriculum Guide To Adult
             Basic Education, Intermediate Level. Washington, D.C.: U.S.
             Department of Health, Education, and Welfare, Office of
             Education, 1966.

23.E.2906   How To Prepare Materials For New Literates. Newark,
             Delaware: International Reading Association, 1986.

23.E.2907   Inventory For Readiness For Literacy. Phase 1: Visual
             Discrimination and Select Cognitive Abilities. Albany, New
             York: New York State Education Department, Bureau of
             Continuing Education Curriculum Development, 1972.
             ED 069 959.

23.E.2908   Ivanic, T.R., and Lesirge, R. "Help Yourself To Reading:
             Materials For Literacy Groups." Times Educational Supplement
             3396, (July 24, 1981): 22.

23.E.2909   Johns, Jerry L. "A List of Basic Sight Words For Older Disabled
             Readers." English Journal 61, 7(October 1972): 1057-1059.

23.E.2910   Kapel, Marilyn B. "Improving Reading Competence of City
             Housing Authority Personnel: A Diversified Approach."
             Lifelong Learning 8, 3(November 1984): 16-20.

23.E.2911   Khawar, Rafiq, ed. Writing For New Readers; A Handbook on
             Writing, Translation, and Adaptation of Books. Karachi,
             Pakistan: National Book Center of Pakistan, 1963.

23.E.2912   Literacy Review, No. 1 - 1980. Teheran: International Institute
             For Adult Literacy Methods, n.d.

23.E.2913   Lyman, Helen H. Library Materials In Service To The Adult
             New Reader. Phase I, The Planning Year. Final Report.
             Madison, Wisconsin: University of Wisconsin, Library School,
             1968. ED 024 436.

23.E.2914   Management Handbook For Volunteer Programs. N.P.: n.p.,
             1984.

23.E.2915   Marshall, Ann. "Material Availability . . . Late Hour, Small Lot
             Production." Canadian Library Journal 37, 4(August 1980): 255-
             256.

23.E.2916   McKillian, K.R. A Handbook For Literacy Teachers. Nairobi,
             Kenya: East African Literature Bureau, 1964.

23.E.2917   Neijs, Karel. Literacy Primers; Construction, Evaluation and
             Use. Paris: UNESCO, 1961.

23.E.2918   Neijs, Karel. The Construction of Literacy Primers For Adults; A
             Handbook. Noumea, New Caledonia: South Pacific
             Commission, 1954.

23.E.2919   Nickse, Ruth S. Administrator's Handbook. N.P.: n.p., 1985.

23.E.2920   Otto, Wayne, and Ford, David. "Materials For Teaching Adults
             To Read." 1966. ED 015 108.

23.E.2921   Periodicals For New Literates; Seven Case Histories; Editorial
             Methods. Paris: UNESCO, 1957.

23.E.2922   Periodicals For New Literates; Editorial Methods. Paris:
             UNESCO, 1957.

23.E.2923   Planning, Administration & Monitoring In Literacy: Portfolio of
             Literacy Materials, 3 Volumes. Lanham, Maryland: Bernam -
             Unipub, 1984.

23.E.2924   Publishers of Easy-To-Read Materials: A Survey. Teheran:
             International Institute For Adult Literacy Methods, 1977.
             ED 141 774.

23.E.2925   Pyrczak, Fred. "Reducing Reading Illiteracy by Improving
             Reading Materials." Reading Improvement 13, 3(Fall 1976):
             159-162.

23.E.2926   Richards, Charles Granston, ed. The Provision of Popular
             Reading Materials; A Collection of Studies and Technical Papers.
             Paris: UNESCO, 1959.

23.E.2927   Shacklock, Floyd. World Literacy Manual. N.P.: n.p., 1970.

23.E.2928   Simple Reading Material For Adults: Its Preparation And Use.
             Paris: UNESCO, 1963.

23.E.2929   Smoker, D.E. "Southwestern Cooperative Educational
             Laboratory; Adult Basic Education Project." Adult Leadership
             17, (June 1968): 73-74.

23.E.2930   Teaching Materials. Teheran: International Institute For Adult
             Literacy Methods, 1971.

23.E.2931   Venning, P. "Group To Get L1m Litercy Hand-out." Times
             Educational Supplement 3103, (November 15, 1974): 5.

23.E.2932   Wallace, Mary C. Literacy Instructor's Handbook: An Adventure
             In Teaching. Chicago: Follett Publishing Company, 1965.

F.   THEORIES AND PRINCIPLES

23.F.2933   Akinnaso, F. Niyi. "The Consequences of Literacy in Pragmatic
             and Theoretical Perspectives." Anthropology and Education
             Quarterly 12, 3(Fall 1981): 163-200.

23.F.2934   Bertelson, Paul. The Onset of Literacy: Cognitive Processes In
             Reading Acquisition. Boston: Massachusetts Institute of
             Technology Press, 1987.

23.F.2935   Betsileo, Celestin. Conscientisation et Revolution de Paulo
             Freire. N.P.: n.p., 1980.

23.F.2936   Boston, Bruce O. "Conscientization and Christian Education."
             Learning For Living 13, (January 1974): 100-105.

23.F.2937   Brown, Cynthia. "Literacy in Thirty Hours: Paulo Freire's
             Process." Urban Review 7, 3(July 1974): 245-256.

23.F.2938   Brownhill, R.J. "Polanyi's Philosophy And Adult Reading
             Problems." Adult Education (London) 50, 5(January 1978): 289-
             293.

23.F.2939   Bugbee, John A. "The Freire Approach To Literacy: Review and Reflections." Literacy Discussion 4, 4(December 1973): 415-437.

23.F.2940   Cambourne, Brian. "Change and Conflict in Literacy Education: What It's All About." Australian Journal of Reading 8, 2(June 1985): 77-87.

23.F.2941   Cazden, Courtney. "Play With Language and Metalinguistic Awareness: One Dimension of Language Experience." International Journal of Early Childhood 6, 1(1974): 12-24.

23.F.2942   Chafel, Judith A. "Making Early Literacy a Natural Happening." Childhood Education 58, 5(May-June 1982): 300-304.

23.F.2943   "Changes In Teaching Literacy." Australian Journal of Reading 8, 2(June 1985): 104-109.

23.F.2944   Competency Based Adult Education: A Process Model. Sacramento, California: California State Department of Education, 1979. ED 240 391.

23.F.2945   Costigan, Margaret. "'You Have The Third World Inside You.': Conversation With Paulo Friere." Convergence 16, 4(1983): 32-38.

23.F.2946   Craker, G. "Promoting The Language Arts - A Conceptual Framework." Reading Around - A Digest For Teachers 9, 3(September 1981): 61-63.

23.F.2947   Cummings, Ian. "Enemies To Wonder: James Mill and The Diffusionists." Paedagogica Historica 11, 2(1971): 351-368.

23.F.2948   Delalic, Esref. Pre-Service Training For Teachers of Adult Basic Education. Andragogical Model. Handbook. Washington, D.C.: Department of Education, 1981. ED 210 481.

23.F.2949   Duprez, L. "Paulo Freire." Monday Morning 7, (February 1972): 15-16.

23.F.2950   Elias, John L. "Paulo Freire Literacy Method: A Critical Evaluation." McGill Journal of Education 10, 2(Fall 1975): 207-217.

23.F.2951   Enright, Carmel. "Literacy Symposium: Paulo Freire and The Maiden City." Adult Education (London) 47, (March 1975): 347-363.

23.F.2952   Facundo, Blanca. Issues For An Evaluation of Freire - Inspired Programs In The United States and Puerto Rico. Reston, Virginia: Latino Institute, 1984. ED 243 998.

23.F.2953   Fletcher, Philip R. Paulo Freire and Consientizacion In Latin America. New York: Ford Foundation, 1970. ED 072 334.

23.F.2954   Freire, Paulo. Alfabetizacao e Consciencializacao. N.P.: n.p., 198?

23.F.2955   Freire, Paulo. "Literacy and The Possible Dream." Prospects 6, 1(1976): 68-71.
23.F.2956   Freire, Paulo. "Conscientisation." Month 7, (May 1974): 575-578.

23.F.2957   Freire, Paulo. Pedagogy of The Oppressed. New York: Herder and Herder, 1970.

Discussion of the role of conscientizacao and the process of literacy. Examination of the pedagogy of the oppressed. Review of the "banking" concept of education, and how it functions as an instrument of oppression. Explores dialogics, and the essence of education as the practice of freedom. Concludes with an analysis of both dialogics and antidialogics as the matrices from which are generated opposing theories of cultural action.

23.F.2958   Galtung, Johan. "Literacy, Education and Schooling - For What?" Convergence 8, 4(1975): 39-49.

23.F.2959   Gere, Anne Ruggles. "Practise into Theory." English Journal 69, 2(February 1980): 87-90.

23.F.2960   Giroux, H.A. "Literacy and The Pedagogy of Voice and Political Empowerment." Educational Theory 38, (Winter 1988): 61-75.

Examination of the concept of illiteracy as a "cultural marker" within the context of cultural deprivation theory. Presents a brief overview and critique of radical literacy. Discusses the development of an emancipatory theory of literacy. Explores the Freirean Model of emancipatory literacy, critical literacy as a precondition for self - and social empowerment, literacy and the liberation of rememberance, and literacy as a form of cultural politics.

23.F.2961   Grabowski, Stanley M., ed. Paulo Freire: A Revolutionary Dilemma For The Adult Educator. Syracuse, New York: Syracuse University, Publications in Continuing Education, 1972.

23.F.2962   Guthrie, John T. "Research : Equilibrium of Literacy." Journal of Reading 26, 7(April 1983): 668-670.

23.F.2963   Hamadache, Daniel, and Martin, Ali. Theory and Practice of Literacy Work: Policies, Strategies & Examples. Lanham, Maryland: Bernan-Unipub, 1987.

23.F.2964   Hannan, B. "Left, Right, Left, Right, or After Literacy, What." Secondary Teacher, 12(August 15, 1979): 8-9.

23.F.2965   Harste, J., et al. "Examining Our Assumptions: a Transactional View of Literacy and Learning." Research in The Teaching of English 18, (February 1984): 84-108.

23.F.2966   Haverson, Wayne W., and Haynes, Judith L. ESL/Literacy For Adult Learners. Language In Education: Theory and Practice, No. 49. Washington, D.C.: National Institute of Education, 1982. ED 217 703.

23.F.2967   Haviland, R. Michael. "An Introduction To The Writings of Paulo Freire." Adult Education (London) 45, 5(January 1973): 280-285.

23.F.2968   Heyman, R.D. "Theoretical Look At Knowledge, Schools and Social Change." Comparative Education Review 18, (October 1974): 411-418.

23.F.2969   Kazemek, Francis E. "Adult Literacy Education: An Ethical Endeavor." Adult Literacy and Basic Education 8, 2(1984): 61-72.

23.F.2970   Kazemek, Francis E. Toward A Theoretical Framework of Adult Literacy. N.P.: n.p., 1983.

23.F.2971   Kazemek, Francis E. Epistemology and Adult Literacy: An Experientialist, Pragmatic Perspective. N.P.: n.p., 1983.   ED 236 326.

23.F.2972   Kazemek, Francis E. Writing In The Adult Literacy Program: A Theoretical Base. N.P.: n.p., 1983. ED 243 123.

23.F.2973   Kerr, A. "Is Instruction In Literacy Still A Means of Social Control." Australian Journal of Reading 5, 4(November 1982): 223-225.

23.F.2974   Kolers, Paul A., and Perkins, David N. "Spatial and Ordinal Components of Form Perception and Literacy." Cognitive Psychology 7, 2(April 1975): 228-267.

23.F.2975   Lado, Robert. "The Learning-Assimilation-Facility (LAF) Hypothesis in Preschool Literacy." Reading Teacher 38, 6(February 1985): 548-553.

23.F.2976   Lloyd, Arthur S. "Freire, Conscientization, and Adult Education." Adult Education 23, 1(1972): 3-20.

23.F.2977   Mackie, Robert, ed. Literacy and Revolution: Pedagogy of Paulo Freire. London: Pluto Press, 1980.

23.F.2978   Maring, Gerald H. "Freire, Gray and Robinson on Reading." Journal of Reading 21, 5(February 1978): 421-425.

23.F.2979   Mashayekh, Farideh. "Freire, The Man, His Ideas and Their Implications." Literacy Discussion, (Spring 1974): 1-62.

23.F.2980   McDonald, D. "Educating The Oppressed; An Interview With Paulo Freire." Center Magazine 19, (September/October 1986): 16-18.

23.F.2981   Metalinguistic Awareness and Beginning Literacy. N.P.: n.p., 1986.

23.F.2982   Minney, Robin. "Paulo Freire - People Must 'Name The World'." Times Educational Supplement 3052, (November 13, 1973): 4.

23.F.2983   Newton, James. Literature Review of The Writings and Conversations of Paulo Friere. N.P.: n.p., 1985. ED 262 207.

23.F.2984   O'Neill O'Flaherty, Patricia. "Paulo Friere On Literacy and Conscientization." Journal of Applied Educational Studies 4, (Summer 1975): 28-33.

23.F.2985   Owen, Robert. Revolution In The Mind & Practice of The Human Race New York: Kelley, 1973.

23.F.2986   Parker, Robert P. "Are Our Standards Slipping?" English in Australia 40, (May 1977): 5-19.

23.F.2987   Pryor, John. "Education For Humanization And The Theology
             of Liberation: Thoughts on The Writings of Paulo Freire."
             Learning For Living 13, (January 1974): 106-109.

23.F.2988   Reid, Jessie F. "Towards A Theory of Literacy." In Reading and
             Related Skills: Proceedings Of The Ninth Annual Study
             Conference Of The United Kingdon Reading Association,
             Hamilton 1972. London: Ward Lock Educational, 1973. 28-36.

23.F.2989   Ryan, John W. ed. Paulo Freire, Literacy Through
             Conscientization. Teheran: International Institute For Adult
             Literacy Methods, 1974. ED 114 790.

23.F.2990   Salinger, Terry S. A Brief Background of Non-Formal Education
             And Two Applications In Reading. N.P.: New Mexico State
             University, 1978. ED 182 702.

23.F.2991   Sanders, T.G. "The Paulo Freire Method: Literacy Training and
             Conscientization." Dialogue 7, 1(April 1973): 19-31.

23.F.2992   Sanders, Thomas G. The Paulo Freire Method. American
             Universities Field Staff Reports. Hanover, New Hampshire:
             American Universities Field Staff, Inc., 1968. ED 101 294.

23.F.2993   Spencer, Margaret. "Emergent Literacies: A Site For Analysis."
             Language Arts 63, 5(September 1986): 443-453.

23.F.2994   Starratt, Robert J. "On Paulo Freire And The Reform Move-
             ment." National Elementary Principal 52, 6(April 1973): 28-30.

23.F.2995   Street, Brian V. Literacy In Theory And Practice. Cambridge:
             Cambridge University Press, 1985.

23.F.2996   Timpson, William M. "Paulo Freire: Advocate of Literacy
             Through Liberation." Educational Leadership 45, 5(February
             1988): 62-66.

23.F.2997   "Towards a Theory of Literacy." Times Educational Supplement
             2803, (February 7, 1969): 396.

23.F.2998   Wick, Thomas Mead. Theories of Reading. N.P.: n.p., 1980.

23.F.2999   Winch, C.A. "Education, Literacy and The Development of
             Rationality." Journal of Philosophy of Education 17,
             2(December 1983): 187-200.

23.F.3000   Winterowd, W. Ross. "Literacy: 'Kultur' and Culture."
             Language Arts 64, 8(December 1987): 869-874.

23.F.3001   Worpole, Ken. "The Gates': Writing Within The Community."
             Children's Literature in Education 17, (Summer 1975): 76-87.

23.F.3002   Wren, Brien. "Introducing Paulo Freire." Learning for Living
             13, (January 1974): 96-99.

24

Literacy Instruction

24.3003   Anzalone, Stephen, and McLaughlin, Stephen. Making Literacy Work: The Specific Literacy Approach. Amherst, Massachusetts: University of Massachusetts, Center For International Education, 1983.

24.3004   Bassano, Sharon, and Christison, Mary Ann. "Multi-Sensory Language Teaching." TESL Talk 14, 3(Summer 1983): 15-24.

24.3005   Bleich, David. "Teaching Literacy." Teaching English in The Two-Year College 6, 2(Winter 1980): 161-181.

24.3006   Calfee, Robert. "Literacy and Illiteracy: Teaching The Nonreader To Survive In The Modern World." Annals Of Dyslexia 32. (1982); 71-91.

24.3007   Carbo, Marie. "Matching Reading Styles: Correcting Ineffective Instruction." Educational Leadership 45, 2(October 1987): 55-62.

24.3008   Cashdan, A. Literacy: Teaching and Learning Language Skills. Oxford: Blackwell, 1985.

24.3009   "Consequences of Initial Failure in Learning To Read, The." H. Esson. IN SPELD, Victoria. Reading Difficulty and The Intelligent Under-Achiever. (Melbourne, 1971). pages 24-27.

24.3010   Curtis, Redmond. "Literacy and The Subject Teacher." Journal of Education (Halifax, Nova Scotia) 7, 3(1982): 1-5.

24.3011   Darkenwald, G. "Literacy Education For Non-English Speaking Adults In The U.S.A." Literacy Discussion 2, 4(Autumn 1971): 155-169.

24.3012   DeCastell, S. and Luke, A. "Literacy Instruction: Technology and Technique." American Journal of Education 95, (May 1987): 413-440.

24.3013   de Clerck, Marcel. The Operational Seminar: A Pioneering Method of Training For Development. Educational Studies and Documents No. 20. Paris: UNESCO, 1976. ED 134 674.

24.3014   Doak, Cecilia Canrath. Teaching Patients With Low Literacy Skills. N.P.: n.p., 1985.

24.3015   Evans, David R. Games and Simulations In Literacy Training. Teheran: International Institute For Adult Literacy Methods, 1979.   ED 174 957.

24.3016   Farr, Roger, and Olshavsky, Jill Edwards. "Is Minimum Competency Testing The Appropriate Solution To SAT Decline?" Phi Delta Kappan 61, 8(April 1980): 528-530.

24.3017   Feathers, K.M. and Smith F.R. "Meeting The Reading Demands of The Real World: Literacy Based Content Instruction." Journal of Reading 30, (March 1987): 506-511.

24.3018   Franklin, Elizabeth Anne. "Literacy Instruction For LES Children." Language Arts 63, 1(January 1986): 51-60.

24.3019   Functional Literacy: A Method of Training For Development. Paris: UNESCO, 1970. ED 051 485.

24.3020   Gambell, Trevor J. "Literacy, Curriculum and Teacher Education." English in Australia, 67 (March 1984): 3-9.

24.3021   Goodman, Yetta, and Goodman, Kenneth. "Twenty Questions About Teaching Language." Educational Leadership 38, 6(March 1981): 437-442.

Presents what the authors believe to be their scientific base of knowledge upon which a developmental literacy program can be constructed. Format is in the form of twenty true-false statements, followed by the answer, and then supported with a discussion. Authors encourage other professionals to share their thoughts with their colleagues.

24.3022   Harste, Jerome C., et al. Language Stories and Literacy Lessons. Portsmouth, New Hampshire: Heinemann Educational Books, Inc., 1984. ED 257 113.

24.3023   Hayden, H.M.R., and Fagan, W.T. "Keeping It In Context:
           Strategies For Enhancing Literacy Awareness." First Language 7,
           Part 2, 20(1987): 159-171.

24.3024   Holdaway, Don. Stability and Change in Literacy Learning.
           London, Ontario: University of Western Ontario, Faculty of
           Education, 1983.

24.3025   Holmes, Elizabeth. "Report From a Teacher." Canadian Library
           Journal 37, 4(August 1980): 273-274.

24.3026   Hoover, Wesley A. Language and Literacy In Bilingual
           Instruction: Preliminary Report. Cantonese Site Analytic Study.
           Washington, D.C.: National Institute of Education, 1982. ED
           245 572

24.3027   Hunter-Grundin, Elizabeth. Literacy: A Systematic Start.
           London: Harper & Row, 1979.

           Presents the author's belief regarding beginning reading and
           literacy. Examines the concepts of reading readiness, and the
           development of language skills. Looks at the nature of the
           pupil-teacher relationship, and how that relationship is further
           related to reading. Argues that the development of systematic
           language and reading - communication skills - are central to the
           curriculum of and infant school. Concludes with the analysis of
           a research project which the author states, empirically supports
           her approach.

24.3028   Kliger, Samuel. "Transformational-Generative Grammar and
           Literacy Education." Literacy Discussion 3, 2(June 1972): 259-
           276.

24.3029   Koenke, Karl. "ERIC/RCS: Libraries Take An Active Role in
           Literacy Training." Reading Teacher 39, 9(May 1986): 940-943.

24.3030   Langer, Judith, ed. Literacy and Culture: Issues of Society and
           Schooling. Norwood, New Jersey: Ablex Publishing
           Corporation, 1987.

24.3031   Language and Literacy Learning In Bilingual Instruction:
           Executive Summary. Washington, D.C.: National Institute of
           Education, 1983. ED 245 573.

24.3032   Last, Mary J. "A Staff-Resident Literacy Training Programme."
           Education 60, 3(December 1987): 240-244.

24.3033   Luke, Allan. "The Non-Neutrality Of Literacy Instruction: A
           Critical Introduction." Australian Journal of Reading 11, 2(June
           1988): 79-83.

24.3034   Mace-Matluck, Betty J., et al. Language and Literacy Learning In
           Bilingual Instruction: Preliminary Report. Descriptive Studies -
           Asian, Spanish, Navajo. Washington, D.C.: National Institude
           of Education, 1982. ED 245 571.

24.3035   Mace-Matluck, Betty J., et al. Language and Literacy Learning In
           Bilingual Instruction: A Case Study of Practices and Outcomes.
           Washington, D.C.: National Institude of Education, 1982. ED
           245 574.

24.3036   Maguerez, Charles. La Promotion Technique du Travailleur
           Analphabete. Paris: n.p., 1966.

24.3037   McKillian, K.R. A Handbook for Literacy Teachers. Nairobi,
           Kenya: East African Literture Bureau, 1964   ED 018 689.

24.3038   Meeting on Literacy Training, Berlin (West). Final Report. July
           11-17, 1975. Bonn: German Foundation For International
           Development, 1976. ED 132 288.

24.3039   Mellott, Robert S. "Another Dimension, a Publisher
           Comments." Canadian Library Journal 37, 4(August 1980): 259-
           260.

24.3040   Morris, Betty Ruth. "Basic Considerations For Teaching Reading
           In The ESL Classrooms." Adult Literacy and Basic Education 5,
           2(Summer 1981): 97-105.

24.3041   Myers, Miles. "The National Writing Project: Literacy and
           Teaching." National Forum: Phi Kappa Phi Journal 65, 4(Fall
           1985): 32-34.

24.3042   Newman, Anabel P. Literacy Instructor Training. N.P.: n.p.,
           1978.

24.3043   Norman, Charles A., and Malicky, Grace V. "Application of
           Adult Learning Principles To Literacy Instruction." Adult
           Literacy and Basic Education 6, 2(Summer 1982): 61-72.

24.3044   Out Of The Shadows: Starting Points For Planning Literacy
           Projects. Toronto: TVOntatio, 1983.

24.3045   Paton, James M. "Literacy and Teachers of English." Teacher Education, 11(October 1977): 80-87.

24.3046   Patterson, Karalyn, and Kay, Janice. "Letter-by-Letter Reading: Psychological Descriptions of a Neurological Syndrome." Quarterly Journal of Experimental Psychology. A Human Experimental Psychology 34A, Part 3 (August 1982): 411-441.

24.3047   Peck, S.D. "Teaching Literacy Training." Library Journal 113, (April 15, 1988): 56.

24.3048   Perry, Joseph A., Jr. "Phonemics and Literacy." Literacy Discussion 3, 2(June 1972): 187-198.

24.3049   Pritchard, N.A., and Chamberlain, R.G.D. "Special Purpose English: Changing Approaches To English Language Teaching. RECL Journal 5, 2(December 1974): 48-57.

24.3050   Rahnema, Majid. "Literacy: To Read The Word or The World?" Prospects 6, 1(1976): 72-82.

24.3051   Ritter, Ellen M. "'Back To Basics' and Accountability Issues in Secondary School Speech Education." Communication Education 27, 2(March 1978): 119-126.

24.3052   Robinson, Richard D. "How To Present A Reading Lesson." Literacy Work 2, 4(May 1973): 55-59.

24.3053   Rockas, Leo. "Teaching Literacy." College Composition and Communication 28, 3(October 1977): 273-275.

24.3054   Sachs, Murray. "Literacy, Learning, and Foreign Language Study." ADFL Bulletin 13, 3(March 1982): 13-16.

24.3055   Singh, Sohan. Learning To Read and Reading To Learn. N.P.: n.p., 1976.

24.3056   Sofo, Francesco. "A Different Approach To Literacy - Graphics." Australian Journal of Adult Education 25, 2(July 1985): 27-34.

24.3057   Stimpson, Catharine R. "Is There A Core In This Curriculum? And Is It Really Necessary?" Change 20, 2(March-April 1988): 26-31.

24.3058   Stoodt, Barbara D. Reading Instruction. Boston: Houghton Mifflin, 1981.

24.3059   Thiagarajan, Sivasailam. Programmed Instruction For Literacy
               Workers; A Guide For Developing Self-Instructional Materials
               and Strategies For Adult Learners, Literacy Teachers and
               Discussion Leaders. Literacy In Development: A Series of
               Training Monographs. Teheran: International Institute For
               Adult Literacy Methods, 1976. ED 138 114.

24.3060   Unsworth, Len. "Whole Language or Procedural Display? The
               Social Context of Popular Whole Language Activities."
               Australian Journal of Reading 11, 2(June 1988): 127-137.

24.3061   Vinegrad, M.D. "Learning by Example: A CBT Approach."
               Programmed Learning and Educational Technology 21,
               3(August 1984): 218-222.

24.3062   "World Drive At Crucial Point." School & Society 99,
               2337(December 1971): 461-462.

25

Literacy Organizations, Campaigns and Volunteers

25.3063   Adam, C. "Campaign For All Seasons." <u>New Statesman</u> 90, (November 14, 1975): 601-602.

25.3064   Arnove, R.F. and Graff, H.J. "National Literacy Campaigns: Historical and Comparative Lessons." <u>Phi Delta Kappan</u> 69, (November 1987): 202-206.

25.3065   Bernstein, Judith. <u>People, Words and Change. Literacy Volunteer Handbook</u>. Ottawa, Ontario: Algonquin College, 1980. ED 198 310.

25.3066   "Beyond The Ringing Phrase: An Interview With Ruth Love Holloway." <u>Reading Teacher</u> 25, 2(November 1971): 118-128.

25.3067   Bhola, H.S. <u>Campaigning For Literacy</u>. N.P.: n.p., 1984.

25.3068   Bhola, H.S., et al. <u>The Promise of Literacy. Campaigns, Programs and Projects. Report of The International Seminar on Campaigning For Literacy (Udaipur, India, January 4-11, 1982)</u>. Bonn: German Foundation For International Development, 1983. ED 237 730.

25.3069   Brown, Barbara E. "The Identification of Major Competencies and Attributes Needed By Volunteer Literacy Tutors of Adults." <u>Adults Literacy and Basic Education</u> 6, 1(Spring 1982): 27-34.

25.3070   Burger, W.E. and Kennedy, E.M. "A Literacy Corps For The 90's." <u>Teacher Educator</u> 23, (Winter 1987-1988): 25-27.

25.3071   Buttz, John Raymond. "Educational Goals and Motivational Deter-minants Inherent In Participants In Volunteer Literacy Education." Ed. D. dissertation, Indiana University, 1968. 29/06-A, p.1747.

25.3072   "Campaign Against Illiteracy." International Bureau of
            Education Bulletin 14, (1st Quarter 1940): 16.

25.3073   Cleland, Donald L. "Education's Moonshot: Our Challenge."
            Reading Teacher 25, 2(November 1971): 133-137.

25.3074   Cohen, R. "Partners For Literacy; Literacy Volunteers, Inc.
            Syracuse, New York." American Education 6, (June 1970): 36.

25.3075   Cohn, William L. "Meeting Adult Literacy Needs." Catholic
            Library World 52, 2(September 1980): 54-56.

25.3076   Comings, John, and Kahler, David. Peace Corps Literacy
            Handbook. Appropriate Technologies For Development.
            Manual M-21. Washington, D.C.: Peace Corps, 1984. ED 251
            696.

25.3077   Community Relations Handbook. Syracuse, New York: Literacy
            Volunteers, Inc., 1977. ED 188 465.

25.3078   Contribution To Study of The Rural Environment Within The
            Framework of Functional Literacy Operations. Paris: UNESCO,
            1979. ED 194 244.

25.3079   Correa, Hector, and Reimer, Everett. "Planning A Literacy
            Campaign And Other Educational Programs." Scientia
            Paedagogica Experimentalis 7, 1(1970): 15-22.

25.3080   Curle, A. "World Literacy Campaign; Plea For Integration."
            Times Educational Supplement 2536, (March 6, 1964): 571.

25.3081   Curle, Adam. World Campaign For Universal Literacy;
            Comment And Proposal. Cambridge, Massachusetts: Harvard
            University, 1964.

25.3082   "Dana W. Allen Heads Literacy Commission." Adult Leadership
            12, (January 1964): 209.

25.3083   Directory of 338 Literacy Projects And Institutions In 96
            Countries. Teheran: International Institute For Adult Literacy
            Methods, 1971. ED 068 777.

25.3084   Directory of Literacy And Adult Learning Programs. N.P.: n.p.,
            1979?

25.3085   Emery, Donald G. "The National Reading Center." Reading
           Teacher 25, 2(November 1971): 138-141.

25.3086   Experimental World Literacy Programme, The. N.P.: n.p., 1976.

25.3087   Fakouri, Ebrahim. "Some Psychological Aspects of Literacy
           Programs." Literacy Work 2, 4(May 1973): 19-27.

25.3088   Geyer, John J. "When Static Becomes Theory." Journal of
           Reading Behavior 3, 3(Summer 1971): 1-8.

25.3089   Gibb, Frances. "Adult Literacy Campaign Draws The Crowds."
           Times Higher Education Supplement 220, (January 9, 1976): 9.

25.3090   Gold, K. "DES To Take Over From Adult Body." Times Higher
           Education Supplement 549, (May 13, 1983): 1.

25.3091   Gold, P.C. and Horn, P.L. "Intelligence and Achievement of
           Adult Illiterates In A Tutorial Project: A Preliminary Analysis."
           Journal of Clinical Psychology 39, (January 1983): 107-113.

25.3092   Haendle, Connie. Organizational Management Handbook.
           Syracuse, New York: Literacy Volunteers, Inc., 1976. ED 188
           464.

25.3093   Haendle, Connie. "The Community Link: Libraries and The
           Literacy Volunteers of America." Wilson Library Bulletin 50,
           9(May 1976): 731-733.

25.3094   Haussman, Fay. "Literacy Campaigns Emphasize Informal
           Methods." Times Educational Supplement 3116, (February 14,
           1975): 17.

25.3095   Hinzen, Heribert, et al. "Cooperating or Campaigning For
           Literacy? Invitation To Dialogue." Convergence 17, 3(1984):
           52-63.

25.3096   Huus, Helen. "Right To Read, IRA, and What You Can Do."
           Reading Teacher 25, 2(November 1971): 112-117.

25.3097   Imel, S. "Volunteers and Adult Literacy Education (Ideas From
           ERIC)." Adult Literacy and Basic Education 10, 2(1986): 117-128.

25.3098   "Interview (With) Dr. Theodore L. Harris." Reading Newsreport
           6, 1(October 1971): 4-9.

25.3099   Issues In Planning And Implementing National Literacy
           Programmes. London: International Institute For Educational
           Planning, H.M.S.O., 1985.

25.3100   Jacobs, Bella. Tutoring Older Adults In Literacy Programs. N.P.:
           n.p., 1986.

25.3101   Karunaratne, Garvin. "Developing a Functional Literacy
           Programme." Literacy Work 5, 4(Winter 1976-1977): 45-51, 53,
           54.

25.3102   Kaston, Carren. The Community of The Book. N.P.: n.p., 1986.

25.3103   Kirkaldy, Kohn. "Major Campaigns To Stamp Out Illiteracy."
           Times Educational Supplement 2989, (September 1, 1972): 12.

25.3104   Land, C.O. "Social Research and Literacy Campaigns."
           International Review of Education 9, 4(1963/1964): 418-429.

25.3105   Laubach Literacy. Syracuse, New York: Laubach Literacy Fund,
           n.d.

25.3106   Lawson, V.K., et al. Read All About It! Tutor Adults With Daily
           Newspaper. Tutor Handbook. Syracuse, New York: Literacy
           Volunteers of America, Inc., 1984. ED 244 518.

25.3107   "Literacy Campaign Snowballs." Times Educational Supplement
           2551, (April 10, 1964): 898.

25.3108   Literacy Trainer Handbook. Syracuse, New York: New Readers
           Press, 1980.

25.3109   "Major Groups Merge To Form New African Association For
           Literacy and Adult Education." Convergence 16, 3(1983): 73-74.

25.3110   Martin, Larry G. "Student's Life-Style Classifications: Key To
           Improved Literacy Programs." Lifelong Learning 10,
           1(September 1986): 12-15.

25.3111   Mathies, Lorraine. "Citings On The Educational Horizon."
           Educational Horizons 54, 2 (Winter 1975-1976): 107-108.

25.3112   Mattleman, M.S. and Gaige, M. "Literacy." Media & Methods
           24, (January/February 1988): 9-10.

25.3113   Meyer, Valerie, et al. "Some Basic Principles of The Reading
            Process Required of Literacy Volunteers." Journal of Reading
            29, 6(March 1986): 544-548.

25.3114   Moore, Allen B. "Reading Literacy Development To Career
            Development." Adult Literacy and Basic Education 2, 3(Fall
            1978): 190-200.

25.3115   Muyoba, G.N. Literacy Workers' Guide. N.P.: n.p., 1972?

25.3116   Norris, W. "Fighting Illiteracy in US (With College Students)."
            Times Higher Education Supplement 767, (July 17, 1987): 8.

25.3117   Quezada, Shelley, and Soolman, Roberta. "Establishing and
            Evaluating Library Literacy Programs." Catholic Library World
            57, 6(May-June 1986): 267-270.

25.3118   Rauch, Sidney J., and Sanacore, Joseph, eds. Handbook For The
            Volunteer Tutor, 2nd Edition. Newark, Delaware: International
            Reading Association, 1985.

25.3119   Reducing Functional Illiteracy: A National Guide To Facilities
            and Services. Lincoln, Nebraska: American Association of
            Advertising Agencies Contract Center, n.d. ED 170 511.

25.3120   Richards, M. "Extension For Unit." Times Higher Education
            Supplement 592, (March 9, 1984): 1.

25.3121   Richards, M. "Literacy Unit Counts on the Next Ten Years."
            Times Higher Education Supplement 590, (February 24, 1984):
            11.

25.3122   Rogers, Joy J. "Maintaining Volunteer Participation In Adult
            Literacy Programs." Lifelong Learning 8, 2(October 1984): 22-24.

            Presents data on the incidence of functional illiteracy. Examines
            the roll of the adult literacy tutor, and the depletion of the pool
            of potential volunteer tutors. Discusses six strategies designed to
            retain the volunteer tutor. Concludes with a brief discussion of
            the Laubach paradigm pertaining to the relationship between
            student and tutor.

25.3123   Ross, Lorraine N., and Lidoff, Lorraine. Senior Volunteer
            Literacy Tutors. Washington, D.C. : National Concil on The
            Aging, 1984.

25.3124   Scoble, J., et al. "Training Family and Friends as Adult Literacy Tutors." Journal of Reading 31, (February 1988): 410-417.

25.3125   Smith, Eleanor Touhey. "Adult Functional Illiteracy: A Pervasive Problem." Catholic Library World 55, 3(October 1983): 117-121.

25.3126   Spencer, D. "Question of ACACE Successor in Doubt." Times Education Supplement 3511, (October 14, 1983): 5.

25.3127   Straley, Walter W. "On The Morning of The Fifth Day." Reading Teacher 25, 2(November 1971): 129-132.

25.3128   Swick, Kevin J., and Driggers, R. Kim. "Educational Needs and Programs: A Common Sense Approach For Educational Leaders." Education 96, 3(Spring 1976): 276-277.

25.3129   "The Right To Read: Report of Forum 7." Reading Teacher 25, 6(March 1972): 592.

25.3130   Thomas, Audrey M. "Organizational Models For Literacy Programs." Canadian Library Journal 37, 4(August 1980): 261-264.

25.3131   United Nations. World Campaign For Universal Literacy: Note. New York: United Nations, 1965.

25.3132   Universities and Institutes Offering Literacy Training Programmes: Directory. Teheran: International Institute For Adult Literacy Methods, 1977. ED 150 406.

25.3133   Vafa, Annette. "Volunteer Tutors Must Have Training and Support." Canadian Library Journal 37, 4(August 1980): 267-269.

25.3134   Villaume, John M. "Theory-Informed Middle-Range Eveluation of Literacy Programs." Literacy Discussion 5, 3(Fall 1974): 471-506.

25.3135   Williams, Margaret, et al. Read All About It! Tutor Adults With Daily Newspaper. Leader Handbook. Syracuse, New York: Literacy Volunteers of America, 1984. ED 244 519.

25.3136   Witty, P.A. "Campaign Against Illiteracy." National Parent-Teacher 53, (November 1958): 20-23.

25.3137   Wolf, Evelyn, and Kavanagh, Catherine. "Adult Illiteracy: A
           Public Library Responds." Catholic Library World 55, 3(October
           1983): 125-128.

25.3138   Workshop Leader's Handbook. Syracuse, New York: Literacy
           Volunteers, Inc., 1977.   ED 188 463.

25.3139   World Directory of Literacy Organizations. New Delhi: Literacy
           International Committee, 1973?

25.3140   "World Literacy Congress-Teheran." Canadian National
           Commission For UNESCO Bulletin 8, (February 1966): 7.

26

Literacy Research

A.   LITERACY RESEARCH

26.A.3141   Albaugh, Thomas A., and Porreca, Anthony G. "Accounting
            Instruction Builds Economic Literacy." Business Education
            Forum 39, 5(February 1985): 31-34.

26.A.3142   Allington, Richard L., and Walmsley, Sean A. "Functional
            Competence in Reading Among The Urban Aged." Journal of
            Reading 23, 6(March 1980): 494-497.

26.A.3143   Altus, W.D. "Relationship Between Vocabulary and Literacy
            When Intelligence Is Held Constant." Journal of Social
            Psychology 31, (May 1950): 299-301.

26.A.3144   Altus, W.D., and Bell, H.M. "Analysis of Four Orally
            Administered Measures of Adjustment." Educational and
            Psychological Measurement 7, 1(1947): 101-115.

26.A.3145   Badry, Fatima. "Acquisition of Derivational Rules In Moraccan
            Arabic: Implications For The Development of Standard Arabic
            As A Second Language Through Literacy." Ph.d. dissertation,
            University of California, Berkeley, 1983. 44/08-A, p. 2392.

26.A.3146   Brown, Don A., and Newman, Anabel P. "Research In Adult
            Literacy." Journal of Reading Behavior 2, 1(Winter 1970): 19-
            46.

26.A.3147   Clark, Jack Manning. "The Prediction of Gain In Reading
            Among Adult Illiterated From An Analysis of Items on The
            Wechsler, Leiter and Davis-EELLs Scales." Ed. D. dissertation,
            University of New York at Buffalo, 1971. 32/05-A, p. 2512.

26.A.3148   Cook, Jacqueline, and Quinones, Anisia. <u>Spanish Literacy</u> <u>Investigation Project</u>. Albany, New York: New York State Education Department, 1983. ED 234 182.

26.A.3149   Davidoff, J.B., et al. "Information Extraction From Brief Verbal Displays: Half-Field and Serial Position Effects For Children, Normal and Illiterate Adults." <u>British Journal of Psychology</u> 73, Part 1(February 1982): 29-39.

26.A.3150   Davidson, Judith. "Adolescent Illiteracy: What Libraries Can Do To Solve The Problem - A Report on The Research of The Project on Adolescent Illiteracy." <u>Journal of Youth Services in Libraries</u> 1, 2(Winter 1988): 215-218.

26.A.3151   de M.P. Parante, M.A., and Lecours, A.R. "The Influence of Cultural Factors In Neuropsychology and Neurolinguistics." <u>International Social Science Journal</u> 40, (February 1988): 97-108.

26.A.3152   Dickinson, W., and Hembrough, A.R. "The Design and Implementation of Research: With Reference to Research into Numeracy and Literacy of Engineering Students." <u>Coombe Lodge Reports</u> 9, 12(1976): 429-433.

26.A.3153   Downing, John. "An Application of The Comparative Method To A Practical Educational Problem: Literacy Learning." <u>School Review</u> 83, 3(May 1975): 449-459.

26.A.3154   Dyson, Anne Haas. "'Learning To Write/Learning To Do School: Emergent Writers' Interpretations of School Literacy Tasks." <u>Research in The Teaching of English</u> 18, 3(October 1984): 233-264.

26.A.3155   Dyson, Anne Haas. "Research Currents: Who Controls Classroom Writing Contexts?" <u>Language Arts</u> 61, 6(October 1984): 618-626.

26.A.3156   Ewoldt, Carolyn. "A Descriptive Study of The Developing Literacy of Young Hearing-Impaired Children." <u>Volta Review</u> 87, 5(September 1985): 109-126.

26.A.3157   Gee, James P. "Orality and Literacy: From The Savage Mind To Ways With Words." <u>TESOL Quarterly</u> 20, (December 1986): 719-746.

Examines how the dichotomy literate/illiterate has replaced the civilized/primitive dichotomy. Continues on to discuss how the current dichotomy can be applied to social groups in a modern society. Reviews some of the literature on orality and literacy. Discusses language and literacy acquisition as a form of socialization, different literacy practices, and literacy and the English teacher.

26.A.3158   Gibbons, Beryl. "Language and Literacy: An Investigation Into An LEA Instigated School-Focused In-Service Exercise." British Journal of In-Service Education 13, 2(Spring 1987): 90-94.

26.A.3159   Gold, Patricia Cohen, and Johnson, John A. "Entry Level Achievement Characteristics of Youth and Adults Reading Below Fifth Level: A Preliminary Profile and Analysis." Adult Literacy and Basic Education 5, 4(Winter 1981): 197-208.

26.A.3160   Goudreau, N. "Improve Your Adult Literacy Instruction by Vitalizing The Research." Lifelong Learning 10, (November 1986): 17-20; (January 1987): 11-14.

26.A.3161   Grohsmeyer, Frederick, and Johnson, Richard R. A Comparison of Two Techniques of Teaching Scientific Method In Introductory Psychology Laboratories: Stage 1, The Development of An Evaluative Instrument. Final Report. Washington, D.C.: Office of Education, 1968. ED 035 941.

26.A.3162   Guthrie, John T. "Research Views: Acquisition of Newspaper Readership." Reading Teacher 34, 5(February 1981): 616-618.

26.A.3163   Guthrie, John T. "Research Views: Three Facts of Reading Achievement." Reading Teacher 33, 6(March 1980): 750-752.

26.A.3164   Guthrie, John T. "Research: Being Literate." Journal of Reading 22, 5(February 1979): 450-452.

26.A.3165   Hall, Budd. "Notes on Literacy Research: The State of The Art." Convergence 8, 4(1975): 14-22.

26.A.3166   Hartley, M., and Swanson, E. Achievement and Wastage: An Analysis of The Retention of Basic Skills In Primary Education. Washington: The World Bank, 1984.

26.A.3167   Holmes, John. "Thoughts On Research Methodology " Studies In Adult Education 8, 2 (October 1976): 149-163.

26.A.3168   Literacy and Education For Adults; Research In Comparative Education. Geneva: International Bureau of Education, 1964.

26.A.3169   Literacy Projects. Report on The Replies Received To The
             Institute's Questionnaire. Final Report. Teheran: International
             Institute For Adult Literacy Methods, 1971. ED 057 351.

26.A.3170   McPhail, Irving P. "Toward an Agenda For Urban Literacy: The
             Study of Schools Where Low-Income Black Children Read At
             Grade Level." Reading World 22, 2(December 1982): 132-149.

26.A.3171   Meek, Margaret. Achieving Literacy: Longitudinal Studies of
             Adolescents Learning To Read. New York: Methuen, Inc. 1983.

26.A.3172   Newman, Anabel P. Twenty Lives Nineteen Years Later: A
             Longitudinal Study (1964-1983) of The Impact of Literacy on The
             Occupations, Schooling, and Educational Growth of Young
             Adults Who Were Low Reading Readiness In First Grade With
             Special Attention Given To Model, Motivation, Interest,
             Perseverance, and Pressure As Aspects of Background and
             Mental Environment. Bloomington, Indiana: Indiana
             University, Language Education Department, 1985. ED 262 390.

26.A.3173   Norman, Charles A., and Malicky, Grace V. "A Comparison of
             Two Approaches For Teaching Reading To Adults." Adult
             Literacy and Basic Education 8, 2(1984): 91-101.

26.A.3174   Otto, Wayne. "Research: Wondering Why is Weyauwega, WI."
             Journal of Reading 30, 8(May 1987): 752-755.

26.A.3175   Otto, Wayne. "Research: Peter Johnston, We Salute You."
             Journal of Reading 29, 7(April 1986): 700-703.

26.A.3176   Pettit, Neila T., and Cockriel, Irvin W. "A Factor Study of The
             Literal Reading Comprehension Test And The Inferential
             Reading Compre-hension Test." Journal of Reading Behavior 6,
             1(April 1974): 63-75.

26.A.3177   Phillips, C.J.; Stott, D.H.; and Birrell, Heather V. "The Effects of
             Learning Style on Progress Towards Literacy and Numeracy."
             Educational Review 39, 1(1987): 31-40.

26.A.3178   Proceedings of The Great Literacy Crisis Symposium, San Diego
             State University, October 2, 1978. Washington, D.C.: National
             Endowment For The Humanities, 1978. ED 169 519.

26.A.3179   Qutub, Ishaq Y., et al. Illiteracy As An Impediment To
             Production: An Empirical Investigation. Sirs-El-Layyan,

Menoufia, Egypt: Regional Centre For Functional Literacy In Rural Areas For The Arab States, 1972. ED 068 764.

26.A.3180   "Research Summaries." Action in Teacher Education 5, 4(Winter 1983-1984): 53-61.

26.A.3181   Rodgers, Bryan. "Change in The Reading Attainment of Adults: A Longitudinal Study." British Journal of Development Psychology 4, 1(March 1986): 1-17.

26.A.3182   Sawyer, Wayne. "Literature and Literacy: A Review of Research." Language Arts 64, 1(January 1987): 33-39.

26.A.3183   Shaughnessy, Mina. "Some Needed Research on Writing." College Composition and Communication 28, 4(December 1977): 317-320.

26.A.3184   Spaulding, S. "Research on Content, Methods, and Techniques in Education For Development." Review of Educational Research 38, (June 1968): 277-292.

26.A.3185   Survival Literacy Study. New York: Harris and Associates, Inc., 1970. ED 068 813.

26.A.3186   Van Dongen, Richard. "Children's Narrative Thought, at Home and at School." Language Arts 64, 1(January 1987): 79-87.

26.A.3187   Vogt, Dorathee K. Literacy Among Youths 12-17 Years, United States. Rockville, Maryland: National Center For Health Statistics, 1973.

B.   LITERACY STATISTICS

26.B.3188   Abel, J.F. Graphic Presentation of Statistics of Illiteracy By Age Groups. N.P.: Superintendent of Documents, 1930.

26.B.3189   Caliver, Ambrose. Literacy Education; National Statistics and Other Related Data. Washington, D.C.: U.S. Department of Health, Education, and Welfare, Office of Education, 1953.

26.B.3190   Caughran, Alex M., and Lindlof, John A. "Should The 'Survival Literacy Study' Survive?" Journal of Reading 15, 6(March 1972): 429-435.

26.B.3191   "Census Returns on Illiteracy and School Attendance." School Review 39, (November 1931): 641-3.

26.B.3192   Comparative Analysis of Male and Female Enrolment and Illiteracy. N.P.: n.p., 1980.

26.B.3193   "Decrease In Illiteracy As Shown By The Census." School and Society 34, (July 11, 1931): 49-50.

26.B.3194   de S. Brunner, E. "Trends In Educational Attainment, 1940-1950." Teachers College Record 55, (January 1954): 191-196.

26.B.3195   Educational Trends In 1970, An International Survey. Geneva: International Bureau of Education, 1970. ED 049 950.

26.B.3196   Grant, W.V. "Comparative Statistics on School Attendance and Illiteracy." American Education 7, (December 1971): 45.

26.B.3197   Literacy Education; National Statistics and Other Related Data. Washington, D.C.; United States Office of Education, 1953.

26.B.3198   Literacy 1967-1969; Progress Achieved In Literacy Throughout The World. Paris: UNESCO, 1970. ED 043 820.

26.B.3199   "Literacy Program; Concern Expressed As Result of Census Report." Education For Victory 1, (July 1, 1942): 12.

26.B.3200   Literacy Projects. N.P.: International Institute For Adult Literacy Methods, 1971.

26.B.3201   Literacy Projects; Report On The Replies Received To The Institute's Questionnaire. Teheran: International Institute for Adult Literacy Methods, 1971.

26.B.3202   Literacy Statistics From Available Census Figures. Paris: UNESCO, 1950.

26.B.3203   McGrail, Janet. Adult Illiterates and Adult Literacy Programs: A Summary of Descriptive Data. Washington, D.C.: National Institute of Education, 1984. ED 254 756.

26.B.3204   Rycroft, W. Stanley, and Clemmer, Myrtle M. The Struggle Against Illiteracy. New York: United Presbyterian Church in The U.S.A., 1964.

26.B.3205   Sopher, D.E. "Measure of Disparity." The Professional
              Geographer 26, (November 1974): 389-392.

26.B.3206   Statistics of Educational Attainment and Illiteracy: 1945-1974.
              Paris: UNESCO, 1977.

26.B.3207   Towards A Methodology For Projecting Rates of Literacy and
              Educational Attainment. N.P.: n.p., 1978.

26.B.3208   Vaugrante, Christiane. Techniques For Analysing Changes In
              Literacy Rates and In The Number of Illiterates. N.P.: n.p., 1970.

26.B.3209   World Illiteracy At Mid-Century, A Statistical Study. Paris:
              UNESCO, 1957.

26.B.3210   World Literacy At Mid-Century, A Statistical Study. N.P.:
              UNESCO, 1957.

27

Mathematical Literacy

27.3211   Barron, A. and Murray, J. "Problems of Numeracy and Literacy
           in Undergraduates." European Journal of Engineering
           Education 4, 2, 3(February 1980): 175-179.

27.3212   Battista, M.T. "The Relationship of Mathematics Anxiety and
           Mathematical Knowledge to The Learning of Mathematical
           Pedagogy by Preservice Elementary Teachers." School Science
           and Mathematics 86, (January 1986): 10-19.

27.3213   Beattie, I.D. "Modeling Operations and Algorithms."
           Arithmetic Teacher 33, (February 1986): 23-28.

27.3214   Beckmann, M.W. "Eighth-grade Mathematical Competence; 15
           Years Ago and Now." Arithmetic Teacher 17, (April 1970): 334-
           335.

27.3215   Beckmann, M.W. "Ninth Grade Mathematical Competence: 15
           Years Ago and Now." School Science and Mathematics 69,
           (April 1969): 315-319.

27.3216   Bednarz, N., and Janvier, B. "A Constructivist Approach To
           Numeration In Primary School: Results of A Three Year
           Intervention With The Same Group of Children." Educational
           Studies in Mathematics 19, (August 1988): 299-331.

27.3217   Behr, M.J., et al. "Order and Equivalence of Rational Numbers:
           A Clinical Teaching Experiment." Journal for Research in
           Mathematics Education 15, (November 1984): 323-341.

27.3218   Bell, A., et al. "Choice of Operation in Verbal Arithmetic
           Problems: The Effects of Number Size, Problem Structure and
           Context." Educational Studies in Mathematics 15, (May 1984):
           129-147.

27.3219   Berry, John W. "Learning Mathematics in a Second Language: Some Gross-Central Issues." For The Learning of Mathematics - An International Journal of Mathematics Education 5, 2(June 1985): 18-23.

27.3220   Bondl, H. "Mathematics, The Universities and Social Change." Universities Quarterly 20, (September 1966): 407-419.

27.3221   Brunner, R.B. "Reading Mathematical Exposition." Educational Research (Great Britain) 18, (June 1976): 208-213.

27.3222   Burton, G.M., and Knifong, J.D. "What Does Division Mean?" School Science and Mathematics 83, (October 1983): 464-473.

27.3223   Byers, V., and Erlwanger, S. "Memory in Mathematical Understand-ing." Educational Studies in Mathematics 16, (August 1985): 259-281.

27.3224   Byers, V., and Erlwanger, S. "Content and Form in Mathematics." Educational Studies in Mathematics 15, (August 1984): 259-275.

27.3225   Cauley, K.M. "Construction of Logical Knowledge: Study of Borrowing In Subtraction." Journal of Educational Psychology 80, (June 1988): 202-205.

27.3226   Cobb, P. "An Investigation of Young Children's Academic Arithmetic Contexts." Educational Studies in Mathematics 18, (May 1987): 109-124.

27.3227   Comber, G. "Math and Science - The Easy Liberal Arts." Improving College & University Teaching 31, (Winter 1983): 4.

27.3228   Cox, P.L. "Informal Geometry - More Is Needed." Mathematics Teacher 78, (September 1985): 404-405.

27.3229   Curcio, F.R. "Comprehension of Mathematical Relationships Expressed in Graphs." Journal For Research in Mathematics Education 18, (November 1987): 382-393.

27.3230   D'Ambrodio, U. "Mathematics Education In A Cultural Setting." International Journal of Mathematical Education In Science And Technology 16 (July/August 1985): 469-477.

27.3231   Davis, P.J. "What Do I Know? A Study of Mathematical Self-Awareness." College Mathematics Journal 16, (January 1985): 22-41.

27.3232   De Corte, E., et al., "Influence of Rewording Verbal Problems on Children's Problem Representations and Solutions." Journal of Educational Psychology 77, (August 1985): 460-470.

27.3233   Denvir, B. and Brown, M. "The Feasibility of Class Administered Diagnostic Assessment in Primary Mathematics." Educational Research 29, (June 1987): 95-107.

27.3234   Denvir, B. and Brown, M. "Understanding of Number Concepts In Low Attaining 7-9 Year Olds: The Teaching Studies." Educational Studies in Mathematics 17, (May 1986): 143-164.

27.3235   Denvir, B., and Brown, M. "Understanding of Number Concepts in Low Attaining 7-9 Year Olds: Development of Descriptive Framework and Diagnostic Instrument." Educational Studies in Mathematics 17, (February 1986): 15-36.

27.3236   Downing, D. "Time To Look and Listen One-To-One." Times Educational Supplement 3750, (May 13, 1988): B 30.

27.3237   Ernest, P. "A Model of The Cognitive Meaning of Mathematical Expressions." Journal of Educational Psychology 57, (November 1987): 343-370.

27.3238   Forbes, J.E. "Some Thoughts on Minimal Competencies." Mathematics Teacher 71, (February 1978): 94-100.

27.3239   Frankenstein, M. "Critical Mathematics Education: An Application of Paulo Freire's Epistemology." Journal of Education 165, (Fall 11983): 315-339.

27.3240   Galbraith, P.L. "The Use of Mathematical Strategies: Factors and Features Affecting Performance." Educational Studies in Mathematics 17, (November 1986): 413-441.

27.3241   Galbraith, P.L. "Mathematical Vitality of Secondary Mathematics Graduates and Prospective Teachers: A Comparative Study." Educational Studies in Mathematics 13, (February 1982): 89-112.

27.3242   Ginther, J.L. et al. "Three Decade Comparison of Elementary Teachers' Mathematics Courses and Understandings." School Science and Mathematics 87, (November 1987): 587-597.

27.3243   Good, T.L. and Grouws, D.A. "Increasing Teachers' Understanding of Mathematical Ideas Through Inservice Training." Phi Delta Kappan 68, (June 1987): 778-783.

27.3244   Goodwin, R. "Even Contest; Education and Industry." Times Educational Supplement 3219, (February 11, 1977): 32.

27.3245   Greenberg, Herbert J. "The Objectives of Mathematics Education." Mathematics Teacher 67, 7(November 1974): 639-643.

27.3246   Kane, R.B. "School Mathematics: Where To Now?" Arithmetic Teacher 14, (February 1967): 126-131.

27.3247   Kennedy, L.M. "A Rationale (For Using Manipulative Materials)." Aritmetic Teacher 33, (February 1986): 6-7.

27.3248   Kirkman, S. "Weak Maths No Barrier To New Technology." Times Educational Supplement 3608, (August 23, 1985): 3.

27.3249   Lauda, D.P. "Technology Education: A Fundamental Framework For Improved Capability in Math and Science." Technology Teacher 45, (November 1985): 3-6.

27.3250   Leinhardt, G. "Getting To Know: Tracing Students' Mathematical Knowledge From Intuition To Competence." Educational Psychologist 23, (Spring 1988): 119-144.

27.3251   Leinhardt, G., and Smith, D.A. "Expertise in Mathematics Instruction: Subject Matter Knowledge." Journal of Educational Psychology 77, (June 1985): 247-271.

27.3252   Leinhardt, G., and Smith, D. "Why Johnny Can't Fractionate." Phi Delta Kappan 67, (September 1985): 68-69.

27.3253   Le Roux, A.A. "Numeracy: An Alternate Definition." International Journal of Mathematical Education in Science and Technology 10, 3(July-September 1979): 343-354.

27.3254   Lichtenberg, B.K. "Mathematical Literacy For Teachers? Of Course!" Arithmetic Teacher 34, (December 1986): Inside Cover.

27.3255   Madell, R.L. "Children Can Understand Mathematics."
Arithmetic Teacher 29, (January 1982): 18-21.

27.3256   "Mathematical and Scientific Literacy For The High Tech
Society." (Symposium). Educational Leadership 41, (December
1983/January 1984): 4-18.

27.3257   "Mathematical Competencies and Skills Essential For
Enlightened Citizens." National Council of Teachers of
Mathematics. Committee on Basic Mathematical Competencies
and Skills." Arithmetic Teacher 19, (November 1972): 601-607.

27.3258   Moody, W.B. "Arithmetic: Must It Be Mechanical Monotony
and Individualized Boredom?" Arithmetic Teacher 24, (January
1977): 65-69.

27.3259   Mullen, G.S. "How Do You Measure Up?" Aritmetic Teacher
33, (October 1985): 16-21.

27.3260   Nesher, P., et al. "Development of Semantic Categories For
Addition and Subtraction." Educational Studies in Mathematics
13, (November 1982): 373-394.

27.3261   Nicholson, A.R. "Mathematical Literacy." Mathematics in
School 9, 2(March 1980): 33-34.

27.3262   Orton, A. "Students' Understanding of Differentation."
Educational Studies in Mathematics 14, (August 1983): 235-250.

27.3263   Orton, A. "Students' Understanding of Integration."
Educational Studies in Mathematics 14, (February 1983): 1-18.

27.3264   Osborne, Alan. "Mathematical Literacy and Teacher Education."
Journal of Research and Development in Education 15,
(Summer 1982): 19-29.

Reviews the call of three position papers on the mathematics
curriculum, and their recommendations. Raises the question,
then, that if there is a shift in the goals of the mathematics
curriculum, will this necessitate a change in teacher education
programs. Discusses the goal shifts in mathematical literacy, the
relationship between teachers and curriculum development,
and mathematical literacy and habituated behaviors.

27.3265   Phillips, J.M. "Mathematical Literacy, Junior Grade." Instructor
81, (February 1972): 59-61.

27.3266   Pigge, F.L., et al. "Updated Comparison of The Number Of
           Mathematics Courses Taken By Elementary Teachers and Their
           Mathematical Understandings." School Science and
           Mathematics 80, (December 1980): 643-650.

27.3267   Pigge, F.L., et al. "Today's Elementary School Teachers Are
           Better Prepared in Mathematics." Arithmetic Teacher 26,
           (March 1979): 48-51.

27.3268   Post, T.R. "Order and Equivalence of Rational Numbers: A
           Cognitive Analysis." Journal For Research in Mathematics
           Education 16, (January 1985): 18-36.

27.3269   Presmeg, N.C. "School Mathematics In Culture-Conflict
           Situations." Educational Studies In Mathematics 19, (May
           1988): 163-177.

27.3270   Pribnow, R. "Why Johnny Can't Read World Problems."
           School Science and Mathematics 69, (October 1969): 591-598.

27.3271   Rosin, R.T. "Gold Medallions: The Arithmetic Calculations of
           an Illiterate." (Reprinted From The Council on Anthropology
           and Education Newsletter, July 1973). Anthropology &
           Education Quarterly 15, (Spring 1984): 38-50.

27.3272   Saxe, G.B. "Effects of Schooling on Arithmetical
           Understandings: Studies With Oksapmin Children In Papua
           New Guinea." Journal of Educational Psychology 77, (October
           1985): 503-513.

27.3273   Schoenfeld, A.H. "When Good Teaching Leads To Bad Results:
           The Disasters of 'Well Taught Mathematics Courses.'"
           Educational Psychologist 23, (Spring 1988): 145-166.

27.3274   Schultz, K.A. "Representational Models From The Learners'
           Perspective." Arithmetic Teacher 33, (February 1986): 52-55.

27.3275   Senechal, M., and Fleck, G. "Two-Dimensional Math in a Three-
           Dimensional World." Education Digest 51, (October 1985): 50-
           52.

27.3276   Simon, M.A. "The Teacher's Role In Increasing Student
           Understanding of Mathematics." Educational Leadership 43,
           (April 1986): 40-43.

27.3277   Stiff, L.V. "Understanding Word Problems." Mathematics
            Teacher 79, (March 1986): 163-165.

27.3278   Taylor, D.H. "Alternatives To Social Promotion." Arithmetic
            Teacher 30, (November 1982): 6.

27.3279   Wheeler, M.M., and Feghali, I. "Much Ado About Nothing:
            Preservice Elementary School Teachers' Concept of Zero."
            Journal for Research in Mathematics Education 14, (May 1983):
            147-155.

27.3280   Wilderman, A. "Math Skills For Survival In The Real World."
            Teacher, The Professional Magazine of The Elementary Grades
            94, (February 1977): 68-70.

27.3281   Zacharias, J.R. "Importance of Quantitative Thinking."
            National Elementary Principal 53, (January 1974): 8-13.

28

Media Literacy

28.3282   Haynes, W.L. "Of That Which We Cannot Write: Some Notes on The Phenomenology of Media." <u>Quarterly Journal of Speech</u> 74, (February 1988): 71-101.

28.3283   Houk, Annelle, and Bogart, Carlotta. <u>Media Literacy: Thinking About</u>. Cincinnati, Ohio: Pflaum Order Department, 1974. ED 091 390.

28.3284   Morrow, James. "Media Literacy in The 80's" <u>English Journal</u> 69, 1(January 1980): 48-51.

Examines the concept of media literacy. Defines said concept as both ". . . critical viewing and creative production. . ." Discusses what the author identifies as the death of technological determinism. Surveys the transformation of visual literacy. Presents a list of skills and abilities with which secondary school students should exit a 1980s media literacy curriculum unit. Finally, reviews a number of possibilities by which to resurrect classroom production.

28.3285   Olson, D.R. "Mind and Media: The Epistemic Functions of Literacy." <u>Journal of Communication</u> 38, (Summer 1988): 27-36.

29

Military Service
and Mental Fitness

29.3286   Altus, W.D. "Constipation and Adjustment Among Illiterate
Males." Journal of Consulting Psychology 14, (February 1959):
25-31.

29.3287   Altus, W.D. "Adjustment and food Aversions Among Army
Illiterates." Journal of Counseling Psychology 3, (December
1949): 429-432.

29.3288   Altus, W.D. "Some Correlates of Enuresis Among Illiterate
Soldiers." Journal of Consulting Psychology 10, (September
1946): 246-259.

29.3289   Altus, W.D. "Validity of The Terman Vocabulary For Army
Illiterates." Journal of Consulting Psychology 10, (September
1946): 268-276.

29.3290   Altus, W.D., and Bell, H.M. "Validity Of A General Information
Test For Certain Groups of Army Illiterates." Journal of
Consulting Psychology 11, (May 1947): 120-132.

29.3291   Altus, W.D., and Clark, J.H. "Some Sectional Differences
Among Negro and White Illiterate Soldiers." Journal of Social
Psychology 30, (August 1949): 97-104.

29.3292   "Armed Forces Rejections During The First Year Of The Korean
War." School and Society 77, (January 3, 1953): 12.

29.3293   "Arms and The Manual." Journal of Education (London) 77,
(June 1945): 290.

29.3294   Baer, M.F. "Medical Rejectees." Personnel and Guidance
Journal 42, (June 1964): 956-957.

29.3295   Baer, M.F. "One-Third of a Nation Rejected; Mental Rejectees."
            Personnel and Guidance Journal 42, (May 1964): 852-853.

29.3296   Bagley, W.C. "Proposed Continuation of The Draft and Its
            Educational Implications." School & Society 62, (September 8,
            1945): 148.

29.3297   Bagley, W.C. "Illiteracy and Near-Illiteracy In The Selective-
            Service Age Groups." School & Society 55, (June 6, 1942): 633-
            634.

29.3298   Bain, June W. "Reading Achievement Gains of Adults In Air
            Force Program." Journal of Reading 14, 7(April 1971): 467-472,
            500.

29.3299   "Basic Education Centers; an Army Experiment." Times
            Educational Supplement 1567, (May 12, 1945): 219.

29.3300   "Basic Education Courses; Army Approach To Problems of
            Illiteracy." Times Educational Supplement 1547, (December 23,
            1944): 615.

29.3301   Blanchard, Jay S. "U.S. Armed Services Computer Assisted
            Literacy Efforts." Journal of Reading 28, 3(December 1984): 262-
            265.

29.3302   Bradley, G.H. "Review of Educational Problems Based on
            Military Selection and Classification Data In World War II."
            Journal of Educational Research 43, (November 1949): 161-174.

29.3303   Brownfield, Sharon, and Vik, Gretchen. "Teaching Basic Skills
            With Computer Games." Training and Development Journal
            37, 12(December 1983): 52-56.

29.3304   Cornish, D.T. "Union Army As A School For Negroes." Journal
            of Negro History 37, (October 1952): 368-382.

29.3305   Deiss, J. "Cost of Illiteracy: 15 Army Divisions." Christian
            Science Monitor Weekly Magazine Section, (August 15, 1942): 6.

29.3306   de Kiewiet, C.W. "Education For Survival." Scientific Monthly
            76, (February 1953): 57-62.

29.3307   De Vries, Deborah Davisson. "A Study of An Adult Basic
            Literacy Program For Military Personnel." Ed.D. dissertation,
            University of Southern California, 1981. 42/10-A, p. 4250.

29.3308   Duffy, T.M. "Literacy Instruction In The Military." Armed
           Forces and Society 11, (Spring 1985): 437-467.

           Examines efforts by the military to identify literacy needs and to
           provide measures to meet these needs. Discusses literacy within
           a military context. Reviews literacy programs in the military,
           both past and present. Within said overview are discussions on
           literacy policy, instructional design, the measurement of reading
           requirements, the instructional objective, and the instructional
           content. Surveys current literacy curricula in the armed forces.

29.3309   Duffy, Thomas M. Literacy Instruction In The Armed Forces.
           CDC Technical Report No. 22. Pittsburgh, Pennsylvania:
           Carnegie-Mellon University, Communications Design Center,
           1985. ED 276 882.

29.3310   Duffy, Thomas M., et al. Language Skills: A Prospectus For The
           Naval Service. San Diego: Navy Personnel Research and
           Development Center, 1975. ED 133 683.

29.3311   Farley, B.M. "Alphabet and The Army." Journal of The
           National Education Association 32, (March 1943): 77-78.

29.3312   Firestone, R.W. "Education, Intelligence, and Military Recruit
           Performance." Journal of Clinical Psychology 13, (January 1957):
           93-95.

29.3313   Fisher, Allan H., Jr., and Brown, George H. Army 'New
           Standards' Personnel: Effect of Remedial Literacy Training on
           Performance In Military Service. Alexandria, Virginia: Human
           Resources Research Organization, 1971. ED 056 272.

29.3314   Fisher, Allan H., Jr., and Brown, George H. Army 'New
           Standards' Personnel: Relationships Between Literacy Level and
           Indices of Military Performance. Alexandria, Virginia: Human
           Resources Research Organization, 1971. ED 056 273.

29.3315   Fletcher, John D., et al. Historical Antecedents and
           Contemporary Trends In Literacy and Readability Research In
           The Navy. San Diego: Navy Personnel Research and
           Development Center, 1977. ED 134 968.

29.3316   Foster, R.M., and Ballard, J.F. "Navy's Literacy Training
           Program." School Life 36, (November 1953): 31-32.

29.3317   Fox, Lynn C., and Sticht, Thomas G. A Program For Job Related Reading Training. Monterey, California: Human Resources Research Organization, 1974   ED 157 014.

29.3318   Goffard, S. James. An Experimental Evaluation of A Basic Education Program In The Army. Washington, D.C.: George Washington University, Human Resources Research Office, 1956.

29.3319   Goldberg, Samuel. Army Training of Illiterates In World War II. New York: Bureau of Publications, Teachers College, Columbia University, 1951.

29.3320   Goldberg, Samuel. "Army Training of Illiterates In World War II." Ph.D. dissertation, Columbia University, 1952. W1952, p. 170.

29.3321   Greene, M. "Open Letter To Robert S. McNamara, Secretary of Defense." Teachers College Record 68, (November 1966): 150-154.

29.3322   Guthrie, John T. "Research: Classrooms and Battalions." Journal of Reading 24, 4(January 1981): 364-366.

29.3323   Harding, Lowry W., and Burr, James B. Servicemen Learn To Read. Practice Book Numbers I and II. Madison, Wisconsin: Armed Forces Institute, 1956. ED 012 838.

29.3324   Holberg, Anne. The Role of Remedial Training In The Naval Service: One Last Chance For Many Recruits. Report No. 75-17. San Diego: Naval Health Research Center, 1975.   ED 120 404.

29.3325   Hull, Jr., J.D. "Secondary School Curriculum Adjustments For The National Emergency." School Life 34, (November 1951): 19-20.

29.3326   HumRRO Work Unit FLIT (Functional Literacy); Fort Ord, California. Carmel, California: Human Resources Research Organization, 1974. ED 108 146.

29.3327   HumRRO's Literacy Research For The U.S. Army: Progress and Prospects. N.P.: n.p., 1973.

29.3328   "It's Called Multimedia, Multimodal, Multilevel Communication Skills System -- But It Can Still Teach Near

Illiterates To Read and Write." Educational Media Magazine 1,
8(December-January 1969/1970): 14-15.

29.3329   Jones, Paul L., and Medley, Vickie. Memphis-Defense Logistics
Agency Reading Improvement Program. Report No. 87-2.
Memphis, Tennessee: Memphis Literacy Coalition, 1987.   ED
284 996.

29.3330   Kaplan, N. "Salvaging Illiterates In The Army." Occupations
23, (November 1944): 74-76.

29.3331   Kern, Richard P. Usefulness of Readability Formulas For
Achieving Army Readability Objectives: Research and State-of-
The-Art Applied To The Army's Problem. Alexandria, Virginia:
Army Research Institute For The Behavioral and Social Sciences,
1980. ED 189 563.

29.3332   Kidd, C.V. "Mobilization of Scientific, Engineering, and Medical
Manpower: An Interim Report." Science 113, (June 29, 1951):
737-741.

29.3333   Kniffin, J. Douglas, et al. Operational Consequences of Literacy
Gap. Final Report. Hunt Valley, Maryland: Westinghouse
Electric Corporation, 1979. ED 179 942.

29.3334   Koenig, F.J., and Smith, J. "Preliminary Study Using A Short
Objective Measure For Determining Mental Deficiency in
Selective Service Registrants." Journal of Educational
Psychology 33, (September 1942): 443-448.

29.3335   Kozol, Jonathan, "Literacy Instruction in The U.S. Military:
Some Reflections on The Words of C.P. Snow." Journal of
Education 167, 2(1985): 42-49.

29.3336   Kuenzli, I.R. "Federal Aid For National Defense and The
General Welfare." American Teacher 37, (March 1953): 4-5.

29.3337   Kuhlen, R.G. "Nervous Symptoms Among Military Personnel
As Related To Age, Combat Experience, and Marital Status."
Journal of Consulting Psychology 15, (August 1951): 320-324.

29.3338   Larson, Gordon A. "Evaluating Military Literacy Programs."
New Directions For Continuing Education, 3 (1979): 75-80.

29.3339   Lynde, S.A. "Help Wanted - For The Under-Educated Veteran."
Secondary Education 12, (September 1945): 7-8.

29.3340   Lynde, S.A., and Schuler, E.A. "Undereducated Serviceman and the G.I. Bill of Rights." Adult Education Bulletin 9, (December 1944): 35-40.

29.3341   Maier, Milton H. Effects of English Language Training On Aptitude Test Performance of Insular Puerto Ricans. Arlington, Virginia: Behavior and Systems Research Lab, 1972.   ED 099 892.

29.3342   McGoff, R.M., and Harding, F.D. A Report On Literacy Training Programs In The Armed Forces. Report No. MR-74-6. Alexandria, Virginia: Air Force Human Resources Lab, 1974. ED 096 536.

29.3343   McGrath, E.J. "Selective Service Rejectees; A Challenge To Our Schools." School Life 35, (December 1952): 35-36.

29.3344   Nelson, L. "Man Cannot Live By The Sword Alone." Arizona Teacher 39, (May 1951): 15.

29.3345   O'Brien, G.E. "What The War Has Taught Me About Education." Educational Method 22, (March 1943): 250-253.

29.3346   Ohlsen, M.M., and Smith, A.E. "Educational-Vocational Planning In Terms of Military Service." Personnel and Guidance Journal 34, (February 1956): 366-368.

29.3347   Petersen, B. "Special Literacy Activities in The Danish Armed Forces." Prospects 17, 2(1987): 251-258.

29.3348   Philippi, Jorie W. "Matching Literacy to Job Training: Some Applications From Military Programs." Journal of Reading 31, 7(April 1988): 658-666.

Examines the need for job literacy training for entry-level employment positions. Discusses the efforts of the United States military to incorporate job literacy programs into the job training of new recruits. Reviews three literacy programs used by the U.S. military. Asks why it is important to teach job literacy, and how to teach it. Presents a list of reading processes and competencies, and a suggested lesson format.

29.3349   Poor Design and Management Hamper Army's Basic Skills Education Program. Report To The Secretary of The Army. Washington, D.C.: General Accounting Office, 1983.   ED 233 179.

29.3350   Rienow, R. "Salvaging Benefits From A Conscript Army."
            Social Education 11, (January 1947): 16-18.

29.3351   Ritchie, M.A.F. "Sam Jones, Seaman First Class." Journal of
            Education 127, (December 1944): 309-310.

29.3352   Robinson, H.M. "Training Illiterates In The Army." Elementary
            School Journal 52, (April 1952): 440-442.

29.3353   Ross, C.S. "Literacy Training In The Navy." School and Society
            63, (March 23, 1946): 203-204.

29.3354   Shawyer, R.C. "Army Fights Illiteracy." Adult Education 17,
            (December 1944): 74-83.

29.3355   Sticht, Thomas G. Basic Skills In Defense. Professional Paper 3-
            82. Alexandria, Virginia: Human Resources Research
            Organization, 1982. ED 237 776.

29.3356   Sticht, Thomas G. Evaluation of The "Reading Potential"
            Concept For Marginally Literate Adults. Alexandria, Virginia:
            Human Resources Research Organization, 1982.   ED 217 168.

29.3357   Sticht, Thomas G., et al. Literacy, Oracy and Vocational Aptitude
            As Predictors of Attrition and Promotion In The Armed
            Services. Alexandria, Virginia: Human Resources Research
            Organization, 1982. ED 217 169.

29.3358   Sticht, Thomas G., et al. Job-Related Reading Tasks: Teaching
            Marginally Literate Adults To Read. HumRRO Professional
            Paper 10-78. Alexandria, Virginia: Human Resources Research
            Organization, 1978. ED 163 189.

29.3359   Sticht, Thomas , et al. "Project REALISTIC: Determination of
            Adult Functional Literacy Skill Levels." Reading Research
            Quarterly. 7, 3(Spring 1977): 424-265.

29.3360   Sticht, Thomas G., and Beck, Lawrence J. Development of An
            Experimental Literacy Assessment Battery. Final Report.
            Alexandria, Virginia: Human Resources Research Organization,
            1976. ED 129 900.

29.3361   Sticht, Thomas G., and Zapf, Diane Welty, eds.. Reading and
            Readability Research In The Armed Services. Final Report.
            Alexandria, Virginia: Human Resources Research Organization,
            1976. ED 130 242.

29.3362   Sticht, Thomas G., ed. A Program of Army Functional Job
           Reading Training: Development, Implementation, and Delivery
           Systems. Final Report. Alexandria, Virginia: Human Resources
           Research Organization, 1975. ED 116 161.

29.3363   Sticht, Thomas G., ed. Reading For Working: A Functional
           Literacy Anthology. Alexandria, Virginia: Human Resources
           Research Organization, 1975. ED 102 532.

29.3364   Sticht, Thomas G. "Research Toward The Design, Development
           and Evaluation of A Job-Functional Literacy Training Program
           For The United States Army." Literacy Discussion 4,
           3(September 1973): 339-369.

29.3365   Sticht, Thomas G., et al. HumRRO's Literacy Research For The
           U.S. Army: Developing Functional Literacy Training.
           Alexandria, Virginia: Human Resources Research Organization,
           1973. ED 091 596.

29.3366   Sticht, Thomas G., et al. HumRRO's Literacy Research For The
           U.S. Army: Progress and Prospects. Alexandria, Virginia:
           Human Resources Research Organization, 1973. ED 073 369.

29.3367   Scott, P. "Hard-up Army Takes on The Backward." Times
           Educational Supplement 2838, (October 10, 1969): 10.

29.3368   Seidenfeld, M.A. "Training Linquistically Handicapped and
           Mentally Limited Personnel In The Military Service." Journal of
           Educational Psychology 34, (January 1943): 26-34.

29.3369   Standlee, Lloyd S. "A Follow-up and Comparison of Three
           Groups of Navy Enlisted Men; Marginal-and-Illiterate, Marginal-
           But-Literate, and Typical Recruits." Ph.D. dissertation, Columbia
           University, 1955. W 1955, p. 188.

29.3370   Stevenson, Colin. Adult Illiteracy: Reading and Writing
           Disability In The British Army. New York: Teachers College
           Press, 1986.

29.3371   "3R's For 1-A's." Time 43, (June 12, 1944): 81.

29.3372   Trytten, M.H. "Deferments and Induction." Phi Delta Kappan
           48, (May 1967): 439.

29.3373   Waggoner, R.E. "ABC's For GI Joe." Educational Screen 25,
           (February 1945): 58-59.

29.3373   Waggoner, R.E. "ABC's For GI Joe." Educational Screen 25, (February 1945): 58-59.

29.3374   Wall, W.D. "Reading Backwardness Among Men In The Army." British Journal of Educational Psychology 15, (February 1945): 28-40.

29.3375   Wetmore, F.K. "Educational Rehabilitation Classes For Illiterate Registrants." Adult Education Bulletin 8, (December 1943): 37-38.

29.3376   Wheldon, Jack. "Army School 'Gets Mechanized.'" Times Educational Supplement 2930, (July 16, 1971): 28.

29.3377   Willard, Joanne B. "Low-Aptitude Trainees Can Succeed." Instructional Innovator 26, 7(October 1981): 18-20.

29.3378   Witty, P.A. "Army Experiences With Readers and Reading and Their Implications For Postwar Education." (In Conference on Reading. Appraisal of Current Practices In Reading. p 10-14).

29.3379   Witty, P.A. "Principles of Learning Derived From The Results Of The Army's Program For Illiterate and Non-English-Speaking Men." Adult Education Bulletin 11, (June 1947): 131-136.

29.3380   Witty, P.A. "G.I. Education and The English Program." Bulletin of The National Association of Secondary School Principals 30, (February 1946): 170-175.

29.3381   Witty, P.A. "Education For G.I. Joe." Progressive Education 23, (November 1945): 52.

29.3382   Witty, P.A. "Army Teaches Reading." Educational Outlook 19, (March 1945): 115-122.

29.3383   Witty, P.A. "Teaching The Three R's In The Army." English Journal 34, (March 1945): 132-136.

29.3384   Witty, P.A., and Cruze, W.W. "3R's Go To War." Progressive Education 20, (December 1943): 364-365.

29.3385   Woellner, R.C. "Youths Facing Military Service." School Review 58, (October 1950): 384-386.

30

Moonlight Schools

30.3386 Fletcher, S.S. "Moonlight School For Colored Adults in Southwest Virginia." Virginia Journal of Education 26, (December 1932): 157.

30.3387 Jones, S. "Report of A Moonlight School In Virginia." Virginia Journal of Education 26, (October 1932): 43-44.

30.3388 Rose, Harold, and Curtis, Mike. "The Cora Wilson Stewart Moonlight Schoolhouse." Community Education Journal 4, 2(March-April 1974): 43-45.

Discussion of the efforts of Mrs. Cora Wilson Stewart in establishing moonlight schools for adults in Rowan County Kentucky. Contains information on enrollment, course of study, and the use of The Rowan County School Messenger as a reading text. Reports on the 1914 establishment of the Kentucky Illiteracy Commission.

30.3389 Stephens, C.P. "Moonlight School" (In World Federation of Education Associations. Proceedings, 1933. p. 123-6).

31

Right to Read Programs

31.3390   Allen, Gary G. "Right To Read: Rhetoric or Reality?" Phi Delta
           Kappan 53, 4(December 1971): 217-220.

31.3391   Allen, J.E., Jr. "Right to Read - Target for The 70's." Language
           Arts 60. (January 1983): 100-101.

31.3392   Allen, James E., Jr. "The Role of The Elementary Principal In
           Achieving The Right To Read Goal." Address before the
           Convention of The National Association of Elementary School
           Principals, Philadelphia, Pennsylvania, 1970.   ED 044 262.

31.3393   Allen, James E., Jr. "The Right To Read - Target For The 70's."
           Speech presented to The National Association of State Boards of
           Education Los Angeles, California, 1969.   ED 033 840.

31.3394   Berenger, R. D. "Ambitious Goal of Right To Read." Compact 9
           (April 1975): 2-5.

31.3395   Brown, Sandra M., ed. New Books In Reading Instruction:
           Series I. New York: MultiMedia Education, Inc., 1971. ED 053
           899.

31.3396   Canning, Sheila. "Right To Read." Saturday Review: Education
           1, 1(January 1973): 25-29.

31.3397   Cortright, R.W. "Right To Read." Elementary English 40,
           (March 1963): 299-302.

31.3398   Criscuolo, N. "Homemade Teachers; Project GRASP (Good
           Readers Are Successful People)." School and Community 64,
           (December 1977): 22-23.

31.3399   Emery, Donald. "The Need To Read." School Libraries 21,
           1(Fall 1971): 25-30.

31.3400   Emery, Donald G. "[A Barnraising For Reading: How Business
           Can Help The Right To Read Effort.]" Address To The American
           Association of Publishers, Washington, D.C., 1971. ED 053 896.

31.3401   Fay, Leo. "The Issues and The Challenge of The Right To Read."
           Address delivered to the Ohio Council of the International
           Reading Association, Toledo, Ohio, 1969. ED 042 567.

31.3402   Fedo, Michael W. "Minnesota's All Out Drive On Reading."
           American Education 10, 9(November 1974): 6-11.

31.3403   Goldstein, Judith E. "Right To Read Summer." Parks and
           Recreation 11, 6(June 1976): 16-17.

31.3404   Harman, David. "The 'Right To Read': An Assessment."
           Educational Horizons 54, (Winter 1975-1976): 71-76.

           Overview of the goal of "Right-To-Read." Examines whether
           the goal is being attained. Suggests that the goal lacks clarity.
           Discusses the relationship between reading level and the act of
           reading. Also reviews the behavior known as reading, and its
           relationship to social and economic life in the United States.
           Examines the question of whether there is a reading crisis in the
           U.S., and whether said crisis can be remediated. Concludes that
           gaps between readers and non-readers are widening. Calls for a
           new look at reading strategies and instructional mechanisms.

31.3405   Holloway, R.L. "Role of the States In Right to Read." State
           Government 48, (Summer 1975): 189-193.

31.3406   Holloway, Ruth Love. "Right To Read - A Chance To Change:
           Report From Washington" Reading Teacher 27, 1(October
           1973): 33-36.

31.3407   Isaacs, Mary Ann Lorenz. "ERIC/RCS Report: Right To Read:
           Ten Years Later." Language Arts 56, 8(November-December
           1970): 954-958.

31.3408   Jennings, F. G. "Reflection and Renewal: 1974, The Year of
           Print." New England Reading Association Journal 24, (Winter
           1988): 19-20.

31.3409   McGarry, Florence A. "The Right To Read: Be Wary." Reading
            Newsreport 5, 5(March 1971): 30-33.

31.3410   "National Right To Read Effort, The." Reading Teacher 25,
            7(April 1972): 616-617.

31.3411   Olsen, Turee. "ERIC/RCS: The Right To Read Effort." Journal
            of Reading 18, 6(March 1975): 500-501, 503.

31.3412   Pearpoint, Jack C. "The Right To Read: A Key to Community
            Living." Canadian Journal of Mental Retardation 34,
            4(Autumn 1984): 34-39.

31.3413   Reid, "National Right To Read Campaign Really on The Move."
            Times Higher Education Supplement 260, (October 15, 1976): 7.

31.3414   "Right To Read: New Director, New Approach. An Interview."
            Phi Delta Kappan 53, 4(December 1971): 221-224.

31.3415   Right To Read. N.P.: n.p., 1965.

31.3416   Schneiderman, P. "Without Reading You Ain't Nothing; Ohio
            State University Right To Read Program." Lifelong Learning 1,
            (September 1977): 16-18.

31.3417   Sisson, Roger L. "The Design of A National Right-To-Read
            Effort." Socio-Economic Planning Sciences 6, 5(October 1972):
            477-488.

31.3418   Swiss, T. "Right To Read? Model Programs; ERIC/RCS
            Report." Journal of Reading 19, (October 1975): 89.

31.3419   Wagner, J. "Focusing on Reading." American Education 12,
            (November 1976): 27-30.

31.3420   Wells, Alan. "Recognising The Right To Read." Special
            Education: Forward Trends 2, 1(March 1975): 8-11.

31.3421   Winkeljohann, R. "Right To Read: Effective Reading Programs;
            ERIC/RCS Report." Journal of Reading 19, (November 1975):
            188-189.

31.3422   Wooden, S.L., and Backer, J.C. "Right To Read." Journal of
            American Indian Education 15, (January 1976): 1-6.

32

Scientific Literacy

32.A.3423   "AAAS News: Questions of Science Literacy Addressed by
             Rutherford/AAAS; 1982 Exhibit; Energy and Health to Be
             Discussed in Berkeley; Short Courses at Pacific Division, Annual
             Meeting." Science 212, 4494 (May 1981): 532-533.

32.A.3424   Agin, Michael L. "Education For Scientific Literacy: A
             Conceptual Frame of Reference and Some Applications."
             Science Education 58, 3(July-September 1974): 403-415.

32.A.3425   Aguirre J., and Erickson, G. "Student's Conceptions About The
             Vector Characteristics of Three Physics Concepts." Journal of
             Research in Science Teaching 21, (May 1984): 439-457.

32.A.3426   Aikenhead, Glen S. "High-School Graduates' Beliefs About
             Science-Technology-Society. III. Characteristics and Limitations
             of Scientific Knowledge." Science Education 71, 4(July 1987):
             459-487.

             Examines the scientific literacy of high-school graduates.
             Specifically explores the responses of Canadian students to
             questions 13 to 19 of Views on Science-Technology-Society
             (VOSTS). Said questions focus on the characteristics and
             limitations of a student's scientific knowledge. Provides a
             discussion for each question. Concludes that the high school
             graduates examined had beliefs about scientific knowledge
             which were both diverse and contradictory.

32.A.3427   Aikenhead, Glen S. "Science: A Way of Knowing." Science
             Teacher 46, 6(September 1979): 23-25.

32.A.3428   Andrews, T.F. "Science Education of The Nonscientist."
             Educational Technology 10, (January 1970): 29-32.

32.A.3429   Arca, M., and Vicent-Missioni, M. "A Reflection on Some
             Meanings of 'Interdisciplinary' and 'Integration Among The
             Sciences'." European Journal of Science Education 3, 2(April-
             June 1981): 117-126.

32.A.3430   Aurd, Paul DeHart. "Scientific Enlightenment For An Age of
             Science." Science Teacher 37, 1(January 1970): 13-15.

32.A.3431   Babb, Patricia. "The President's Report on Science and
             Engineering Education." Technological Horizons in Education
             8, 5(September 1981): 64-66.

32.A.3432   Bakaya, R.M. "Opyt Sostavlenija Uchebno-Spravochnogo
             Slovarja Dlja Chtenija Nauchno-Technicheskoj Literatury
             (Methods of Compiling A Scientific Reference Dictionary For
             Reading Scientific and Technical Literature)." Russkij Yazyk Za
             Rubezham, 2(1973): 33-37.

32.A.3433   Bauman, R.P. "We Can Do Better To Help Students Understand
             Physics." Physics Teacher 23, (September 1985): 377-378.

32.A.3434   Bengelsdorf, Irving S. "The Adventures of Janus In Mass-Media
             Land." Journal of Chemical Education 46, 9(September 1969):
             543-546.

32.A.3435   Bennett, Jack. "Americans Lack Basic Science Knowledge."
             BioScience 30, 12(December 1980): 860.

32.A.3436   Bevan, William. "The Sound of The Wind That's Blowing."
             American Psychologist 31, 7(July 1976): 481-491.

32.A.3437   Bibby, Cyril. "Towards a Scientific Culture." Education in
             Science 59, (September 1974): 14-20.

32.A.3438   Bloom, Robert B. "Science, Humanities, and Society." NASSP
             Bulletin 57, 370(February 1973): 50-57.

32.A.3439   Blum, Abraham. "Science Magazine For Youth in Five
             Countries - Different Approaches." Science Education 65,
             1(January 1981): 65-70.

32.A.3440   Bonham, G.W. "Some Questions About Science Literacy."
             Change 15, (July/August 1983): 10-11.

32.A.3441   Booth, N. "Science in School." Trends in Education 17, (January 1970): 19-23.

32.A.3442   Bork, A.M. "Two Examples of Computer-Based Learning on Personal Computers." AEDS Journal 17, (Fall/Winter 1983): 49-53.

32.A.3443   Bowden, Gordon T. "Becoming a Scientifically Literate Nation." Educational Record 63, 4(Fall 1982): 5-8.

32.A.3444   Bracey, G.W. "Science Without Sense." Phi Delta Kappan 69, (May 1988): 685-686.

32.A.3445   Braddock-Rogers, Kenneth, and Braddock, Kenneth Mackenzie. "Science Errors in The Communication Media." School Science and Mathematics 78, 7(November 1978): 593-602.

32.A.3446   Bromley, D. Allan. "The Other Frontiers Science." Science 215, 4536(February 1982): 1035-1044.

32.A.3447   Brovey, D.J. "Science Among Ordinary Citizens." Journal of College Science Teaching 10, (November 1980): 88-91.

32.A.3448   Brown, Jr., G.E. "Biotechnology and Science Literacy: A Federal Perspective." American Biology Teacher 46, (November/December 1984): 447-448.

32.A.3449   Brunschwig, F., and Breslin, R.D. "Scientific and Technological Literacy - A Major Innovation and Challenge." Liberal Education 68, (Spring 1982): 49-62.

32.A.3450   Burt, Cyril. "Personal Knowledge, Art and The Humanities." Journal of Aesthetic Education 3, 2(April 1969): 29-46.

32.A.3451   Champagne, A.B., and Klopfer, L.E. "Actions in a Time of Crisis." Science Education 66, (July 1982): 503-514.

32.A.3452   Chen, D., and Novik, R. "Scientific and Technological Education in an Information Society." Science Education 68, (July 1984): 421-426.

32.A.3453   Cleaver, Thomas J. "Science and Education: A Shaky Partnership." American Biology Teacher 38, 2(February 1976): 110-111.

32.A.3454   Cobb, David. "Aural Comprehension Materials for Tertiary
             Level Science/Technical Students." RELC Journal 3, 1-2(June-
             December 1972): 70-87.

32.A.3455   Collins, H., and Shapin, S. "Uncovering The Nature of Science."
             Times Higher Education Supplement 612, (January 27, 1984):
             13.

32.A.3456   Collins, P.M.D., and Bodmer, W.F. "The Public Understanding
             of Science." Studies in Science Education 13, (1986): 96-104.

32.A.3457   Comber G. "Math and Science - The Easy Liberal Arts."
             Improving College and University Teaching 31, (Winter 1983):
             4.

32.A.3458   "Contemporary Issues Related to Chemistry." Journal of
             Chemical Education 58, 1(January 1981): 4-6.

32.A.3459   Cook, William B. "AAAS Symposium: Chemistry and Social
             Concern. Should Chemistry Instruction Reflect Social Concern."
             Journal of Chemical Education 48, 10(October 1971): 642-643.

32.A.3460   Cookson, C. "Report Warns of Growth in Science Illiteracy;
             United States." Times Educational Supplement 3359,
             (November 7, 1980): 13.

32.A.3461   Cossman, G.W. "Effects of a Course in Science and Culture For
             Secondary School Students." Journal of Research in Science
             Teaching 6, 3(1969): 274-283.

32.A.3462   Danon-Boileau, L. "Caracterisations de l'Anglais Scientifique
             Ecrit (Characterization of Written Scientific English)." Langues
             Modernes 69, 2-3(1975): 124-139.

32.A.3463   Daugs, Donald R. "Scientific Literacy - Re-examined." Science
             Teacher 37, 8(November 1970): 10-11.

32.A.3464   Dennis, Everette E., and McCartney, James. "Science Journalists
             on Metropolitan Dailies." Methods, Values and Perceptions of
             Their Work." Journal of Environmental Education 10,
             3(Spring 1979): 9-15.

32.A.3465   DeRoche, E.F. "Is Science Education Coming of Age?" Science
             Education 51, (April 1967): 292-294.

32.A.3466   de Roulet, Lionel. "Science Within Man's Grasp: A Precondition To Progress." Out-of-School Scientific and Technical Education, 2(1972): 5-8.

32.A.3467   DeSieno, Robert P. "Provocative Opinion: A Quest For Unity." Journal of Chemical Education 49, 1(January 1972): 31-33.

32.A.3468   Dickson, D. "French Plan For Science and Technology Without Tears." Times Higher Education Supplement 680, (November 15, 1985): 10.

32.A.3469   "Directory and Proceedings, Academy - Conference - 1966." N.P.: American Association For The Advancement of Science, 1966. ED 014 437.

32.A.3470   Downie, R. "'Deliberate Mistakes' Articles and Scientific Literacy." Journal of Biological Education 17, (Winter 1983): 303-306.

32.A.3471   Dyrenfurth, M.J. "Route To Technological Literacy." VocEd 58, (January/February 1983): 42-44.

32.A.3472   Dyrenfurth, M. "Technological Literacy For a Changing World." VocEd 56, (March 1981): 48-51.

32.A.3473   Eder, Alan H. "Equal Time for Religion in Public Schools." Humanist 42, 2(March-April 1982): 20-28, 54.

32.A.3474   Eiss, A.F. "Systems Approach to Developing Scientific Literacy." Educational Technology 10, (January 1970): 36-40.

32.A.3475   Eiss, A.F. "NSTA Conference on Scientific Literacy." Science Teacher 35, (May 1968): 30-32.

32.A.3476   Elliott, David, et al. "Scientific Illiteracy In Elementary School Science Textbook Programmes." Journal of Curriculum Studies 19, 1(January-February 1987): 73-76.

32.A.3477   Etzional, Amitai. "Understanding of Science." Science 177, 4047 (August 1972): 391.

32.A.3478   Evans, J. Daryll. "Putting Names to Concepts in Biology." Journal of Biological Education 12, 4(December 1978): 261-266.

32.A.3479   Evans, Thomas P. "Scientific Literacy: Whose Responsibility?" American Biology Teacher 32, 2(February 1970): 80-84.

32.A.3480   Fensham, P.J. "Science For All." Educational Leadership 44, (December 1986/January 1987): 18-23.

32.A.3481   Fisher, K.M. and Lipson, J.I. "Twenty Questions About Student Errors." Journal of Research in Science Teaching 23, (December 1986): 783-803.

32.A.3482   Friedman, Sharon M. "Training Reporters To Cover Science and Technology." Professional Engineer 51, 3(September 1981): 22-27.

32.A.3483   Gardner, M.H., and Yager, R.E. "How Does The U.S. Stack Up?" Science Teacher 50, (October 1983): 22-25.

32.A.3484   Garrett, Alfred B. "For The Next Quarter of A Century." Science Teacher 36, 6(September 1969): 20-21.

32.A.3485   Gelpi, E. "Politiques et Activites d'education Permanente: Reflexions sur l'education Scientifique et La Societe Moderne." International Review of Education 28, 3(1982): 357-366.

32.A.3486   Gibbons, James Patrick. "Scientific Literacy: Basic Concepts, Skills and Attitudes." Ph.D. dissertation, Texas A & M University, 1976, 1976. 37/12-A, p. 7660.

32.A.3487   Gordon, D. "The Image of Science, Technological Consciousness, and The Hidden Curriculum." Curriculum Review 14, (Winter 1984): 367-400.

32.A.3488   Gray, Paul E. "American's Ignorance of Science and Technology Poses A Threat To The Democratic Process Itself." Chronicle of Higher Education 34, (May 18, 1988): B 1-2.

32.A.3489   Greenberg, S. "Does Scientific Illiteracy Begin in The Doll Corner?" Instructor 96, (November/December 1986): 18.

32.A.3490   Gross, Bernard F. "Scientific Literacy and The Nonscience Major." Journal of College Science Teaching 2, 3(February 1973): 10-14.

32.A.3491   Guthrie, J.T. "Literacy for Science and Technology." Journal of Reading 27, (February 1984): 478-480.

32.A.3492   Guthrie, J.T. "Scientific Literacy." Journal of Reading 27, (December 1983): 286-288.

32.A.3493   Haddad, W.D. "Interaction Between Science and Society in The Arabic Press of The Middle East." Science Education 58, (January 1974): 35-39.

32.A.3494   Haddad, W.D. "Analysis of the Science Content of The Arabic Press in The Middle East." School Science and Mathematics 71, (May 1971): 411-422.

32.A.3495   Hahn, Walter von. "Numerische Untersuchungen In Der Fachsprachenforschung (Numerical Investigations In Technical - Language Research)." Zeitschrift Fur Dialektologie Und Linguistik 40, 2(1973): 184-191.

32.A.3496   Hall, David, et al. "Patterns of Thought in Scientific Writing: A Course in Information For Engineering Students." English For Specific Purposes 5, 2(1986): 147-160.

32.A.3497   Hamilton, David. "Writing Science." College English 40, 1(September 1978): 32-40.

32.A.3498   Harmand, Arlette, and Harmand, Jean-Marie. "L'Anglais Scientific: Un Faux Probleme (Scientific English: A False Problem)." Langues Modernes 69, 2-3 (1975): 149-154.

32.A.3499   Harrison, Anna J. "In Search of New Initiatives." Journal of Chemical Education 59, 9(September 1982): 713-716.

32.A.3500   Hashweh, Maher. "Descriptive Studies of Students' Conceptions in Science." Journal of Research in Science Teaching 25, 2(February 1988): 121-134.

32.A.3501   Helms, S.J.S. and Montague, E.J. "Study of College Nonscience Majors' Expectations of The Scientific Enterprise." Journal of Research in Science Teaching 17, (November 1980): 553-558.

32.A.3502   Hendrix, J.R., and Mertens, T.R. "NSF's New Positon: Panacea or Pandemonium?" Phi Delta Kappan 54, (June 1973): 702.

32.A.3503   Hermens, R.A., ed. "Chemistry, Scientific Thought, and Public Communication (Symposium)." Journal of Chemical Education 63, (August 1986): 695-698.

32.A.3504   Herron, J.D. "Science, Society, and The Reformation." Journal of Chemical Education 59, (July 1982): 560-562.

32.A.3505   Hersh, R. "Are American Schools Turning Out Techno-peasants?" Instructor (New York, New York) 92, (May 1983): 26-29.

32.A.3506   Hersh, R.H. "Schools Can Help Fight Technological Illiteracy." Education Digest 49, (December 1983): 6-9.

32.A.3507   Hersh, R.H. "Education and The Corporate Connection." Educational Horizons 62, (Fall 1983): 5-8.

32.A.3508   Hersh, R.H. "How To Avoid Becoming A Nation of Technopeasants." Phi Delta Kappan 64, (May 1983): 635-638.

32.A.3509   Hinerman, Charles Ovalee. "The Level of Achievement of Graduating Missouri High School Seniors on Two Referents of Scientific Literacy." Ph.D. dissertation, The University of Wisconsin, 1971. 31/12-A, p. 6430.

32.A.3510   Hirschhorn, Howard H. Technical & Scientific Reader In English [Temas tecnicos y cientificos en ingles, con ejercicios para aumentar el vocabulario]. New York: Simon and Schuster, 1970. ED 042 166.

32.A.3511   Hoddeson, Lillian Hartmann. "The Living History of Physics and The Human Dimension of Science." Physics Teacher 12, 5(May 1974): 275-282.

32.A.3512   Hodson, D., and Reid, D.J. "Science For All: Motives, Meanings and Implications." School Science Review 69, 249(June 1988): 821-826.

32.A.3513   Hofman, Helenmarie. "Energy Crisis - Schools to The Rescue Again." School Science and Mathematics 80, 6(October 1980): 467-478.

32.A.3514   Holmes, Chauncey D. "Geology and Liberal Education." Journal of Geological Education 17, 3(October 1969): 142-144.

32.A.3515   Holton, Gerald. "Issues For The Seventies." Physics Teacher 8, 5(May 1970): 229-232.

32.A.3516   "How Schools Handled The Last Science Scare (Sputnik Era)." American School Board Journal 169, (September 1982): 19.

32.A.3517   Howder, Murray L., et al. "Academic Training of Translator: A Debatable Issue." Federal Linguist 5, 1-2(Summer 1973): 2-17.

32.A.3518   Hufstedler, S.M., and Langenberg, D.N. "Science and
             Technology Education For All Americans (Report of National
             Science Foundation and Department of Education." Journal of
             College Science Teaching 10, (February 1981): 245-248.

32.A.3519   Hurd, P.D. "Science Education For a New Age: The Reform
             Movement." NASSP Bulletin 69, (September 1985): 83-92.

32.A.3520   Hurd, P.D. "Scientific Enlightenment For an Age of Science."
             Science Teacher 37, (January 1970): 13-15.

32.A.3521   Hurd, P.D., and Gallagher, J.J. "Goals Related To The Social
             Aspects of Science." School Science and Mathematics 68, (May
             1968): 358-360.

32.A.3522   Innocent, G. "L'Anglais dans une Universite Scientifique
             (English in a Scientific University)." Langues Modernes 69, 2-
             3(1975): 161-165.

32.A.3523   Jaffarian, William Armand. "An Evaluation of The Relative
             Levels of Scientific Literacy Possessed by Twelfth Grade Students
             In Wisconsin." Ph.D. dissertation, The University of Wisconsin,
             1968.   30/01-A, p. 61.

32.A.3524   Jenkin, R.G. "Scientific Literacy and The Role of Practical
             Work." SASTA Journal, 852(October 1985): 10-13.

32.A.3525   Jerome, Fred. "Prime Time Science and Newsstand Technology:
             Is It All Just Hoopla?" Professional Engineer 51, 3(September
             1981): 12-14.

32.A.3526   Jones, Haskell Lee. "The Development of Certain Aspects of
             Scientific Literacy In College Freshman Physical Science
             Students." Ph.D. dissertation, The Ohio State University, 1969.
             30/04-A, p. 1337.

32.A.3527   Jones, Katherine Maurice. "The Attainment of Understandings
             About The Scientific Enterprise, Scientists, and the Aims and
             Methods of Science By Students In A College Physical Science
             Course." Journal of Research In Science Teaching 6, 1: 47-49.

32.A.3528   Jungck, John R. "Bio-Logical Dissection of Rhetorical Flora."
             American Biology Teacher 39, 3(March 1977): 142-147, 154.

32.A.3529   Kahle, J.B., et al. "An Assessment of The Impact of Science
             Experiences on The Career Choices of Male and Female Biology

Students." Journal of Research in Science Teaching 22, (May 1985): 385-394.

32.A.3530   Kahle, J.B., and Lakes, M.K. "Myth of Equality in Science Classrooms." Journal of Research in Science Teaching 20, (February 1983) 131-140.

32.A.3531   Karplus, Robert. "Science for Young Pupils." Prospects 8, 1(1978): 48-57.

32.A.3532   Keilin, Charles. "A Course Designed For The Non-Scientist." Journal of Chemical Education 46, 2(February 1969): 66-68.

32.A.3533   Klein, Judy. "The Medium Gets a Message." Science News 115, 22(June 1979): 361,365.

32.A.3534   Klopfer, L.E. "Scientific and Technological Literacy for All: A National Policy?" (Science and Engineering Education For The 1980's and Beyond: Report of National Science Foundation and Department of Education). Science Education 65, (January 1981): 1-2.

32.A.3535   Klopfer, Leopold E. "Individualized Science: Relevance For The 1970's." Science Education 55, 4(October/December 1971): 441-448.

32.A.3536   Klopfer, Leopold E. Science Education in 1991. Pittsburgh, Pennsylvania: University of Pittsburgh, Learning Research and Development Center, 1969.   ED 035 557.

32.A.3537   Klopfer, Leopold E. "The Teaching of Science and The History of Science." Journal of Research In Science Teaching 6, 1: 87-95.

32.A.3538   Kondo, Allan K. "Scientific Literacy: A View From A Developing Country." NASSP Bulletin 56, 360(January 1972): 28-37.

32.A.3539   Korth, Willard W. "Test Every Senior Project: Understanding The Social Aspects of Science." Paper presented at The National Association For Research In Science Teaching Conference, Pasadena, California, 1969.   ED 028 087.

32.A.3540   Krick, E.V. "Engineering For Non-Engineering Students." Engineering Education 62, 3(December 1971): 252-254.

32.A.3541   Kriegbaum, Killier. Science and The Mass Media. New York: New York University Press, 1967.   ED 028 920.

32.A.3542   Kurland, D.J. "Underprepared Student, Scientific Literacy and Piaget; Reflections on the Role of measurement in Scientific Discussion." Journal of Chemical Education 59, (July 1982): 574-576.

32.A.3543   Lagowski, J., et al. "Improving Scientific Literacy." USA Today 110, (December 1981): 16.

32.A.3544   Lagowski, J.J. "Scientific Literacy and Education." Journal of Chemical Education 64, (November 1987): 905.

32.A.3545   Lagowski, J.J. "On Becoming Scientifically Literate." Journal of Chemical Education 64, (October 1987): 821.

32.A.3546   Lagowski, J.J. "Primary School, Science, and Scientific Literacy." Journal of Chemical Education 60, (April 1983): 257.

32.A.3547   Lagowski, J.J. "Declining Science Literacy." Journal of Chemical Education 58, (January 1981): 1.

32.A.3548   Lagowski, J.J. "Declining Science Literacy." Journal of Chemical Education 58, (May 1980): 327.

32.A.3549   Lagowski, J.J. "Current Needs of Science Education." Journal of Chemical Education 57, (May 1980): 327.

32.A.3550   Lagowski, J.J. "Literacy." Journal of Chemical Education 64, (September 1977): 733.

32.A.3551   Lahti, Arnold M. "Comments on The Teaching and The History of Science." Journal of Research In Science Teaching 6, 1: 96-98.

32.A.3552   Landreman, Dolores. "English Teachers and The Advancement of Science and Engineering." English Journal 61, 3(March 1972): 389-404.

32.A.3553   Larkin, P.G. "Science, Math Key to High Tech." Community and Junior College Journal 53, (April 1983): 43-44.

32.A.3554   Lauda, D.P. "Technology Education: A Fundamental Framework For Improved Capability in Math and Science." Technology Teacher 45, (November 1985): 3-6.

32.A.3555   Lawrenz, Frances. "Misconceptions of Physical Science Concepts Among Elementary School Teachers." School Science and Mathematics 86, 8(December 1986): 654-660.

32.A.3556   Layton, David, et al. "Science For Specific Social Purposes (SSSP): Perspectives on Adult Scientific Literacy." Studies in Science Education 13, (1986): 27-52.

32.A.3557   Leake, John B., and Hinerman, Charles O. "Scientific Literacy and School Characteristics." School Science and Mathematics 73, 9(December 1973): 772-282.

32.A.3558   Lederman, L.M. "Sermon for Science Teachers." Physics Teacher 24, (September 1986): 331-333.

32.A.3559   Leonard, W.H. "Does The Presentation Style of Questions Inserted Into Text Influence Understanding and Retention of Science Concepts?" Journal of Research in Science Teaching 24, (January 1987): 27-37.

32.A.3560   Lijnse, Piet. "Does Science Education Improve The Image of Science?" Science Education 67, 5(October 1983): 575-582.

32.A.3561   Lippincott, W.T. "Scientific Literacy: Its Time Is Now." Journal of Chemical Education 55, (December 1978): 751.

32.A.3562   Lippincott, W.T. "Editorially Speaking: The Citizen's Science." Journal of Chemical Education 48, 12 (December 1971): 781.

32.A.3563   Lucas, A.M. "Public Knowledge of Elementary Physics." Physics Education 23, 1(January 1988): 10-16.

32.A.3564   Lucas, Arthur. "Public Knowledge of Biology." Journal of Biological Education 21, 1(Spring 1987): 41-45.

32.A.3565   Lucas, Stephen B., and Burlando, Andrew A. "The 'New Science Methods' and Reading." Language Arts 52, 6(Septmeber 1975): 769-770.

32.A.3566   Lux, Donald G. "Science and Technology: A New Alliance." Journal of Epsilon Pi Tau 10, 1(Spring 1984): 16-21.

32.A.3567   Markow, P.G. "Teaching Chemistry Like the Foreign Language It Is." Journal of Chemical Education 65, (January 1988): 57-58.

32.A.3568   Martin, Michael. "The Use of Pseudo-Science In Science
             Education." Science Education 55, 1(January/March 1971): 53-
             56.

32.A.3569   Mason, Peter. "Speaking Scientific." Australian Science
             Teachers Journal 17, 3(October 1971): 39-42.

32.A.3570   McCrory, D.L., and Maughan, Jr., G.R. "Instructional Resources
             For Technological Literacy." Man/Society/Technology A
             Journal of Industrial Arts Education 42, (May/June 1983): 13-14.

32.A.3571   McDonald, K. "Cooperation Urged in War on Scientific
             Illiteracy." Chronicle of Higher Education 24, (May 26, 1982):
             11.

32.A.3572   Mertens, T.R., and Hendrix, J.T. "Responsible Descisionmaking:
             A Tool For Developing Biological Literacy." American Biology
             Teacher 44, (March 1982): 148-152.

32.A.3573   Miller, J.D., and Barrington, T.M. "Acquisition and Retention of
             Scientific Information." Journal of Communication 31, (Spring
             1981): 178-179.

32.A.3574   Miller, Paul A. "Adult Education, Science and Technology."
             Convergence 13, 3(1980): 39-45.

32.A.3575   Miller, R.M. "Science Teaching For The Citizen of The Future."
             Science Education 68, (July 1984): 403-410.

32.A.3576   Mallinson, G.G. "Supercilious Cats, Gasoline and Washing
             Machines, and Scientific Literacy." School Science and
             Mathematics 79, (February 1979): 91-92.

32.A.3577   "Mathematical and Scientific Literacy For The High Tech
             Society." Educational Leadership 41, (December 1983/January
             1984): 4-18.

32.A.3578   Missimer, William C., Jr. "Business and Industry's Role in
             Improving The Scientific and Technological Literacy of
             American's Youth." American Education 20, 4(May 1984): 6-9.

32.A.3579   Missimer, W.C., Jr. "Business and Industry's Role in Improving
             The Scientific and Technological Literacy of America's Youth."
             T.H.E. Journal 11, (February 1984): 89-93.

32.A.3580   Mitman, Alexis L., et al. "Instruction Addressing The Components of Scientific Literacy and Its Relation To Student Outcomes." American Educational Research Journal 24, 4(Winter 1987): 611-633.

Study of seventh-grade life science teachers. Study predicated on the hypothesis that the linkages, in the teachers, between science content and broader societal ramifications, ultimately had a facilitative effect on student' scientific literacy. Results indicate a gap between the goal of scientific literacy and current teaching practice. Concludes with a list of five components of scientific literacy.

32.A.3581   "More Science! Why Now?" Instructor 96, Special Issue (Spring 1987): 4-7.

32.A.3582   Moriber, G. "Are Applications Capable of Creating An Interest in Chemistry?" Journal of Chemical Education 61, (September 1984): 807.

32.A.3583   Morrow, J. "Is There a Cure For Scientific Illiteracy?" Media & Methods 17, (October 1980): 22-25.

32.A.3584   Mowyer, J.B., and Linn, M.C. "Effectiveness of The Science Curriculum Improvement Study in Teaching Scientific Literacy." Journal of Research in Science Teaching 15, (May 1978): 209-219.

32.A.3585   Moyer, Albert E. "Don't Never Plant Corn On The New of The Moon." Physics Teacher 9, 4(April 1971): 168-174.

32.A.3586   "News: State and Society." Physics Today 33, 12(December 1980): 53-56.

32.A.3587   Nicholls, M. "A Little Knowledge . . ." Times Educational Supplement 3748, (April 29, 1988): 160-161.

32.A.3588   Noce, G., et al. "The Floating of Objects On The Moon: Prediction From A Theory of Experimental Facts." International Journal of Science Education 10, 1(January-March 1988): 61-70.

32.A.3589   Norris, W. "Americans Mistrust Appliance of Science." Times Higher Education Supplement 710, (June 13, 1986): 8.

32.A.3590   Ogden, W.R. "Scientific Literacy: A Recommitment." High School Journal 57, (May 1974): 351-355.

32.A.3591   Ogunniyi, M.B. "Conceptions of Traditional Cosmological Ideas Among Literate and Nonliterate Nigerians." Journal of Research in Science Teaching 24, 2(February 1987): 107-117.

32.A.3592   O'Hearn, G.T. "Science Literacy and Alternative Futures." Science Education 60, (January 1976): 103-114.

32.A.3593   O'Loughlin, M.J., et al. "Solar Energy As A Theme For Relating Science and Technology To Society." Journal of Science and Mathematics Education In Southeast Asia (MALAYS) 7, 2(December 1984): 15-18.

32.A.3594   Orr, Verne. "Are We A Nation of Scientific Illiterates?" American Education 19, 3 (April 1983): 24-25, 35-36.

32.A.3595   Osborne, J. "Scientific Literacy Essential." Times Educational Supplement 3118, (February 18, 1975): 70.

32.A.3596   Osborne, R. "Children's Science Meets Scientists' Science." Lab Talk 28, 1(February 1984): 2-7.

32.A.3597   Ostlund, K., et al. "A Naturalistic Study of Children and Their Parents In Family Learning Courses in Science." Journal of Research in Science Teaching 22, (November 1985): 723-741.

32.A.3598   Overington, Michael A. "The Scientific Community as Audience: Toward a Rhetorical Analysis of Science." Philosophy and Rhetoric 10, 3(Summer 1977): 143-163.

32.A.3599   Padilla, M.J., et al. "An Examination of The Line Graphing Ability of Students in Grades Seven Through Twelve." School Science and Mathematics 86, (January 1986): 20-26.

32.A.3600   Paldy, Lester G., ed. "National & Legislative View." Journal of College Science Teaching 10, 4(February 1981): 245-248.

32.A.3601   Palmer, Glenn A. "Teaching the Nature of the Scientific Enterprize." School Science and Mathematics 79, 1(January 1979): 13-21.

32.A.3602   Paske, G.H. "Science For Humanists." Liberal Education 53, (May 1967): 252-263.

32.A.3603   Patrick, John J. "Science and Society in The Education of Citizens." BSCS Journal 3, 4(December 1980): 1-6.

32.A.3604   Pella, M.O. "Place or Function of Science For A Literate
             Citizenry." Science Education 60, (January 1976): 97-101.

32.A.3605   Pella, M.O. "Scientific Literacy and The H.S. Curriculum."
             School Science and Mathematics 67, (April 1967): 346-356.

32.A.3606   Pella, M.O. "Scientific Literacy: Its Referents." Science Teacher
             33, (May 1966): 44.

32.A.3607   Phillips, Melba. "Science and Progress." Physics Teacher 12,
             4(April 1974): 199.

32.A.3608   Pine, T.S., and Shapiro, A.F. "Science Literacy." Teacher 94,
             (November 1976): 56-58.

32.A.3609   Plapp, Grederick W. "Chemical Insecticides." American Biology
             Teacher 38, 4(April 1976): 239-241.

32.A.3610   Preece, B.P. "Why A Bulletin On Science and Technology?"
             Delta Kappa Gamma Bulletin 50, (Spring 1984): 13-14.

32.A.3611   Prewitt, Kenneth. "Civic Education and Scientific Illiteracy."
             Journal of Teacher Education 34, 6(November-December 1983):
             17-20.

32.A.3612   Porter, Sir George, F.R.S. "One Hundred and Eighty Years of
             Education in Popular Science At The Royal Institutions."
             Journal of Chemical Education 59, 2(February 1982): 97-98.

32.A.3613   Prisk, D.P., and Stauer, J.R. "Science Literacy For Science
             Teachers (Exerpt From The 1982 Yearbook of The Association for
             The Education of Teachers in Science)." Curriculum Review 21,
             (May 1982): 205-209.

32.A.3614   "Program Objectives and Scientific Literacy FUSE (Australia)."
             South Australian Science Teachers Journal 753, (September
             1975): 44-47.

32.A.3615   Rabinowitch, Eugene. "Who Will Be The Decision-Maker?"
             BioScience 21, 23(December 1971): 1149.

32.A.3616   Rakow, S.J., and Walker, C.L. "The Status of Hispanic American
             Students in Science: Achievement and Exposure." Science
             Education 69, (July 1985): 557-565.

32.A.3617   "Report of The Fifth Diennial Conference on Chemical
             Education: Plenary Lectures." Journal of Chemical Education
             56, 1 (January 1979): 2-3.

32.A.3618   Riechard, Donald E. "Politics and Scientific Literacy." Education
             106, 1(Fall 1985): 108-111.

             Discusses the crisis the scientific enterprise finds itself involved
             in. Identifies the causes for said crisis. Contends that there is a
             need for the scientific enterprise and scientific education to be
             formulators of policy rather than reactors to political changes.
             Identifies the establishment of nationwide scientific literacy as a
             policy goal. Concludes with a discussion of why such a goal is
             important.

32.A.3619   Ritz, John M. "Technology as The Content Base For Industrial
             Arts." Man/Society/Technology 41, 1(September-October 1981):
             2-4.

32.A.3620   Rowell, J.A. "What is Science . . .???" Australian Science
             Teachers Journal 23, 3(November 1977): 53-55.

32.A.3621   Rubba, P.A., and Andersen, H.O. "Development of An
             Instrument To Assess Secondary School Students'
             Understanding of The Nature of Scientific Knowledge." Science
             Education 62, (October/December 1978): 449-458.

32.A.3622   Rubba, Peter A., et al. "A Study of Two Misconceptions About
             The Nature of Science Among Junior High School." School
             Science and Mathematics 81, 3(March 1981): 221-226.

32.A.3623   Sanford, Julie P., and Crawley, Frank E. "The Forum." Science
             Teacher 44, 4(April 1977): 25-26.

32.A.3624   Sawyer, Thomas M. "The Common Law of Science and The
             Common Law of Literature." College Composition and
             Communication 21, 5(December 1970): 337-341.

32.A.3625   Schilling, Irmgard. "Sachverhalte und Syntax Beim Erwerb
             Fachorientierter Fremdsprachenkenntnisse (Facts and Syntax In
             Acquiring Technical Orientation In A Foreign Language)."
             Deutsch Als Fremsprache 10, 3(1973): 176-182.

32.A.3626   Schodde, P. "Barriers To Concept Formation Or Confessions of
             A One Time Science Student." SASTA Journal, 872 (September
             1987): 37-38.

32.A.3627   Schoenfeld, Clay. "Environmental Communications Today: An Educator's Perspective." Journal of Environmental Education 10, 3(Spring 1979): 43-44.

32.A.3628   "School Science Education For The 70's" Science Teacher 38, 8(November 1971): 46-51.

32.A.3629   "Scientific Illiteracy Target of Curriculum." News & Views (Wisconsin) 20, (October 19, 1984): 9.

32.A.3630   Seaborg, Glen T. "The Public Understanding of Science." Out-of-School Scientific and Technical Education, 1(1971): 13-16.

32.A.3631   Seeger, Raymond J. "Provocative Opinion: On Teaching Secondary School Science to The Humanistically Oriented." Journal of Chemical Education 57, 12(December 1980): 880-881.

32.A.3632   Seitz, Sue, and Marcus, Sally. "Die Rolle der Wortbildung im Studienbegleitenden Deutschunterricht. (The Role of Word-Building in Teaching Scientific German)." Zielsprache Deutche, 4(1975): 7-13.

32.A.3633   Shamos, M.H. "The 'Crisis' In Science Education." Education Digest 54, (October 1988): 19-22.

32.A.3634   Shamos, M.H. "Toward Technological Literacy." Journal of College Science Teaching 12, (May 1983): 367.

32.A.3635   Shamos, Morris H. "A False Alarm In Science Education." Issues In Science and Technology 4, 3(Spring 1988): 65-69.

32.A.3636   Shamos, Morris H. "You Can Lead a Horse To Water . . ." Hoosier Science Teacher 9, 4(May 1984): 104-110.

32.A.3637   Shamos, Morris H. "Exposure To Science vs. Scientific Literacy." Journal of College Science Teaching 13, 5(March-April 1984): 393.

32.A.3638   Shamos, Morris H. "Science For Everyone?" New York University Education Quarterly 13, 4(Summer 1982): 2-10.

32.A.3639   Sharafuddin, A.M. "Science Popularization: A View From The Third World." Impact of Science on Society, 144 (1986): 379-385.

32.A.3640   Sharefkin, Belle D. "Science and Social Values." Urban Review 4, 2(October 1969): 29-31.

32.A.3641   Shea, James Herbert. "Science, Geology, Geography and
             'Cultural Literacy'." Journal of Geologoical Education 35,
             5(November 1987): 244-245.

32.A.3642   Shneour, Elie A. "Science: Too Much Accountability." Science
             195, 4282(March 1977): 939.

32.A.3643   Shortland, Michael. "Networks of Attitude And Belief: Science
             and The Adult Student." Scientific Literacy Papers, 1(Summer
             1987): 37-66.

32.A.3644   Shortland, Michael. "Scientific Literacy and Political Literacy:
             Examining The Common Ground." Scientific Literacy Papers,
             1(Summer 1987): 15-29.

32.A.3645   Shrigley, R.L. "Correlation of Science Attitude and Science
             Knowledge of Preservice Elementary Teachers." Science
             Education 58, (April 1974): 143-151.

32.A.3646   Shyarnas, V. "Mathodicheskie Osnovy Slovarnoj Raboty I
             Uchebnaja Leksikografij (A Methodology For Compiling A
             Scientific Lexicography)." Russkij Yazyk Za Rubezhom, 2(1973):
             29-32.

32.A.3647   Silha, Stephen. "Citizens and Science." Community and Junior
             College Journal 49, 4(December - January 1978-1979): 26-28.

32.A.3648   Simpson, Ronald D. "National Attentiveness To Science: An
             Educational Imperative For The Eighties and Beyond."
             Education 104, 1(Fall 1983): 7-11.

32.A.3649   Slaughter, J.B. "Frightening Public Attitude." USA Today 110,
             (April 1982): 16.

32.A.3650   Smalley, Robert L., and Brand, John R. "College Workshop For
             Secondary-School Students." Journal of College Science
             Teaching 3, 4(April 1974): 283-284.

32.A.3651   Smith, C. "Phlogiston Rules OK, or Some Parallels Between
             Children's Views of Chemistry and Historical Scientific Ideas."
             Lab Talk 30, 2(April 1986): 11.

32.A.3652   Smith, John P. "The Popularization of Science in The People's
             Republic of China." Science Education 65, 1(January 1981): 71-
             77.

32.A.3653   Smith, F.R., and Feathers, K.M. "Role of Reading in Content
             Classrooms: Assumption vs. Reality, The." Journal of Reading
             27, (December 1983): 262-267.

32.A.3654   Smith Norman F. "The Challenge of Scientific Literacy."
             Science Teacher 41, 6(September 1974): 34-35.

32.A.3655   Sorenson, Juanita S., and Voelker, Alan M. "Attitudes of a
             Selected Group of High School Seniors Toward The United
             States Space Program." Science Education 56, 4(October-
             December 1972): 459-470.

32.A.3656   Spencer, J.N. "Where Have All The Students Gone?" Journal of
             Chemical Education 61, (October 1984): 906-907.

32.A.3657   Spratt, Frederick. "Art Production in Discipline-Based Art
             Education." Journal of Aesthetic Education 21, 2(Summer
             1987): 197-204.

32.A.3658   Stahl, Frieda Axelrod. "Teaching Physics for Scientific Literacy."
             Ph.D. dissertation, Claremont Graduate School, 1969. 30/03-A,
             p. 938.

32.A.3659   Steinhauer, Gene D., and Peden, Blaine F. "Artificial Behavior:
             An Idea." Collegiate Microcomputer 3, 3(August 1985): 255-262.

32.A.3660   Stevens, R.A. "Africa in a Hurry." Out-of-School Scientific and
             Technical Education, 2(1972): 26-28.

32.A.3661   Stiles, William B. "Science, Experience, and Truth: A
             Conversation with Myself." Teaching of Psychology 8,
             4(December 1981): 227-230.

32.A.3662   Sullivan, Walter. "Books and Journals, A Special Report."
             Physics Today 23, 8(August 1970): 51-71.

32.A.3663   Swartz, Ronald. "Alternative Learning Strategies As Part of The
             Educational Process." Science Education 66, 2(April 1982): 269-
             279.

32.A.3664   Swetz, Frank J., ed. "Popular Science Readers: An Aid For
             Achieving Scientific Literacy in The PRC." Chinese Education
             11, 1(Spring 1978): 3-106.

32.A.3665   Tagliacozzo, Renata. "Levels of Technicality in Scientific Communication." Information Processing and Management 12, 2(1976): 95-110.

32.A.3666   Tarp, John R. "Toward Scientific Literacy For All Our Students." Science Teacher 45, 9(December 1978): 38-39.

32.A.3667   Tatum, E.L. "Science and Citizen: Horizons For The 70's." Science Teacher 36, (May 1969): 10-16.

32.A.3668   "Technological Literacy." (Symposium). Action in Teacher Education 5, (Winter 1983-1984): 1-7.

32.A.3669   Tichenor, Phillip J., et al. "Community Control and Care of Scientific Information." Communication Research - An International Quarterly 3, 4(October 1976): 403-424.

32.A.3670   Trowbridge, Leslie W. "A Decade of Promise." Science Teacher 41, 5(May 1974): 25-28.

32.A.3671   Turney, J. "Reaching A Public Understanding." Times Higher Education Supplement 614, (August 10, 1984): 10.

32.A.3672   Veltman, John. "An Oviparous Vertebrate Need Not Be A Strange Bird." Instructor 81, 5(January 1972): 60-61.

32.A.3673   Vitrogan, D. "Scientific Literacy and The Socially Disadvantaged Youth: A Laboratory-Demonstration Project." School Science and Mathematics 69, (October, 1969): 618-623.

32.A.3674   Walberg, H.J., et al. "A Test of A Model Of Educational Productivity Among Senior High School Students." Journal of Educational Research 79, (January/February 1986): 133-139.

32.A.3675   Walker, C.N. "Scientific Literacy: Another Dimension." School Science and Mathematics 71, (December, 1971): 767-768.

32.A.3676   Walker, J.T. "Dinosaurs, Nuclear Winter, and Kaniza Figures: In Defense of Pure Science and Intellectual Curiosity." Teaching of Psychology 14, (February 1987): 48-50.

32.A.3677   Weiss, Thomas M. "The Spirit of Science." Science Education 53, 4(October 1969): 365-367.

32.A.3678   Weyland, Jack. "Tell Me Why: The Science Version of Ann Landers." Physics Teacher 19, 7(October 1981): 451-455.

32.A.3679   Widdowson, H.G. "Description du Langage Scientifique
             (Description of Scientific Language)." Francais dans le Monde
             129, (May-June 1977): 15-21.

32.A.3680   Windler, K.J. "Concerned Over Scientific Illiteracy, Scholars
             Enter Creationist Debate." Chronicles of Higher Education 25,
             (December 15, 1982): 33-34.

32.A.3681   Wolfe, J.K. "Industry: An Unnoticed Consumer." Compact 6,
             (February 1972): 7-8.

32.A.3682   Wood, N. "Royal Society Launches Inquiry into Public Scientific
             'Literacy'."Times Educational Supplement 3516, (November 18,
             1983): 4.

32.A.3683   Wood, Roger L. "University Education Student's
             Understanding of The Nature and Processes of Science." School
             Science and Mathematics 72, 1(January 1972): 73-79.

32.A.3684   Woolpy, Jerome H. "Information Retrieval for Introductory
             Science Courses." American Biology Teacher 39, 3(March 1977):
             162-164, 171.

32.A.3685   Yager, R.E. "Let Kids Experience Science, and Watch The Crisis
             in Science Education Subside." American School Board Journal
             170, (June 1983): 26-27.

32.A.3686   Yager, R.E. "What Are The Basics in General Biology?"
             American Biology Teacher 43, (March 1981): 154-156.

32.A.3687   Yager, R.E., and Penick, J.E. "School Science in Crisis."
             Education Digest 49, (April 1984): 40-42.

32.A.3688   Yager, R.E., and Penick, J.E. "School Science in Crisis."
             Curriculum Review 22, (August 1983): 67-70.

32.A.3689   Yager, R.E., and Yager, S.O. "The Effect of Schooling Upon
             Understanding of Selected Science Terms." Journal of Research
             in Science Teaching 22, (April 1985): 359-354.

32.A.3690   Yager, Robert E. "Perspectives: What Are 'The Basics' in
             General Biology?" American Biology Teacher 43, 3(March
             1981): 154-156.

32.A.3691   Zeidler, D.L. "Moral Issues and Social Policy in Science
             Education: Closing The Literacy Gap." Science Education 68,
             (July 1984): 411-419.

32.A.3692   Zinberg, Dorothy. "A Strategy for Science Education in The
             1970's." Science 179, 4079 (March 1973): 1187.

B.   NATURE OF SCIENTIFIC KNOWLEDGE SCALE

32.B.3693   Lederman, N.G. "Students' and Teachers' Understanding of the
             Nature of Science: A Reassessment." School Science and
             Mathematics 86, (February 1986): 91-99.

32.B.3694   Lederman, N.G. "Relating Teaching Behavior and Classroom
             Climate to Changes in Students' Conceptions of The Nature of
             Science." Science Education 70, January 1986): 3-19.

32.B.3695   Lederman, N.G., and Druger, M. "Classroom Factors Related to
             Changes in Students' Conceptions of the Nature of Science."
             Journal of Research in Science Teaching 22, (October 1985): 649-
             662.

32.B.3696   Yankelovich, Daniel. "Changing Public Attitudes to Science and
             the Quality of Life: Edited Exerpts from a Seminar." Science
             Technology & Human Values 7, 39(Spring 1982): 23-29.

C.   PHILOSOPHY OF SCIENCE

32.C.3697   Adams, David L., et al. "Science, Technology, and Human
             Values: An Interdisciplinary Approach to Science Education."
             Journal of College Science Teaching 15, 4(February 1986): 254-
             258.

32.C.3698   Auger, Pierre. "Science and Humanism." Out-of-School
             Scientific and Technical Education, 1(1971): 27-30.

32.C.3699   Broudy, H.S. "Can Research Provide a Rationale for The Study
             of Science?" Journal of Research in Science Teaching 10,
             3(1973): 227-233.

32.C.3700   Carter, Paul A. "Science and The Common Man." American
             Scholar 45, 1(Winter 1975-1976): 778-794.

32.C.3701   Connelly, F. Michael. "Philosophy of Science and The Science Curriculum." Journal of Research In Science Teaching 6, 1: 108-113.

32.C.3702   Cutcliffe, Stephen H., and Goldman, Steven L. "Science, Technology, and the Liberal Arts: Report on a National Conference Held at Lehigh University." Science, Technology, and Human Values 10, 1(Winter 1985): 80-87.

32.C.3703   Dolby, R.G.A. "Three Hundred Years of Newton's Principia." Physics Education 22, 6(November 1987): 337-342.

32.C.3704   "Editorially Speaking: Scientific Growth and Moral Enlightenment." Journal of Chemical Education 49, 12(December 1972): 785.

32.C.3705   Gosling, David. "Some Aspects of the Impact of Science on Religion." New Frontiers in Education 4, 3(July/September 1974): 19-28.

32.C.3706   Grobman, A.B. "Science Education Today: Public Policy Tomorrow." NEA Journal 56, (March 1967): 8-10.

32.C.3707   Hawkins, David. "Science and the Public." Outlook, 35(1980): 40-46.

32.C.3708   Jacobsen, Marion S. "Relating Science and Values." Science Teacher 39, 3(March 1972): 52-53.

32.C.3709   "Knowledge of Science Declines." Science News 107, 13(March 1975):206.

32.C.3710   Lagowski, J.J. "Two Cultures: The Paradox Continues." Journal of Chemical Education 64, (March 1987): 193.

32.C.3711   Lightner, Jerry P. "Comment: The Cancer of Ignorance." Journal of Biological Education 8, 5(October 1974): 247-248.

32.C.3712   Master, John, and Elza, Betty. "Science and Culture." Science Teacher 37, 7(October 1970): 62-63.

32.C.3713   Moravesik, Michael J. "The Transmission of A Scientific Civilization." Bulletin of The Atomic Scientists 29, 3(March 1973): 25-28.

32.C.3714   Morison, Robert W. "Proposals For Achieving The World We Want." Science Teacher 37, 5(May 1970): 21-26.

32.C.3715   O'Hearn, George T. "Science Literacy and Alternative Futures." Science Education 60, 1(January-March 1976): 103-114.

32.C.3716   Pella, Milton O. "The Place or Function of Science For a Literate Citizenry." Science Foundation 60, 1(January-March 1976): 97-101.

32.C.3717   Prewitt, Kenneth. "The Public and Science Policy." Science Technology & Human Values 7, 39(Spring 1982): 5-14.

32.C.3718   Raman, Varadaraja. "The Three Planes of Science In Society." Impact of Science on Society 25, 1(January-March 1975): 9-17.

32.C.3719   Saunders, W.L. "Alternative Conceptions of The Nature of Science Responses Form Students, Teachers and Professors." Education 107, (Fall 1986): 98-105.

32.C.3720   Silverstone, Roger. "Science in the Frame: The Challenge of Translating the Private World of the Laboratory For a Mass Audience." Times Higher Education Supplement, 779 (October 9, 1987): 15.

32.C.3721   Smith Ralph A. "The Two Cultures Debate Today." Oxford Review of Education 4, 3(October 1978): 257-265.

32.C.3722   Thomas, Geoffrey, and Durant, John. "Why Should We Promote The Public Understanding of Science?" Scientific Literacy Papers, 1(Summer 1987): 1-14.

32.C.3723   Wartell, Michael A. "Science and The Liberal Arts." Liberal Education 70, 1(Spring 1984): 21-25.

32.C.3724   Willett, Richard E., and Roy, Paula A. "Crossing The Cultural Divide." Science Teacher 49, 5(May 1982): 32-36.

32.C.3725   Yager, Robert E. "The Major Crisis in Science Education." School Science and Mathematics 84, 1(March 1984): 189-198.

D.   SCIENCE CURRICULUM

32.D.3726   Anderson, Kenneth E. "U.S. Science Education: Last in The World Race?" Science Teacher 49, 4(April 1982): 47-48.

32.D.3727   Andrews, Ted F. "Science Education For The NonScientist." Educational Technology 10, 1(January 1970): 29-32.

32.D.3728   Bentley, Diana, et al. "Where Are We Going? An Examination of Some Secondary Science Curriculum Review Philosophies of Science Education." School Science Review 66, 237(June 1985): 658-667.

32.D.3729   Bernstein, Jeremy. "Science Education For The Non-Scientist." American Educator: The Professional Journal of The American Federation of Teachers 8, 3(Fall 1984): 46.

32.D.3730   Bowyer, Jane B., and Linn, Marcia C. "Effectiveness of the Science Curriculum Improvement Study in Teaching Scientific Literacy." Journal of Research in Science Teaching 15, 3(May 1978): 209-219.

32.D.3731   Dumbrill, Derek, and Birley, Graham. "Secondary School Pupils' Understanding of Some Key Physics Concepts." Research in Education, 37(May 1987): 47-59.

32.D.3732   Dykstra, D., Jr. "Science Education in Elementary School: Some Observations." Journal of Research in Science Teaching 24, (February 1987): 179-182; Discussion: 183-186; (October 1987): 679-682.

32.D.3733   Elliott, David, et al. "Scientific Illiteracy in Elementary School Science Textbook Programmes." Journal of Curriculum Studies 19, 1(January-February 1987): 73-76.

32.D.3734   Gauld, Colin. "The Scientific Attitude and Science Education: A Critical Reappraisal." Science Education 66, 1(January 1982): 109-121.

32.D.3735   Girard, G. Tanner. "Impact of NSF Science Curriculum Projects." School Science and Mathematics 79, 1(January 1979): 3-6.

32.D.3736   Gross, Bernard Francis. "The Design of an Auto-Tutorial Genetics Course to Increase Scientific Literacy Among Nonscience Majors and Its Evaluation Using A Science-Related Semantic Differential Instrument." Ph.D. dissertation, Syracuse University. 1971. 32/08-A, p. 4442.

32.D.3737   Hewson, M.G.A. "The Acquisition of Scientific Knowledge:
             Analysis and Representation of Student Conceptions
             Concerning Density." Science Education 70, (April 1986): 159-
             170.

32.D.3738   Heylin, Michael. "High School Science Problems Gain
             Spotlight." Chemical and Engineering News 60, 21(May 24,
             1982): 39-41.

32.D.3739   Leake, J.B., and Hinerman, C.O. "Scientific Literacy and School
             Characteristics." School Science and Mathematics 73,
             (December 1973): 772-282.

32.D.3740   Lewis, John L. "Energy Education and The Environment in The
             Science Curriculum." Environmental Education and
             Information 1, 3(July-September 1981): 189-196.

32.D.3741   Marshall, William L. "Implementing Cultural Science in The
             High Schools." Journal of Chemical Education 58, 10(October
             1981): 770-772.

32.D.3742   Rosenblum, Yeshayahu, and Markovits, Arieh. "Scientific Prose
             or Narrative Style in a Science Program For The Culturally
             Disadvan-taged." Studies in Educational Evaluation 2, 1(Spring
             1976): 53-56.

32.D.3743   "Scientific Literacy: Imperative For Survival; Some Thoughts
             For The Principal in Developing The Science Curriculum;
             Symposium." National Association of Secondary School
             Principals Bulletin 56, (January 1972): 1-99.

32.D.3744   Showalter, Victor. New Directions For Science Curriculum
             Development. Cleveland, Ohio: Educational Research Council
             of America, 1968.   ED 025 436.

32.D.3745   Thomas, F.J., and Kondo, A.K. Towards Scientific Literacy: A
             Core Curriculum For Adult Learners and Literacy Teachers.
             Teheran: International Institute For Adult Literacy Methods,
             1978.

32.D.3746   Yager, Robert E., and Cossman, George. Guidelines For The
             Development of A Course for Secondary Schools Emphasizing
             The Interaction of Science and The Culture of Man. Iowa City,
             Iowa: Iowa University, 1966.   ED 018 400.

E.   SCIENCE TEACHING

32.E.3747   Boylan, C. "Year 7 Students Understanding of Heat and
            Temperature." Scios 22, 3(September 1987): 10-18.

32.E.3748   Cisar, Vaclav, and Petracek, Svatopluk. Scientific and Technical
            Education In Czechoslovakia. Paris: UNESCO, 1982. ED 238
            089.

32.E.3749   Collins, R. "Science Teaching In The School." Science
            Education News 34, 1(Autumn 1985): 18-21.

32.E.3750   Cossman, George W. "The Effects of a Course In Science and
            Culture For Secondary School Students." Journal of Research In
            Science Teaching 6, 3(1969): 274-283.

32.E.3751   Dumbrill, Dere, and Birley, Graham. "Secondary School Pupils'
            Understanding of Some Key Physics Concepts." Research in
            Education, 37(May 1987): 47-59.

32.E.3752   Dunathan, Harmon, et al. "Discourse Science Instruction."
            Liberal Education 74, 2(March-April 1988): 2-19.

32.E.3753   Ewing, M.S., et al. "Improving Student Attitudes Toward
            Biology by Encouraging Scientific Literacy." American Biology
            Teacher 49, (September 1987): 348-350.

32.E.3754   Friedman, Sharon M. "Using Real World Experience to Teach
            Science and Environmental Writing." Journal of
            Environmental Education 10, 3(Spring 1979): 37-42.

32.E.3755   Goldsmith, Robert H. "Changes in the Importance of Certain
            Popular Science Misconceptions." School Science and
            Mathematics 78, 1(January 1978): 31-36.

32.E.3756   Hetherington, Norriss S. "The History of Science and The
            Teaching of Science Literacy." Journal of Thought 17,
            2(Summer 1982): 53-66.

32.E.3757   James, Rosemarie, "Science Teaching and Career Education - A
            Joint Venture." Science Teacher 48, 6(September 1981): 32-35.

32.E.3758   Kass, Heidi. "Science Activities in The Development of Basic
            Reading and Number Skills." Elements 9, 2(October 1977): 3-5.

32.E.3759   Lange, C.T. "Helping Students Become More Scientifically
Literate." American Biology Teacher 50, (January 1988): 51-52.

32.E.3760   Lederman, Norman G., and Zeidler, Dana L. "Science Teachers'
Conceptions of the Nature of Science: Do They Really Influence
Teaching Behavior?" Science Education 71, 5(October 1987):
721-734.

32.E.3761   Lucas, Arthur. "Public Knowledge of Biology." Journal of
Biological Education 21, 1(Spring 1987): 41-45.

32.E.3762   Maarschalk, J. "Scientific Literacy and Informal Science
Teaching." Journal of Research in Science Teaching 25,
(February 1988): 135-146.

32.E.3763   Maarschalk, Jan. "Scientific Literacy Through Informal Science
Teaching." European Journal of Science Education 8, 4(October-
December 1986): 353-360.

32.E.3764   MacMahan, Horace. "A Plea For Honesty In Science Classes."
Science Education 55, 4(October/December 1971): 449-450.

32.E.3765   Markow, G. "Teaching Chemistry Like The Foreign Language It
Is." Journal of Chemical Education 65, (January 1988): 57-58.

32.E.3766   Massey, W.E. "Making Science Accessible." Liberal Education
74, (March/April 1988): 16-19.

32.E.3767   Mertens, Thomas R. "New Directions in Science Teaching:
Human Genetics Education." Phi Delta Kappan 64, 9(May 1983):
628-631.

32.E.3768   Osborne, R.J. "'I Understand, But I Don't Get It': Some
Problems of Learning Science." Queensland Science Teacher,
(November 1980): 1-9.

32.E.3769   Petroski, Henry J. "Biology Education in The People's Republic
of China." American Biology Teacher 43, 2(February 1981): 82-
95.

32.E.3770   Phillips, D.C. "Can Scientific Method Be Taught?" Journal of
College Science Teaching 15, 2(November 1985): 95-101.

32.E.3771   Priestley, Herbert. "Science For The Non Science Major - -
Problem and Partial Prescription." American Journal of Physics
39, 12(December 1971): 1498-1503.

32.E.3772   Rawis, Rebecca L. "Concept of Quasicrystalline Metal Alloys Becoming Clearer." Chemical and Engineering News 64, 25(June 23, 1986): 37-38.

32.E.3773   Ritterbush, Philip C. "Science Teaching and The Future." Science Teacher 36, 6(September 1969): 32-39.

32.E.3774   Robinson, James T. The Nature of Science and Science Teaching. Belmont, California: Wadsworth Publishing Co., Inc., 1968. ED 031 395.

32.E.3775   Shakhashiri, Bassam Z. "The Need For Science Instruction inYour Child's School." PTA Today 10, 5(March 1985): 7-9.

32.E.3776   Swartz, Cliff. "On Teaching That We Do Not Know." Physics Teacher 13, 7(October 1975): 390, 438.

32.E.3777   Swetz, Frank J., ed. "Popular Science Readers: An Aid For Achieving Scientific Literacy In The PRC." Chinese Education 11, Special Issue (Spring 1978): 3-105.

32.E.3778   Zietsman, A.I., and Hewson, P.W. "Effect of Instruction Using Microcomputer Simulations and Conceptual Change Strategies on Science Learning." Journal of Research in Science Teaching 23, (January 1986): 27-39.

F.   TESTS AND SCALES

32.F.3779   Andersen, H.O., et al. "Nature of Science, 1969 and 1984: Perspective of Preservice Secondary Science Teachers (Use of Nature of Science Scale)." School Science and Mathematics 86, (January 1986): 43-50.

32.F.3780   Doran, Rodney L., et al. "An Analysis of Several Instruments Measuring 'Nature of Science' Objectives." Science Education 58, 3(July-September 1974): 321-329.

32.F.3781   Fisher, K.M. and Lipson, J.I. "Twenty Questions About Student Errors." Journal of Research in Science Teaching 23, (December 1986): 783-803.

32.F.3782   Fraser, Barry J. Test of Enquiry Skills [and] Handbook. Hawthorn, Australia: Australian Council For Educational Research, 1979. ED 181 082.

32.F.3783   Rubba, Peter A., and Andersen, Hans O. "Development of An Instrument to Assess Secondary School Students' Understanding of the Nature of Scientific Knowledge," Science Education 62, 4(October-December 1978): 449-458.

G.   RESEARCH

32.G.3784   Allen, Leslie R. "An Evaluation of Children's Performance on Certain Cognitive, Affective, and Motivational Aspects of the Systems and Subsystems Unit of the Science Curriculum Improvement Study Elementary Science Program." Journal of Research in Science Teaching 10, 2(1973): 125-134.

32.G.3785   Barrington, B.L., and Hendricks, B. "Attitudes Toward Science and Science Knowledge of Intellectually Gifted and Average Students In Third, Seventh, and Eleventh Grades." Journal of Research in Science Teaching 25, (November 1988): 679-687.

32.G.3786   Bowes, John E., and Stamm, Keith R. "Science Writing Techniques and Methods: What the Research Tells Us." Journal of Environmental Education 10, 3(Spring 1979): 25-28.

32.G.3787   Brown, Talbert W., et al. "Research on The Development of Scientific Literacy." Science and Children 12, 4(January 1975): 13-15.

32.G.3788   Crane, Robert. Science Achievement In The Schools: A Summary of Results From The 1976-77 National Assessment of Science. Denver: Education Commission of The States, 1978. ED 164 337.

32.G.3789   Downie, Roger. "'Deliberate Mistakes, Articles and Scientific Literacy." Journal of Biological Education 7, 4(Winter 1983): 303-306.

32.G.3790   Elliott, David; Nagel, Kathleen; and Woodward, Arthur. "Scientific Illiteracy in Elementary School Science Textbook Programmes." Journal of Curriculum Studies 19, 1(January-February 1987): 73-76.

32.G.3791   Falk, J.H., et al. "The Things of Science: Assessing The Learning Potential of Science Museums." Science Education 70, (October 1986): 503-508.

32.G.3792   Fisher, K.M., and Lipson, J.I. "Twenty Questions About Student
            Errors." Journal of Research in Science Teaching 23, (December
            1986): 783-803.

32.G.3793   Gabel, Lawrence Lee. "The Development of a Model To
            Determine Perceptions of Scientific Literacy." Ph.D. dissertation,
            The Ohio State University, 1976. 37/08-A, p. 5013.

32.G.3794   Gennaro, E.D., et al. "A Study of The Latent Effects of Family
            Learning Courses in Science," Journal of Research in Science
            Teaching 23, (December 1986): 771-781.

32.G.3795   Guthrie, John T. "Research: Literacy For Science and
            Technology." Journal of Reading 27, 5(February 1984): 478-480.

32.G.3796   Guthrie, John T. "Research: Scientific Literacy." Journal of
            Reading 27, 3(December 1983): 286-288.

32.G.3797   Harbeck, Mary B. "Instructional Objectives In The Affective
            Domain." Educational Technology 10, 1(January 1970): 49-52.

32.G.3798   Hawkins, J. and Pea, R.D. "Tools For Bridging The Cultures of
            Everyday and Scientific Thinking." Journal of Research in
            Science Teaching 24, (April 1987): 291-307.

32.G.3799   Jerkins, Kenneth F. "Measurement of Understanding Science
            and Scientists In Selected Junior High School Classes." Science
            Education 53, 5(December 1969): 399-401.

32.G.3800   Jerkins, Kenneth F. "Measurement of Understanding Science
            and Scientists In Selected Collegiate Academic Groups." Science
            Education 53, 3(April 1969): 225-226.

32.G.3801   Maxwell, Martha J. "The Value of Skimming and Scanning In
            Studying Science Textbooks." Journal of The Reading Specialist
            9, 3(March 1970): 116-117.

32.G.3802   Mitman, A.L., et al. "Instruction Addressing The Components
            of Scientific Literacy and Its Relation To Student Outcomes."
            American Educational Research Journal 24, (Winter 1987): 611-
            633.

32.G.3803   Norris, B. Science Report Shows Russia Is Years Ahead [Survey
            by the National Science Teacher Association]." Times
            Educational Supplement 3747, (April 22, 1988): 14.

32.G.3804   Renner, John W., and Coulter, Vivian Jensen. "Science
Achievement is Above Expectations in Norman, Oklahoma."
Science and Children 13, 7(April 1976): 26-27.

32.G.3805   Riner, Phillip S. "Establishing Scientific Methodology With
Elementary Gifted Children Through Field Biology." G/C/T, 28
(May-June 1983): 46-49.

32.G.3806   Scharmann, L.C. "Locus of Control: A Discriminator of The
Ability To Foster An Understanding of The Nature of Science
Among Preservice Elementary Teachers." Science Education 72,
(July 1988): 453-465.

32.G.3807   Singer, Daniel M., and Singer, Maxine Frank. "Ethical Problems
at The Frontiers of Biological Research." American Biology
Teacher 37, 9(December 1975): 528-529, 539.

33

Technological Literacy

33.3808   Adams, D.L., and Baker, R.E. "Science, Technology, and Human
             Values: An Interdisciplinary Approach to Science Education."
             Journal of College Science Teaching 15, (February 1986): 254-
             258.

33.3809   Adams, Dennis M., and Hamm, Mary. "Teaching Students
             Critical Viewing Skills."Curriculum Review 26, 3(January-
             February 1987): 29-31.

33.3810   Bailey, John. "Evolution Not Revolution: Whatever Happened
             To Design and Technology." Programmed Learning and
             Educational Technology 20, 4(November 1983): 228-242.

33.3811   Baird, William E. "Conference Abstracts: EdComCon '84."
             Journal of Computers in Mathematics and Science Teaching 5,
             1(Fall 1985): 62-63.

33.3812   Balistreri, Jerry, and Hammer, Douglas E. "Technology
             Education in Utah." Technology Teacher 47, 8(May-June 1988):
             11-14.

33.3813   Barber, Betsy Sue. "Technological Change and English Teaching:
             A Delphi Study of American, British, and Canadian English
             Educators' Views of the Future of Secondary English Teaching
             (Word-Processing, Media, Literacy)." Ph.D. Dissertation, The
             University of Connecticut, 1985.   46/06-A, p. 1493.

33.3814   Batey, Andy, et al. "Developing an Understanding of
             Technology Through The Application of Science and
             Mathematics." Technology Teacher 43, 8(May-June 1984): 27-
             29.

33.3815   Bender, Myron. "Technology Education and Traditional Industrial Arts." Journal of Epsilon Pi Tau 8, 2(Fall 1982): 55-68.

33.3816   Bensen, M.J. "Today's Students Need a Future-Based Technology Education." School Shop 45, (April 1986): 26-27.

33.3817   Borchardt, Frank. "Tur(n)ing The Tables: A Quiet Polemic." CALICO Journal 4, 4(June 1987): 31-35.

33.3818   Boucher, F.C. "Increasing America's Competitiveness Through Technology Education." Technology Teacher 47, (May/June 1988): 3-5.

33.3819   Bowen, Blannie E., et al. "Theme: Staying Current - High Technology." Agricultural Education Magazine 59, 3(September 1986): 3-19.

33.3820   Bowser, Hal. "Technology and the Human Dimension: An Interview With Elting E. Morison." American Heritage of Invention and Technology 1, 1(Summer 1985): 34-41.

33.3821   Branscomb, Anne W. "Knowing How to Know." Science Technology, and Human Values 6, 36(Summer 1981): 5-9.

33.3822   Breslow, Gail. "AAAS: The Mass Media Science Fellows." Science, Technology, and Human Values 6, 36(Summer 1981): 41-44.

33.3823   Brown, Peter D. "English and The Computer." English Quarterly 16, 4(Winter 1984): 55-62.

33.3824   "Business and Industry's Role in Improving The Scientific and Technological Literacy of America's Youth." American Education 20, 4(May 1984): 6-9.

33.3825   Butler, M. "Selected Annotated Bibliography." (Technological Literacy). Action in Teacher Education 5, (Winter 1983-1984): 63-79.

33.3826   Caporael, Linnda R., and Thorngate, Warren. "Introduction: Towards The Social Psychology of Computing." Journal of Social Issues 40, 3(1984): 1-13.

33.3827   Caravella, Joseph R. "Coping With The Challenge of Change." Arithmetic Teacher 30, 6(February 1983): 50.

33.3828   Chen, David, and Novik, Ruth. "Scientific and Technological Education in an Information Society." Science Education 68, 4(July 1984): 421-426.

33.3829   Colelli, Leonard A. "Industrial Arts and Elementary Education: An Integrated Approach Toward Cultural Development." Man/Society/Technology 40, 1(September-October 1980): 8-10.

33.3830   Compaine, Benjamin. "The Evolution of the 'New Literacy'." National Forum: Phi Kappa Phi Journal 63, 3(Summer 1983): 10-12.

33.3831   Considine, David. "Media, Technology, and Teaching: What's Wrong and Why?" School Library Media Quarterly 13, 3-4(Summer 1985): 173-182.

33.3832   Declercq, Guido V. "A Third Look at The Two Cultures: The New Economic Responsibility of The University." International Journal of Institutional Management in Higher Education 5, 2(July 1981): 117-122.

33.3833   DeVore, Paul W. "Technology - An Examen." Journal of Industrial Teacher Education 25, 3(Spring 1988): 7-18.

33.3834   DeVore, Paul W. "Science and Technology: An Analysis of Meaning." Journal of Epsilon Pi Tau 13, 1(Winter-Spring 1987): 2-9.

33.3835   Dyrenfurth, Michael. "Technological Literacy For a Changing World." VocEd 56, 2(March 1981): 49-51.

           Examines the issue of technological literacy for postsecondary and adult industrial arts education students. Reviews the major thrusts for said classification of students. Discusses the use of cluster laboratories and its application to occupational/technical preparation; the providing of basic education; and recreational and leisure activities of post-secondary and adult education students. Concludes with a call for vocational educators to speak to the needs of adults who find themselves in an increasingly technological world.

33.3836   Dyrenfurth, Michael J. Literacy For A Technological World. Columbus, Ohio: Ohio State University, National Center For Research In Vocational Education, 1984.

33.3837   Dyrenfurth, Michael J. "The Route To Technological Literacy."
            VocEd 58, 1(January-February 1983): 42-44.

33.3838   Dyrenfurth, Michael J., and Lemons, Dale. "Vocational
            Education's Role in Developing Technological Literacy."
            Canadian Vocational Journal 18, 1(May 1982): 32-35.

33.3839   Foster, Phillip R., and Perreault, Raymond J., Jr. "Characteristics
            of Technological Literacy: Perspectives From The Industrial and
            Educational Sectors." Journal of Epsilon Pi Tau 12, 1(Summer-
            Fall 1986): 55-58.

33.3840   Frazier, Robert. "Man Quests The Future." Action in Teacher
            Education 5, 4(Winter 1983-1984): 1-7.

33.3841   Friedman, Madeleine. "Robotics Literacy Captivates Elementary
            Students." TechTrends 31, 1(January 1986): 12-14.

33.3842   Friedman, Sharon. "Training Reporters To Cover Science and
            Technology." Professional Engineer 51, 3(September 1981): 22-
            27.

33.3843   Fullinwider, Robert K. "Technological Literacy and
            Citizenship." Scientific Literacy Papers, 1(Summer 1987): 31-35.

33.3844   Garner, Douglas. "Course Syllabus: Science, Technology and
            Society." Science, Technology and Society, 46(February 1985): 6-
            10.

33.3845   Gault, Michel. The Future of The Book: Part II - The Changing
            Role of Reading No.9. Paris: UNESCO, 1982.   ED 234 348.

33.3846   Gies, Joseph C. "Technology: A New Liberal Art?" AGB
            Reports 24, 1(January-February 1982): 17-20.

33.3847   Goetsch, D.L. "Understanding High Technology." Technology
            Teacher 45 [47], (March 1988): 29-31.

33.3848   Goldberg, A.L. "The Eclectic Technologist: Computer Literacy or
            Technological Literacy?" Educational Technology 24, (July
            1984): 33-34.

33.3849   Goldberg, Albert L. "A Few Words About Technological
            Literacy." Michigan Social Studies Journal 2, 1(Fall 1987): 71-72.

33.3850   Goldberg, Samuel. "The Sloan Foundation's New Liberal Arts
           Program." Change 18, 2(March-April 1986): 14-15.

33.3851   Guthrie, John T. "Research, Literacy For Science and
           Technology." Journal of Reading 27, 5(February 1984): 478-480.

33.3852   Hartman, J. Paul, et al. The Warp and The Woof: 1984
           Conference For Universities." Weaver of Information and
           Perspectives on Technological Literacy 3, 1(Fall 1984): 3-4.

33.3853   Hazeltine, Barrett. "Logic Circuits as a Vehicle For Technological
           Literacy." The Weaver of Information and Perspectives on
           Technological Literacy 4, 1(Fall 1985): 4-5.

33.3854   Hersh, Richard H. "Education and The Corporate Connection."
           Educational Horizons 62, 1(Fall 1983): 5-8.

33.3855   Hersh, Richard H. "How To Avoid Becoming a Nation of
           Technopeasants." Phi Delta Kappan 64, 9(May 1983): 635-638.

33.3856   Hutson, B.A. "Developing Student's Technical Literacy As A
           Tool For Work." Delta Kappa Gamma Bulletin 51,
           (Winter/Spring 1985): 26-32.

33.3857   Ircha, M.C., and McLaughlin, J.D. "Teaching Public Policy In An
           Engineering College." Engineering Education 78, 7(April 1988):
           703-704.

33.3858   Isherwood, Geoffrey B. "The Principal and The Pauper:
           Administrator Training in Computer Technology." Education
           Canada 25, 4(Winter 1985): 4-9.

33.3859   Jarcho, Irma S. "S/T/S in Practice: Five Ways To Make It
           Work." Curriculum-Review 24, 3(January-February 1985): 17-
           20.

33.3860   Jones, Allan C. "Technical Illiteracy: Treat The Cause, Not The
           Symptom." Engineering Education 78, 8(May 1988): 741-743.

33.3861   Kanigel, Robert. "Technology As A Liberal Art: Scenes From the
           Classroom" Change 18, 2(March-April 1986): 20-27, 30.

33.3862   Keohane, Nannerl O. "Business as Usual or Brave New World?
           A College President's Perspective." Change 18, 2(March-April
           1986): 28-29.

33.3863   Krieger, James. "Science and Society Programs Fuel Drive For Technological Literacy." Chemical and Engineering News 65, 8(February 23, 1987): 26-27.

33.3864   Lacroix, William J. "The Future in Review." Journal of Epsilon Pi Tau 9, 2(Fall 1983): 15-21.

33.3865   Lang, Berel. "Commentary: Preliteracy, Postliteracy, and the Cunning of History." Journal of Reading 26, 7(April 1983): 581-585.

33.3866   Lauda, Donald. "Three Scenarios on The Technology Education Base." Journal of Epsilon Pi Tau 9, 2(Fall 1983): 7-14.

33.3867   Lauda, Donald P. "Technology Education: A Fundamental Framework For Improved Capability in Math and Science." Technology Teacher 45, 2(November 1985): 3-6.

33.3868   Ley, Connie J. "Technological Literacy and Investigative Imperatives For Vocational Education Researchers." Journal of Vocational Education Research 12, 1(Winter 1987): 1-9.

33.3869   Liao, Thomas T. "Microcomputers: Tools for Developing Technological Literacy." Weaver of Information and Perspectives on Technological Literacy 1, 2(Spring 1983): 13.

33.3870   Lindauer, George, and Hagerty, Joseph. "Technology and Society - An Upper-Level Course." Engineering Education 74, 7(April 1984): 666-668.

33.3871   Lovedahl, Gerald G. "Robotics: A New Challenge For Industrial Arts." Man/Society/Technology 42, 7(April 1983): 14-15.

33.3872   Magazine, Alan H. "The Journal From 'Here' to 'There'." Journal of the Society of Research Administrators 15, 1(Summer 1983): 5-13.

33.3873   Maley, Donald. "Technology Literacy as a Major Thrust For Technology Education." Journal of Epsilon Pi Tau 13, 1(Winter-Spring 1987): 44-49.

33.3874   Maley, Donald. "Teaching the Heritage of Technology: Past, Present, and Future." The Technolgy Teacher 43, 3(December 1983): 3-7.

33.3875   Markert, Linda Rae. "Technology Education: Its Place and
           Importance in the Curriculum." NASSP Bulletin 68, 472(May
           1984): 27-34.

33.3876   Mathews, J., et al. Towards Flexible Skill Formation and
           Technological Literacy: Challenges Facing The Education
           System. Melbourne: Ministry of Education, 1987.

33.3877   "Matters of Course." Weaver of Information and Perspectives
           on Technological Literacy 3, 1(Fall 1984): 5-8.

33.3878   McClure, Larry. "High Tech for Your Home, School and
           Community." Wisconsin Vocational Educator 8, 3(Summer-
           Fall 1984): 18.

33.3879   McCrory, David L., and Maughan, George R., Jr. "Instructional
           Resources For Technological Literacy."
           Man/Society/Technology 42, 8(May-June 1983): 13-14.

33.3880   Menefee, Robert. "Society for College Science Teachers: High
           Technology." Journal of College Science Teaching 13,
           2(November 1983): 70-71.

33.3881   Mestel, Gayle S. "University of Arizona Research on MIS Looks
           to the Future." School Business Affairs 52, 1(January 1986): 30,
           58-59.

33.3882   Missimer, William C., Jr. "Business and Industry's Role in
           Improving The Scientific and Technological Literacy of
           America's Youth." Technological Horizons in Education 11,
           5(February 1984): 89-93.

33.3883   Missner, W.C., Jr. "Industry Must Lead The Fight To Improve
           Technological Literacy." Montana School Boards Association
           Bulletin 15, (November 1983): 3-4.

33.3884   Mohammed, Mowafak A.H., and Swales, John M. "Factors
           Affecting The Successful Reading of Technical Instructions."
           Reading in a Foreign Language 2, 2(Fall 1984): 206-217.

33.3885   Morrison, Raymond, and Brandt, Linda. "Keeping Skills
           Current Through Continuing Education." Technological
           Horizons in Education 15, 7(March 1988): 82-85.

33.3886   Murchland, B. "Facing Technology Through Education."
           Education Digest 51, (January 1986): 44-45.

33.3887   Murchland, B. "Facing Technology." Educational Horizons 63, (Spring 1985): 113-116.

33.3888   Murchland, Bernard. "Citizenship in a Technological Society: Problems and Possibilities." Journal of Teacher Education 34, 6(November-December 1983): 21-24.

33.3889   O'Donnell, Holly. "ERIC/RCS: Beyond Computer Literacy." Journal of Reading 27, 1(October 1983): 78-80.

33.3890   Ost, David H. "The Nature of Technologic Literacy." School Science and Mathematics 85, 8(December 1985): 689-696.

33.3891   Page, Ray, et al. "The Schools Council's 'Modular Courses in Technology' Project." Research in Science and Technological Education 1, 2(1983): 239-245.

33.3892   Pellegrino, James P. "Literacy Is Vital To Survival In The Technical Classroom and Workplace." NASSP Bulletin 72, 509(September 1988): 88-94.

33.3893   Perritt, R.D., ed. "Staying Current - Agricultural Mechanics." (Sym-posium). Agricultural Education Magazine 58, (February 1986): 4-16.

33.3894   Peterson, I. "Knowing Little About How Things Work." Science News 129, 8(February 22, 1986): 118.

33.3895   Rennie, L. "Teacher's Perception of Technology." Scios 22, 2(June 1987): 8-12.

33.3896   Richman, Ellen. "Equity in Technology." Computing Teacher 15, 5(February 1988): 33-37.

33.3897   Rooke, Denis. "Presidential Address: Science - Fundamental to the School Curriculum and the Nation's Future." School Science Review 62, 221(June 1981): 625-630.

33.3898   Roy, Rustum. "The Science/Technology/Society Connection." Curriculum Review 24, 3(January-February 1985): 16.

33.3899   Ruina, Jack. "Coping With Nuclear Weapons Policy: How Expert Do You Have To Be?" Weaver of Information and Perspectives on Technological Literacy 1, 2(Spring 1983): 8-9.

33.3900   Selby, Cecily Cannan. "Integrated Mathematics, Science and
           Technology Education: Opening Doors and Opening Minds."
           Technology Teacher 47, 5(February 1988): 3-5.

33.3901   "Science and Technology: A New Alliance." Journal of Epsilon
           Pi Tau 10, 1(Spring 1984): 16-21.

33.3902   "Scientific and Technological Education in an Information
           Society." Science Education 68, 4(July 1984): 421-426.

33.3903   Scriven, M. "The Rights of Technology In Education: A Need
           For Consciousness Raising." SASTA Journal, 873(December
           1987): 20-31.

33.3904   Selland, Larry G. "'Principles of Technology' - The First Two
           Years'." Vocational Education Journal 61, 4(May 1986): 47-49.

33.3905   Sharon, D., et al. "Robotics Literacy Curriculum." Industial
           Education 76, (March 1987): 18.

33.3906   Sharon, D., et al. "Robotics and Automation Literacy Project."
           Industiral Education 76, (February 1987): 44-46.

33.3907   Sharon, Dan, et al. "The ORT Open Tech Robotics and
           Automation Literacy Course." Programmed Learning and
           Educational Technology 24, 3(August 1987): 200-216.

33.3908   Sharples, Brian. "Values: The Forgotten Dimension in
           Administration." Education Canada 24, 3(Fall 1984): 32-37.

33.3909   Stannard, C.R. "Technology-Oriented Science For
           Nonspecialists." Journal of College Teaching 15, (February
           1986): 267-273.

33.3910   Staudenmaier, J.M. "Technological Literacy In Context."
           Momentum 19, (Summer 1988): 13.

33.3911   Taylor, W.D. and Johnson, J.B. "Resisting Technological
           Momentum." Yearbook (National Society for the Study of
           Education) 85th, pt.1(1986): 216-233.

33.3912   "Technical Illiteracy Threatens U.S. Science." Science News 118,
           18(November 1980): 276.

33.3913   "Technological Literacy." (Symposium). Teacher Educator 5,
           (Winter 1983-1984): 1-7.

33.3914   Tenner, Edward. "The Computer and Higher Education: A New Definition of Education?" Change 16, 3(April 1984): 22-27.

33.3915   Thiel, David V. "Science With Microprocessors: Flexibility in an Interdisciplinary School." Higher Education 11, 6(November 1982): 635-643.

33.3916   Trachtman, Leon E. "The Public Understanding of Science Effort: A Critique." Science, Technology, and Human Values 6, 36(Summer 1981): 10-15.

33.3917   Truxal, John B. "The Warp and The Woof." Weaver of Information and Perspectives on Technological Literacy 2, 2(Spring 1984): 2-3.

33.3918   Truxal, John G. "Learning to Think Like an Engineer: Why, What, and How?" Change 18, 2(March-April 1986): 10-19.

33.3919   Tsurumi, Toshi. "Insights: Too Many U.S. Managers Are Technologically Illiterate." High Technology 4, 4(April 1984): 16.

33.3920   Tucker, Marc S. "Computers in The Schools: What Revolution?" Journal of Communication 35, 4(Fall 1985): 12-23.

33.3921   Uhlig, George. "Dimensions of Technology Literacy in Teacher Education." Journal of Teacher Education 34, 5(September-October 1983): 2-5.

33.3922   Van Laatum, Henk, and Waijer, Jan. "Outline of a Teaching - Learning Package on Information Technology For Use in Teacher Education." European Journal of Teacher Education 6, 2(1983): 151-156.

33.3923   Visich, Marian, Jr. "Energy at Stony Brook." Weaver of Information and Perspectives on Technological Literacy 2, 2(Spring 1984): 8-9.

33.3924   Waetjen, Walter B. "The Autonomy of Technology. A Challenge to Education." Technology Teacher 46, 6(March 1987): 13-14.

33.3925   Wedemeyer, Dan J. "The New Age of Telecommunication: Setting the Context for Education." Educational Technology 26, 10(October 1986): 7-13.

33.3926   Wiens, A. Emerson. "Teaching Technology as a Liberal Art."
           Journal of Industrial Teacher Education 25, 1(Fall 1987): 7-16.

33.3927   Wiens, A. Emerson. "Technological Education in The Liberal
           Arts." Journal of Epsilon Pi Tau 13, 2(Summer-Fall 1987): 16-
           23.

33.3928   Wiens, A. Emerson. "Technology and The Liberal Arts."
           Technology Teacher 45, 2(November 1985): 13-14.

33.3929   Williams, B. "Brave New Classrooms." Media & Methods 21,
           (November 1984): 50.

33.3930   Winter, Metta L. "Nuclear Education Update." School Library
           Journal 32, 5(January 1986): 22-26.

33.3931   Yager, Robert E. "The Major Crisis in Science Education."
           School Science and Mathematics 84, 3(March 1984): 189-198.

33.3932   Yager, Robert E. "Goals Provide Direction in Science Education."
           Science Education in Ohio 2, 1(Winter 1983): 1-5.

34

Technology and Literacy

34.3933   Bernard, H.R. "The Power of Print: The Role of Literacy In Preserving Native Cultures." <u>Human Organization</u> 44, (Spring 1985): 88-93.

34.3934   Bolter, J. David. "Text and Technology: Reading and Writing in the Electronic Age." <u>Library Resources and Technical Services</u> 31, 1(January-March 1987): 12-23.

34.3935   Clarkson, P. "Technical Education: Some Overseas Trends and Ideas." <u>Educational Magazine</u> 41, 5(1984): 14-15.

34.3936   Covert, James R. "Use of Post-Literate Technology in a Pre-Literate Culture: Examples and Implications." <u>Canadian and International Education</u> 6, 1(June 1977): 15-32.

        Focuses on the bringing together of both teaching styles and learning styles. Specifically, examines a pre-literate learning style being matched with a post-literate teaching approach. Discusses the content of formal, non-formal and informal education. Presents three assumptions which must be examined before discussing the matching of pre-literate learning styles with post-literate teaching techniques. Provides three examples, and attendant discussions, on said attempts to match. Examples are (1) Newfoundland, (2) Sky River, and (3) Southern Appalachia. Concludes with a discussion of implications for the future.

34.3937   Fawns, R. "Setting Out To Make Things Work: Technological Literacy and Sensibility In The Curriculum." <u>Lab Talk</u> 23, 5(October 1979): 19-22.

34.3938   Friedman, Edward A., ed. <u>Technological Literacy and The Liberal Arts</u>. Washington, D.C.: Association of American Colleges, 1980.   ED 196 350.

34.3939   Gardner, John, and Mitchell, John. "Kilroy Was Here: Being A Dissertation On The Measures Needed To Combat The Present Illiteracy of Technical Students." <u>Technical Education</u> 9, (June 1967): 252-253, 256.

34.3940   Hall, W. "Science, Technology and Society." <u>Education News</u> 18, 5(July 1983): 34-35.

34.3941   Malcolm, C. "Technology Education In General Education." <u>Educational Magazine</u> 41, 5(1984): 3-5.

34.3942   Mikulecky, L., and Ehlinger, J. "The Influence of Metacognitive Aspects of Literacy on Job Performance of Electronics Technicians." <u>Journal of Reading Behavior</u> 18, 1(1986): 41-62.

34.3943   Ohmann, R. "Literacy, Technology, and Monopoly Capital." <u>College English</u> 47, (November 1985): 675-689.

34.3944   Ong, Walter J. <u>Orality and Literacy: The Technologizing of the World</u>. New York: Methuen, Inc., 1982.

34.3945   "Pennsylvania's Information Technology Education Programs." <u>Technological Horizons in Education</u> 13, 10(June 1986): 70-73.

34.3946   Rennie, Leonie J. "Teachers' and Pupils' Perceptions of Technology and the Implications for Curriculum." <u>Research in Science and Technological Education</u> 5, 2(1987): 121-133.

34.3947   Stephens, M. "Technology Education and Curriculum Change." <u>Educational Magazine</u> 41, 5(1984): 6-8.

34.3948   Ungerleider, Charles. "Teaching, Technology and Literacy." <u>B.C. Teacher</u> 63, 1(September-October 1983): 36-37.

34.3949   Ungerleider, Charles. "Illiteracy and the New Technology." <u>Canadian Journal of Educational Communication</u> 11, 3(1981): 17-18.

34.3950   Valgardson, W.D. "Technology and Literacy." <u>B.C. English Teacher Journal</u> 27, 1(1983-1984): 58-61.

34.3951   White, H. Loring. "A Technological Model of Global History."
            History Teacher 20, 4(August 1987): 497-517.

34.3952   Willis, A.H. The Impact of Technology On The Teaching Process
            In Australian Universities. Canberra: Tertiary Education
            Commission. 1983.

35

Use of Television and Radio in Literacy

35.3953   Abelman, R. "Television Literacy Programs for Gifted Children." Education Digest 52, (May 1987): 30-32.

35.3954   Abelman, Robert. "Children and TV: The ABC's of TV Literacy." Childhood Education 60, 3(January-February 1984): 200-205.

35.3955   Allen, Dwight W., and Anzalone, Stephen. "Learning by Radio: The First Step to Literacy." Prospects 8, 2(1978): 202-210.

Discusses the use of radio education as a means of providing basic education for those in rural areas not being served by schools. Examines the legacy of literacy, the concern for basic education, and the need and technical feasibility of basic education by radio.

35.3956   Amey, L.J. Visual Literacy: Implications For The Production of Children's Television. London: Vine Press, 1976.

35.3957   Barnes, Neil H. "BBC and Adult Literacy in Britain: The Campaign Begins." Educational Broadcasting International 8, 4(December 1975): 179-182.

35.3958   Bazemore, Judith S. "Two-Way TV Technology and The Teaching of Reading." Journal of Reading 21, 6(March 1978): 518-524.

35.3959   Bowers, John. "Television and Functional Literacy: A Presentation of the Problems." Educational Television International 3, 4(December 1969): 239-243.

35.3960   Burke, Richard C. The Use of Radio In Adult Literacy Education.
             Teheran: International Institute For Adult Literacy Methods,
             1976.   ED 154 334.

35.3961   Cass, Angelica W. "Materials and Methods For Adult Literacy
             Programmes." Literacy Discussion 2, 3(Summer 1971): 9-25.

35.3962   Cass, Angelica W. "Television's Future In Reducing Illiteracy."
             Educational Broadcasting Review 4, 2(April 1970: 39-43.

35.3963   Cass, Angelica Watson. "The Role of Television in Reaching
             Illiterate Adults With a Literacy Program Series." Ed. D.
             dissertation, Columbia University, 1969. 31/02-A, p. 602.

35.3964   Cave, D. "Teaching Literacy by T.V. (in Italy, 1960-1968)."
             Secondary Teacher, 197(July 1974): 116.

35.3965   Conference of Executives From Radio and T.V. Organizations,
             Held in Ankara, November 27-29, 2978. Ankara: Central Treaty
             Organization, 197?

35.3966   Culkin, John, and Drexel, John. "Building a New Literacy."
             Teacher 96, 5(January 1981): 45-47.

35.3967   Dornish, J. Robert. "A Study of The Effectiveness of ITV as a
             Supplement to Face-to-Face Teaching of Functional Illiterates."
             Ed.D. dissertation, Lehigh University, 1969. 30/12-A, p. 5220.

35.3968   Edington, A.B. "What Can Television Do For Us? The ARLO-
             CETO Seminar On The Use of Television In Literacy
             Campaigns." Educational Television International 4, 2(June
             1970): 144-147.

35.3969   Experiment, With Evaluation, In The Eradication of Adult
             Illiteracy By Use of Television Instruction Over A State
             Educational Television Network Supplemented By Supervised
             Group Viewing and By The Related Use of Project-Supplied
             Materials of Instruction; An. Florence, Alabama: Alabama State
             College, 1961.

35.3970   Gagne, Robert, and Burkman, Ernest. Promotion Science
             Literacy In Adults Through Television. Final Report.
             Washington, D.C.: National Science Foundation, 1982.   ED 229
             234.

35.3971   Hargreaves, David H. Adult Literacy and Broadcasting: The
            B.B.C.'s Experience. London: F. Pinter, Publishers, Ltd., 1980.

35.3972   Hargreaves, David. Adult Literacy and Broadcasting: The BBC's
            Experience. A Report To The Ford Foundation. London:
            British Broadcasting Corp., 1980.   ED 191 013.

35.3973   Hargreaves, D. "Auntie Moves On: BBC Literacy
            Programming." Times Educational Supplement 3289, (July 14,
            1978): 36.

35.3974   Harvey, Jennifer. "Educational TV: Linkup to Literacy." Orbit 9,
            3(June 1978): 3-5.

35.3975   Highton, D. "Broadcasting Support Services." Media In
            Education and Development 18, (June 1985): 90-92.

35.3976   Hilliard, Robert L. Curriculum's Technology Lag (Curricula and
            Television Literacy). N.P.: n.p., 1981 ED 220 941.

35.3977   Kasdon, L.M., and Kasdon, N.S. "Television: Vehicle for
            Literacy Training in Mexico." Adult Leadership 16, (September
            1967): 91-92.

35.3978   Kinnamon, Sue. "Commercial Television and Adult Reading."
            Journal of Reading 18, 6(March 1975): 470-474.

35.3979   Kirby, Brian. "Television and Functional Literacy: Some
            Comments." Educational Television International 3,
            4(December 1969): 244-245.

35.3980   "Latin America Plans E.T.V. Network." Times Educational
            Supplement 2764, (May 10, 1968): 1589.

35.3981   "Literacy Through Radio and Television In Jamaica."
            Educational Television International 4, 1(March 1970): 50-54.

35.3982   Lowry, Dennis T. "Radio, T.V. and Literacy In Mexico." Journal
            of Broadcasting 14, 2(Spring 1970): 239-244.

35.3983   Luke, R.A. "Literacy Through Television; Operation Alphabet."
            Audiovisual Instruction 11, (April 1966): 260-262.

35.3984   Luke, R.A. "Operation Alphabet: Literacy Through Television."
            International Journal of Adult and Youth Education 16, 1(1964):
            11-14.

35.3985   Maddison, John. Radio and Television In Literacy. A Survey of The Use of The Broadcasting Media In Combating Illiteracy Among Adults. Paris: UNESCO, 1971.   ED 061 493.

35.3986   Marchilonis, Barbara A., and Niebuhr, Herman. Television Technologies In Combating Illiteracy. A Monograph. Washington, D.C.: National Institute of Education, 1985.   ED 253 772.

35.3987   Matiwichuk, Ed. "Television's Assault on Literacy." ATA Magazine 58, 2(January 1978): 22-23.

35.3988   Metcalf, Lawrence E. "The CBS Programs, Reflectively Speaking." High School Journal 62, 3(December 1978): 142-147.

35.3989   Morrow, James, and Suid, Murray. "Media in the English Classroom: Some Pedagagical Issues." English Journal 63, 7(October 1974): 37-44.

35.3990   Muller, Josef, comp. Radio for Literacy. A Reader On The Use of Radio In Literacy Programmes. Bonn: German Foundation For International Development, 1985. ED 265 372.

35.3991   Neri, Italo. "Radio and Television For Literacy." Indian Journal of Adult Education 32, 11(November 1971): 16-18.

35.3992   Olson, David R. "The Consequences of Television." Interchange on Educational Policy 12, 1(1981-1982): 53-60.

35.3993   Peerson, Nell. "An Experiment With Evaluation, In The Eradication of Adult Illiteracy By Use of Television Instruction Over A State Educational Television Network Supplemented By Supervised Group Viewing."   ED 003 561.

35.3994   Project For Training Literacy Instructors By Radio. N.P.: Movimento Brasileiro de Alfabetizacao, 1975.

35.3995   "Radio's Predominant Role in Literacy Drive." Literacy Work 4, 1(July/September 1974): 1-32.

35.3996   Rossman, Mark H. "Recruiting Illiterates Via The Media." Adult Leadership 23, 7(January 1975): 223-224.

35.3997   Salomon, Gavriel. "Television Literacy and Television vs. Literacy." Journal of Visual/Verbal Languaging 2, 2(Fall 1982): 7-16.

35.3998   Shannon, Patrick, and Fernie, David E. "Print and Television: Children's Use of the Medium Is The Message." Elementary School Journal 85, 5(May 1985): 663-672.

35.3999   Spence, Peter, and McManus, Jim. Next Move. London: British Broadcasting Corporation, 1977.

35.4000   Spindler-Brown, Angela. "Broadcasting and Literacy: Recent BBC Contributions." Educational Broadcasting International 14, 1(March 1981): 20-24.

35.4001   Stauffer, John, et al. "Literacy, Illiteracy, and Learning From Television News." Communication Research - An International Quarterly 5, 2(April 1978): 221-232.

35.4002   Stauffer, John, et al. "Recall and Comprehension of Radio News in Kenya." Journalism Quarterly 57, (Winter 1980): 612-617.

            Study of the use and effectiveness of radio as a source of news. Examined for groups of radio listeners as a function of educational level. Said groups were adult illiterates, tenth-graders, college students, and out-of-school adults. Results found that the college students recalled significantly more news stories than any of the other three groups. Concludes with a discussion of the relationship between the educational process - and attainment in it - and the ability to decode oral language.

35.4003   Stevens, Jenny. "BBC Adult Literacy Project." Convergence 10, 1(1977): 20-28.

35.4004   Tyler, I.K. "Conbating Illiteracy With Television." AV Communication Review 13, (Fall 1965): 309-324.

35.4005   Valgardson, W.D. "Technology and Literacy." Skylark 21, 1(Fall 1984): 15-17.

36

Visual Literacy

36.4006   Abetman, R. "Television Literacy for Gifted Children." Roeper Review 9, (February 1987): 166-169.

36.4007   Adams, D.M., and Hamm, M. "Changing Gateways To Knowledge: New Media Symbol Systems." TechTrends 33, (January 1988): 21-23.

36.4008   Ausburn, F.V., and Ausburn, L.J. "Visual Analysis Skills Among Two Populations In Papua New Guinea." Educational Communication and Technology 31, 2(Summer 1983): 112-122.

36.4009   Bell, J. "Communication - The Essence of Education [symposium]." Educational Media International 24, (September 1987): 121-169.

36.4010   Beswick, Norman W. "Visual Literacy: A Vital Skill." Education Libraries Bulletin 24, part 1 (Spring 1981): 29-37.

36.4011   Bowker, Jeanette E., and Sawyers, Janet K. "Influence of Exposure on Preschoolers' Art Preference." Early Childhood Research Quarterly 3, 1(March 1988): 107-115.

36.4012   Buckle, L., and Kelley, P. "Candid Camera [Television Literacy Project and Kodak (UK)]." Times Educational Supplement 3748, (March 1988): 139.

36.4013   Burton, L. "First Steps In Decoding Ads." Metro, 72(Summer/Autumn 1987): 33-35.

36.4014   Castello, Charlene G.M. "Words Are Not Enough: An Introduction to Visual Literacy." Ed.D. dissertation, Fairleigh Dickinson University, 1980 X 1980.

36.4015   Colle, Royal, and Glass, Sandra. "Pictorial Conventions in
Development Communication in Developing Countries."
Media in Education and Development 19, 4(December 1986):
159-162.

36.4016   Considine, D.M. "Visual Literacy and The Curriculum: More
To It Than Meets The Eye." Language Arts 64, 6(October 1987):
634-640.

Reviews the nature of the traditional classroom in relation to
the expanding electronic environment. Argues that teachers
must adapt their classrooms to the - and with - the changes in
technology. Discusses the need for the teacher to help students
understand the visual elements which they may be watching.
Presents a teacher's analysis of the relationship between print
and image.

36.4017   Considine, D.M. "Visual Literacy & Children's Books: An
Integrated Approach." SLJ 33, (September 1986): 38-42.

36.4018   Considine, David M. "Visual Literacy and Children's Books: An
Integrated Approach." School Library Journal 33, 1(September
1986): 38-42.

36.4019   Corcoran, Farrel, and Schneider, Michael J. "Correlates of the
Interpretation of Televised Drama: A Study of Young Children's
Abilities." Early Child Development and Care 20, 4(1985) 301-
313.

36.4020   Cranny - Francis, A. "Visual Literacy." Metro, 71(Spring 1986):
8-13.

36.4021   Cromer, J. "Art Criticism and Visual Literacy." School Arts 86,
(April 1987): 22-25.

36.4022   Dondis, Donis A. Primer of Visual Literacy. London: M.I.T.
Press, 1974.

36.4023   Evans, B. "Photography and The Retarded Child: An Approach
To Visual Literacy." Education (WA) 34, 2(1985): 18-19.

36.4024   Feldman, Edmund B. "Visual Literacy." Journal of Aesthetic
Education 10, 3 & 4(July/October 1976): 195-200.

36.4025   Flores, J.G. "Becoming Visually Literate." Media & Methods 23,
(September/October 1986): 82.

36.4026   Fransecky, Roger Barnum. "A Multivariate Study of a Visual Literacy Training Strategy for Extending Language Study in Elementary Classrooms." Ph.D. dissertation, University of Cincinnati, 1972. 33/06-A, p. 2691.

36.4027   Grbevski, S. "Vision Development and Learning." Orana 21, 3(August 1985): 132-136.

36.4028   Guerin, David V. "Visual Literacy." Educational Resources and Techniques 10, 2(Summer 1970): 24-26.

36.4029   Gumpert, Gary, and Cathcart, Robert. "Media Gramnars, Generations, and Media Gaps." Critical Studies in Mass Communication 2, 1(March 1985): 23-53.

36.4030   Hewett, Gloria J., and Rush, Jean C. "Finding Buried Treasures: Aesthetic Scanning With Children." Art Education 40, 1(January 1987): 41-43.

36.4031   Hill, F.E. "Perception or Deception: Being Literate in a Subliminal World." International Journal of Instructional Media 13, 4(1986): 257-262.

36.4032   Hortin, John Arthur. "Visual Literacy - The Theoretical Foundations: An Investigation of The Research Practices and Theories." Ed.D. dissertation, Northern Illinois University, 1980. 41/12-A, p. 4944.

36.4033   "ICEM Conference, Cardiff, 26-27 October 1987." Educational Media International 25, (March 1988): 5-41.

36.4034   Jones, P.W. "The Visual and Dramatic in Religious Education." Spectrum 17, 2(Spring 1985): 29-35.

36.4035   Learmont, J., et al. Reading Ability and Skills In Analyzing Visuals. Hawthorn, Australia: Swinburne Technical College, 1980.

36.4036   "Learning to Interpret Visual Communication." Ohio Schools 53, (November 28, 1975): 21-24.

36.4037   Le Franc, Robert, et al. "The Audio-Visual Media: Some Proposed Solutions to Literacy Problems." Visual Education, (August-September 1972): 87-92.

36.4038   McGee, C. "Children's Perceptions of Symbols On Maps and
           Aerial Photographs." Geographical Education 4, 2(June 1982):
           51-59.

36.4039   Meisel, Timothy Joseph. "Increasing Visual Literacy Through
           The Structural Analysis of Film." Ph.D. dissertation, State
           University of New York at Buffalo, 1979. 40/09-A, p. 4857.

36.4040   Mercer, John. "Optical Effects and Film Literacy." Ph.D.
           dissertation, The University of Nebraska, Lincoln, 1953. W1953,
           p. 210.

36.4041   Shenkman, Harriet. "Reversing the Literacy Decline by
           Controlling the Electronic Demons." Educational Leadership 42,
           5(February 1985): 26-29.

36.4042   Sinatra, Richard. Visual Literacy Connections To Thinking,
           Reading, and Writing. N.P.: n.p., 1986.

36.4043   Sinatra Richard, and Venezia, Jennie F. "A Visual Approach To
           Improved Literacy Skills For Special Education Adolescents: An
           Exploratory Study." Exceptional Child 33, 3(November 1986):
           187-192.

           Study of special education students, in three different IQ level
           groupings, in a visual literacy approach to reading and writing
           develop-   ment. Results tended to indicate a usefulness of
           using a visual compo-sition approach. This was especially true
           in the dull-normal borderline IQ students' writing proficiency.
           The students in the 70-89 IQ grouping did not demonstrate a
           significant increase in reading ability.

36.4044   Sless, D. "Visual Literacy: A Failed Opportunity." Educational
           Communication and Technology 32, 4(Winter 1985): 224-228.

36.4045   Sofo, F. "Graphic Literacy: Part 1. A Review of the Literature."
           Vocational Aspects of Education 37, 98(December 1985): 107-113.

36.4046   "Visual Literacy Connections: An Interview With Richard
           Sinatra." Academic Therapy 23, (November 1987): 169-171.

36.4047   Zimmer, Anne, and Zimmer, Fred. Visual Literacy In
           Communication: Designing For Development. Teheran:
           International Institute For Adult Literacy Methods, 1978. ED
           163 424.

37

Women and Literacy

37.4048   Bhasin, Kamla. "The Why and How of Literacy For Women: Some Thoughts In The Indiana Context." Convergence 17, 4(1984): 37-43.

Discusses the basis on which a literacy campaign should be established. Argues that said campaign must be based on an analysis of socioeconomic conditions, political realities, the causes of poverty, and the usefulness of becoming literate. States that there is ". . . no casual relationship between illiteracy and poverty . . ." Points out that previous literacy campaigns in India were designed to domesticate, not liberate, the poor. Reports that materials used in literacy campaigns perpetuate stereotypes about women. Concludes that a literacy campaign should empower the oppressed.

37.4049   Brayfield, Clotean Helm. "Social Literacy Education For Women Educators: Will It Facilitate Their Entry Into Public School Administration?' Ed.D. dissertation, University of Massachusetts, 1978. 39/01-A, p. 35.

37.4050   Chabaud, Jacqueline. The Education and Advancement of Women. Paris: UNESCO, 1970. ED 054 437.

37.4051   Chandler, Judith B. "Another Kind of Returning Student." Journal of The National Association of Women. Deans, Administrators, and Counselors 47, 4(Summer 1984): 3-7.

37.4052   Craig, Gillian Mary. "The Development of a Freire-Based Literacy/Conscientization Program For Low-Literate Women In Prison." Ph.D. dissertation, The Pennsylvania State University, 1981. 42/01-A, p. 68.

37.4053   "Creating A Favourable Climate For Promoting Literacy Among Women." Report of Seminar held in Karachi, Pakistan, 1968. Mimeographed. London: International Alliance of Women, 1968.

37.4054   Ellis, Pat. "Women, Adult Education and Literacy: A Caribbean Perspective." International Journal of Lifelong Education 6, 1(January-March 1987): 61-68.

37.4055   Ellis, Pat. "Women, Adult Education and Literacy: A Caribbean Perspective." Convergence 17, 4(1984): 44-53.

37.4056   Ellowitch, Azi. A Curriculum In Employment: Women and The World of Work. Harrisburg, Pennsylvania: Pennsylvania State Department of Education, 1983. ED 246 214.

37.4057   Empacher, Marjorie, R.P. A Case Study Using Oral History In The Analysis of Factors Contributing To Illiteracy. Boston: Boston University, 1977. ED 173 769.

37.4058   Equity of Access of Women To Literacy: Comparative Study. Paris: UNESCO, 1970. ED 051 486.

37.4059   Fonseca, C. "Functional Literacy For Village Women: An Experiment In Upper Volta." Prospects 5, 3(1975): 380-386.

37.4060   Homayounpour, P. The Experimental Functional Literacy Project For The Social and Economic Promotion of Rural Women: The Final Report. Tehran: National Centre For Adult Education and Training, 1977.

37.4061   Homayounpour, P. "The Experimental Functional Literacy Project of The Women's Organization In Iran." In The Design of Educational Programmes For The Promotion of Rural Women Tehran: International Institute For Adult Literacy Methods, 1975.

37.4062   Innovative Education For Preliterate Rural Women: A Project Proposal. New York: World Education, 1974.

37.4063   International Institute For Adult Literacy Methods. Literacy Programmes For Women. Tehran: International Institute For Adult Literacy Methods, 1977.

37.4064   International Seminar on Eradication of Illiteracy Among Women. N.P.: n.p., 1966.

37.4065   Jackson, L.M., and Yamanaka, E. "Measuring Women's
            Attitudes, Goals, and Literacy Toward Computers and Advanced
            Technology." Educational Technology 25, (February 1985): 12-
            14.

37.4066   Jeffrey, R. "Governments and Culture: How Women Made
            Kerala Literate." Pacific Affairs 60, (Fall 1987): 447-472.

37.4067   Junge, Barbara Jackson, and Tegegne, Debebe. "The Effects of
            Liberation From Illiteracy on the Lives of 31 Women: A Case
            Study." Journal of Reading 28, 7 (April 1985): 606-613.

            Discusses illiteracy in Ethiopia, and the mass literacy campaign
            which began in 1979. Examined 31 women who took part in said
            literacy campaign. Reviews the selection of the sample of
            women. Also presents the fourteen questions which were asked
            of the women involved regarding both their participation in and
            outcome of their taking part in the literacy campaign. Concludes
            with a discussion of the value of literacy for the participating
            women. Lists several areas for additional research and action.

37.4068   Kazemek, Francis E. "Women and Adult Literacy: Considering
            The Other Half of The House." Lifelong Learning 11, 4(January
            1988): 23-24, 25.

37.4069   Mathews, Walter M., and Winkle, Linda Wyrick. "Computer
            Equity for Young Women in Rural Schools." Research in Rural
            Education 1, 1(Fall 1982): 37-41.

37.4070   Mathur, Anita, and Tandon, Rajesh. "Participatory Training For
            Illiterate Women Trainees In India." Convergence 19, 1(1986):
            20-23.

37.4071   McCall, Cecelia. "Women and Literacy: The Cuban Experience."
            Journal of Reading 30, 4(January 1987): 318-324.

37.4072   Mirzadek, M. "Case Study: The Experimental Functional
            Literacy Projects For The Social and Economic Promotion of
            Rural Women (Saxek Project)." Mimeographed. Tehran:
            National Centre For Adult Education and Training, 1977.

37.4073   Mulay, Sumah. "Literacy and Family Planning Behavior of
            Rural Women." Indian Journal of Adult Education 37,
            (January 1976): 9-10.

37.4074   New Trends In Adult Education For Women. Report of The
           National Seminar (New Delhi, India, February 19-22, 1980).
           Series No. 135. New Delhi: Indian Adult Education Association,
           1980. ED 205 810.

37.4075   Nimer, Kamal K. The Role of Women's Organizations In
           Eradicating Illiteracy In Jordan. N.P.: n.p., 1986.

37.4076   Pathak, Yogini. Child-to-Mother, A Strategy Based On Children
           As Vectors of Taking Science and Technology To Rural Women.
           [and] Realities of Rural Life. N.P.: n.p., 1982 ED 232 765.

37.4077   Rockhill, Kathleen. "Gender, Language and The Politics of
           Literacy." British Journal of Sociology of Education 8, 2(1987):
           153-167.

37.4078   Rutherford, F. James. The Role of The National Science
           Foundation. N.P.: n.p., 1978. ED 168 819.

37.4079   Sagasti, H. de. "Social Implications of Adult Literacy: A Study
           Among Migrant Women In Peru." Ph.D. dissertation,
           University of Pennsylvania, 1972.

37.4080   Senbel, A. Aziz. "The Goals of Women's Literacy Education In
           Saudi Arabia As Preceived By Saudi Arabian University
           Professors, Female Literacy Teachers and Female Adult Learners
           (Functional, Curriculum, Philosophy)." Ph.D. dissertation,
           University of Nebraska, Lincoln, 1984. 46/03-A, p. 585.

37.4081   Weisinger, R. "Economic Development and Functional Literacy
           For Women: A Pilot Project in Iran; WOAL Programmes for
           Women." International Review of Education 19, 1(1973): 96-
           101.

37.4082   Weisinger, R.J. Light Me A Candle: Two Years of Literacy and
           Adult Education Work Among The Women of Khuzistan, Iran.
           Bombay: Shakuntala Publishing Hours, 1973.

37.4083   "Women - - A Majority With Minority Rights To Education."
           Literacy Discussion 6, 4(Winter 1975/1976): 9-16.

37.4084   Women's Organization of Iran and International Institute For
           Adult Literacy Methods. "The Design of Educational
           Programmes For The Social and Economic Promotion of Rural
           Women." Report of an Internation Seminar held in Tehran,
           April 19-24, 1975. Tehran: IIALM, 1975.

37.4085   "Women's Role In Future Development." <u>Literacy Work</u> 4, 3(January/March 1975): 1-26.

Author Index

The author index includes authors and joint authors. Since the bibliography is numbered consecutively throughout the chapters, the numbers refer to individual entry numbers.

Subject Index

Numbers below refer to entry numbers.

Aborigines, 2567

Adult Literacy, 1-239, 398, 534, 1178, 1259, 2697, 2703, 2777, 2969-2972, 3097, 3122, 3124, 3146, 3160, 3307, 3556, 3960-3961, 3971-3972

Adult Reading Programs, 240-298, 1802, 1809, 3171, 3181

Africa, 306, 1652, 2899, 3660

Aliteracy, 299-303

Amish, 1319, 2611

Appalachia, 731

Arab World, 312, 3145, 3493-3494

Arizona, 1189

Assessment of Literacy, 40

Audio-Visual Aids, 62, 2889

Australia, 400, 423, 1080, 1995, 3614, 3952

Austria, 1447

Bahrain, 460

BBC Computer Literacy Project, 908-915

BBC Literacy Project, 294, 3973

Bibliographies on Literacy, 304-377, 916-922, 3825

Bilingual Literacy, 3031, 3035

Biliteracy, 378-388,

Blacks, 354, 654, 1422, 1655, 2565, 2600-2602, 2607-2608, 2615, 2628, 2638, 2641-2642, 3170, 3291, 3304, 3386

Brazil, 318

Burkina Faso, 4059

Business, Industry and Corporations, 66, 126, 135, 1959, 1966-1968, 1988, 2200, 3400, 3507, 3578-3579, 3812, 3854, 3882-3883

California, 448, 805, 841, 2690, 3326,

Cambridge House, 1781

Canada, 446, 603, 643, 1335

Caribbean, 4054-4055

China (PRC), 3652, 3664, 3769, 3777

Competency Testing, 1142, 1190, 1221, 1269, 3016

Computer Literacy, 389-1059

Computer Literacy; Bibliographies, 916-922

Computer Literacy; Computer Aptitude, Literacy and Interest Profile, 923-960

Computer Literacy; General, 389-907

Computer Literacy; Research, 1008-1059

Computer Literacy; Tests and Scales, 961-985

Computer Literacy; Textbooks and Materials, 986-1007

Computers and Literacy, 8, 224, 234, 241, 245, 293, 296, 298, 309, 323, 353, 355, 389-1059, 1302, 1790, 1947, 2618, 3301, 3303, 3778, 3869, 3889, 3915, 4069

Connecticut, 475

Content Areas, 43

Correctional Facilities and Illiteracy, 293, 1060-1101, 1554, 4052

Critical Literacy, 2751

Cuba, 4071

Cultural Literacy, 1102-1129, 3641

Curriculum, 150, 857, 897, 1975, 2905, 3020, 3057, 3584,3605, 3629, 3728, 3730, 3735, 3740, 3743-3745, 3905, 3937, 3946-3947, 3976, 4016, 4056

Definitions of Literacy, 151, 187, 537, 669,

About the Compilers

JOHN HLADCZUK and SHARON HLADCZUK are with the Center for Interdisciplinary Studies in Knoxville, Tennessee and East Amherst, New York. WILLIAM ELLER is a professor at the State University of New York at Buffalo, Department of Learning and Instruction.